AMERICAN
POCKET WATCH
IDENTIFICATION AND PRICE GUIDE
BOOK 2

INTRODUCTION

This book contains carefully selected actual pages from original factory sales catalogs, factory advertisements, supply house catalogs and sales brochures. It covers American pocket watches from 1857 to the 1960's. The following information is given for each watch — the year it was offered for sale, the factory description, the price it sold for originally and the present retail value.

Over 95% of all pocket watches manufactured in the United States since 1857 can be identified and a reasonably close retail value arrived at by comparing your watch with an actual picture of it in this book.

You are holding a very unique book. The original antique and historic material has not been altered. Long after the current retail prices no longer apply to the watches shown herein, it will still be very valuable to anyone interested in pocket watches for research and identification.

REVISED PRICE GUIDE SECTION
JUNE 1980

HEART OF AMERICA PRESS
POST OFFICE BOX 9808
KANSAS CITY, MISSOURI 64134

First Printing October, 1974
ISBN 0—913902—09—8
Author — Roy Ehrhardt

INDEX

READ PAGE 9

NEW UP–DATED PRICES for SPRING 1980 for the AMERICAN POCKET WATCH IDENTIFICATION & PRICE GUIDE BOOK 2 (Published in 1974)

READ PAGE 9

The up-dated prices on the following pages are generally the prices realized on sales by N.A.W.C.C. dealers, both at the local and regional meetings and through mail order lists. Trades or sales by individuals, antique dealers, auctions, or antique shows will generally be too high or too low to use. I have attended all of the National Association of Watch and Clock Collector regional meetings this year and quite a few antique shows and flea markets. I use only prices from sales between dealers and collectors who have a good knowledge of watches and their values. These prices can generally be regarded as high wholesale to low retail.

I would suggest you take a pen and go through your book and mark the changes. Most of the values have increased but those that have decreased in value were priced too high to start with, and some of the 12 Size are not as popular as they were in 1974.

PAGE 15

Hampden Watch Company

NO.	1974 Price	1980 Price
1	$ 75	$ 100
2	60	125
3	50	
4	50	
5	75	100
6	65	150
7	75	60
8	75	100

Keywind-Keyset from back are scarce and hard to case.

PAGE 16

NO.	1974 Price	1980 Price
Railway	75	100
Perry	50	100
31	35	
70	30	
Spgfd.	30	
Spgfd.	30	
36	30	40
34	30	
71	45	30
60	55	65
59	45	
57	35	
56	30	35
55	30	
54	30	

Hampden watches have not caught on & there are only a few serious collectors. See Pages 26-29 of the 1977 Indicator for a complete listing of all known Hampden watch grades.

PAGE 17

NO.	1974 Price	1980 Price
1	75	85
2	60	75
3	60	
4	60	
5	60	
6	40	45
7	40	45
8	40	45
9	35	
10	35	
11	35	
12	30	
13	30	
14	25	
15	25	
16	30	
17	30	
18	30	
19	35	
20	25	

PAGE 18

NO.	1974 Price	1980 Price
1	25	35
2	25	
3	25	
4	20	
5	20	
6	20	
7	20	
8	20	
9	70	150
10	60	150
11	40	
12	35	
13	30	
14	25	

PAGE 19

NO.	1974 Price	1980 Price
1	15	
2	$ 40	$ 60
3	35	40
4	30	
5	25	
6	20	
7	15	

PAGE 20

NO.	1974 Price	1980 Price
1	130	150
2	130	150
3	120	140
4	75	85
5	75	85
6	70	75
7	70	80
8	70	80
9	70	80
10	40	75
11	40	75
12	35	
13	35	
14	35	
15	35	

PAGE 21

NO.	1974 Price	1980 Price
1	30	
2	30	
3	25	
4	25	
5	15	
6	15	
7	75	100
8	75	100
9	30	35
10	30	35
11	30	25
12	30	25
13	15	
14	15	
15	40	
16	40	

PAGE 22

NO.	1974 Price	1980 Price
23J		130
1	50	
2	50	
3	35	
4	35	
5	25	
6	25	
7	20	
8	15	
9	15	
10	40	
11	30	
12	15	
13	20	
14	15	

PAGE 23

NO.	1974 Price	1980 Price
1	130	140
2	75	85
3	70	85
4	70	80
5	40	
6	30	
7	20	

PAGE 24

NO.	1974 Price	1980 Price
1	150	210
2	70	100
3	70	100
4	70	100
5	70	100

PAGE 25

NO.	1974 Price	1980 Price
1	$ 40	$ 30
2	35	25
3	25	
4	20	15
5	15	

PAGE 26

NO.	1974 Price	1980 Price
1	55	
2	35	
3	35	
4	25	
5	20	
6	15	
7	40	
8	30	
9	20	

PAGE 27

NO.	1974 Price	1980 Price
(The Paul Revere)		
19J-18K	200	150
19J-14K	180	140
19J-14K	160	130
17J-14K	100	130
17J-14K	100	130
17J-14K	110	130
17J-14K	120	130
17J-25Y	70	
17J-25Y	70	
17J-25Y	80	
(The Minute Man)		
25Y	60	
25Y	60	
25Y	60	
(The Nathan Hale)		
All	50	

PAGE 29

Hamilton Watch Company

NO.	1974 Price	1980 Price
1	250	650
2	225	375
3	700	1400
4	40	65
5	40	65
6	40	65
7	40	65
8	60	175
9	60	175
10	40	75
11	40	125
12	125	650
13	150	800
14	70	80
15	80	100

PAGE 30

NO.	1974 Price	1980 Price
1	125	200
2	125	300
3	225	400
4	300	5000
5	125	200
6	100	500
7	175	350
8	150	250
9 gold	175	500
9 gilded	140	425
10	100	450
11	100	500
12	100	200
13	100	200
14	70	75
15	70	75
16	35	175
17	125	250
18	125	300
19	100	500
20	100	500

PAGE 31

NO.	1974 Price	1980 Price
1	$ 35	$
2	35	
3	40	50
4	90	150
5		175
6	70	175
7	70	180
8	70	125
9	90	175
10	75	175
11	175	1200
12	40	200
13	70	100
14	50	75

PAGE 32

NO.	1974 Price	1980 Price
1	20	20
2	20	
3	20	
4	20	
5	75	
Marked Masterpiece		
5A	100	250
6	60	75
Marked Masterpiece		
6A	100	250
7	20	
8	30	
9	50	100
10	125	250
11	50	60
12	75	100
13	50	60
14	50	60
15	30	30

PAGE 33

NO.	1974 Price	1980 Price
1	225	400
2	300	5000
3	70	80
4	70	125
5	100	500
6	40	65
7	40	65
8	40	65
9	40	65

PAGE 34

NO.	1974 Price	1980 Price
1	175	350
2	150	250
3	90	150
4	70	100
5	90	200
6	80	
7	80	100
8	40	50
9	35	
10	35	
11	70	75
12		125

PAGE 35

See Note No. 1, Page 15

NO.	1974 Price	1980 Price
1	300	550
2	275	525
3	200	425
4	200	375
5	325	950
6	225	850
7	225	850
8	70	100
9	300	350
10	275	325
11	175	250
12	175	250
13	260	275

PAGE 35 (Cont.)

NO.	1974 Price	1980 Price
14	$235	$245
15	145	175
16	145	175

PAGE 36

NO.	1974 Price	1980 Price
18K	250	200
14K	220	190
14K	220	190
14K	220	180
14K	200	180
14K	200	170
Perm.	150	100
Perm.	150	100
(No. 900)		
14K	185	200
14K	185	200
14K	165	180
14K	165	180
14K	150	170
Perm.	100	
Perm.	100	
(No. 914)		
14K	140	
14K	140	
14K	110	
14K	110	
14K	100	
14K	100	
Perm.	60	
Perm.	60	
(No. 910)		
	60	70

PAGE 37

NO.	1974 Price	1980 Price
1	90	125
2	85	110
3	90	120
4	90	125
5	190	400
6	300	425
7	175	300
8	115	240
9	120	250
10	125	250
11	160	300
12	450	750
17	60	
18	60	
19	120	200
20	125	200
21	225	225
22	450	700

See Note No. 1, Page 15

PAGE 38

NO.	1974 Price	1980 Price
1	600	900
2	350	800
3	450	900
4	1500	4000
5	175	150
6	150	
7	200	160
8	300	400
9	140	175
10	110	160
11	100	
12	100	
13	150	200

See Note No. 1, Page 15

PAGE 39

NO.	1974 Price	1980 Price
1	85	100
2	100	115
3	130	145
4	60	
5	70	
6	85	
7	60	70
8	35	
9	40	
10	50	
11	55	
12	40	
13	50	
14	35	
15	45	
16	50	
17	80	100

See Note No. 1, Page 15

PAGE 40

NO.	1974 Price	1980 Price
1	200	
2	120	
3	120	
4	165	

NO.	1974 Price	1980 Price
5	$110	$
6	120	
7	85	
8	85	
6	65	
7	65	

PAGE 41

NO.	1974 Price	1980 Price
1	110	200
2	110	180
3	110	200
4		350
5	70	100
6	70	60
7	60	75
8	700	1400

These three cases, No. 1,2 & 3, are very desirable. Collectors want their watches in these factory marked Hamilton cases. Knowledgeable collectors will pay near $100 for one of these in mint condition. There has not been any recent production of these cases. I do not picture all of the marked Hamilton cases and you should watch for them. Somewhere around 1900 Webb C. Ball began selling watches in Ball marked factory cases, followed closely by Howard in 1905. One by one the other companies making railroad watches followed Ball's lead, with all of them offering the 16 Size railroad watches where the movement was cased and timed at the factory. These original cases are just about as important to the collector as the movement. Since Ball was about the only company who sold 18 Size cased railroad watches, any cases by the other makers are scarce but you can occasionally find one.

PAGE 42

NO.	1974 Price	1980 Price
1	750	
2	300	350
3	350	

PAGE 43

NO.	1974 Price	1980 Price
1	200	
3	200	135
4	185	150
6	75	
7	185	150
8	75	
9	110	120
12	110	120

PAGE 44

NO.	1974 Price	1980 Price
1	90	200
2	300	800
3	225	600
4	190	500
5	100	250
6	85	175
9	50	70
3	60	100

CASES

The Hamilton marked cases on this page are the last models Hamilton used to case their railroad watches before they left the factory. They were also sold empty as replacement cases by Hamilton through material houses. About three years ago, Star Watch Case Co. began producing these cases and selling them wholesale to material houses without Hamilton's name in them. The cases are exactly the same quality and workmanship. Star manufactures these cases using the old methods but with today's cost for materials, labor and profit margins. These cases fill a definite need in the industry and thousands have been sold in the last couple of years. A good idea of today's costs can be gotten by looking at the current retail price of $100. for a new case like the one on Page 44 of Book 2 pictured above the description of railroad watch No. 17 in 10K YGF. It seems to me that if buyers are willing to pay $100 without Hamilton markings, a collector would readily pay $100 or so for a mint one with Hamilton markings. A few new cases are still around with the Hamilton markings and you should look for them.

DIALS

Unlike the new cases, the new dials that are being made by at least two manufactures ARE NOT a continuation of production by the original makers. None of the dials that I have seen are as good quality and do not look original. You need to familiarize yourself with what the old dials look like and don't pay top price for watches with new dials. The dials certainly make a watch worth more than one with a bad dial but not as much as one with a mint original. For my collection, I would rather have a bad original than a new one that is not right. Dials are being made for almost all of the 16 Size and 18 Size railroad watches made by Elgin, Hamilton, Waltham, Illinois, South Bend and Howard, and maybe others. These dials usually retail for under $15. There is a maker around Chicago making decorated dials that appear to be of good quality and really does dress up a watch. I think it will have to be a personal decision as to what dial and case you want on the watches in your collection. Collectors who are willing to pay top dollars will always want originals.

PAGE 45

NO.	1974 Price	1980 Price
1	100	80
2	300	350
3	500	
4	70	
5	50	
6	50	
7	35	40
8	35	40
9	150	110
10	150	110
11	120	90
12	120	110
13	100	90

PAGE 47

NO.	1974 Price	1980 Price
No changes except 9		250

PAGE 48

No changes.

PAGE 49

No changes except

NO.	1974 Price	1980 Price
12	450	450

PAGE 50

Aurora Watch Co.

NO.	1974 Price	1980 Price
38	50	75
36	40	60
35	30	50
33	30	50

PAGE 51

NO.	1974 Price	1980 Price
10	95	400
8	70	125
113	60	90
26	50	80
109	40	50
22	40	50
4½	40	70
6	50	
3½	40	
2	40	
1	40	

Open Face Lever Set

NO.	1974 Price	1980 Price
10	95	400
8	75	150
113	100	
26	50	90
109	40	60
22	40	50
4½	40	50
6	50	70
3½	40	50
2	40	
1	40	

PAGE 52

Illinois Watch Company

The value I have placed on some of these Illinois movements is based on production figures, and the collectors are not yet willing to pay these somewhat higher prices based on rarity.

K-1= Keywind Model 1
H-2= Hunting Model 2
O-3= Open Face Model 3

NO.	1974 Price	1980 Price
1—K-1	90	550
1—H-2		450
1—O-3		500
2—K-1	100	1200
2—H-2		800
2—O-3		1000
3—K-1	85	1100
3—H-2		700
3—O-3		900
4—K-1	75	150
4—H-2		150
4—O-3		200
5—K-1	65	125
5—H-2		125
5—O-3		150
6—K-1	40	50
6—H-2		40
6—O-3		100
7—K-1	65	40
7—H-2		100
8—K-1	65	100
8—H-2		200
9—K-1	65	40
9—H-2		200
10—K-1	65	75
10—H-2		200
11—K-1	30	30
11—H-2		75
11—O-3		200

PAGE 53

NO.	1974 Price	1980 Price
1—K-1	40	40
2—K-1	30	100
2—H-2		100
3—K-1	35	40
3—O-2	35	40
4—K-1	45	
6—H-2	35	
7—K-1	30	35
7—H-2	30	50
8—K-1	30	

PAGE 54

NO.	1974 Price	1980 Price
1—H-2	125	200
1—O-3		400
2—H-2	90	450
2—O-3		500
3—H-2	100	800
3—O-3		1000
4—H-2	85	100
4—O-3		100
5—H-2	65	150
5—O-3		200
6—H-2	40	
6—O-3		100
7—K-1	35	50
7—H-2		35
7—O-3		35
8	35	
9—H-2	100	150
9—O-3		200
10—K-1	40	
10—H-2		40
10—O-3		50
11—K-1	35	
11—H-2		35
11—O-2		35
12—K-1	30	

NO.	1974 Price	1980 Price
PAGE 54 (Cont.)		
12—H-2	$	$ 30
12—O-3		30
13	65	100
14	40	
15	25	
16—K-1	15	45
16—H-2		15
PAGE 55		
Bunn—H-2	100	800
Bunn—O-3		1000
Miller—K-1	65	150
Miller—H-2	65	200
107—H-2	70	200
107—O-3		200
5—K-1	65	
5—H-2	40	50
5—O-3		65
60—K-1	30	60
60—H-2		35
60—O-3		35
6—K-1	10	40
2—K-1	20	30
2—H-2	20	
2—O-3		20
I.W.Co.—K-1	35	
I.W.Co.—H-2	20	
I.W.Co.—O-3		40
105—H-2	125	200
105—O-3		400
65—K-1	90	50
65—H-2		50
65—O-3		50
99—K-1	40	
99—H-2	30	40
99—O-3		40
101—K-1	40	30
101—H-2		30
101—O-3		30
146	80	
144	35	
142	30	
143	30	
141	25	
140	25	
136	80	
134	35	
132	30	
133	30	
131	30	
130	30	
PAGE 57		
1	125	200
2	100	200
3	80	1000
4	90	50
5	40	
6	30	
7	30	
8	25	
9	30	
10	25	
11	25	
12	20	
13	35	
14	80	125
15	35	
16	35	
17	30	
18	30	
19	25	
20	20	
21	80	
22	35	
23	30	
24	30	
25	25	
26	25	
27	25	
PAGE 58		
1	400	700
2	100	150
3	35	
4	30	
5	25	
6	30	
7	25	
8	25	
PAGE 59		
1	125	

NO.	1974 Price	1980 Price
1A (23J)	$	$ 150
2	100	
3	100	150
3A (21J)		200
4	40	
5	35	
6	30	
7	25	
8	20	
9	35	
10	30	
11	20	
12	25	20
PAGE 60		
1	20	65
2	30	55
3	30	50
4	85	150
5 (21J)	85	200
5A (19J)		200
6	35	85
7	35	85
8 (23J)	110	500
8A (25J)		3500
9	40	75
10 (21J)	90	175
10A (19J)		175
11	400	1750
12	40	75
PAGE 61		
1	165	550
2	100	125
3	125	125
4	125	400
5	100	200
6	50	35
7	30	

PAGE 62

NOTE: The Model 9, 23J Sangamo Special and 21J Bunn Special on this page are rare models. Do not confuse with the common models. Look at the damaskeen patterns to see the difference.

NO.	1974 Price	1980 Price
1	150	500
2	110	350
3	70	300
4	100	
5	110	450
6	150	650
7	85	115
8	85	125

PAGES 63, 64 & 65

No Changes.

PAGE 66

These cases are probably not marked Illinois. The 16 Size movements shown here are fairly scarce and are worth more than the common ones you see everywhere.

NO.	1974 Price	1980 Price
1	85	215
2	120	270
3	90	220
4	100	230
5	140	290
6	100	130
7	140	290
8	90	220
9	130	280
10	95	225
11	135	285
12	115	125
13	125	135
14	140	150
15	130	140
16	135	145
PAGE 67		
1	95	225
2	135	285
3	90	220
4	130	280
5	100	235
6	140	285
7	100	235

NO.	1974 Price	1980 Price
8	$ 140	$ 285
9	90	120
10	125	265
11	130	140
12	140	150
13	130	140
14	140	150
15	100	100
16	70	200
17	110	250

PAGE 68

No Changes.

PAGE 69

This solid bow case shown at No. 1, 2 and 3, is the most desirable of all marked Sangamo cases.

NO.	1974 Price	1980 Price
1 GF		750
2 SG	350	1200
Mint Case		500
3, 23 SS	150	250
4	200	550
Mint Case		250
5	150	300
6	200	550
Mint Case		250

PAGE 70

NO.	1974 Price	1980 Price
1, 21J 60H	135	300
Mint Case		200
2, 21J 60H	135	300
Mint Case		200
3, 21J 60H	130	300
Mint Case		200
3A, 21J 60H		100
4, M29 10K	130	300
5, M29 14K	130	300
6, M29 10K	140	300
7, M29 14K	140	300
Mint Case 10K		200
Mint Case 14K		200

All collectors of railroad watches want their 60 Hour Bunn Specials in these factory marked, original mint cases. The case is worth more than the movement, on 21 Jewel, 60 Hour Bunns.

PAGE 71

No Changes.

PAGE 72

NO.	1974 Price	1980 Price
1	25	40
2	25	40
3	55	70
4	25	50
5	25	40
6	40	100
7	40	
	80	130
8	30	
	70	130
9	40	100
10	40	100
11	40	100

PAGES 73 & 74

No Changes.

PAGE 75

NO.	1974 Price	1980 Price
1	250	425
2	135	
3	275	750
4	200	350
5	250	475
6	100	150

PAGE 76

Many of the watches on this page have gone up in value since 1974. It is too difficult to try and up-date these in a meaningful way.

PAGE 77

It seems to me that since writing the paragraph at the bottom of

this page five years ago, the facts are still true and I will not change anything.

PAGE 78

18 Size Elgin Keywinds with grade names are being looked for and gathered up by Early American watch collectors.

NO.	1974 Price	1980 Price
1 — 4	No Changes.	
Mat Laflin	$ 50	$ 50
J. T. Ryerson	50	50
W. H. Ferry	60	60
Chas. Fargo	50	50
PAGE 79		
1	50	75
2	50	75
3	40	
4	30	
5	50	75
6	50	75
7	50	75
8	45	
PAGE 80		
97	20	30
B.W.R.	50	75
B.W.R.	50	75
H.H.T.	50	75
H.H.T.	50	75
G.M.W.	25	
G.M.W.	20	
80	40	
82	20	
10	20	
96	10	
33	40	50
103	20	
102	15	
B.W.R.	40	
H.H.T.	40	
G.M.W.	20	
76	35	
75	20	
74	15	
73	10	
G.M.W.	25	
44	20	
43	15	
104	15	
92	15	
2	20	
3	30	
4	40	60
50	50	
72	250	700
86	75	
95	15	
94	15	
65	15	
101	20	
45	20	
67	25	
71	140	
PAGE 81		
1	50	75
2	50	75
3	25	
4	20	
5	10	
6	15	
7	10	
8	40	60
9	75	
10	15	
11	15	
12	15	
PAGE 82		
149	100	
150	100	
91	250	700
72	250	700
50	50	60
86	75	
16-S, 21J	40	
19J	40	
17J	30	
17J	20	
15J	20	
10-S, 21J	10	
17J	10	
15J	10	

6

NO.	1974 Price	1980 Price

PAGE 83

No Changes.

PAGE 84

NO.	1974 Price	1980 Price
1	$ 200	$ 275
2	100	100
3	40	100
4	75	125
5	35	
6	30	
7	15	
8	15	
9	120	100

PAGE 85

No Changes.

PAGE 86

NO.	1974 Price	1980 Price
1	160	
2	100	
3	95	
4	65	
5	60	
6	30	
7	25	
8	20	
9	15	
10	10	
11	350	2200
12	160	450
13	100	400
14	75	100

PAGE 87

NO.	1974 Price	1980 Price
1	55	65
2	65	100
3	30	
4	25	
5	15	
6	10	
7	250	150
7A, Lord Elgin		250
8		100
9		35
10		30
11		20
12		10

PAGE 88

NO.	1974 Price	1980 Price
1	160	200
2	100	
3	95	125
4	95	100
5	60	65
6	60	
7	65	100
8	30	50
9	25	

PAGE 89

No Changes except

ELGIN 16 SIZE UP-DOWN INDICATORS

19J B.W. Raymond (372)	325
19J B.W. Raymond (455)	325
21J B.W. Raymond (391)	350
21J B.W. Raymond (472)	350
21J B.W. Raymond (478) Military (Cased)	500
21J B.W. Raymond (47?)	350
21J B.W. Raymond (?) Military SS Hack (Cased)	500
21J Father Time (?4)	375
21J Father Time (454)	375
21J Veritas (?5)?	450
23J B.W. Raymond (376)	400
23J B.W. Raymond (494)	400
23J B.W. Raymond (494) P.S. Military (Cased)	600
23J B.W. Raymond (540)	400
23J B.W. Raymond (540) P.S. Military (Cased)	600
23J Veritas (376)	600
23J Veritas (453)	600

ELGIN 18 SIZE UP-DOWN INDICATORS

19J B.W. Raymond (240)	550
21J B.W. Raymond (390)	700
21J Father Time (367)	700
21J Father Time Free Sprung	750
21J Veritas (239)	800
21J Veritas (274) Htg.	1400
23J Veritas (214)	1200
21J Elgin Natl.W.Co.(?2)	700
21J Elgin Natl.W.Co.(412) Free Sprung 3P	750
21J Father Time (367)	1500

(Free Sprung cased in original 6 oz. open face case with large deck watch dial—SCARCE).

21J Father Time (367)	600

(Mounted in Gimballs with both boxes.)

21J Elgin Natl.W.Co.(412)	600

(Mounted in Gimballs with both boxes.)

The statement at the bottom of this page, "Add $150 for winding indicator on either 18 Size or 16 Size" is no longer valid and will not apply.

PAGE 90

NO.	1974 Price	1980 Price
1		Rare
2	160 ?	300
3	100	125
4	75	100
5	100	
6	55	100
7	65	100
8	30	
9	25	

PAGE 91

NO.	1974 Price	1980 Price
1	20	
2	15	
3	10	
4	60	100
5	150	

PAGE 92, 93, 94 & 95

No Changes.

PAGE 96

Cannot be Up-Dated.

PAGE 99

See Page 27 of the 1978 Indicator for more info.

PAGE 100

CORNELL

Cornell watches are scarce and not traded enough to really get a handle on their actual value. The Chicago Cornells run from $300 to $600, with the California Cornells at least $100 higher.

WESTERN WATCH CO.

The last of the Cornells made when the machinery came back to Chicago are marked "Western Watch Co." and are very scarce and desirable collector pieces.

PAGE 101

No interest—No change except

NO.	1974 Price	1980 Price
9	150	800

PAGE 102

No activity—No change except

NO.	1974 Price	1980 Price
1	150	800

PAGE 103

No Changes.

PAGE 104

Columbus Watch Co.

For complete breakdown of all Columbus watches, see Page 32 to Page 37 in the 1977 Indicator.

NO.	1974 Price	1980 Price
1	200	150
2	85	125
3	85	125
4	65	40
5	$ 65	$ 40
6	35	20
7	35	20
8	25	50
9	85	75
10	85	75
11	50	30
12	50	50
13	60	50
14	45	40
15	200	
16	200	150
17	75	85
18	75	85
19	50	30
20	50	30
21	40	35
22	40	35

PAGE 105

NO.	1974 Price	1980 Price
1	110	
2	110	
3	90	
4	90	
5	70	40
6	70	40
7	140	150
8	100	50
9	100	50
10	90	75
11	50	40
12	40	35
13	35	25

PAGE 106

NO.	1974 Price	1980 Price
1, 21J	160	225
1, 23J	225	450
1, 17J	115	175
1, 25J	800	1600
2	80	
3	100	
4	70	

PAGE 107

NO.	1974 Price	1980 Price
1	50	
2	35	
3	40	
RKW	150	

PAGE 108

NO.	1974 Price	1980 Price
1	200	250
2	120	150
3	85	
4	65	50

PAGE 109

NO.	1974 Price	1980 Price
1	60	
2	85	
3	40	
4	70	

PAGE 110

NO.	1974 Price	1980 Price
1	65	
2	40	20
3	50	30

The production date serial numbers on this page have been revised and are shown on Page 37 of the 1977 Indicator. On Pages 32 to 37 of the 1977 Indicator there is a much more complete illustrated listing with price guide of all the known Columbus grades.

PAGE 111

Seth Thomas

NO.	1974 Price	1980 Price
1	200	1000
2	165	135
3	150	125
4	175	125
5	100	60
6	100	60
7	60	40
8	70	50
9	175	1000
10	75	
11	75	
12	60	
13	70	
14	50	
15	50	
16	$	$ 60
17	50	
18	50	
19	40	
20	75	
21	55	
25J Maiden	1000	2500

PAGE 112

The model numbers on this page are confusing. The Maiden Lane is Model 5 and all Model 5's are open face. This is a beautiful movement with most of the 17J and above done in 2-tone (gold & nickel) damaskeened. The lever set is more desirable and brings more money, but the pendant set can (I believe) be considered railroad grade also.

	1974 Price	1980 Price
1, 21J Maiden L.	200	800
1A, 21J		400
2, 17J LS 2-tone	175	200
2A, 17J PS 2-tone	175	
3	150	
4	80	
5	80	
6, 15J gilded	60	
7, 7-11J gilded	50	
8	250	1000
9	70	60
10	70	40
11	60	35
12	60	35

The Henry Molineux shown on this page is a Model 2 and all Model 2's are hunting case, and I believe are well represented on Page 111 of Book 2.

	1974 Price	1980 Price
13	100	
14	100	
15	80	
16	80	
17	140	300
18	80	
19	80	
20	80	
21	80	
22	60	
23	60	

PAGE 113

NO.	1974 Price	1980 Price
1	200	800
2	175	400
3	150	200

PAGES 114—118

No Changes.

PAGE 119

New England Watch Co.

	1974 Price	1980 Price
Girl	75	150
Flag	75	150
Ship	75	150
Horse	75	150

Raise All Enamel $50
No change on others.

PAGE 120

	1974 Price	1980 Price
Skelton	225	300
Cards	125	200

Raise all Enamel $50
No changes on others.

PAGE 121

	1974 Price	1980 Price
Train, 12-S	60	125
Flag, 12-S	60	125
Dog, 12-S	60	125
Horse, 16-S	75	150
Dog, 16-S	75	150
Riding, 16-S	75	150

Raise all Enamel $50

PAGE 122

Non-Magnetic W. Co.

	1974 Price	1980 Price
101		1100
110		1500
102		1000
112		1200
103		900
120		1500
125		1800

See Note No. 1, Page 15

PAGE 122 (Cont.)

NO.	1974 Price	1980 Price
130	$	$2500
135		2200
140		2200
145		1800
150		1700
155		1600
210		3000
215		2400

To bring these prices retail, watches would have to be mint and heavy cases.

PAGE 123, 124 & 125

No Interest—No Changes.

PAGE 126

NO.	1974 Price	1980 Price
1, 21J	100	150
1, 23J		600
1, 24J	400	1200
2, 17J		150
3, 17J	50	85
4, 15J	45	55
5, 15J	35	45
6, 21J	85	300
7, 17J	70	150
8, 17J	40	75
9, 15J	30	65
10, 15J	25	50
11, 11J	25	50

PAGE 127

South Bend Watch Co.

NO.	1974 Price	1980 Price
1	40	75
2	40	75
3	40	75
4	30	65
5	40	100
6	40	100
7	30	50
8	30	50
9	20	50
10	35	50
11	35	50

PAGE 128

NO.	1974 Price	1980 Price
1	80	
2	80	
3	70	250
3A, Pol.		800
4	70	250
4A, Pol.		800
5	100	175
6	80	150
7	70	200
8	50	150
9	40	
10	40	

PAGE 129

No Changes.

PAGE 130

NO.	1974 Price	1980 Price
1	150	200
2	150	200
3	130	175
4	40	
5	40	60
6	35	
7	35	
8	35	
9	35	
10	30	
11	30	

PAGE 131

NO.	1974 Price	1980 Price
1	20	40
2	15	30
3	15	20
4	40	60
5	30	50
6	20	40

PAGE 132, 133 & 134

Trenton Watch Co.
No Interest—No Changes except
No.13 on P. 133. RARE-$300

ROCKFORD SECTION
PAGE 135 – 144

See Page 22 of the 1978 Indicator for report on Rockford Research.

If you are a Rockford collector or dealer who needs more information, I have a book for sale called, "Rockford Grade & Serial Numbers with Production Figures and Price Guide", for $10.00 plus postage.

PAGE 135

Some of these higher prices are based on rarity as indicated by Production Figures, and only a few collectors are willing to pay them.

NO.	1974 Price	1980 Price
1	$ 200	$1000
2	75	35
3	100	50
4	90	50
5	50	35
6	140	100
7	50	35
8	140	100
9	55	35

PAGE 136

NO.	1974 Price	1980 Price
1	100	200
2	100	150
3	90	150
4	90	200
5	70	
6	70	
7	50	
8	50	
9	40	
10	40	
11	50	
12	50	
13	80	
14	80	
15	75	
16	75	
17	75	100
18	75	125
19	50	200
20	50	200
21	45	
22	45	
23	40	30
24	40	30

PAGE 137

NO.	1974 Price	1980 Price
1	40	30
2	40	30
3	45	30
4	45	30
5	40	30
6	40	30
7	30	25
8	30	25
9	125	150
10		Not Made
11	65	40
12		Not Made
13	30	40
14		Not Made

Some of the Rockford Grade Numbers advertised by Rockford and shown in this book, were never manufactured. These are indicated by the notation "Not Made".

PAGE 138

NO.	1974 Price	1980 Price
1	40	
2	Not Made	
3	40	
4	Not Made	
5	35	25
6	Not Made	
7	40	
8	40	250
9	30	
10	Not Made	
11	30	
12	Not Made	
13	100	
14	75	100
15	75	
16	50	75
17	50	
18	40	

NO.	1974 Price	1980 Price
19	$ 20	$

PAGE 139

NO.	1974 Price	1980 Price
1	550	1500
2	550	1550
3	200	250
4	200	250
5	185	150
6	165	140
7	165	140
8	165	175
9	165	175
10	70	
11	70	
12	70	50
13	70	50
14	70	40
15	70	40
16	50	40
17	50	40

PAGE 140

NO.	1974 Price	1980 Price
23J, Doll		500
1, 21J	200	400
1, 23J	265	750
2, 21J	200	450
3	165	200
4	165	200
5	150	175
6	150	175
7	140	165
8	140	165
9	140	150
10	140	150
11	120	175
12	120	175
13	50	40
14	50	40
15	40	30
16	40	30
17	40	30
18	40	30

PAGE 141

No Changes.

PAGE 142

NO.	1974 Price	1980 Price
572	40	30
573	40	30
570	40	30
575	40	30
584	35	25
585	35	25
590	35	25
595	35	25
140	75	
150.0	60	
160	50	

PAGE 143

NO.	1974 Price	1980 Price
340 H	125	250
3450	125	175
350 H	70	
3550	70	
190 H	50	75
185 H	75	
16-S, 17J - P	550	700
16-S, 17J - L		750
16-S, 21J	450	700
18-S, 21J	550	3500

PAGE 144

NO.	1974 Price	1980 Price
620 H	125	200
630 H	70	200

No Other Changes.

PAGE 145

Waltham Watch Co.
Model 57

NO.	1974 Price	1980 Price
1	40	25
2	35	25
3	35	25
4	40	50

PAGE 146

NO.	1974 Price	1980 Price
5	40	50
5½	50	
7	35	
8	35	
9	35	

PAGES 147 & 148

No Changes except

NO.	1974 Price	1980 Price
2, P. 148	$ 300	$ 1250

On the Waltham Chronographs at the bottom of the page, there has been some increase in value because of the jump in gold price. Mostly, only the highest grade movements are sought by collectors. The low grade in silver or gold filled will seldom bring over $200.

PAGE 149

NO.	1974 Price	1980 Price
AT Co.		40
PSB		25
RER		40
Wm. E.		25
Sterling		25
Broadway		30
15		25
3		20
1		10
Crescent		50
AT Co.		50
W.W. Co.		30
35		40
25		30
15		25
3		25

PAGE 150

No Changes.

PAGE 151

NO.	1974 Price	1980 Price
1		80
2		50
3		50
4		30
5		25
6		20
7		15
8		15
9	90	120
10		35
11		20

PAGE 152

NO.	1974 Price	1980 Price
1	275	400
1-A, 19J		400
2	300	500
3		75
4	60	50
5	50	30
6	35	25
7	30	25
8		15
9	300	400
10	310	500
11	70	50

PAGE 153

NO.	1974 Price	1980 Price
1	200	300
2		50
3		40
4		30
5	125	200
6		25
7		20
8		15
9		20
10		50
11		50
12		40
13		25
14		25
15		20
16	200	225
17		40
18		25

PAGE 154

NO.	1974 Price	1980 Price
1	Vanguard	
23J	160	125
23J	160	125
21J	80	
21J	80	
19J	80	
19J	80	
23J	180	130

NO.	1974 Price	1980 Price

PAGE 154 (Cont.)

23J	$ 180	$ 130
17J	150	

With Up—Down Indicator

21J		1200
23J		1250
Premier		100
4, A.T. & Co.	70	
5	45	
	45	

PAGE 155

1 to 6	No Changes	
7 PS	300	400
7 LS	300	550
8 Up-Down	220	425

WALTHAM 16 SIZE UP-DOWN INDICATORS

21J Crescent St. (1908)		400
21J Crescent St. (1912)		425
23J Vanguard (1908) 5P		425
23J Vanguard (1908) 6P		425
23J " (1908) 6P Lossier		425
23J Vanguard (1899) PS		475
23J Vanguard (1912)		425
23J Vanguard (1912) PS Military (Cased)		600
23J Riverside Maximus 100 Damaskeened		3000
23J Riverside Maximus 200 Not Damaskeened		2500
19J Ball Model		3250
23J Premier Maximus Original marked case		8500

WALTHAM 18 SIZE UP-DOWN INDICATORS

19J Vanguard		1200
21J Vanguard		1200
23J Vanguard		1250
9, 23J LS	110	120
9, 23J PS	90	100
9, 21J LS		500
9, 19J PS	80	100
9, 19J LS	90	175

PAGE 156

No Changes.

PAGE 157

No Changes except

1	225	250
11	120	150

PAGES 158 & 159

See Note No. 1, Page 15

PAGE 160

1	300	200
2	1250	8000
3	100	100
4	250	185
5	250	175

PAGE 161

1	100	
2	100	
3	100	
4	80	
5	90	
6	85	
7	70	60

PAGE 162

Cases Only

1	30	100
2	30	90
3	30	60
4	15	40
5	15	40
6	15	40
7	5	15
8	7.50	10

Adjust the other watches accordingly. Old original cases in mint or new condition are becoming more and more desirable, as collectors would rather have a mint old case than a new one. More cases in my "Foreign & American Pocket Watch Id. &

Price Guide, Book 3," and my "1976 Price Indicator."

PAGE 163

1	$ 300	$ 200
2	110	90
3	65	55
4	80	70
5	50	
6	80	
7	45	
8	40	
9	40	

PAGE 164

Cannot be Revised.

PAGE 165 — 168

No Changes.

PAGES 169 & 170

Howard Watch Co.
See Note No. 1, Page 15

PAGE 171

Adjust these prices according to Page 170. Lots of interest for Howard cases and watches.

PAGE 172

No Changes.

On Page 22 of the "1977 Price Indicator" is a full report on the Howard Watch Co., by Howard Gunderson. Contains Production Dates and Figures. A must for the Howard collector!

PAGE 173

No change except, No. 8 and 10 will not now bring these prices until the collectors discover that they are the highest grade watch made by the old Howard Company.

PAGE 174

No Changes, and must be original case. Add the value of the case to these prices.

PAGE 175

1	225	400
2	225	400
3	175	
4	185	
5	175	200
6	140	
7	140	
8	150	
9	125	175
10	120	175
11	120	
12	120	100

Deduct $50 off Railroad grades for pendant set.

PAGE 176

1	50	
3	1500	9500
4	150	
5	150	
6	100	75
7	100	75
8	75	
9	75	
10	75	
11	75	
12	70	50
13	70	50
14	70	50
15	70	50

PAGE 177

No Changes except

1	225	400

See Note No. 1, Page 15

PAGE 178

1	$ 150	$
2	120	100
3	100	120
4	100	

PAGE 179

1	175	
2	70	

All of the watch case values on this page should be doubled.

992	400	800
923	475	950
925	140	300
926	150	300

PAGE 180

1	550	600
2	250	450
3	125	150
4	125	150

PAGE 181

Open Face	50	125
Hunting	70	200

PAGE 182

Webb C. Ball

1, OF		150
1, H		200
2		450
2A, 23J Hamilton		450
2B, 23J Hamilton Bridge Model		450
3		150
4		125
5		100
6		150

PAGE 183

CORRECTION: "Waltham Pictured" is really a 16 Size, 23J Hamilton.

16-S, Up-Down Indicator 3500

All of the following priced as if in original, mint Ball cases. Ball watches were working watches and show heavy use. An early mint, 16 Size Ball case is a rarity and is worth $125 to $150 by itself. Collectors want all of the Ball watches in their collection to be in original marked Ball cases. I think as railroad collectors become more knowledgeable, Ball watches will become more important to them and therefore increase in value more rapidly. I recommend that you hold on to them if you can.

1,16-S 21J Silver	100	175
2,18-S,21J Silver	100	250
3,16-S,21J 20Y	125	200
4,18-S,21J 20Y	125	275
5,16-S,21J 25Y	135	200
6,18-S,21J 25Y	135	275

The Silveroid is the most scarce but very little attention is given them. The early Silveroid with the gold shield inlaid are really to be treasured.

One of the later styles with the Butler finish back in 16 Size is now being manufactured by the Star Watch Case Co., using the old methods. So far, collectors have been slow to accept them. The 1979 wholesale price is $72. each.

7, 16-S, 23J Hamilton Bridge	275	700
7A, 16-S, 23J Hamilton	300	700
8, 16-S, 23J Waltham	RARE	

No 23J, Waltham made, Ball watches have shown up that I am aware of.

9, 16-S, 23J Ill.	$325	$ 700
10, 18-S, 23J Hamilton (5 known)	400	5000

NOTE: I believe at the present time that railroad watch collectors should have at least one each of the three different 23J, 16 Size Ball watches in their collection. Also, be watching for a 16 Size, 23J Waltham, and dreaming of a 23J, 18 Size Hamilton Ball. Ball played a very important role in the development of the American railroad watch, and when the full story of Webb C. Ball is told, the watches will take on more importance.

PAGE 184

From recent research, I believe the hole in the bow (Patent Safety Bow) was later advertised as the "20th Century Model". 16 Size watches with the brotherhood markings, such as BofLE, BofRT, ORC, etc., are worth about $100 more if marked on the dial, and $100 additional if also marked on the movement. There is a large selection of these watches in the "1977 Indicator." 18 Size brotherhood markings value about $200 extra for markings on both the plate and dial.

16, 17J, Silver		150
16, 19J, Silver	90	175
18, 17J, Silver	70	250
18, 19J, Silver	90	300
16, 17J, 20Y	90	200
16, 19J, 20Y	120	225
18, 17J, 20Y	90	250
18, 19J, 20Y	120	400
16, 17J, 25Y	110	200
16, 19J, 25Y	130	225
18, 17J, 25Y	110	250
18, 19J, 25Y	130	425
16, 17J, 14K (Rare)		600
16, 19J, 14K "		625
18, 17J, 14K (Rare)		1000
18, 19J, 14K "		1100

NOTE: Hamilton made 16 Size Ball watches in 19, 21 & 23 Jewel. All were railroad grade and seem to be preferred by collectors over the watches Waltham made for them.

PAGE 185

Manhattans are interesting watches to add to a general collection. In their original, nickel silver case, $125; Gold filled $150 to $175. It is very important that the watch be mint and running, because they are hard to repair.

KEYSTONE WATCH CO.

All are older and predecessors to Hamilton, but nobody seems to be collecting them. Therefore, the value remains low and mostly depends on the case.

TERSTEGEN 5-MINUTE REPEATERS

I have seen three of these, two Elgins and one Howard, neither of them cased nor working well. I think one of these working and in an original appearing case, might bring $1500 to $2000. On the other hand, I may be misjudging them as I have no actual sales on which to base this value.

PAGE 186

No Changes.
Watches of this type are shown in "Book 3."

PAGE 187

I have in my collection a hand-made watch by Charles DeLong. A full description with pictures is shown on Page 89 of the "1978 Indicator." My watch is a very desirable addition to any collection, and from the offers I have had, a very valuable one. To my knowledge, this is the only DeLong that has turned up. If, as you read this, you find that you have a watch of the type (one of a kind handmade), drop me a line and tell me about it. I attend most of the NAWCC regionals to gather information and to try and keep track of what collectors and dealers will pay for all kinds of watches and clocks. Bring your watch with you so I can examine it and we can talk about it. The watches shown on this page (and others like them) are made by famous prototype, pattern, and model makers who were important to the development of the American watch. They are very desirable and valuable watches to collectors and museums.

PAGE 188

THE CHESHIRE WATCH: *This watch is pretty scarce and old. No one seems to be willing to pay much for one except the collector who wants one for his collection of watches made by American watch factories. Mint,*

original in Nickel—$125.

PHILADELPHIA WATCH CO.:
Arguments are still going on as to whether this is an American or Swiss made watch. A Bill of Lading has recently been found that indicates they are Swiss. They are made in Swiss sizes from about 10 Size through 19 Size, in both high grade gilt and nickel. Most I have seen are uncased, and if running, sold for about $100 to $150. Cased in silver, hunting, 18 Size—$350 to $450.

Most serious collectors seem to have decided during the past year or so that they should have one in their collection, no matter who made them, and the watches find ready buyers. They are Keywind & Set from the back and will not fit American style cases. If you buy an uncased movement, you should be prepared to wait a while for the case.

AUBURNDALE TIMER: *I have had about 10 of these in my lifetime because I have gone out of my way to buy them. When I put this book out in 1974, they would bring about $300. Since that time, interest has fallen off. I don't understand why because this is an early and important watch, even though of low quality. Most do not work well and are cased mostly in nickel. The other models of the Auburndale, such as the Rotary, Bentley and Lincoln, are even more rare and I don't have a record of any sales.*

BRISTOL WATCH CO.: *Even though this ad says "American Made Watches and Cases", I have serious doubts about this. The quality and finish looks like cheap Swiss import to me. If anyone reading this has facts to the contrary I would like to hear from me. Most of these sell for $35 to $60 cased in nickel and running.*

NEW HAVEN WATCH CO.:
This movement shown is, I believe, Swiss made. The real New Haven looks like the Trenton Movement No. 20 on Page 132 of "Book 2." The New Haven still brings the price of a Swiss fake, about $35 cased in nickel and running.

PAGE 191

NO.	1974 Price	1980 Price
F1	$ 150	$ 650
F2	525	1200
F3	385	1000
F4	175	300
F5	600	750
F6 Mvt.		20
F6 Dial		25
F7	300	450
B1	200	
B2	225	450
B3	100	125
B4	165	200
B5	150	
B6	150	175
B7	525	2000
B8	525	950
B9 Mvt.		30
B9 Case	150	
B10	450	550
B11	200	300
B12		1000

NO.	1974 Price	1980 Price
B13	$ 200	$ 300
B14	150	
B15	100	
B16	300	450
B17	200	350
B18	225	425
B19	150	200
B20	350	

PAGE 192

This picture was taken in the summer of 1974. I have since sold the old brown Travco Motor Home and now have a blue and white, 29 foot F.M.C. (Food Machinery Co.) Motor Home. Larry, sitting in the door and now 23, has finished high school and one year of college, and is now working full time for me in the Land Survey Company as a Party Chief. Our survey work has been rather slow due to the money market, and Larry has been trying to learn the gold, silver, and pocket watch business this Fall and Spring. Sherry, now 21, is still working for me as Secretary and Girl Friday, and comes with me occasionally to the NAWCC Marts and antique shows to help out. Alpha is still on the road to recovery and has made really good progress this year. Most of her double vision and other paralysis problems have corrected themselves and we're looking forward to a safe and healthy year. I wish all the best of health for you and your loved ones.   *ROY*

EXPLANATION OF THESE PAGES (3 — 18)

This is the fifth in a series of price indicators: the 1976, 1977, 1978, 1979 Pocket Watch Price Indicators, and this one, the 1980 Pocket Watch Price Indicator. I have issued these yearly publications as a means of updating the prices for the **1974 American Pocket Watch Identification & Price Guide, Book 2**, (red, white & blue cover), and presenting all of the new knowledge that I gained during the year. So, if you are interested and would like to have everything I have published on American pocket watches, you will need to have the **American Pocket Watch Identification & Price Guide, Book 2** (published in 1974), and all of the **Indicators**. I believe the next most important book you should have is the **Trademark**. A full description of each of these books can be found elsewhere in this book.

You will find these eighteen (18) pages in both the 1980 Pocket Watch Price Indicator and in the Revised (June, 1980) issues of the 1974 American Pocket Watch Identification & Price Guide, Book 2. In the 1974 book, these pages will be inserted after Page 2.

The following explanation is directed to you folks who are reading one of my watch price guides for the first time. Prices have been steadily increasing on most models since I started issuing these price guides in 1972. This applies mostly to the high grades (which are railroad), and the watches that have been determined to be rare or unusual by ongoing research projects conducted by individuals scattered throughout the United States. Everyone has known about railroad watches from the beginning and there has always been an active market because so many people collect railroad watches. The watches that have been proven rare or unusual, or those desirable for any other reason, are reflected by the higher prices shown (without an explanation.) It would take a book by itself to present the explanations.

For those of you who are just beginning or just getting interested in watch collecting, you might keep in mind that those watches priced $100 and above are easier to find a buyer for. Those priced below $100 are generally not collectible watches and are traders. So, you can consider it safe if you buy original, mint condition watches at 75% or below the prices shown.

There are some watches listed in this update section that do not appear in the **American Pocket Watch Identification & Price Guide, Book 2**, and this will cause you a little trouble until you understand more about collecting watches. An example is on Page 6, under Page 89. Listed here are more Up-Down Indicators than are shown on that page in Book 2.

If there are no new prices shown under the **1980 Price** column, that means there has been no appreciable changes.

NEW UP—DATED PRICES FOR 1980
for the
1976 PRICE INDICATOR (Published in 1975)

PAGE 13

Illinois Keywinds

K-1= Keywind Model
H-2= Hunting Model 2
O-3= Open Face Model 3

NO.	1976 Price	1980 Price
1, K-1	$300	$550
1, H-2		450
1, O-3		500
3, K-1	100	1100
3, H-2		700
3, O-3		900
4, K-1	150	1200
4, H-2		800
4, O-3		1000
5, K-1	75	150
5, H-2		150
5, O-3		200
1, K-1	140	150
1, H-2		150
1, O-3		200

PAGE 14

Illinois Keywinds

NO.	1976 Price	1980 Price
2, K-1	40	
2, H-2		100
3, K-1	40	50
3, H-2	40	
3, O-3		100
4, K-1	40	
4, H-2		75
Mary Stuart, 15J		200
Rose Leland, 13J		200
Sunnyside, 11J		100
Arlington, 11J, K-1		100
Arlington, 11J, H-2		100

PAGE 15

18 Size Illinois

NO.	1976 Price	1980 Price
24J Bunn S.	400	750
26J Bunn S.	2000	6000
26J Lafayette		6000
26J Ben Franklin		6000
26J C & O Special		8000
24J B & O Spl	600	2600
21J Bunn S.	80	125
17J Bunn	135	150
79	35	
69	30	
59	25	

PAGE 16

16 Size Illinois

NO.	1976 Price	1980 Price
1	200	600
2	150	200
3	125	150
4	150	200
5	60	
6	40	
7	30	
8	25	
9	20	

PAGE 17

Bunn Special

NO.	1976 Price	1980 Price
1	160	250
2	175	300
3	175	300
4, SG	500	900
4A, GF	350	750
5	175	300

PAGE 18

Bunn Specials 163-A, 161-A

NO.	1976 Price	1980 Price
1	350	850
2	330	750
3	225	400
4	225	400
5	225	425
6	65	
7	35	

PAGE 19

Benjamin Franklin

NO.	1976 Price	1980 Price
1	175	
2	2000	3500

NO.	1976 Price	1980 Price
3	$75	$100
4	250	350
5	90	
6	30	50
7	35	50

PAGES 20, 21

1877 Watch Case Brochure.
1877 Howard Watch Company Brochure.

PAGES 22, 23

1864 Waltham Watch Company Brochure.

PAGES 24 — 30

Waltham Model Identification showing 80 different movements.

PAGE 31

Waltham cased watches (1942) No Changes.

PAGE 32

Waltham cased RR watches. (1933) No Changes except

NO.	1976 Price	1980 Price
1	120	
2	275	425

PAGE 33

Cased Ball Watches (1916) See Page 183 & 184 of BOOK 2 for values of the top three watches. No other changes.

PAGE 34, 35, 36

Webb C. Ball Serial Numbers & Production Figures.

PAGE 37

Columbus Watch Co. (1904)

NO.	1976 Price	1980 Price
1, 25J	1250	1500
2	400	600
3	200	225
4	200	150
5	70	
6	50	
7	50	

PAGE 38

Hampden Watch Co. (1902) No Changes except

NO.	1976 Price	1980 Price
3	130	150

PAGE 39

1905 Mixed American 18-S

NO.	1976 Price	1980 Price
1	130	150
2, 23J	125	
2, 21J	80	
2, 19J		80
2, 17J	150	
3	1500	2500
4, 23J	160	
4, 21J	100	
5	120	
6	75	

PAGE 40

1905 Mixed American 18-S

NO.	1976 Price	1980 Price
1	300	350
2	75	100
3	200	250
4	75	
5	70	
6, 19J	60	
6, 17J	100	

PAGE 41

1905 Mixed American 18-Size
No Changes except

NO.	1976 Price	1980 Price
1	$150	$200

PAGE 42

1905 Mixed American 18-Size
No Changes.

PAGE 43

1905 Mixed American 16-Size
No Changes except

NO.	1976 Price	1980 Price
1	300	500
2	200	225

PAGE 44

1905 Mixed American 12-Size
No Changes.

PAGE 45

1905 Mixed American 16-Size
No Changes.

PAGE 46

1905 Mixed American 12-Size and 6-Size
No Changes.

PAGE 47

1905 Mixed American 6-Size and 0-Size
No Changes except

NO.	1976 Price	1980 Price
Riverside M.	125	150

PAGE 48

1905 Mixed American 0-Size
No Changes.

PAGE 49

0-Size Solid Gold Cases.

NO.	1976 Price	1980 Price
3	155	200
4	165	200
5	175	300
6	175	300
7	175	300
8	175	300
9	175	300
10	225	500
11	225	500
12	225	500
13	225	500
14	225	500
15	225	500
16	150	250
16A	175	300

See Note No. 1, Page 15

PAGE 50

18-Size Gold Filled Cases

NO.	1976 Price	1980 Price
1	45	75
2	50	75
3	75	90
4	65	90
5	75	90
6	65	90
7	65	90
8	65	90

PAGE 51

18-Size Gold Filled Cases.

1980 Prices	OF	HC
1	75	120
2	85	140
3	85	150
4	85	150
5	85	150
6	85	150
7	85	150
8	85	150

PAGE 52

18 Size Gold Filled Cases.

1980 Prices	OF	HC

NO.	1976 Price	1980 Price
1	$70	$120
2	85	140
3	85	150
4	85	150
5	85	150
6	120	170
7	85	150
8	85	150

PAGE 53

18-Size Gold Filled Cases.

1980 Prices	OF
1	70
2	80
3	95
4	90
5	95
6	120
7	120
8	100

Subtract $10 for Swing Ring.

PAGE 54

16-Size Gold Filled Cases.

1980 Prices	OF	HC
1	80	120
2	85	125
3	85	130
4	90	145
5	90	145
6	90	145
7	90	170
8	105	170
9	105	170

PAGE 55

16-Size 14K Solid Gold Cases.

1980 Prices	OF	HC
1, LT	125	
1, M	160	
1, H	175	
2, LT	135	
2, M	160	
2, H	185	
3, LT	125	
3, M	150	
3, H	175	
4	225	325
5	135	
6	225	325
7	225	325
8	200	300
9	225	325

See Note No. 1, Page 15

PAGE 56

16-Size 14K Solid Gold Cases.

1980 Prices	OF	HC
1, LT	235	
1, M	260	
1, H	385	
2, LT	225	
2, M	250	
2, H	275	
3, LT	275	
3, M		325
3, H	225	375
4		375
5		375
6		450
7		1000
8		800
9		525

See Note No. 1, Page 15

PAGE 57

16-Size Gold Filled Cases

1980 Prices	OF	HC
1	100	160
2	100	160
3	100	170
4	100	160
5	100	170
6	100	170
7	100	
8	90	
9	95	

PAGE 58

16-Size Gold Filled Cases.

PAGE 58 (Cont.)

1980 Prices	OF	HC
1	$ 100	$ 175
2	100	175
3	100	175
4	100	180
5	100	180
6	100	190
7	100	
8	90	
9	90	

PAGE 59

16 Size Gold Filled Cases.

1980 Prices	OF	HC
1	80	150
2	95	155

1980 Prices	OF	HC
3	$ 95	$ 155
4	95	165
5	95	175
6	90	175
7	120	200
8	95	185
9	95	185

PAGE 60

16 Size Gold Filled Cases.

1980 Prices	B&B	SR
1	90	75
2	95	80
3	95	80
4	120	100
5	105	90

1980 Prices	OF	HC
6	$ 140	$ 120
7	95	80
8	95	80
9	95	80

PAGE 61

16 Size Gold Filled Cases.

1980 Prices	B&B	SR
1	85	75
2	90	80
3	90	80
4	125	115
5	105	95
6	105	95
7	115	105
8	80	80
9	100	90

PAGE 62

12 Size Gold Filled Cases.
No Changes.

PAGE 63

NO.	1976 Price	1980 Price

16-Size Hamilton Elinvar Cased Watches.

1	$ 160	$ 250
2	80	175
3	170	275
4	160	225
5	60	80
6	200	425
7	400	1400

NEW UP—DATED PRICES FOR 1980
for the
1977 PRICE INDICATOR (Published in 1976)

NO.	1977 Price	1980 Price

PAGE 15

1895 Model Howard
No Changes.

PAGE 16

1895 Howard
No Changes.

PAGE 17

18-Size Muhr Howard Cases.
No Changes.

PAGE 18

16-Size Howard Cased Watches.

1, Box	$ 50	$ 60
2		275
3, 21J	200	250
4, 23J	325	650
5, 23J	500	900
6, 23J	475	850
7, 21J	300	450
8, 23J	325	650
9, 21J	200	250

PAGES 19 — 20 — 21

10 & 12-Size Howard Cased Watches.
No Changes.

PAGES 22 — 23

Research progress report on the E. Howard Watch Co., showing total and accurate production.

PAGES 24 — 25

Ferguson Railroad Dial and Abbott Sure Time.
No Changes.

PAGES 26 — 29

All known Hampden Grades with Price Guide.
No Changes except

23J		Add 10%

PAGE 30

Hampden Watch Co.
No Changes.

PAGE 31

Atlas, Marvin, Peerless, Sundial.

NO.	1977 Price	1980 Price

No Changes.

PAGES 32 — 35

Columbus Watch Company
No Changes.

PAGES 36 — 37

All known Columbus Watch Co. Grades with Prices and New Production Date Chart.
No Changes Except

18 Size, 25J	$	$1600
16 Size, Ruby		300
18 Size, 23J		600

PAGES 38 — 39

Washington Watch Co.

1	40	
2	20	
3	70	100
4	60	75
5, 23J	200	350
5, 25J		2500
6	400	600
7	40	75
8	50	65
9	75	
10	85	65
11, 21J	135	200
11, 19J		200
12	50	75
13, 21J	200	150
13, 19J		150
0 Size		60
6 Size		50

Plus Case

PAGES 40 — 41

Sears, Roebuck & Co. (1905)
Illinois & Seth Thomas.
No Changes.

PAGE 42

Montgomery Ward (1904)
No Changes except

6, 24J	400	600

PAGES 43 — 44

Montgomery Ward (1904)
No Changes.

PAGES 45 — 48

Benjamin Franklin
No Changes except

NO.	1977 Price	1980 Price
No. 200	$	$ 6000
No. 300		3500

PAGES 49 — 53

United States Watch Co. Marion, NJ.
See Page 27 of the 1978 Price Indicator for complete listing & Price Guide.

PAGES 54 — 58

South Bend Watch Co.
12-Size Cased Watches.
No Changes.
Pg. 57 - Production Date Table.
Pg. 58 - Price Guide to all known grades.

PAGES 59 — 65

Ball Watch Co. (1902) Original Catalog showing old model Ball cases and the railroad Union & Order Dials, etc.
No Changes.

PAGES 66 — 67

Ball Watch Co. (1934) Cased Watches.

1	150	210
2	65	110
3	75	120
4	75	130
5	75	130
6	75	130

PAGE 68

Ball Watch Co. (1934) Cased Watches.

1, Dial	25	
2	350	550
3	65	110
4	75	130
5	75	130
6	75	130

PAGE 69

Ball Watch Co. (1934) Cased Watches.

1	135	250
2, Box	25	50
3	125	150
4	30	50
5	30	50
6	30	50
7	30	50

NO.	1977 Price	1980 Price

PAGES 70 — 73

Watch Keys.
No Changes.

PAGE 74 — 75

Independent Watch Co. Fredonia, N.Y.

PAGES 76 — 82

1862 Waltham Factory Catalog. (Earliest Known.)
No Changes.
One watch like No. 1 on Pg. 79 is known to be in a collection.

PAGES 83 — 88

Watches by names not otherwise listed, with rough Price Guide.
No Changes.

PAGES 89 — 90

Railway Trademarks.

PAGE 91

Up-Down Indicators. See 1979 Price Indicator for revised list and new values.

PAGES 92 — 93

Burlington & Sante Fe Watch Company.
No Changes.

PAGE 94

Special Railroad Watches.

1		RARE
2	$	900
3		600
4		RARE
5		60
6		600

PAGE 95

Special Railroad Watches.

Up-Down		3500
ORC		3500
A.K.J.		600
E.F.B.		1000
S.T. Ball		RARE
H. Ball		1200

NEW UP—DATED PRICES FOR 1980
for the
1978 PRICE INDICATOR

PAGE 20

Mermod Jaccard, Hampdens, and Cases. No Changes.

PAGE 21

See Index in 1979 Indicator for page of revised values.

PAGE 22

Rockford Research by Roger Weiss, Jr.

PAGE 23

Illinois Research by Bill Meggers & Charles Sweeting.

PAGE 24

Freeport Watch Company

PAGE 27

United States Watch Co. Marion Watch Co., Marion, NJ Add 10% to 20% to most values. Research Project by Maylene Rabeneck.

PAGE 28

1872 Model Waltham. No Changes.

PAGE 29

72 Model Research by Tom Fowler.

PAGE 30 — 31

Up-Down Indicator Parts List for 16-Size & 18-Size Waltham.

PAGE 32 — 33

Mainspring Charts for all major watch companies.

PAGE 34 — 38

H. Muhr's Sons 1887 Price List of Cases and all watch company movement.

PAGE 39

Howard Watch Co. 1886 Brochure of Movements.

PAGE 40 — 43

N. H. White's 1887 Price List of American Watches and gold, silver, and filled cases.

PAGE 44

Non-Magnetic W. Co., Peoria, & Imported movements. No Changes.

PAGE 45

Non-Magnetic W. Co. made by Illinois No Changes except

NO.	1978 Price	1980 Price
2	155	150
7	240	500
1	550	1750

NO.	1978 Price	1980 Price
8	$ 155	$ 150

PAGE 46

Rockford No Changes.

PAGE 47

NO.	1978 Price	1980 Price
6S, 15J	125	150
6S, 17J	150	175
12S, 15J	125	150
12S, 17J	150	175
16S, 23J	350	700
16S, 17J	150	200
18S, 23J	500	1600
18S, 17J	150	250

PAGE 48

18-Size E. Howard Cases, 14K Marked Howard.

NO.	1978 Price	1980 Price
1	400	500
1A	450	550
2	450	550
2A	500	600
3	550	650
4	600	800
5	600	800
6	600	800
7	650	1000
8	1000	1500
9	1500	2000

See Note No. 1, Page 15

PAGE 49

18-Size E. Howard Cases, Gold filled, marked Howard.

NO.	1978 Price	1980 Price
1	200	275
1A	300	425
2	225	300
2A	325	450
3	225	300
3A	325	450
4	225	300
4A	325	450
5	300	425
5A	450	600
6	250	375
6A	350	550
7	200	325
7A	300	475
8	225	350
8A	325	500
9	225	350
9A	325	500

See Note No. 1, Page 15

PAGE 50

18-Size & 14-Size E. Howard 14K Marked Cases.

NO.	1978 Price	1980 Price
1	450	550
1A	500	600
2	500	600
3	600	800
4	500	600
5	650	800
6	800	1000
7	240	275
8	300	350
9	350	400
10	450	600

See Note No. 1, Page 15

PAGE 51

6-Size E. Howard Cases. 14K marked Howard.

NO.	1978 Price	1980 Price
1	525	725
2	675	875
3	1000	1500
4	400	500
5	200	
6	200	
7	240	

See Note No. 1, Page 15

NO.	1978 Price	1980 Price
8	200	
8A	225	
8B	250	

PAGE 52 — 53

Waterbury Rotary.

PAGE 54 — 55

Standard American W. Co. Pittsburg, Pa. No changes.

PAGE 56 — 57

Monarch Watch Co. made by Seth Thomas and Illinois. No Changes.

PAGE 58

NO.	1978 Price	1980 Price
25 Yr. Greenwich	600	2000

PAGE 59

Marshall Field Watches by Illinois.

NO.	1978 Price	1980 Price
1	200	450

PAGE 60

16-Size Cased Ball Watches (1929)

NO.	1978 Price	1980 Price
21J	$ 200	$
23J	500	700
Case	120	140

PAGE 61

16-Size Cased Ball Watches (1929)

NO.	1978 Price	1980 Price
21J	200	
23J	500	700
Case	120	140

PAGE 62

12-Size & 16-Size Ball Presentation Watches (1929).

NO.	1978 Price	1980 Price
19J, 12-S	250	Gold
21J, 16-S	325	Not
23J, 16-S	650	Revised

PAGE 63

12-Size Ball Complete Watches.

NO.	1978 Price	1980 Price
Cases	40	50
19J	150	

PAGES 64 — 65

12-Size Ball Cased Watches. No Changes.

PAGE 67

Ball Watches. No Changes except

NO.	1978 Price	1980 Price
1	75	200
4	100	125

PAGE 68

Ball Watches. No Changes except

NO.	1978 Price	1980 Price
1	1000	800
4	200	250
5	200	250
6	500	600

PAGE 69

Ball Watches

NO.	1978 Price	1980 Price
1	$ 375	$ 450
2	375	600
3		RARE
4	3000	4000
5	500	600
6	500	600
7	220	250
8	75	100
9	75	100

PAGE 70

No Changes.

PAGE 71

NO.	1978 Price	1980 Price
2	500	550
3	500	650
9		1500

PAGE 72

NO.	1978 Price	1980 Price
4	175	125
5	150	200
8	50	200

PAGE 73

NO.	1978 Price	1980 Price
2	150	200
3	150	200
7	600	500
8	450	400

PAGE 74

NO.	1978 Price	1980 Price
8		2000

PAGE 75

NO.	1978 Price	1980 Price
1		325
2		150
3		75
4		
5		75
6		160
7		150
9		200
10		450

PAGE 76

NO.	1978 Price	1980 Price
3	2000	3000
4	350	250
7	260	350

PAGE 77

NO.	1978 Price	1980 Price
1	200	375
2	2500	3500
3	260	350
4	75	25
8	240	225

PAGE 78

NO.	1978 Price	1980 Price
2	1000	
3	375	600
6	600	800
8	1050	2000

PAGE 79

NO.	1978 Price	1980 Price
2	260	375
9	155	250

PAGE 80

NO.	1978 Price	1980 Price
1	700	1200
2	700	1200

NO.	1978 Price	1980 Price	NO.	1978 Price	1980 Price	NO.	1978 Price	1980 Price	NO.	1978 Price	1980 Price
	PAGE 80 (Cont.)			*Premier Maximus.*		7, JR	$ 475	$ 600	2	$ 500	$ 900
4	$155	$200		*No Changes.*		8, PRS	600	1100	3	260	325
5		1500		**PAGE 89**		9, RR	300	300	4	150	200
7	155	225		*Borrenson — C.E. Delong.*			**PAGE 96**		5	180	240
8	300	400		*No Changes.*		1	600	RARE	6	200	220
	PAGE 81			**PAGE 90**		2	475	575	7	500	RARE
1	625	700		*First American made Railroad*		3	475	575	8	350	
2	325	400		*Watch.*					9	450	550
8	220	150		*No Changes.*			**PAGE 97**			**PAGE 104**	
	PAGE 82			**PAGE 91**			*No Changes.*			*No Change except*	
1	375	450		*Pennsylvania Railroad.*			**PAGE 98**		2	475	550
2	160	175		*No Changes.*		1	200	225	9	125	175
3	260	275		**PAGE 92**		2	500	900		**PAGE 105**	
	PAGE 83		1	80	100	3	600	1400		*No Change Except*	
1	450	350	2	80	100		**PAGE 99**		1	400	450
2	220	250	3	80	100				3	500	RARE
6	200	150	4	425	800	1	425	575	7	125	RARE
7	450	550	9	240	300	2	900	1400	8	195	RARE
8	350	225		**PAGE 93**		3	35	450		**PAGE 106 – 107**	
	PAGE 84 – 85			*No Changes.*			**PAGE 100**			*No Changes.*	
	No Changes.			**PAGE 94**		1	150	300		**PAGE 108**	
	PAGE 86		1	200	300	4	150	175		*No Change Except*	
1	650	1100	2	350	400	6	175	200	1	525	1000
2	650	1100	3	3250	8000		**PAGE 101**		2	300	500
3	650	1100	4	125	250	1	125	175	3	240	RARE
4	1200	RARE	5	675	2000	2	150	300	6	425	600
6	155	800		**PAGE 95**		4	75	100	7	525	900
7	800	1550	1, BRT.	500	600	5	200	225	8	195	250
8	5000	RARE	2, B&O	600	2200		**PAGE 102**		9	300	375
	PAGE 87		3, SR5	625	1000	1	800	RARE		**PAGE 109**	
351P		2200	4, Dial	200	300	2	190	200	1	200	250
351L		2500	5, C&O	900	2400	3	500	550	3	400	550
350		450	6, RRD	200	250		**PAGE 103**		4	600	650
360		400				1	400	RARE	5	425	600
361		250							6	260	350
									7	155	200
									8	260	350
									9	(3 known)	RARE

NEW UP–DATED PRICES FOR 1980
for the
1979 PRICE INDICATOR (Published in 1979)

NO.	1979 Price	1980 Price	NO.	1979 Price	1980 Price	NO.	1979 Price	1980 Price	NO.	1979 Price	1980 Price
	PAGE 13 – 19			**PAGE 36**		6	$ 450	$ 1000	7	$ 800	$ 1400
	O'Hara Waltham Dial Co.		105 H	$ 300	$ 800	7	200	275	8		200
	No Changes.		105 O	400	1000	8	200		9	1250	1600
	PAGE 20		Bunn H	400	800	9	200			**PAGE 44**	
	Webb C. Ball Watch Co.		Bunn O	450	1000		**PAGE 41**		1	900	
	No Changes.		107	200	600		*No Changes Except*		2	900	
	PAGE 21		65	50	100	1	200		3	SCARCE	900
	Louisville & Nashville RR Co.		5	40	80	2	240		4	625	
	General Instruction for Watch		5 KW	40	80	3	200		5	625	
	Inspection. No Changes.		60	40		4	220		6	700	
	PAGE 22 – 23		99	40		5	100		7		700
	Hamilton Watch Co.		99 KW	40		6	350	400	8	100	
	See Page 16 & 17 of the		61	40	80	7	325	400	9	1500	1850
	1980 Indicator.		64	40	80	8	200			**PAGE 45**	
	PAGE 24 – 33		101	30		9	200		1	1250	1850
	See Note No. 1, Page 14.		2	40			**PAGE 42**		2	1250	1850
	Gold values change so rapidly		6	40		1	125		3	1150	1750
	it would serve no purpose to		IWC	25		2	125		4	1150	1750
	revise these prices.		IWC-KW	25		3	125		5	100	200
	PAGE 34			**PAGE 37**		4	150		6	1150	1750
	Waltham Non-Magnetics.			*See Page 15 of the*		5	100		7	1250	1850
	No Changes.			*1980 Indicator.*		6	150		8	100	200
	PAGE 35			**PAGE 38 – 39**		7	SCARCE	1000	9	1250	1850
	Waltham Various Models.			*Illinois Decision Diagrams.*		8	SCARCE	1000		**PAGE 46**	
	No Changes.			*No Changes.*		9	SCARCE	1000	1	RARE	5000
				PAGE 40			**PAGE 43**		2	100	200
			1	750	1200	1	125		3	1500	
			2	1500	2000	2	125		4	1500	
			3	550	800	3	140		5		
			4	260		4	450		6	2500	3000
			5	400	750	5	500		7	350	550
						6	625	1000	8		100

14

NO.	1979 Price	1980 Price
PAGE 46 (Cont.)		
9	$ 975	$1100
PAGE 47		
1	650	900
2	100	200
3	525.	900
4	500	600
6	100	200
7	750	1250
8	2500	3000
9	500	RARE
PAGE 48		
1	500	575
2	100	200
3	450	550
4	500	550
5	500	600
6	450	550
7	450	550
8	500	550
9	450	550
PAGE 49		
1	475	575
2	600	850
3	100	200
4	500	650
5	350	
6	500	
7	350	
8	500	
9	350	
PAGE 50		
1	200	
2		75
3	125	200
4	125	
5		75
6	125	
7	200	150
8		50
9	150	
PAGE 51		
1	125	
2		50
3	600	800
4	85	
5	100	
6	85	
7	260	300
8	75	
9	200	
PAGE 52		
1	155	
2	125	
3	60	
4	85	125
5	500	
6	150	200
7	SCARCE	
8	750	1250
9	RARE	5000
PAGE 53		
1	200	
2	150	200
3	150	175
4	175	200
5	200	
6	SCARCE	
7	SCARCE	
8	200	
9	280	
PAGE 54		
1	220	300
2	220	300
3	280	300
4	350	
PAGE 55		
1	220	
2	300	

NO.	1979 Price	1980 Price
3	$ 300	$
4	SCARCE	4000
5		200
6	775	1000
7	775	1000
8	100	200
9	85	100
PAGE 56		
1	650	
2	100	
3	650	
4		650
5	500	550
6	500	650
7	400	550
PAGE 57		
21J	850	1200
23J	600	750
PAGE 58		
23J	1350	1750
23J	1000	1250
PAGE 59		
23J	1200	1500
PAGE 60		
1	125	
2	SCARCE	
3	125	
4	375	475
5	325	425
6	SCARCE	
7	240	
8	100	
9	125	
PAGE 61		
1	240	
2	300	
3	450	500
4	400	
5	675	
6		600
7	500	550
8	675	
9	150	200
PAGE 62		
1	350	
2	300	450
3	150	
4	125	150
5	280	300
6	375	
7	280	300
8	RARE	3000
9	280	300
PAGE 63		
1	175	
2	50	100
3	175	
4	220	
5	50	100
6	75	
7	75	
8	75	
9	75	
PAGE 64		
1	175	
2	175	
3	325	
4	125	
5	120	
6	475	
7	RARE	3000
8	240	
9	150	
PAGE 65		
1	75	
2		40
3	130	
4	200	

NO.	1979 Price	1980 Price
5	$ 200	$
6	65	
7	200	
8	75	
9	100	
PAGE 66		
1	775	900
2	150	
3	75	100
4	525	600
5	75	100
6	75	
7	SCARCE	
8	SCARCE	
PAGE 67		
1	425	500
2		50
3	130	
4	75	
5	200	
6	120	
7	115	
8	60	
9	130	
PAGE 68		
1	525	600
2	525	600
3	240	250
4	775	800
5	775	600
6	105	
7	200	
8	300	
9	130	
PAGE 69		
1	75	
2	75	
3	100	
4	75	
5	240	
6		50
7	200	
8		50
9	240	
PAGE 70		
1	150	100
2		50
3		50
4	100	
5	100	
6	100	
7	35	
8	200	
9	55	
PAGE 71		
1	325	
2	100	
3	SCARCE	
4	400	
5		100
6	240	250
7	SCARCE	350
8	50	100
PAGE 72		
1, RR	120	
2, RRD	50	
3, Pit	RARE	
4, Ball	140	
5		
6, 21J	RARE	
7, WWC	75	
8, WNCD		35
9, HB	200	
PAGE 73		
1	325	
2		100
3	475	
4	325	
5	120	
6		200
7		150
8	150	

NO.	1979 Price	1980 Price
9	$ 750	$1250
PAGE 74		
1	220	200
2		100
3	160	60
4	SCARCE	200
5	SCARCE	200
6	SCARCE	375
7	220	
8	30	
9	325	
PAGE 75		
1		150
2	110	200
3	110	200
4	240	90
5	925	
6	950	
7	950	100
8	120	200
9	975	1350
PAGE 76		
1	RARE	
2	RARE	
3	240	
4	425	
5		275
6		200
7	SCARCE	400
8	200	
9	SCARCE	400
PAGE 77		
1	725	1000
2	450	
3	400	500
4	425	200
5	325	
6	700	
7	140	
8	425	
9	425	
PAGE 78		
1859 Model Research		
PAGE 79		
Frank Leslie Watch		
PAGE 80		
RF	425	500
ELW	725	
TNW	400	500
Dial		100
Ball		RARE
NWC	400	500
PAGE 81		
Dudley Masonic		
PAGE 82		
Fasoldt & Potter		
PAGE 83		
McIntyre—Fasoldt—Rotary		
PAGE 84		
HGA	475	
Dial		100
HGA	475	
Dial		100
Otay	SCARCE	
Otay Dial		200
USWC	SCARCE	1000
EHF	RARE	4000
PAGE 85		
Seth Thomas Serial Numbers.		
PAGE 86 — 88		
Seth Thomas Research.		

NO.	1979 Price	1980 Price
PAGE 89		
1	$1750	$
2	150	
3	SCARCE	
4		50
5	110	
6		50
7	375	
8	SCARCE	
9	150	
PAGE 90		
1	425	250
2		200
3	95	
4	150	
5	1500	
6	400	500
7	150	175
8		30
9	95	
PAGE 91		
1	240	
2		50
3	85	
4	280	300
5	120	
6	80	
7	80	
8	260	400
9	260	300
PAGE 92		
1	525	
2		200
3	575	400
4	425	

NO.	1979 Price	1980 Price
5	$ 165	$
6		200
7	325	
PAGE 93		
1, BLE	700	
2, Dial	300	
3, BRT	700	
4, BLFE	700	
5, RWG	1000	800
6, BS	SCARCE	
7, SR	150	250
PAGE 94		
1	RARE	
2	1000	800
3	1000	800
4	RARE	
5	RARE	4000
6	200	
7	SCARCE	
8	700	
9	200	250
PAGE 95		
1	RARE	4000
2		200
3	SCARCE	
4		400
5		200
6	200	
7	SCARCE	
8	SCARCE	
9	725	700
PAGE 96		
G. P. Reed — No Changes.		

NO.	1979 Price	1980 Price
PAGE 97		
Potter — M.S. Smith, Freeport. No Changes.		
PAGE 98		
1	$ 475	$
2	475	
3	SCARCE	
4	SCARCE	300
5	SCARCE	250
6	75	
7	RARE	
8	RARE	
9	160	125
PAGE 99		
1	300	200
2	SCARCE	
3	SCARCE	
4	750	
5	260	
6	110	80
7	110	80
8	SCARCE	450
9	130	
PAGE 100		
French—Delong—Reed No Changes.		
PAGE 101		
1		200
2		300
3		5
4		300

NO.	1979 Price	1980 Price
5	$	$ 100
6		
7		100
8		100
9		20
PAGE 102		
J. P. Stevens — No Changes.		
PAGE 103		
Bowman—Mozart—Goddard. No Changes.		
PAGE 104		
1		550
PAGE 105		
1		425
PAGE 106		
S-I	SCARCE	
S-K	SCARCE	
S-K	SCARCE	
S-111	220	200
S-One	SCARCE	
S-111	SCARCE	
Exp.	RARE	
S-One	SCARCE	
S-One	SCARCE	
PAGE 107		
H & R	5000	
EH & Co.	3250	
P.S.B.	800	

NOTE NO. 1: I have not revised the values of gold cased pocket watches. The prices shown herein are based on $250.00 per ounce gold. Gold cases have to be historically important, rare, or mint condition to bring even scrap value from watch collectors. Slightly worn, unpopular sizes (6, 8, 10, 12 sizes), and cases that are not pretty are very difficult to sell with gold at or above $450.00 per ounce. Ladies 0 Size and smaller, and big mint 18 Size solid gold cases are the most popular with gold watch buyers now, with gold approximately $550.00.

NOTE NO. 2:

SCRAP GOLD — HOW MUCH SHOULD I SELL FOR?

The following formula is close to what would be used to determine what a buyer who sells to the smelter would pay to an individual who has less than 100 (DWT) pennyweights of scrap gold to sell.

Example: 40 DWT scrap gold watch case.

Formula: $\text{Spot} \times \text{karat constant} \times \dfrac{.85}{20} = \text{Price per DWT.}$

Karat Constant: 18K = .72 Dental 16K = .65
14K = .55 10K = .36

Example worked out with gold spot of $500.00

$$\$500.00 \times .55 \times \frac{.85}{20} = \$11.69 \text{ Per DWT of 14K}$$

NOTE NO. 3: During this past year I have been using my Nikon 35mm camera at the various NAWCC regionals, as well as various individual collections. Collectors and dealers from all over the United States have brought their unusual or unique watches for me to photograph. Many of these pictures appear in this 1980 Indicator, or will be used in future issues or for advanced research. I will continue to bring my camera to the meetings and if any of you have interesting watches that you would like to talk about or see them in a future issue of the Indicator, please bring them by. ROY

CORRECTIONS TO 1979 PRICE INDICATOR

Page No.	Watch No.	Listing	Correction
38		Note at lower right should read: "The 4th wheel will have 70 teeth on the 2nd model and 80 teeth on the 5th model.	
40	5	17J ON4L	15J HG2L
40	7	ON4L	ON6L
40	9	ON4L	ON6L
48	4	OG2L	OG3L
	6	ON4L	ON4P or ON6L
	7	ON4L	ON4P or ON6L
49	6	ON4L	ON4P or ON6L
	7	ON4L	ON4P or ON6L
50	6	HN1K	HN2L
51	1	S/N 781,800	S/N 731,800
	3	S/N 1,334,645	S/N 1,334,045
	4	HN5L—A	HN5L—U
52	Manhattan Fenderson & Mitchell	HN1K	HN2L
		ON4L	ON4P
56	Bottom SS	16S	17S
59	SS	16S	17S
60	3	ON9L	ON11L
	4,5	ON9L	ON14L
	9	21J ON9L	23J ON9L
61	1	ON9L	ON11L
	3	ON15L	ON14L
62	3	S/N 3,252,690	S/N 5,252,690
63	6	ON9L	ON7L
	7	G185	G174
	8	S/N 2,445,086	S/N 2,495,086
64	2	ON5L	ON6L
	6	HN8L	HN6P
65	9	12S, ON1P	13S, ON2P
67	1	G995	G99-S
68	Bottom, G187	21J	17J
69	2	ON1L	ON3L
	4	No Grade	G-G
70	4	HN2L—A—G60	ON1L—A—G439
	5	ON1P	ON2P

18 SIZE AND 16 SIZE MOVEMENTS

RAILROAD GRADE: This is a very important part of collecting American watches. Railroad watches were generally of higher grade and were more expensive to buy. At this point in time, the majority of railroad collectors consider nearly all other watches as traders, unless the watch has a special dial or case.

LOW SERIAL NUMBER: Serial numbers under 1,000 are more desirable collector pieces, and the closer to number one, the higher the value.

ABBREVIATIONS:

O=Open   H=Hunting   L=Lever Set   P=Pendant Set
RG=Railroad Grade

18 SIZE MOVEMENTS

All 18 Size Movements are Lever Set. All values are for mint movements only.

Grade	Description	Production	1980 Value
	7-OL	1,300	$2000
	11-OL & HL	250	2500
(4 Types of 11 Jewel Movements. Plates are Gilt & Nickel in both Hunting and Open Face)			
922	15-OL	1,171	1600
923	15-HL	1,260	1500
924	17-OL	138,306	65
925	17-HL	72,020	65
926	17-OL	80,815	65
927	17-HL	45,781	65
928	15-OL	4,997	175
929	15-HL	5,900	175
930	16-OL	4,200	175
931	16-HL	4,000	175
932	16-OL	600	1250
933	16-HL	650	1250
934	17-OL	3,310	175
935	17-HL	1,700	175
936	17-OL-RG	18,336	75
937	17-HL-RG	4,930	175
938	17-OL-RG	2,198	650
939	17-HL-RG	1,310	800
940	21-OL-RG	205,815	80
941	21-HL-RG	25,411	125
942	21-OL-RG	5,418	200
943	21-HL-RG	2,399	300
944	19-OL-RG	6,600	250
946	23-OL-RG	10,692	400
947	23-HL-RG	308	5000
948	17-OL-RG	1,500	500
999	19-OL-RG	4,500	300
999	21-OL-RG	6,789	200
999	23-OL-RG	100	5000
999E	-OL-RG	1,098	1000
999F	-OL-RG	502	1000
999H	-OL-RG	7,000	100
999	17-OL-RG	1,799	150

All 999 grade watches were produced for the Webb C. Ball Watch Co. of Cleveland, Ohio, and were used exclusively by them. Specifications met the standards of Ball's Railroad Inspection Service. The majority of these watches having been used on the railroads. Available factory records do not yield complete data on these movements.

16 SIZE MOVEMENTS

Grade	Description	Production	1980 Value
950	23-OP-RG	4,401	$ 350
950	23-OL-RG	17,902	350
951	23-HP-RG	44	3500
951	23-HL-RG	97	3000
950E	23-OL-RG	7,001	400
950B	23-OL-RG	30,000	425
952	19-OP-RG	1,499	200
952	19-OL-RG	5,800	250
954	17-OP	2,700	125
954	17-OL-RG	1,898	175
956	17-OP	51,298	60
960	21-OP	1,918	250
960 Marked	(Add $60)		
960	21-OL-RG	3,045	250
961	21-HP	1,152	225
961 Marked	(Add $50)		
961	21-HL-RG	1,100	350
962	17-OP	350	500
963	17-HP	380	500
964	17-OP	340	500
965	17-HP	410	500
966	17-OP	307	500
967	17-HP	300	500
968	17-OP (Some Marked)	1,037	450
969	17-HP	930	500
970	21-OP	2,806	200
971	21-HP	2,497	200
972	17-OP-RG (1st Model Detent)	935	100
972	17-OP-RG	10,800	75
972	17-OL-RG	35,652	75
973	17-HP	6,640	75
973	17-HL	3,619	75
974	17-OP	204,088	35
974	Gilt	14,000	60
974	17-OL	93,645	35
974 Spl.	17-OP-3P (Scarce)	11,500	75
974 Spl.	17-OL-3P (Scarce)	12,903	75
974B	17-OL	(No Information)	
1974B	17-OP	(No Information)	
2974B	17-OP	16,095	150
975	17-HP	68,700	35
975	17-HP Gilt Trim (Add $10)		
975	17-HL	31,573	35
976	16-OP	4,406	75
977	16-HP	5,730	75
978	17-OL	24,500	50
990	21-OL-RG	16,489	150
991	21-HL-RG	2,521	175
992	21-OP-RG - 1st	2,520	120
992	21-OP-RG - 2nd	3,601	120
992	21-OL-RG - 1st	104,067	100

16 SIZE MOVEMENTS (Cont.)

Grade	Description	Production	1980 Value
992	21-OL-RG - 2nd	438,217	$ 100
992E	21-OL-RG	63,497	175
992B	21-OL-RG	217,876	175
992B	21-OL-RG-US Gvt.	17,146	150
3992B	22-OP-British Navy	2,494	250
4992B	22-OP	96,082	125
6992B	21-OL	(No Information)	
993	21-HP	2,000	150
993	21-HL-RG	11,476	125
993	21-HL-RG	6,700	125
994	21-OP	301	1200
994	21-OL-RG	800	1100
996	19-OL-RG	23,497	200
HWW	17-OP	208	400
HWW	17-HP	192	500
HWW	17-OL	30	1200
HWW	21-OP	336	500
HWW	21-HP	293	600
HWW	21-OL-RG	228	650
999	21-OL-RG	43,728	175
999-Elinvar	21-OL-RG	40	300
999B	21-OL-RG	8,208	225
999	23-OL-RG	6,697	600
998B	23-OL-RG	2,700	600
161	21-OL-RG	(161 to 163A are all	300
161-Elinvar	21-OL-RG	60 Hour Bunn Specials	350
161A	21-OL-RG	finished by Hamilton.)	300
161B	21-OL-RG		Rare
163	23-OL-RG		550
163-Elinvar	23-OL-RG		600
163A	23-OL-RG		550

SPECIALTY PRODUCTS

Grade	Description	Production	1980 Value
23	19-OP-Stop Watch	25,291	125
22-35 Size	21-OP-Navy Deck (2 Boxes)	28,127	375
22-35 Size	21-OP-Gimballs (2 boxes)		650
-36 Size	21-O-KWKS-Gimballs (2 Boxes)	966	1400
-36 Size	21-O-Silver Pocket Case	250	1500
25	16-Airplane elapsed time	15,641	200
21	14-Naval Chron. (2 boxes)	24,793	1200
121	14-Different Dials		
221	14-Different Dials		

12 SIZE MOVEMENTS

Value is for movement only. Add the value of case. Must be in original marked Hamilton case to have much value.

Grade	Description	Production	1980 Value
900	19-OP, see 1	24,699	$ 100
902a	19-OP, see 2	9,600	75
904a	21-OP, see 2	4,100	75
910	17-OP, see 1	153,793	20
912a	17-OP, see 2	260,900	20
914	17-OP, see 1	43,099	20
916a	17-OP, see 2	33,800	20

Grade	Description	Production	1980 Value
918a	19-OP, see 2	17,700	20
920	23-OP, see 1	13,598	75
920	23-OP (Marked Masterpiece)		250
922	23-OP, see 2&3	15,711	75
922	23-OP (Marked Masterpiece)		250
	23-OP, see 4	1,189	
400	21-OP, see 5	2,301	250

1. Larger than conventional 12 Size. Pillar Plate diameter 1.630''; case opening diameter 1.605''; (12 Size - 1.567''); require special made case.
2. "A" Model; smaller than conventional 12 Size. Pillar Plate diameter 1.565''; case opening diameter 1.537''; (12 Size - 1.567); require special case.
3. During 1924 to 1928 more than 1400, 922's were produced without grade numbers and used for Masterpiece and special cases. In 1928, Masterpiece movements were made a distinctive grade.
4. The Masterpiece grade. Previous to 1928, this grade could be distinguished from the 922 grade in the records only by serial number.
5. Originally an Illinois Watch; a standard 12 Size thin model.

10 SIZE MOVEMENTS

Value is for movement only. Add value of case. Must be in marked Hamilton case to have much value.

Grade	Description	Production	1980 Value
917	17-OP	156,391	$ 20
921	21-OP	37,749	30
923	23-OP	2,077	100
923	23-OP (Marked Masterpiece)		250
H917	17-OP, see 1	11	Rare
945	23-OP		100
945	23-OP (Marked Masterpiece)		200

1. Same as regular 917 except engraved and marketed under Howard name. Larger quantity than indicated believed produced.

0 SIZE MOVEMENTS

Standard size will fit any O Size case. Standard size models manufactured with hunting type faces. Made available for open face cases without a seconds bit by cutting off the fourth pinion staff. Originally sold as Chatelaine Watches for ladies. Later marketed in sterling silver cases as "Men's Strap Watches", and in round or cushion shaped cases as "Military Watches".

Grade	Description	Production	1980 Value
981	17-HP, see 1	2,200	$ 60
982	17-OP, see 2		30
983	17-HP, see 3&4	5,996	60
984	19-OP, see 5		60
985	19-HP, see 3	1,899	100

1. Replaced Models 983 and 985.
2. Finished as Model 983, quantities produced included with that given for Model 983.
3. Bridge Model.
4. Lady Hamilton engraved on train bridge.
5. Finished as Model 985, quantities produced included with that given for Model 985.

AMERICAN POCKET WATCHES WITH UP—DOWN WINDING INDICATORS
(Movement & Dial Only. Add the Value of the Case.)

ELGIN 16 SIZE UP-DOWN INDICATORS

19J B.W. Raymond (372)	$ 375
19J B.W. Raymond (455)	375
21J B.W. Raymond (391)	400
21J B.W. Raymond (472)	400
21J B.W. Raymond (478) Military (Cased)	500
21J B.W. Raymond (478)	400
21J B.W. Raymond (581) Military SS Hack (Cased)	450
21J Father Time (374)	425
21J Father Time (454)	425
21J Veritas (375)?	450
23J B.W. Raymond (376)	600
23J B.W. Raymond (494)	600
23J B.W. Raymond (494) P.S. Military (Cased)	600
23J B.W. Raymond (540)	600
23J B.W. Raymond (540) P.S. Military (Cased)	600
23J Veritas (376)	1000
23J Veritas (453)	1000

ELGIN 18 SIZE UP-DOWN INDICATORS

19J B.W. Raymond (240)	700
21J B.W. Raymond (390)	1200
21J Father Time (367)	950
21J Father Time Free Sprung	1000
21J Veritas (239)	1200
21J Veritas (274) Htg.	RARE
23J Veritas (214)	1600
21J Elgin Natl.W.Co.(412)	750
21J Elgin Natl.W.Co.(412) Free Sprung 3P	800
21J Father Time (367)	1800
(Free Sprung, cased in original 6 oz. open face case with large deck watch dial—SCARCE).	
21J Father Time (367)	700
(Mounted in Gimballs with both boxes.)	
21J Elgin Natl.W.Co.(412)	650
(Mounted in Gimballs with both boxes.)	

WALTHAM 16 SIZE UP—DOWN INDICATORS

21J Crescent Street (1908)	$ 375
21J Crescent St. (1912)	400
23J Vanguard (1908) 5P	350
23J Vanguard (1908) 6P	350
23J Vanguard (1908) 6P Lossier	350
23J Vanguard (1899) PS	400
23J Vanguard (1912)	350
23J Vanguard (1912) PS Military (Cased)	600
23J Riverside Maximus 100 Damaskeened	Scarce
23J Riverside Maximus 200 Not Damask.	Scarce
19J Ball Model	Scarce
23J Premier Maximus. Original marked case.	8000

WALTHAM 18 SIZE UP—DOWN INDICATORS

19J Vanguard	1250
21J Vanguard	1450
23J Vanguard	1750

ROCKFORD 16 SIZE

17J Indicator	750
21J Indicator (655)	750

ROCKFORD 18 SIZE

21J Indicator (950)	4500

LONGINES (SWISS) 18 SIZE

With 24 Hour Dial issued to U.S. War Dept.	325

HAMILTON

36 Size WW I in large silver pocket type case with Bow & Crown	1500
35 Size WW II Grade 22 in Keystone Base metal SB&B OF case with dust cover & no bow -- $300. With both Wood Boxes	400

ADD THE VALUE OF THE CASE TO THESE PRICES

* *

HOW TO READ THE LINE OF CODE SHOWN IN THE DESCRIPTION OF EACH WATCH, THAT IS AN ACTUAL PHOTOGRAPH.

EXAMPLE: 18S—17J—ON1L—A—G-936

Reads like this: 18 SIZE — 17 JEWEL — OPEN FACE, NICKEL MOVEMENT, MODEL ONE, LEVER SET — ADJUSTED — GRADE 936.

18S	21J	O	N	1	L	A	G-936
S = Size	Number of Jewels	O = Open H = Hunting	N = Nickel G = Gilded	Model No. X = Unknown	L = Lever Set P = Pendant Set K = Keywind	A = Adjusted U = Unadjusted P = Positions G = Grade	Grade Name or Number

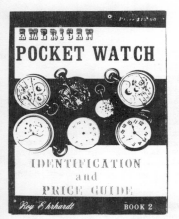

AMERICAN POCKET WATCH IDENTIFICATION & PRICE GUIDE, BOOK 2
EHRHARDT, 1974. 192, 8½x11 Pages. $15.00. No. -09-8
* * * FIRST PRINTING 1974.* * * PRICE GUIDE SECTION REVISED 1979. * * *

1

The **AMERICAN WATCH COLLECTOR'S BIBLE.** *This book was immediately accepted by everyone interested in watches who saw it. You can identify your watch, its age and the retail value by comparing it with an original picture. It contains selected pages from original factory sales, supply house, and parts catalogs, along with various advertisements and brochures dating back to 1865, the beginning of serious watchmaking in the U. S. Over 1900 pocket watches are pictured and described. Completely new and different from the 1972 Edition of BOOK 1— nothing is duplicated. No collector, dealer, or anyone who has a good watch for sale can afford not to look up your watch in this book before acting, if you have any doubts about what you are doing.* **(For beginning collectors. If you own no other watch books, buy this one first.)**

POCKET WATCH PRICE INDICATORS

IF YOU WANT TO KEEP UP TO DATE ON ALL OF THE INFORMATION THAT HAS BEEN PUBLISHED ON AMERICAN MADE POCKET WATCHES AND CASES, YOU NEED TO HAVE ALL OF THE INDICATORS. THE YEARLY PUBLICATIONS ARE DESCRIBED BELOW.

1976 POCKET WATCH PRICE INDICATOR
EHRHARDT, 1975. 64, 8½x11 Pages. $5.00. No. -15-2

This is the first of a yearly "Price Indicator". Mr. Ehrhardt is using this means to make available to the watch collectors and dealers new information acquired during the year. This issue updates the 1974 Edition of **American Pocket Watch Identification & Price Guide, Book 2,** *and contains 40 additional pages of pictures, advertisements and new material not shown in* **BOOK 2.** *1875 Illinois brochure showing all keywinds with descriptions—Four pages of Illinois—Ben Franklin, including 23J—1877 watch cases—1877 Howard—1864 Waltham factory price list with descriptions—All Webb C. Ball serial numbers and production figures and dates—25J Columbus—More Hampdens, Walthams, 14J Seth Thomas, etc.—Elgin, New York Standard, Trenton, Elinvar Hamilton, etc.—Cases (13 page section)—And a 1975 summary of what's been happening to prices of American watches. This book will not make much sense if you do not have* **BOOK 2.**

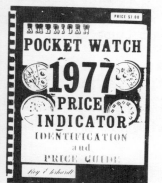

1977 POCKET WATCH PRICE INDICATOR
EHRHARDT, 1976. 96, 8½x11 Pages. $7.00. No. -21-7

Updates prices for the **American Pocket Watch Identification & Price Guide, Book 2,** *published in 1974, and the* **1976 Pocket Watch Price Indicator.** *Additional new material on Hampden—The Ball Watch Company—Ben Franklin 1910 Catalog—United States Watch Company—Special Railroad Watches—Burlington Watch Company—Sears Roebuck watches—Montgomery Ward watches—Columbus Watch Company—E. Howard Watch Company—Waltham —Sante Fe Special—Washington Watch Company—with material on 145 Antique Watch Keys, Chrondrometers, Up-Down Indicators, and a complete price guide to all American companies and individuals who made watches (282 listings).*

1978 POCKET WATCH PRICE INDICATOR
EHRHARDT, 1978. 110, 8½x11 Pages. $10.00. No. -26-8

The third in a series of Indicators updating prices for pocket watches. This book updates prices for the **American Pocket Watch Identification & Price Guide, Book 2,** *published in 1974, the* **1976 Pocket Watch Price Indicator,** *and the* **1977 Pocket Watch Price Indicator.** *Forty-six (46) pages of new reprints never before seen are presented, including pages on Mermod Jaccard—Freeport—Waltham Indicator parts—Mainsprings—E. Howard Cases—Non-Magnetic—Rockford—Interstate Chronometer—Waterbury—Standard American—Monarch—Webb C. Ball. Forty-two (42) pages of* **Unusual, Scarce,** *and* **Rare** *American watches never shown in print before. This last section contains photographs of unusual watches that were taken during the last two years. Finally, the author's comments on "American Watches, 1977 and 1978, in Summary".*

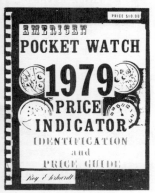

1979 POCKET WATCH PRICE INDICATOR
EHRHARDT, 1979. 120, 8½x11 Pages. $10.00. No. -29-2

The fourth in a series of Indicators updating prices for pocket watches. Updates prices for the American Pocket Watch Identification & Price Guide, Book 2, published in 1974, and the 1976, 1977, and 1978 Pocket Watch Price Indicators. I have been carrying my camera to all the Regionals and collectors have been bringing their watches that, for the most part, I have never seen before. The new material presented in this Indicator consists of photos of these watches. Another very interesting and important section covers the watches shown by drawing in Col. George E. Townsend's book, "Almost Everything You Wanted to Know about American Watches and Didn't Know Who to Ask." He was gracious to give me the original pictures from which he had made the drawings. This is the most interesting of all the Indicators.

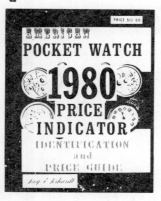

NEW

1980 POCKET WATCH PRICE INDICATOR
EHRHARDT, 1980. 110, 8½x11 Pages. $12.00. - 32-2

The fifth in a series of Indicators updating prices for pocket watches. Updates prices for the American Pocket Watch Identification & Price Guide, Book 2, published in 1974, the 1976, 1977, 1978 & 1979 Pocket Watch Price Indicators, and the Hamilton Pocket Watch Identification & Price Guide, published in 1976. For the past year collectors and dealers have been bringing their unusual watches by my camera at the regionals, making the 1980 Indicator the finest and most interesting picture book of all. Some of the important sections are as follows: Swiss Fakes—English Contract—Interesting and rare Hamiltons, Illinois, Cornell, Newark, Albert Potter, Waltham, with special effort on New York Watch Company, Hampden and Seth Thomas—Rare and scarce movements from all companies and makers. We think the best Indicator ever done.

REMEMBER: In order to have all of the material on American watches that Mr. Ehrhardt has written about, it is necessary to have all of the Indicators. There are no duplications.

WALTHAM POCKET WATCH IDENTIFICATION & PRICE GUIDE
EHRHARDT, 1976. 172, 8½x11 Pages. $10.00. No. -17-9

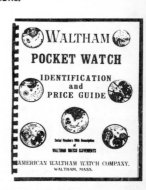

Waltham, being the first American watch factory beginning in the 1850's and continuing to the 1960's and manufacturing over 33 million watches, takes a book by itself to cover their production properly. This book is for the advanced collector or dealer who wants to get the most enjoyment out of his hobby or the most money for his watches. Partial material presented: Complete 1954 Waltham serial numbers with descriptions—Selections from 1890 Waltham Products Catalog (watches & cases)—1874 Waltham Illustrated Price List—1901 Waltham Mainspring Catalog (giving model numbers to KW16, KW20, KW14, etc.)—1948 Waltham Watch & Clock Material Catalog—1952 E. & J. Swigart Co. Manual of Watch Movements. All of the important models, along with all of the grades in each model and a value for each, are given. This book does not leave many questions about Waltham unanswered.

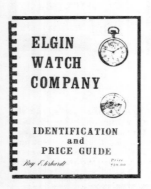

ELGIN POCKET WATCH IDENTIFICATION & PRICE GUIDE
EHRHARDT, 1976. 120, 8½x11 Pages. $10.00. No. -10-1

At last—for the first time ever available—all of the Elgin pocket watch grades with the number of each produced. (A minor miracle in itself). With the help of John Miller of Springfield, Illinois and his computer, I am very proud of this work on Elgin. Partial material presented: All names & numbered grades with classification & description as originally made. Also shown for each grade is the total production, the first and last serial number, and the current value. In addition, the first and last serial number of all the runs for all grades with production of less than 10,000. The complete Elgin serial number list of 50 Million is also included; line drawings of the Elgin models; and on and on with information that the advanced collector and dealer needs to know.

ILLINOIS SPRINGFIELD WATCHES IDENTIFICATION & PRICE GUIDE
EHRHARDT, 1976. 136, 8½x11 Pages. $10.00. No. -20-9

More collectors have asked for this book than any other single company I have done. Contains the following: All of the Illinois serial numbers from 1 to 5,698,801, with the Size, KW, Pendant or Lever Set, Open Face or Hunting, Jewels, Model Number, Grade Number shown for each number—First Serial Number for each model—Line drawing of all 54 different models—Watch dial foot locations—Complete illustrations of 154 watch dials—Production date table—Illustrated watch hands—Mainspring Chart—and 21 pages of movements illustrated with current price guide. Illinois is a very fascinating company and they have done everything that makes it an interesting company to collect. They started early, used names for grades, made high jeweled (24, 25 & 26), made hundreds of watches with other grade names and other company names, and, of course, made a full line of excellent railroad watches. There are a lot of rare grades. Illinois made runs of 5, 10, 15 & 50 watches of one grade, one time. A book any advanced collector will enjoy!

ROCKFORD GRADE & SERIAL NUMBERS WITH PRODUCTION FIGURES
EHRHARDT, 1976. 44, 8½x11 Pages. $10.00. No. -11-X

This Rockford book, and all the other single company books, contains specific information impossible to present in any other way. The 1907 Rockford Serial Number List and Parts Catalog, with all serial numbers up to 824,000, has been completely reproduced. Without a doubt the most important section is the breakdown of how many were produced of each grade. This enormous task was undertaken and completed by Roger Weiss, Jr. of Yorkville, Illinois. Most of you know the value of the 24J, 18S Rockford. There are 50 grades with less production than the 24J Open Face. There are literally hundreds of sleepers out there waiting to be found. Without the proper method of identification, the one you are holding is just another old watch.

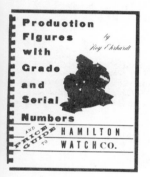

The first pocket watch price guide ever written. Fine book for beginners. Great for dealers to use as a buying reference. Investors use it to see what watches have shown the most improvement in value. Over 2600 watches priced, values from $5.00 to $16,000.00, with 95% being common everyday watches you need to know the value of. Still a very popular, strong selling book. List of all major American and foreign watches showing descriptions and retail prices. Charts of production dates, grading movements and cases; how to determine size; and other useful information.

Book 1 Out of Print

This is the original book and the one that is owned by most of the antique dealers. Because the prices are so low, it is still possible to get good buys from the people who own only this book. When there is a reference needed to aid you in the purchase of a watch, this is the book to use, since (for the most part) the prices shown are only about one-third of today's value.

FOREIGN & AMERICAN POCKET WATCH IDENTIFICATION & PRICE GUIDE, BOOK 3
EHRHARDT, 1976. 172, 8½x11 Pages. $10.00. No. -16-0

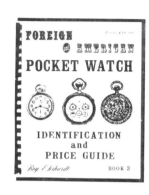

By popular request—everything from "soup to nuts" on foreign watches, including the current collector value. Know how to identify your watches by comparing them with original manufacturers' pictures and descriptions. Also included is a section on American cases of 1893 and one of 1929. Other information covered: How to value cases—Conditions that affect value—Mail order dealers—How current values were determined—Grading of movements & cases—Reproduction of an 18-page illustrated antique watch catalog of expensive watches currently for sale—List of hundreds of foreign watch names—80 Swiss fake railroad names—two pages of American watch company names (merchandisers only). This book contains carefully selected, original, fully illustrated pages from factory sales catalogs and advertisements, supply house catalogs, and sales brochures. The original antique pages have not been altered except for the current value, issue date of page, and author comments added in bold type. A must for every foreign and American watch collector. This book, as well as BOOK 1 and BOOK 2, has a world of information for both beginners and advanced collectors. No duplication in either of the three books.

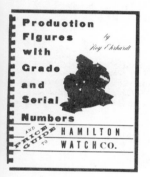

HAMILTON POCKET WATCH IDENTIFICATION & PRICE GUIDE
EHRHARDT, 1976. 53, 8½x11 Pages. $10.00. No. -12-8

How much is my old pocket watch worth? * * How many were made, and when? * * *Three questions very important to anyone interested in pocket watches. With this and the other single company books, you first look up the serial number of your watch to find the grade, then look up how many were made, and finally, how much it is worth. The complete Hamilton serial number list is included, along with everything else you need to know.*

TRADEMARKS
EHRHARDT, 1976. 128, 8½x11 Pages. $10.00. No. -06-3

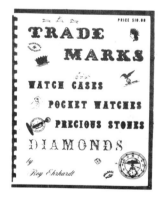

This book is so absolutely necessary to the advanced watch collector, dealer, or trader that you will wonder how you ever managed without it. Contains sections on the following subjects: American Pocket Watch Case Trademark (probably the most important section). Records all of the marks known to the author, and especially the marks used on solid gold cases that do not specifically say gold—American pocket watch trademarks and makers names—Foreign import pocket watch trademarks and makers names—American and foreign clock trademarks and names—Diamonds, How to buy and trade without expensive equipment—Scrap gold, how to find, recognize, buy and sell—Many other useful charts, tables, etc.

 NEW

AMERICAN POCKET WATCH COMPANIES
EHRHARDT, 1979. 96, 3½x5½ Pages. $3.00. No. -30-6

This little pocket book contains all of the following: **Names of all the known companies. * * How many watches were made by each company and when by serial number. * * Inventory space for 80 pocket watches.** *This is a handy "must have" little book for all collectors. Many dealers use this as a "give away" to their customers after marking "Compliments of" and their name on the inside cover.*

This little book is new. If you want a copy, send $3.00 plus 50 cents postage. No postage if you order it with another book. Write for special volume dealer price.

MASTER INDEX

MASTER INDEX TO WATCH BOOKS
R. EHRHARDT, 1979. 16, 8½x11 Pages. $4.00. -31-3.

This is a master index to 13 of the pocket watch books by Roy Ehrhardt. By title, the books included are: **American Pocket Watch Identification & Price Guide, Book 2; Foreign & American Pocket Watch Identification & Price Guide, Book 3; 1976, 1977, 1978 & 1979 Price Indicators; Elgin Pocket Watch Identification & Price Guide; Hamilton Pocket Watch Id. & Price Guide; Illinois-Springfield Identification & Price Guide; Rockford Watch Company Grade & Serial Numbers with Production Figures; Waltham Pocket Watch Identification & Price Guide; Trademarks; and American Pocket Watch Companies.**

CLOCK IDENTIFICATION & PRICE GUIDE, BOOK 1
R. RABENECK & R. EHRHARDT, 1977. 198, 8½x11 Pages. $15.00. No. -23-3
* * * FIRST PRINTED 1977. * * * PRICE GUIDE SECTION REVISED 1979. * * *

This book follows the format of Mr. Ehrhardt's price guides on pocket watches, in that the material is selected from original factory sales catalogs, etc. It covers American and imported clocks from 1850 to the 1940's, with the following information for each clock: The year offered for sale—The factory description—The price it sold for originally—The present retail value. Most of the clocks you see every day are pictured or described (4,000 in all). Over 95% of all clocks manufactured or sold in the United States since 1850 can be identified and a reasonably close retail value determined by comparing your clock with a picture of it or a similar one in this book or in BOOK 2. Of interest is the comments on "Conditions or Considerations as they Affect Value", "Periods in Clock Production", and "Replicas, Reproductions and Fakes". In addition, identification and dating of 150 of the most important clock makers is shown in chart form, beginning with Thomas Harland in 1773, down to the present time. **THE ONLY BOOK OF THIS KIND EVER PUBLISHED. TWO YEARS IN PREPARATION. A MUST FOR EVERY CLOCK COLLECTOR.** *This book is now considered the best all-around for identification and prices, and collectors who have it won't leave home without it. Revised, 1979, to include 1979 Price Up-Date and a complete index.*

1979 CLOCK PRICE UP-DATE & INDEX TO BOOK 1
EHRHARDT, 1979. 18, 8½x11 Pages. $4.00. No. -28-4

Price Revisions for CLOCK IDENTIFICATION AND PRICE GUIDE, BOOK 1 (Published 1977). These 18 pages are punched for insertion in the back of the book. Makes the book current with today's retail prices.

CLOCK IDENTIFICATION & PRICE GUIDE, BOOK 2
R. RABENECK & R. EHRHARDT, 1979. 192, 8½x11 Pages. $15.00. No. -27-6

A continuation of Book 1, with practically all new clocks not pictured in Book 1. Many additional clock companies are covered. Some examples are: Jennings Bros.—Western Clock Company—1873 Terry Clock Company—more complete Ansonia, New Haven, Gilbert, Seth Thomas, Ingraham, Sessions, Welsh—more Jeweler's Regulators and Battery Regulators—Hall—Grandfathers—Calendars—Connecticut Shelf—Novelty and Statue, etc. In addition, a complete unillustrated price guide to all known calendar clocks, with references to all books containing calendar clocks. Also, interesting articles, comments and sidelights to clock collecting and values.

FULL PAGE BROCHURES ARE AVAILABLE BY REQUEST.

ALL BOOKS ARE GUARANTEED TO PLEASE. YOUR MONEY BACK IS ASSURED. JUST RETURN THE BOOK IN GOOD CONDITION.

POCKET KNIFE BOOK 1 & 2 PRICE GUIDE
J. FERRELL & R. EHRHARDT, (Revised, 1977).
128, 8½x11 Pages. $6.95. No. -02-0

Originally published in 1973, with prices and format revised in 1977. A very popular book and a "must have" for anyone interested in buying, selling, or collecting pocket knives. Contains carefully selected pages from old factory and hardware catalogs and sales brochures. Knives are shown actual size with the original factory description and selling price, and, most important, **today's retail value** *shown by each knife. Most knives can be valued by comparing your knife with one in the book, even if made by a different maker. Over 1,790 American and foreign* **Pocket, Bowie,** *and* **Hunting** *knife makers shown, with a mint price by each that will indicate the quality of the known examples. This book was completely revised in September 1977, updating the prices to the current collector value.*

POCKET KNIFE BOOK 3 - PRICE GUIDE TO 2000
WINCHESTER & MARBLES, HARDWARE COLLECTIBLES
LARRY EHRHARDT, 1974. 128, 8½x11 Pages. $6.95. -08-X

This book was compiled of selections from various product sales catalogs of both WINCHESTER and MARBLE companies. The catalogs date from 1903 through the 20's and 30's. Most of the items that are now collectible are shown, along with today's current retail value. **If you are interested in Pocket Knives, Hunting Knives, Fishing Equipment, Sporting Equipment, Hardware Tools, etc., you need this book.** *Hardware Collectibles of WINCHESTER & MARBLES are real sleepers and if you get into any old houses or go to Flea Markets be sure and pick them up.*

Order Form

HEART OF AMERICA PRESS
P. O. Box 9808 — 10101 Blue Ridge Blvd.
Kansas City, Missouri 64134

Telephone: 816-761-0080

ISBN Prefix 9-913902-

QUANTITY	AUTHOR	TITLE	ISBN NO.	PRICE EACH	TOTAL AMT.
	R. Ehrhardt R. Rabeneck	Clock Identification & Price Guide, Book 1	-23-3	$15.00	
	R. Ehrhardt	1979 Clock Price Up-Date and Index to Clock Book 1 (Published 1977) (18 loose sheets to be inserted in your old book)	-28-4	$ 4.00	
	R. Ehrhardt R. Rabeneck	Clock Identification & Price Guide, Book 2	-27-6	$15.00	
	R. Ehrhardt E. Atchley	Violin Identification & Price Guide (1850-1977), Book 1 Violin Identification & Price Guide (1850-1977), Book 2 Violin Identification & Price Guide (Antique), Book 3	-22-5 -24-1 -25-X	$25.00 $25.00 $15.00	
	S. Ehrhardt D. Westbrook	American Collector Dolls Price Guide, Book 1	-14-4	$ 8.95	
	A. Ehrhardt	American Cut Glass Price Guide (Revised 1977)	-04-7	$ 6.95	
	R. Ehrhardt J. Ferrell L. Ehrhardt	Pocket Knife Book 1&2 Price Guide (Revised 1977) Pocket Knife Book 3 Price Guide, Winchester—Marbles—Knives & Hardware	-02-0 -08-X	$ 6.95 $ 6.95	
	R. Ehrhardt	American Pocket Watch Id. & Price Guide, Book 2 (Beginning Collector)	-09-8	$15.00	
	R. Ehrhardt	1976 Pocket Watch Price Indicator	-15-2	$ 5.00	
	R. Ehrhardt	1977 Pocket Watch Price Indicator	-21-7	$ 7.00	
	R. Ehrhardt	1978 Pocket Watch Price Indicator	-26-8	$10.00	
	R. Ehrhardt	1979 Pocket Watch Price Indicator	-29-2	$10.00	
	R. Ehrhardt	1980 Pocket Watch Price Indicator (NEW)	-32-2	$12.00	
	R. Ehrhardt	Foreign & American Pocket Watch Id. & Price Guide, Book 3	-16-0	$10.00	
	R. Ehrhardt	Waltham Pocket Watch Identification & Price Guide	-17-9	$10.00	
	R. Ehrhardt	Elgin Pocket Watch Identification & Price Guide	-10-1	$10.00	
	R. Ehrhardt	Illinois Springfield Watches Identification & Price Guide	-20-9	$10.00	
	R. Ehrhardt	Hamilton Pocket Watch Identification & Price Guide	-12-8	$10.00	
	R. Ehrhardt	Rockford Pocket Watch Identification & Price Guide	-11-X	$10.00	
	R. Ehrhardt	Trademarks (Watch Makers and Case Metal Identification)	-06-3	$10.00	
	Reprint	The Perfected American Watch—Waltham	-19-5	$ 4.00	
	Reprint	The Timekeeper—Hamilton Watch Company	-03-9	$ 3.00	
	Reprint	1858 E. Howard & Company	-18-7	$ 3.00	
	R. Ehrhardt	Master Index to Watch Books (16 loose pages to be inserted in your book)	-31-3	$ 4.00	
	R. Ehrhardt	American Pocket Watch Companies (Pocket Book) (NEW)	-30-6	$ 3.00	
	G. E. Townsend	Everything You Wanted to Know about American Watches and Didn't Know Who To Ask		$ 6.00	
	G. E. Townsend	The Watch That Made The $ Famous		$ 6.00	
	G. E. Townsend	The American Railroad Watch Encyclopedia		$ 6.00	

PLEASE RUSH THIS ORDER TO:

NAME _____

ADDRESS _____

CITY _____

STATE _____ ZIP _____

TOTAL For Books _____

Less Applicable Discount _____

Add 81 cents Postage & Handling 1st Book, 25 cents each additional book   Sub-Total _____

Add 70 Cents for Special Handling _____

Missouri residents add 4.625% tax _____

SEND CHECK OR MONEY ORDER FOR THIS AMOUNT _____

Books for Pocket Watch Collectors

AMERICAN POCKET WATCH IDENTIFICATION & PRICE GUIDE, BOOK 2. Ehrhardt, 1974. **(Prices Revised in 1979).** 192, 8½x11 Pages. $15.00. 1 lb. 10 oz.

FOREIGN & AMERICAN POCKET WATCH IDENTIFICATION & PRICE GUIDE, BOOK 3. Ehrhardt, 1976. 172, 8½x11 Pages. $10.00. 1 lb. 8 oz.

1976 POCKET WATCH PRICE INDICATOR. Ehrhardt, 1975. 64, 8½x11 Pages. $5.00. 14 oz.

1977 POCKET WATCH PRICE INDICATOR. Ehrhardt, 1976. 96, 8½x11 Pages. $7.00. 1 lb.

1978 POCKET WATCH PRICE INDICATOR. Ehrhardt, 1978. 110, 8½x11 Pages. $10.00. 1 lb. 2 oz.

1979 POCKET WATCH PRICE INDICATOR. Ehrhardt, 1979. 110, 8½x11 Pages. $10.00. 1 lb. 2 oz.

1980 POCKET WATCH PRICE INDICATOR. Ehrhardt, 1980. 110, 8½x11 Pages. $12.00. 1 lb. 2 oz.

AMERICAN POCKET WATCH COMPANIES (Pocket Book) Ehrhardt, 1979. 96, 3½x5½ Pages. $3.00. 2 oz.

MASTER INDEX TO POCKET WATCHES. Ehrhardt, 1979. 16, 8½x11 Pages. $4.00. 6 oz.

ELGIN POCKET WATCH ID. & PRICE GUIDE. Ehrhardt, 1976. 120, 8½x11 Pages. $10.00. 1 lb. 2 oz.

ILLINOIS SPRINGFIELD WATCHES ID. & PRICE GUIDE. Ehrhardt, 1976. 136, 8½x11 Pages. $10.00. 1 lb. 4 oz.

WALTHAM POCKET WATCH ID. & PRICE GUIDE. Ehrhardt, 1976. 172, 8½x11 Pages. $10.00. 1 lb. 4 oz.

HAMILTON POCKET WATCH ID. & PRICE GUIDE. Ehrhardt, 1976. 53, 8½x11 Pages. $10.00. 14 oz.

ROCKFORD GRADE & SERIAL NUMBERS WITH PRODUCTION FIGURES. Ehrhardt, 1976. 44, 8½x11 Pages. $10.00. 12 oz.

TRADEMARKS. Ehrhardt, 1976. 128, 8½x11 Pages. $10.00. 1 lb. 2 oz.

THE PERFECTED AMERICAN WATCH—WALTHAM (Reprint). $4.00. 6 oz.

THE TIMEKEEPER—HAMILTON WATCH COMPANY (Reprint). $3.00. 6 oz.

1858 E. HOWARD & COMPANY (Reprint). $3.00. 6 oz.

EVERYTHING YOU WANTED TO KNOW ABOUT AMERICAN WATCHES & DIDN'T KNOW WHO TO ASK. Col. George E. Townsend, 1971. 88, 6x9 Pages. $6.00. 8 oz.

AMERICAN RAILROAD WATCHES. Col. George E. Townsend, 1977. 44, 6x9 Pages. $6.00. 8 oz.

THE WATCH THAT MADE THE DOLLAR FAMOUS. Col. George E. Townsend, 1974. 45, 6x9 Pages. $6.00. 8 oz.

Clock Books

CLOCK IDENTIFICATION & PRICE GUIDE, BOOK 1. R. Rabeneck & R. Ehrhardt, 1977. **(Prices Revised in 1979).** 198, 8½x11 Pages. $15.00. 1 lb. 12 oz.

1979 CLOCK PRICE UP-DATE & INDEX TO CLOCK BOOK 1. Ehrhardt, 1979. 18, 8½x11 Pages. $4.00. 6 oz.

CLOCK IDENTIFICATION & PRICE GUIDE, BOOK 2. M. "Red" Rabaneck & R. Ehrhardt, 1979. 192, 8½x11 Pages. $15.00. 1 lb. 10 oz.

Violin Books

VIOLIN IDENTIFICATION & PRICE GUIDE, BOOK 1. E. Atchley & R. Ehrhardt, 1977. 192, 8½x11 Pages. $25.00 1 lb. 10 oz.

VIOLIN IDENTIFICATION & PRICE GUIDE, BOOK 2. E. Atchley & R. Ehrhardt, 1978. 206, 8½x11 Pages. $25.00 1 lb. 12 oz.

VIOLIN IDENTIFICATION & PRICE GUIDE, BOOK 3. R. Ehrhardt, 1978. 152, 8½x11 Pages. $15.00. 1 lb. 5 oz.

Misc. Books

AMERICAN COLLECTOR DOLLS PRICE GUIDE, BOOK 1. S. Ehrhardt & D. Westbrook, 1975. 128, 8½x11 Pages. $8.95 1 lb. 2 oz.

AMERICAN CUT GLASS PRICE GUIDE, Rev. 1977. Alpha Ehrhardt. 120, 8½x11 Pages. $6.95. 1 lb. 2 oz.

POCKET KNIFE BOOK 1 & 2 PRICE GUIDE. J. Ferrell & R. Ehrhardt, **Rev. 1977.** 128, 8½x11 Pages. $6.95 1 lb. 2 oz.

POCKET KNIFE BOOK 3 — PRICE GUIDE TO 2000 WINCHESTER & MARBLES, HARDWARE COLLECTIBLES. L. Ehrhardt, 1974. 128, 8½x11 Pages. $6.95. 1 lb. 2 oz.

The books listed above are available from HEART OF AMERICA PRESS. All are sold on a satisfaction guarantee. If you are not sure about the books you want, send a self-addressed, stamped envelope and we will send you detailed brochures on all of the publications.

For orders in the U.S. and Canada, send the price of the book plus 81 cents postage and handling for the first book and 25 cents for each additional. Foreign countries—Check with your Post Office for rate, your choice, Air or Sea Mail, Book Rate. Book and carton weights listed above. Send orders to:

HEART OF AMERICA PRESS
P. O. BOX 9808
KANSAS CITY, MISSOURI 64134

I WISH TO THANK THE FOLLOWING FINE PEOPLE FOR THEIR HELP

BERNIE R. NICKELL
Sugar Creek, Mo.

AL GRINER
Overland Park, Kansas

HERBERT LAWSON
Huntington, West Va.

PAUL GUAEHLING
Polo, Illinois

ARTHUR ZIMMERLA
Los Angeles, Calif.

SHIRLEY SHELLEY
Florissant, Mo.

L. H. WOLFE
San Bernardino, Calif.

BILLIE D. BECK
Independence, Mo.

PATTY GLYNN
Kansas City, Mo.

MR. & MRS. E. H. PARKHURST, JR.
Lancaster, Pa.

C. G. BERGER
Washington, D. C.

DR. JOHN N. HOFFMAN
Washington, D. C.

MR. BATTISON
Washington, D. C.

DR. WM. C. HEILMAN, JR.
New Castle, Ind.

STEWART DOW
Akron, Ohio

HART MAYER
Kansas City, Mo.

JOHN D. MILLER
Bartlett, Ill.

THEO McCABE
Manhattan, Kansas

C. W. PELHAM
Kansas City, Mo.

WILLIAM M. CHEAQUI (photos)
Kansas City, Mo.

RON STARNES
Tulsa, Okla.

OTHER SOURCES OF INFORMATION

For those of you who wish to buy books on other areas of timekeeping I would suggest you write the following dealers for lists of books they have available.

ADAMS BROWN AND CO.
P. O. Box 399
Exeter, N. H. 03833

AMERICAN REPRINTS
4656 Virginia
St. Louis, Mo. 63111

ELGIN BOOK CO.
766 South Street
Elgin, Illinois 60120

Most libraries have a good selection of books on watches and clocks and be sure and ask if they have my books. This will help me sell books to them. I have all my books listed in Publishers Trade List Annual.

If you are an interested watch or clock collector you should join the National Association of Watch and Clock Collectors, (NAWCC). Now over 24,000 strong! At the present time the yearly dues are $12.00. Write to NAWCC, Box 33, Columbia, Pa. 17512, and list me as your sponsor.

EXPLANATION OF PRICING

A retail value has been given for every watch pictured on the pages inside this book. The prices apply to the descriptions given by each picture, or somewhere on the page.

Movements are shown on many pages without cases. Most of you will seldom buy or sell a movement by itself without the case. I have given a value for just the movement by itself, then you must add to that a value for the case. For example: I have shown the 23 Jewel, 60 Hour Bunn Special movement only at $150.00, then add $30.00 if it is in a fine or better gold filled case with no brass showing, or $100.00 if it is in a 14Kt solid gold open face case.

If the movement is by itself you should discount it $10.00 or more for having to fit it into a case. A lot of the movements are not standard and will take a special case. Most of these are hard to case because the special cases are very hard to find. A good example of this is 10-Size Keywind Waltham and Elgin cases and 10-Size Waltham Maximum A cases. I will try to indicate this "hard to case" condition on the page by the movement with the initials "HTC".

On pages where movements and cases are shown together, a good idea can be determined by the value added to the movement for each type of case.

The case or condition of the case is, in many instances, the biggest variable in the value of a watch. An example of this would be a 7 Jewel full plate Elgin movement in running condition in a badly worn gold plated or gold filled Hunting case, worth possibly only $20.00, but if it was in a heavy solid 18Kt gold multi-color Hunting case it could be worth $400.00 or $500.00.

Below is a chart to help you get your thinking started. Add to the movement value the following amount if cased similarly:

FIRST, DETERMINE THE SIZE OF THE MOVEMENT. See page __12__ .

ALL CASES TO BE CONSIDERED IN EXTRA FINE CONDITION OR BETTER.

O-S	H.C. Plain polish coin or sterling silver	$ 25.00
O-S	H.C. Plain polish, 20 year	60.00
O-S	H.C. all over engraved or turned, 20 year	80.00
O-S	H.C. all over engraved, 14Kt solid	100.00 Up
O-S	O.F. plain polish, 20 year	15.00
6-S	Similar to O-S but maybe $10 to $20.00 less in 20 year Hunting	
12-S	H.C. plain polish, 20 year	30.00
12-S	H.C. engraved or turned, 20 year	50.00
12-S	O.F. plain polish, 20 year	15.00
12-S	O.F. engraved or turned, 20 year	20.00
16-S	H.C. plain polish, 20 year	50.00
16-S	H.C. engraved or turned, 20 year	65.00

16S	H.C. engraved or turned, 20 year, silver		$ 50.00
16-S	H.C. engraved, 14Kt		100.00 Up
16-S	O.F. plain polish, 20 year		25.00
16-S	O.F. engraved or turned, 20 year		30.00
16-S	O.F. engraved, 20 year original Elgin, Waltham, Illinois, Ball or Hamilton markings in case		35.00 to $45.00
18-S	O.F. plain polish, 20 year		30.00
18-S	O.F. plain polish, silver (according to weight)		30.00 to 45.00
18-S	O.F. engraved or turned, 20 year		40.00
18-S	H.C. plain polished, 20 year		50.00
18-S	H.C. engraved or turned, 20 year		65.00 Up
18-S	H.C. engraved or turned,	14Kt solid	125.00 Up
12-S, 16-S, 18-S	O.F. silveroid, etc.		10.00 to $15.00
12-S, 16-S, 18-S	H.C. silveroid, etc.		15.00 to $20.00
18-S	H.C. or O.F. silveroid, etc.		30.00 Up

Many conditions affect the value of a watch case. In the following paragraphs I will discuss some of them and not necessarily in the order of their importance.

Most collectors want their case to be the original case. This is hard to determine sometimes. A knowledge of the kind of cases that were available when the movement was sold is helpful here. Look for evidence of movement or case screw marks on the case that would indicate another movement has been in the case previously. Some collectors would rather have a worn original than a new case.

Initials on a case usually are not desirable. Ladies O-Size watches sell much better if they have no initials. Large scroll or old English type that are hard to read are not as objectionable as the bold or block letters that you can read easily. Many young families are buying extra fine and mint condition watches and having their initials or children's initials put on them and putting them away to become family heirlooms. Young folks are beginning to realize these superb examples of American craftsmanship. In general, only the value of extra fine or mint condition cases will be affected by initials.

Gold content of gold filled cases is not very important in the final value of a case. A case marked 15, 20, or 25 year is not nearly as important as condition. Of course, a 25 year case would wear much longer than a 15 year case and, if the watch is to be worn, then it should be considered. If you have three cases of different year guarantees but in the same condition, the value will be about the same if it is going to be put in a collection.

Weight of a case is very important, especially in silver or solid gold. As I write this, silver is $5.00 per ounce scrap price and 24kt gold is $150.00 an ounce. This subject is handled in detail in my TRADEMARKS book. But, briefly, gold in the form it is used in 14Kt U.S. Assay cases will bring now, March 1974, about $3.65 per (DWT) pennyweight (20 pennyweights to the ounce).

Lots of solid gold cases change hands the first time or two after the original owner below actual scrap value. A 16-Size 14Kt hunting case weighing 40 DWT is worth at this writing about $140.00 for scrap. Generally, the bigger the case the more desirable.

Condition of the complete watch "movement, dial, crystal and case" is very important especially when in mint plus or factory new condition. Many collectors on the better American grades such as 16 size 23 jewel series 10 or 11 Howards, Lord Elgin or grade 156, Riverside Maximus, etc., will bring a 50% to 100% more if factory new. I saw a collector pay $600.00 for a series 10 Keystone Howard in the factory wood box and outside hard paper cover in factory new condition. I would say in most instances except in the later 10 size and 12 size, you could double the values for factory new.

Decoration is often a matter of taste. Collectors usually like the cases to have as much decoration as possible. The heavy hand engraved is near the top of the list. Multi-color gold decoration probably heads the list, especially when combined with diamonds or other precious stones. At this time it seems for an extra fine or mint condition multi-color, the sky is the limit. The more beautiful a case is the more valuable the watch, especially in ladies and gents Hunting case watches. Only a small percentage of all watches qualify and those really bring a premium when offered to the right buyers.

Marks on cases pertaining to gold content usually are reliable. To really do justice to this subject would take a book by itself. See my book on TRADEMARKS. I'll try to cover some of the more obvious marks that you should watch for. There are quite a few cases which are really gold plated or gold dipped that are marked 10, 15, 20, or 25 year warranted. If these are in extra fine or better condition, they are hard to tell. Most look like they were stamped after they left the factory and the mark will look raw or unpolished. I have an old Brown Bros. catalog that advertised such cases. This will be shown in detail in a future POCKET WATCH PRICE GUIDE, BOOK 3. Such cases will usually have brass showing all over, even if showing only a little wear, and the insides will be bright and look like gold.

An unmarked or mismarked Hunting case can most times be identified by looking at the cut end of the lid of the hinges under 10X magnification. You can see a thin line of gold covering the brass in a gold filled case. A solid gold or brass case will look solid here. The final test, of course, is to use a file on an out-of-the-way place and a touch of acid.

I have tried to cover in detail all phases that relate to the value of watch cases in my book, TRADEMARKS, that is available to you if you wish more information.

Mail order dealers usually have to get a little more for their watches because of the expense and extra trouble they have in the course of doing business. Trading or buying from another collector is a good way to improve your collection. Usually this is less expensive than with a dealer. Get acquainted with as many "hip pocket" traders as you can in your town. They occasionally come up with some good watches.

EXPLANATION OF PRICING OF MOVEMENTS ONLY
(AMERICAN WATCH COMPANIES)

The movements are valued as if they were in extra fine condition.

I offer here what I consider to be extra fine condition. The dial must be original and free of chips and with maybe one or two extremely faint hairlines and no discoloration. Deduct on double sunk railroad watches $10.00 for a bad dial. Deduct $3.00 to $5.00 on 15 Jewel or less, because at present they are usually available with a little looking. High grade original movement dials are expensive when you can find them. Movements over $150.00 value are hard to sell with less than a mint dial. Some collectors like to look for them and will replace them when they can find one. On the other hand, the man who buys watches for investment usually wants watches in extra fine to mint condition because he doesn't want to spend time trying to improve them. A mint dial to an investor and some collectors could be valued at $25.00 plus.

Extra fine condition movement to me means that it is running with a good motion, no wobble in balance, and keeping time; no botched jewel settings or cups, and no evidence of excess cleaning. The movement should have most of its original appearance, allowing for its age and use. Most watches, when they are acquired from the original owner, will at least need cleaning and adjusting and will qualify, all other conditions being equal, as extra fine with allowance being made to clean, a new crystal, etc.

I have not taken into consideration low serial numbers on the pricing of any movement. Some of the early movements shown in this book are of a very low number and would command a much higher price than the one shown. Collectors also like to have the lowest serial number that they can get in the first run of the movement. To my knowledge, serial number lists are only available to Elgin, Waltham and Hamilton Watch Companies. If you have reliable serial number information or lists on any other American Watch Company, I would like to hear from you.

There are a good number of sleeper watches out there to be found. Many collectors, etc. have them and don't know it. As time goes on and more knowledge is acquired by collectors, those movements, of which only a few were made, will increase tremendously in value. For instance: according to Hamilton records, as few as 44 movements were made of Grade 951, 23 Jewel, Hunting, Pendant Set 16-Size.

What Do Collectors Like To Collect? I will list some of the favorite catagories. Some like only mint to factory new of all types. Some only railroads. Many like big Hunting cases; others small Hunting cases. Some, one watch company; and on and on. Collect what appeals to you or what you can get in some instances. Generally, the high grade movements are at the top of the list in the best original case you can get. Be careful not to overlook an early 15 Jewel watch, say Elgin or Waltham, because you didn't know it was the highest grade they made at that time.

Polished gold movement trains add to the beauty of a watch and usually indicates a high grade and originally expensive watch. These make a fine collection.

Beautifully finished and damaskeened movement plates, with gold jewel cups, screws, balance screws, regulators, etc., are also very desirable and are usually accompanied by a gold train.

Most people collect something! I think today the serious collector of watches has an eye on the value of his collection. If he has been at it for as little as 10 years, he has seen his $25.00 watches go up to $100.00 to $200.00 and sometimes more. Since my first Price Guide was published in 1972, there has been a sharp rise in watch values. There are also a lot of new collectors, or maybe just savers. These savers have realized that old watches have a value. They don't necessarily know how much, because the price wasn't very high when they found it and most haven't tried to sell them. It seems to grow on you! First thing you know, you are watching for them. There are still a lot of very good collector watches in dresser drawers of the families of the original owners, waiting for you to find. I think watch collecting is just getting started, and offers a great opportunity for the knowledgeable collector.

How Did I Arrive At the Values Placed on the Watches in this Book?

O.K. Here Goes! I have spent hundreds of hours, driven thousands of miles (in a 27' motor home), attending as many National Association of Watch & Clock Collectors Regional Meetings and Sales as I could; attended hundreds of flea markets, antique shows, swap meets; talked with dealers, collectors, and anybody that could talk watches. I have sent for and received, mail order watch lists from about all the dealers in the United States. I own upward of 700 American and foreign watches myself (all are in the bank, by the way). I set up at flea markets, antique shows, etc., when time permits, offering to buy and sell watches. For the past year I have been selling some of my duplicates by mail. I talk daily with local and distant collectors. For the past few years I have begged, borrowed and bought every bit of research material I could get my hands on. I still will. I was fortunate to have friends and acquaintances who have been at the "gut level" of buying and selling watches for years.

The values I have shown are, I believe, what the watches are bringing today. Some of the movements shown have not been traded enough (that I know of) to really establish a market. On these I tried to value them according to the same or similar grade of another brand. As you have suspected, I have probably made some mistakes. Some are too high - but I suspect many are too low. I did not price a watch high because I knew only a few were made, etc. If it is not common knowledge, until enough people know that a watch is scarce, or a certain type becomes a fad, or something causes a watch to be in demand, it will still only bring so much because only a few are looking for it, and they know they can buy it for less than it is worth when they do find it.

Values in this book are based on the following. The value shown is the price a serious collector or investor, who has the money, will pay another collector or dealer who knows the value of the watch. All other transactions will be, in most cases, below this so called "top price".

I am not infallible and probably have some of these watches priced below their actual market value. As this book gets older, if the past is any indication, the values shown will tend to become low on many of the watches shown. As collector's and investor's knowledge increases and they become more sure of themselves, they will pay more for the watches they want. A case in point: In 1971 at the time I published my first book "Pocket Watch Price Guide", 24 Jewel, 18 Size Illinois watches in gold filled were selling at $180.00 to $200.00 and were moving slow. At this time they are bringing $350.00 to $500.00 to collectors who want one in their collection. I feel there are other watches shown in this book that will show like increases. If I knew which ones they were, I would be buying as many as I could. The man who studies all of the available written material and has the money to take advantage of what he learns, should be able to show a very nice profit in the future.

There are many good watch buys to be made because the owners of most watches that are offered for sale do not know what they are worth. This will always be true because a large number of people in the United States today either do not read at all, or do not like to read. A man who does not read is very limited in his knowledge of anything except his one or two specialties that he has learned by experience. I am not alone in the fact that I have made a great many good buys in watches, and other things, simply because I have read almost every book that has been published recently on antiques of all kinds.

To get a good buy is merely having the ability to recognize one when you see it. Watches are at this time my No. 1 hobby. I have had other in the past. To name a few: fishing, hunting, coins, radio, violins, paper Americana, and other lessor interests. Collecting watches is the most challenging. When I started there was very little written information that was reliable, and no one that I talked to was willing to open up and tell me anything. When they did, a lot of times it proved to be either untrue or only part of the story. I wrote the first book, and for that matter, this book, from material and information I had gotten together for my own use. I felt there was a need for the kind of knowledge I had assembled, and have been encouraged by the letters and comments from strangers who purchased a copy of my first "Pocket Watch Price Guide", to go ahead with this one.

I think the most useful book on pocket watches would be one that pictures as many movements as possible. If this book proves to be profitable and will enable me to search out the material, I will do one some day.

I am a Registered Land Surveyor in the great State of Missouri, and have been lucky enough to earn a little extra money to pursue my hobby of traveling and collecting watches. I have been able also, by using what I have learned, to build up my collection by selling or trading my duplicate finds to other collectors and investors. I have very reliable employees who make it possible for me to be away from my business for short periods of time to attend Flea Markets, NAWCC Shows, and antique shops along the way, in my search for research material and sleeper watches to either add to my collection or sell or trade to other interested people.

If, as you read this, you think that you may have some material or information on any kind of pocket watches or watch companies that you would be willing to sell me or loan to me, drop me a line. There are large vacant areas on many watch companies that need to be filled.

The following few paragraphs are strictly my own personal viewpoints, although I know they are shared by many others.

I hope that many dealers who offer their watches for sale at Antique Shows, Flea Markets, National Association Shows, etc. will read this or someone will tell them about it.

I believe that watches, when displayed for sale, especially in a covered glass case, should have the asking price plainly marked, and, if possible, the number of jewels. Many sales are lost because of a failure to do this. Many buyers will not ask the price because of a number of reasons. I will list a few, and there are others.

1. Collectors and investors who have the money to buy watches did not, in most cases, make it buying and selling pocket watches. They are, on the other hand, talented and very busy people. To name a few: doctors, lawyers, real estate brokers and many other professional and non-professional men whose time is very valuable. They want to be able to see if they are interested in your watches without asking about each watch.

2. Buyers of watches like to have time to make up their mind on whether they are interested in the watches without a conversation with you. Many dealers are unintentionally rude to qualified buyers because of having to put up with so many "tire kickers" who aren't interested anyway. So, once a conversation starts, many times the buyer gets mad and walks away.

3. Put the price you want for the watch on it. Don't put twice the price you really want. Many really serious buyers do not realize that you as the dealer have done this, and therefore never indicate an interest in the watch. Most people do not expect to have to haggle the price down from $200.00 to $100.00. They are used to going in a store to buy a can of beans, chunk of bologna, or a suit of clothes with the price marked, and figure that is what they will have to pay.

No one can ever expect to get the top dollar for all the watches they have for sale. No one will probably ever have that much knowledge about the watches they are selling. If you don't know how much you want for a watch, I doubt if you will be able to find out from your buyer. You must pass some of your good deals on to the next fellow. I have found in my town the dealers who do best add a reasonable amount to their purchase price, even though they suspect it is worth more. This has a tendency to keep buyers coming because the buyer knows the dealer is being fair and can get a sleeper once in a while.

4. Back to time again. I know in my case I have gone to the Flea Market at Brimfield, Mass. and to the one at Renningers & Schoups Grove in Pennsylvania in the same weekend. My family; wife, Alpha; son, Larry; and daughter, Sherry; all either collect something or are interested in looking for something for me. Dealers who have watches displayed and not marked, I sometimes do not ask about them because the dealer is busy with another customer. Or, if I ask his wife she tells me he is somewhere else and she doesn't know the price, etc. Sometimes I never get around to going back. Most of these giant Flea Markets take almost all day to cover, and if you have to haggle, many times you can't make it around. Many people do their most buying of the year when they are on vacation - and you know how short time is then.

I say again - Put the price you want for the watch and as much information as you can in as big letters as is practicable. Many people do not see well. This will help you sell watches.

The idea that all buyers expect you to come down is for the birds. That buyer standing before you, who, in many cases, earns upward of $40.00 an hour, will buy what you have if you make it so that he can, and then be on his way.

Many collectors buy entirely by mail because of their shortage of time. Here again the dealers are losing sales because the watches are not described well enough so that the buyer knows what he is getting. In another instance, there are very few high grade watch parts available to repair watches with. Many parts from lower grade movements will work. If the mail order dealer would list that watch so that it could be identified he would make a sale for parts. I have myself bought watches from $25.00 to $50.00 and used them for parts to fix a couple of $100.00 watches. Collectors who try to get one of each company's watches, need to know what model and grade is being offered. The movement serial number is a must.

Since a great many pocket watches are sold and traded through the mail I have tried to include some help with the descriptions. I have placed a number with a circle around it thus ③ By most of the individual watch descriptions or pictures to help identify which watch you are trying to describe. Use them in this way. Example: 3-20-2 The first number means watch No. 3 (New Railway 23J), the second No. 20 is the page number and the last number is for American Pocket Watch Price Guide Book 2. This should be a great help when writing newspaper ads, mail order lists, or just talking watches on the phone.

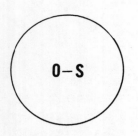

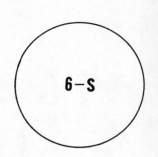

HOW TO DETERMINE THE SIZE OF A WATCH

I will write here mainly of the system used on American watches. The Lancashire Gauge for determining watch sizes is of English origin and is the standard commonly used by watch manufacturers of the United States. By this system one inch was taken as a basing figure and to this was added 5/30 of an inch for fall or drop (the extra width for the dial). English-made watches were usually hinged, swing-ring in the case similar to the swing-ring in modern (1923) swing-ring cases. The top plate was made enough smaller than the pillar plate to permit the movement falling or dropping into position without coming in contact with the case center. Thus, 1 and 5/30 of an inch from the base also forms a size smaller than naught size. Howard watches used letters instead (see Dennison System next page). Their A = 1 inch, B = 1 1/16 inch, C = 1 2/16 inch, etc. The above was taken from a 1923 Illinois Watch parts catalog. Most watch material houses have for sale for under $1.00 a small gauge showing all systems. On the following page I have drawn a gauge to scale.

The plate to measure to determine the size is the one with the dial fastened to it.

Here is how to determine the size or approximately the size of your watch. Take off the cover holding the crystal. Be careful in doing this, some are screwed on – like most RR watches, some are hinged, some pop off – like most hunting cases and dollar watches. The dial in most instances covers about all of the pillar plate, of which you can usually just see the edge. Take a piece of paper and mark the width of the dial or plate if you can see it, then go to the next page and place it on the proper scale. This will tell you the size of the watch. If you remove the works from the case (only experienced people should do this) you can measure it more accurately.

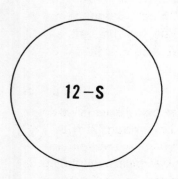

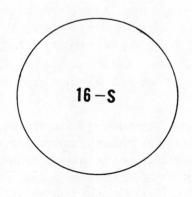

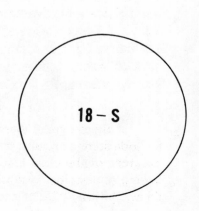

WATCH SIZES

LANCASHIRE SYSTEM – One inch is the base for a 6/0 size and 1/30 inch is added for the next higher size.

DENNISON SYSTEM – One inch is the base for the letter A size and 1/16 inch is added for each following letter.

SWISS SYSTEM – One ligne equals .088814 inches or 2.25583 millimeters. One ligne equals 1/12 of an inch of a Paris foot, which is slightly larger than an English foot.

LANCASHIRE SYSTEM			DENNISON SYSTEM			SWISS SYSTEM		
INCHES	MILLIMETERS	WATCH SIZE	HOWARD LETTER	INCHES	APPRX WATCH SIZE	LIGNES	INCHES DECIMALS	MILLIMETERS
					18-0	7	.622	15.79
					15-0	8	.710	18.05
					12-0	9	.799	20.30
					10-0	10	.888	22.56
1	25.40	6-0	A	1	6-0	11	.977	24.81
1 1/30	26.24	5-0						
1 2/30	27.08	4-0	B	1 1/16	4-0	12	1.066	27.07
1 3/30	27.94	3-0						
1 4/30	28.78	2-0	C	1 2/16	2-0	13	1.154	29.32
1 5/30	29.62	0	D	1 3/16	0	14	1.243	31.58
1 11/30	34.70	6	G	1 6/16	6	15	1.332	33.84
1 13/30	36.40	8	H	1 7/16	8	16	1.421	36.09
1 15/30	38.10	10	I	1 8/16	10	17	1.510	38.35
1 17/30	39.78	12	J	1 9/16	12			
1 19/30	41.48	14	K	1 10/16	14	18	1.599	40.60
1 21/30	43.18	16	L	1 11/16	16	19	1.687	42.86
1 22/30	44.02	17						
1 23/30	44.86	18	N	1 13/16	18	20	1.776	45.11
1 25/30	46.56	20				21	1.865	47.37

WATCH SIZES

BASED ON THE DIAMETER OF AN O SIZE PILLAR PLATE = 35/30 INCHES

SIZE NO. = NUMBER OF THIRTIETHS OF AN INCH IN EXCESS OF 35/30 INCHES

1/30 IN = 1 SIZE = .8466 M.M. = .3753 FRENCH LIGNES = 144/384 FRENCH LIGNES (APPROX.)

1 FRENCH LIGNE = 2.2559 M.M.   1 INCH = 25.40005 M.M.

SIZE (AMERICAN)	SIZE (SWISS)	FRACTIONS OF AN INCH	DECIMALS OF AN INCH	MILLI-METERS	FRENCH LIGNES
36	36	2 11/30	2.367	60.10	26 237/384
35	35	2 10/30	2.333	59.26	26 94/384
34	34	2 9/30	2.300	58.41	25 334/384
33	33	2 8/30	2.267	57.57	25 190/384
32	32	2 7/30	2.233	56.73	25 46/384
31	31	2 6/30	2.200	55.88	24 286/384
30	30	2 5/30	2.167	55.04	24 143/384
29	29	2 4/30	2.133	54.19	23 383/384
28	28	2 3/30	2.100	53.35	23 239/384
27	27	2 2/30	2.067	52.50	23 95/384
26	26	2 1/30	2.033	51.65	22 336/384
25	25	2	2.000	50.80	22 192/384
24	24	1 29/30	1.967	49.96	22 48/384
23	23	1 28/30	1.933	49.11	21 288/384
22	22	1 27/30	1.900	48.26	21 144/384
21	21	1 26/30	1.867	47.42	21 0/384
20	20	1 25/30	1.833	46.57	20 241/384
19	19	1 24/30	1.800	45.72	20 97/384
18	18	1 23/30	1.767	44.87	19 337/384
17	17	1 22/30	1.733	44.03	19 193/384
16	16	1 21/30	1.700	43.18	19 50/384
15	15	1 20/30	1.667	42.33	18 290/384
14	14	1 19/30	1.633	41.49	18 146/384
13	13	1 18/30	1.600	40.64	18 2/384
12	12	1 17/30	1.567	39.79	17 242/384
11	11	1 16/30	1.533	38.95	17 99/384
10	10	1 15/30	1.500	38.10	16 339/384
9	9	1 14/30	1.467	37.25	16 195/384
8	8	1 13/30	1.433	36.41	16 51/384
7	7	1 12/30	1.400	35.56	15 292/384
6	6	1 11/30	1.367	34.71	15 147/384
5	5	1 10/30	1.333	33.87	15 3/384
4	4	1 9/30	1.300	33.02	14 243/384
3	3	1 8/30	1.267	32.17	14 99/384
2	2	1 7/30	1.233	31.33	13 340/384
1	1	1 6/30	1.200	30.48	13 196/384
0	0	1 5/30	1.167	29.63	13 52/384

SIZE (AMERICAN)	SIZE (SWISS)	FRACTIONS OF AN INCH	DECIMALS OF AN INCH	MILLI-METERS	FRENCH LIGNES
0	0	1 5/30	1.167	29.63	13 52/384
00	-1	1 4/30	1.133	28.79	12 293/384
000	-2	1 3/30	1.100	27.94	12 149/384
4/0	-3	1 2/30	1.067	27.09	12 5/384
5/0	-4	1 1/30	1.033	26.25	11 246/384
6/0	-5	1	1.000	25.40	11 102/384
7/0	-6	29/30	.967	24.55	10 343/384
8/0	-7	28/30	.933	23.71	10 199/384
9/0	-8	27/30	.900	22.86	10 56/384
10/0	-9	26/30	.867	22.01	9 296/384
11/0	-10	25/30	.833	21.17	9 152/384
12/0	-11	24/30	.800	20.32	9 8/384
13/0	-12	23/30	.767	19.48	8 249/384
14/0	-13	22/30	.733	18.63	8 106/384
15/0	-14	21/30	.700	17.78	7 341/384
16/0	-15	20/30	.667	16.94	7 193/384
17/0	-16	19/30	.633	16.08	7 49/384
18/0	-17	18/30	.600	15.24	6 290/384
19/0	-18	17/30	.567	14.40	6 147/384
20/0	-19	16/30	.533	13.54	6 2/384
21/0	-20	15/30	.500	12.70	5 242/384
22/0	-21	14/30	.467	11.86	5 98/384
23/0	-22	13/30	.433	11.00	4 338/384
24/0	-23	12/30	.400	10.16	4 192/384
25/0	-24	11/30	.367	9.32	4 48/384
26/0	-25	10/30	.333	8.46	3 299/384
27/0	-26	9/30	.300	7.62	3 145/384
28/0	-27	8/30	.267	6.78	3 1/384
29/0	-28	7/30	.233	5.92	2 240/384
30/0	-29	6/30	.200	5.08	2 97/384
31/0	-30	5/30	.167	4.24	1 336/384
32/0	-31	4/30	.133	3.38	1 191/384
33/0	-32	3/30	.100	2.54	1 48/384
34/0	-33	2/30	.067	1.702	289/384
35/0	-34	1/30	.033	.846	144/384
36/0	-35	0	.0	.000	0

HAMPDEN WATCH CO.

SEE PAGE 4

SPRINGFIELD, MASS. 1878 ADVERTISMENT

H.T.C.

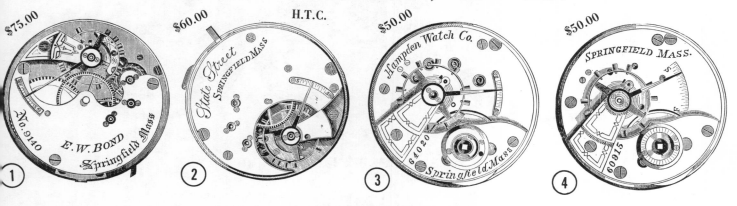

Manufacturers of KEY and KEYLESS
WATCHES.

I have valued the HAMPDEN watches on page 15 to 26 as if they were in extra fine condition complete, running and no hairlines in original dial. I believe most of these movements shown on this page to be NEW YORK WATCH CO. movements complete and sold by HAMPDEN.

Subtract $15.00 Each Movement
For Gilded Finish

Add the following if cased in either of the following in extra fine or better.

O. F. Silver $40.00 H. C. $65 to $85

O. F. Silveroid $20.00 H. C. $30 to $50

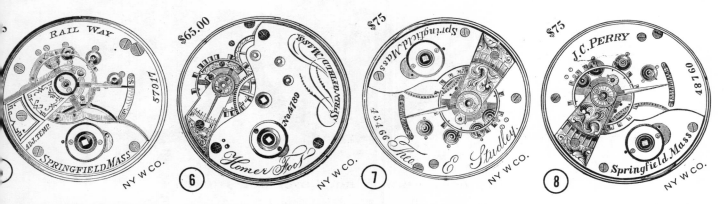

The above are NICKEL, and as samples of SUPERIOR TIMEKEEPERS and for beauty of finish, we respectfully invite the SPECIAL attention of the Trade.

General Office and Factory,
Springfield, Mass.

NEW YORK OFFICE,
No. 12 MAIDEN LANE.

HAMPDEN WATCH MOVEMENTS.

1888 JEWELERS SUPPLY CATALOG

SEE PAGE 4

$75

$50

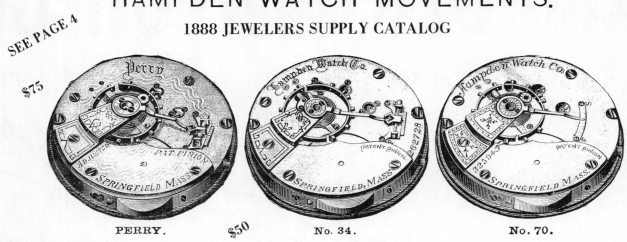

PERRY.   No. 34.   No. 70.

18 Size, Full Plate—Nickel.

		KEY WIND.	STEM WIND.
$75.00 RAILWAY.	15 Ruby Jewels, 4 pairs in settings, adjusted to temperature and isochronism, gold index and red gold trimmings, patent regulator	------	$50.00
$50.00 PERRY.	15 Ruby Jewels, 4 pairs in settings, adjusted to temperature and isochronism, gold index and red gold trimmings, patent regulator	------	37.50
$35.00 No. 31.	Nameless, 11 jewels, 4 upper holes	--- --	15.00

18 Size, Full Plate—Gilt.

		KEY WIND.	STEM WIND.	
No. 70.	Nameless, 11 jewels, 4 upper holes	------	$13.50	$30.00
$35.00 SPRINGFIELD.	7 jewels	$ 7.00	10.00	$30.00
No. 36.	Nameless, 15 jewels, 4 pairs, patent regulator, adjusted	------	24.00	$30.00
" 34.	" 15 " 4 " " "	------	17.00	$30.00
$45.00 " 71.	" 11 jewels	10.50	------	

NOTE: The HAMPDEN WATCH CO. was
moved to Canton, Ohio in 1888.

$55

$45.00

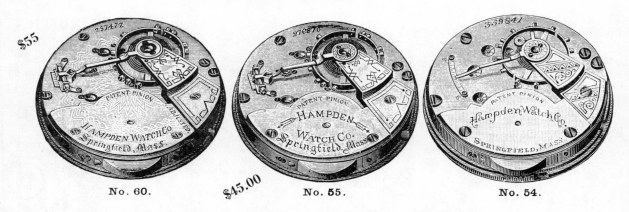

No. 60.   No. 55.   No. 54.

Open Face, Stem Wind, Lever Set—Nickel.

$55.00	No. 60.	Nameless, 15 Ruby Jewels, (same as Railway)	$50.00
$45.00	" 59.	" 15 " " (same as Perry)	37.50
$35.00	" 57.	" 11 jewels, 4 upper holes	15.00

Open Face, Stem Wind, Lever Set—Gilded.

$30.00	No. 56.	Nameless, 15 jewels, 4 pairs, adjusted, patent regulator	$24.00
$30.00	" 55.	" 15 " 4 " patent regulator	17.00
$35.00	" 54.	" 11 " 4 upper holes	13.50

HAMPDEN WATCH COMPANY'S MOVEMENTS.
18 Size, Stem-Wind, Hunting and Open Face.

SEE PAGE 4

1896 A. C. Becken
Supply Catalog

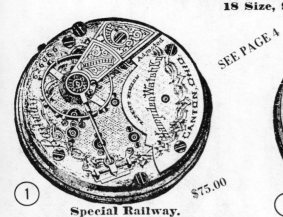

① $75.00
② $60.00
③ ④ ⑤ $45.00

Special Railway.
Nickel, 17 extra fine ruby jewels in solid gold settings, jeweled center, magnificently damaskeened and finished, bevel head gilt screws, 14-k gold patent regulator, expansion balance, perfectly compensated, and accurately timed to all positions and isochronism, double sunk glass enamel dial with red marginal figures, Breguet hair-spring, steel work highly polished, patent center pinion, elegantly engraved and damaskeened, fine escapement, fluer de lis hands, and the "Hampden" back-action main spring.
Open Face or Hunting.................$70 00

New Railway.
Nickel, 17 extra fine ruby jewels, in solid gold settings, 14-k gold patent regulator, compensation balance, accurately adjusted to temperature, isochronism and 6 positions (particularly desirable and especially recommended to meet the requirements of railway service), Breguet hair-spring, patent center pinion, center jeweled, elegantly engraved and damaskeened, fluer de lis hands, and the "Hampden" back-action main spring
Open Face or Hunting.................$50 00

Anchor.
Nickel, 17 extra fine ruby jewels in solid gold settings, patent regulator, compensation balance, accurately adjusted to temperature, isochronism and position, patent center pinion, center jeweled, elegantly engraved and damaskeened, Breguet hair-spring, crescent hands and the "Hampden" back-action main spring.
Anchor. Hunting or Open Face........$32 00
No. 48. Nameless, Hunting.............. 32 00
No. 68. Nameless, O. F................... 32 00

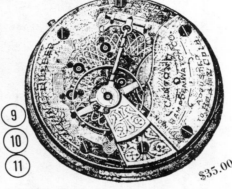

⑥ ⑦ ⑧ $40.00
⑨ ⑩ ⑪ $35.00
⑫ ⑬ $30.00

Nickel, 17 ruby jewels in composition settings, Breguet hair-spring, adjusted compensation balance, gilded patent regulator, gilt screws, double sunk dial with red marginal figures, patent center pinion, elegantly engraved and damaskeened, moon hands, and the "Hampden" back-action main spring. Specially guaranteed to be the best time-keeper in the world for the price, and superior to any other full plate watch made outside the Dueber-Hampden factories.
John C. Dueber. Special, Htg. or O.F. $30 00
No. 47. Nameless, Hunting.............. 30 00
No. 67. Nameless, Open Face........... 30 00

Nickel, 17 ruby jewels in composition settings, adjusted to heat and cold, sunk second and circle dial, Roman or Arabic figures and seconds, Breguet hair-spring, compensation balance, steel patent regulator, patent center pinion, elegantly engraved and damaskeened, moon hands, and the "Hampden" back-action main spring.
John C. Dueber. Hunting or O. F. $24 00
No. 43. Nameless, Hunting............. 24 00
No. 63. Nameless, Open Face........... 24 00

Nickel, 17 ruby jewels in composition settings, sunk second and circle dial, Roman figures and seconds, Breguet hair spring, adjusted, compensation balance, steel patent regulator, patent center pinion, engraved, regular "Hampden" main spring, moon or spade hands.
No. 80. Hunting.........................$20 00
No. 81. Open Face....................... 20 00

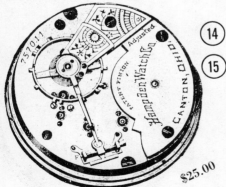
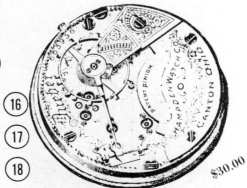
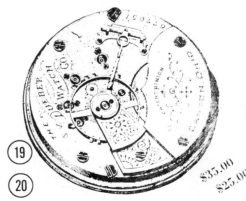

⑭ ⑮ $25.00
⑯ ⑰ ⑱ $30.00
⑲ ⑳ $35.00 $25.00

Gilt, 17 fine ruby jewels in composition settings, adjusted, Breguet hair-spring, steel patent regulator, expansion balance, blue bevel screw throughout, fine escapement, elegantly engraved and gilded, Arabic or Roman red marginal figures, double sunk hard enamel dial, morning glory hands, fine dart seconds, and the "Hampden" back-action main spring.
No. 49. Hunting..............$19 00
No. 69. Open Face............ 19 00

Nickel, 16 ruby jewels in composition settings, sunk second and circle dial, Roman figures and seconds, Breguet hair-spring, compensation balance, steel patent regulator, patent center pinion, elegantly engraved and damaskeened, moon or spade hands, regular "Hampden" main spring.
Dueber. Hunting or Open Face........$16 00
No. 44. Nameless, Hunting.............. 16 00
No. 64. Nameless, Open Face........... 16 00

Nickel, 15 jewels in composition settings, steel patent regulator, Roman circular dial, spade hands, patent center pinion, flat hair spring, elegantly engraved and damaskeened, and the regular "Hampden" main spring.
Dueber Watch Co. 15 jewels, Hunting or Open Face.....................$13 00
Dueber Watch Co. 11 jewels, Hunting or Open Face..................... 12 50

HAMPDEN WATCH COMPANY'S MOVEMENTS.

18 Size, Stem-Wind, Hunting and Open Face.

SEE PAGE 4

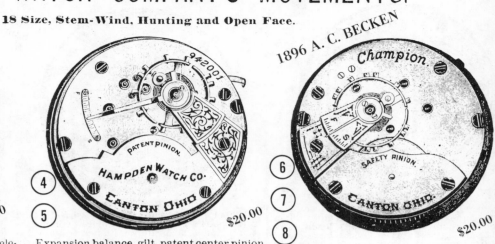

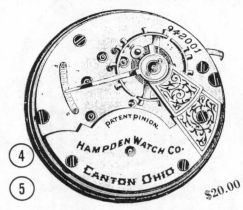

① ② ③ $25.00

Nickel, 11 jewels, patent center pinion, elegantly engraved and gilded, spade hands and regular "Hampden" main spring, patent regulator.

Gladiator. Hunting or Open Face $10 00

No. 45. Nameless, Hunting.......... 10 00

No. 65. Nameless, Open Face 10 00

④ ⑤ $20.00

Expansion balance, gilt, patent center pinion, flat hair spring, elegantly engraved and gilded, spade hands, sunk second dial and regular "Hampden" main spring, patent regulator. The best watch for the price in the world.

No. 46. Hunting, 11 jewels, gilt, plain regulator $9 50

No. 66. Open Face, 11 jewels, gilt, plain regulator 9 50

⑥ ⑦ ⑧ $20.00

Nickel, 7 jewels, expansion balance, patent center pinion, spade hands, sunk second dial and "Regular" main-spring.

Champion, Open Face or Hunting..... $8 00

No. 1. Hunting, gilt 8 00

No. 21. Open Face, gilt .. $15.00.... 8 00

16 Size, Stem-Wind, Hunting and Open Face.

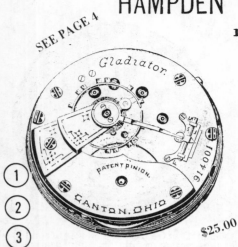

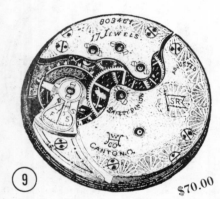

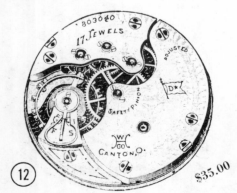

⑨ $70.00

Nickel, 17 extra fine ruby jewels in gold settings, ruby pallets, gilt bevel head screws, magnificent gilt damaskeened, Breguet hairspring, highly finished steel work, micrometer regulator, D. S. glass enamel dial, accurately compensated and timed to position and isochronism.

No. 104...................... $70 00

⑩ $60.00

Nickel, 17 extra fine ruby jewels in gold settings, ruby pallets, gilt bevel head screws, Breguet hair-spring, D. S. glass enamel dial, red marginal figures, micrometer regulator, accurately timed and adjusted to temperature, position and isochronism

No. 105...................... $50 00

⑪ $40.00

Nickel, 17 fine ruby jewels in gold settings, ruby pallets, gilt screws, Breguet hair-spring, micrometer regulator, D. S. hard enamel dial, red marginal figures, adjusted.

No. 106........ $30 00

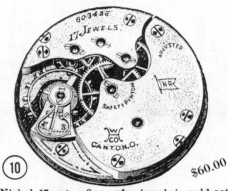

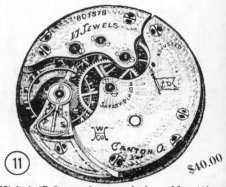

Movements are valued as if they were in a case but you must add the value of the case for the total value of your watch.

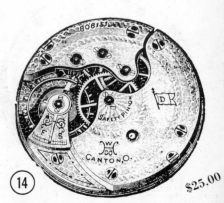

⑫ $35.00

Nickel, 17 ruby jewels in composition settings, ruby pallets, blue bevel head screws, Breguet hair-spring, micrometer regulator, D. S. dial, red marginal figures, patent center pinion, adjusted.

No. 107.................. $24 00

⑬ $30.00

Nickel, 17 ruby jewels in composition settings, ruby pallets, patent center pinion, micrometer regulator, S. S. and imitation double sunk dials.

No. 108   **18** $20 00

⑭ $25.00

Nickel, 13 jewels in composition settings, jeweled center (upper and lower), S. S. dial, patent center pinion.

No. 109.................. $16 00

HAMPDEN WATCH CO.'S MOVEMENTS.

Ladies' size, Stem-Wind and Set. Fit all makes of 6 size Cases.

No extra charge for fancy dials on Hampden movements above 7 jewel. Fancy dials on 7-jewel movements, 70c. extra.

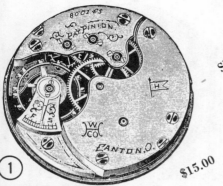

SEE PAGE 4

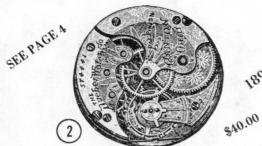

1896 A. C. BECKEN

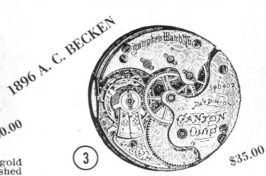

① $15.00

16 size, Stem-wind, Hunting and Open Face.
Gilt, 11 jewels in composition settings, xp. balance, patent center pinion, S. S. ial.
No. 110 ....$10 50

② $40.00

Nickel, 17 fine ruby jewels, raised gold center and train settings, highly polished center and escape wheels, flat hair spring, the "Hampden" back-action main spring, gilt bevel screws throughout, fine gilt spade hands, double sunk glass enamel dial, elegantly painted, neat gilt marginal figures, adjusted to heat, cold and five positions, and very accurately timed. The best 6 size watch on the market.
No. 220. Hunting............$30 00

③ $35.00

Nickel, 16 fine ruby jewels, raised gold center, jewel settings, Arabic double sunk glass enamel dial, red marginal figures, neat gold border on dial, delicate blue spade hands, flat hair spring, gilt bevel screws, gilt regulator, patent center pinion, compensation balance, the "Hampden" back action main spring, and accurately timed.
No. 215. Hunting..............$20 00

Movements are valued as if they were in a case but you must add the value of the case for the total value of your watch.

$30.00

④

Nickel, 15 fine ruby jewels, elegantly engraved and damaskened, at hair spring, compensation balance, blue bev. screws, patent center pinion, fine Roman or Arabic figured double unk dial, red marginal figures, norning glory hands, composition jewel settings, the "Hampden" back action main spring, nd accurately timed.
No. 213. Hunting.......$14 00

⑤ $25.00

Fine nickel movement, 11 jewels, in composition settings, compensation balance, flat hair spring, patent center pinion, sunk second dial, elegantly engraved and damaskeened, fine moon hands, and regular "Hampden" main spring.
No. 206. Hunting........$12 00

⑥ $20.00

Nickel, 7 jewels, expansion balance, patent center pinion, sunk second dial, spade hands, elegantly engraved, and regular "Hampden" main spring.
No. 200.................$10 00

⑦ $15.00

Fine gilded movement, 7 jewels, compensation balance, flat hair spring, patent center pinion, sunk second dial, spade hands, elegantly engraved and gilded, and regular "Hampden" main spring.
No. 200. Hunting........$9 00

HAMPDEN WATCH CO.

APPROXIMATE PRODUCTION DATES

SERIAL No.	DATE	SERIAL No.	DATE	SERIAL No.	DATE
52,000	1877	1,258,000	1889	2,600,000	1903
156,000	1878	1,358,000	1890	2,850,000	1905
260,000	1879	1,458,000	1891	3,050,000	1907
364,000	1880	1,558,000	1892	3,200,000	1909
368,000	1881	1,658,000	1893	3,400,000	1911
472,000	1882	1,758,000	1894	3,600,000	1913
576,000	1883	1,859,000	1895	3,800,000	1915
690,000	1884	1,958,000	1896	4,000,000	1917
854,000	1885	2,150,000	1898	4,200,000	1919
958,000	1886	2,250,000	1899	4,400,000	1921
1,058,000	1887	2,350,000	1900	4,500,000	1923
1,158,000	1888	2,450,000	1901	4,600,000	1925

Hampden Watch Co.'s Movements.

BUSIEST HOUSE IN AMERICA

$130.00 $75.00 $120.00

SPECIAL RAILWAY. 23 J.
Nickel, 23 Extra Fine Ruby and Sapphire Jewels, Gold Settings, Escapement Cap Jeweled, Steel Escape Wheel, Finely Graduated Micrometer Regulator, Breguet Hairspring, Accurately Adjusted to Temperature, Isochronism and Position, Highly Polished Steel Work, Bevel Head Gilt Screws, Gold Lettering, Fine Double Sunk Glass Enamel Dial.
Hunting, Lever Set.... [SALIVARY] $70 00
Open Face, Lever Set.. [SALIVATED] 70 00

NEW RAILWAY. 23 J.
Nickel, 23 Fine Ruby and Sapphire Jewels, Gold Settings, Escapement Cap Jeweled, Steel Escape Wheel, Patent Micrometer Regulator, Breguet Hairspring, Adjusted to Temperature, Isochronism and Position, Polished Steel Work, Gold Lettering, Double Sunk Glass Enamel Dial.
Open Face (only), Lever Set........$56 00
[SALLOWNESS]

SPECIAL RAILWAY. 21 J.
Nickel, 21 Fine Ruby and Sapphire Jewels, Gold Settings, Escapement Cap Jeweled, Steel Escape Wheel, Micrometer Regulator, Breguet Hairspring, Adjusted to Temperature, Isochronism and Position, Highly Polished Steel Work, Bevel Head Gilt Screws, Gold Lettering, Double Sunk Glass Enamel Dial.
Hunting, Lever Set... .....[SALLY] $50 00
Open Face, Lever Set, [SALLYPORT] 50 00

$70.00 $70.00 $70.00

JOHN HANCOCK.
Nickel, 21 Fine Ruby and Sapphire Jewels, Gold Settings, Escapement Cap Jeweled, Steel Escape Wheel, Micrometer Regulator, Breguet Hairspring, Adjusted to Temperature, Isochronism and Position, Polished Steel Work, Bright Bevel Head Screws, Gold Lettering, Double Sunk Glass Enamel Dial.
Hunting, Lever Set......[SALMON] $46 00
Open Face, Lever Set ..[SALOBRAL] 46 00

THE DUEBER WATCH CO. 21 J
Nickel, 21 Fine Ruby Jewels, in Settings, Steel Escape Wheel, Patent Regulator, Breguet Hairspring, Adjusted to Temperature, Isochronism and Position, Double Sunk Dial, Heavy Arabic Figures, for Railway Service.
Open Face, (only), Lever Set...... $37 00
[SALOON]

THE DUEBER WATCH CO. 17 J.
Nickel, 17 Fine Ruby Jewels in Settings, Patent Regulator, Breguet Hairspring, Adjusted to Temperature, Isochronism and Position, Double Sunk Dial, Heavy Arabic Figures, for Railway Service.
Open Face (only) Lever Set........$32 00
[SALPICON]

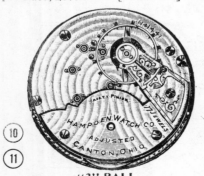

$40.00 $35.00 $35.00

"3" BALL.
Nickel, 17 Fine Ruby Jewels in Settings, Patent Micrometer Regulator, Patent Breguet Hairspring, Accurately adjusted to Temperature, Isochronism and Position, Elegantly Engraved and Damaskeened, Fine Glass Enamel Double Sunk Dial.
Hunting, Lever Set,..[SALSERETA] $24 00
Open Face, Lever Set .[SALTANT] 24 00

Nos. 80 and 81, or DUEBER GRAND.
Nickel, 17 Jewels, in Settings, Adjusted, Patent Regulator, Breguet Hairspring, Elegantly Engraved and Damaskeened, Sunk Second Dial.
No. 80, Hunting, Lever Set....... $20 00
[SALTATION]
No. 81, Open Face, Lever Set...... 20 00
[SALTATORY]

Nos. 44 and 64.
Nickel, 17 Jewels in Settings, Breguet Hairspring, Micrometer Regulator, Bright Flat Screws, Arabic or Roman Dial, Red Marginal Figures and Moon Hands.
No. 44, Hunting, Lever Set........ $18 00
[SALTERIO]
No. 64, Open Face, Lever Set...... 18 00
[SALTISH]

Hampden Watch Co.'s Movements.

SEE PAGE 4

18 Size, Stem Wind, Full Plate.

Fitting All Regular 18 Size Cases.

1904 SUPPLY CATALOG

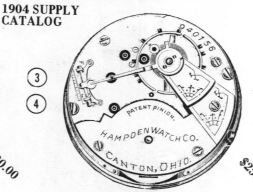

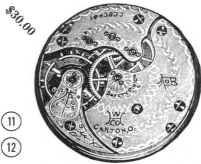

③
④

⑤
⑥

$15.00

$30.00

$25.00

①
②

DUEBER WATCH CO.

Nickel, 15 Jewels in Settings, Breguet Hairspring, Patent Regulator, Sunk Second Dial.

Hunting, Lever Set...[SALTMARSH] $13 50
Open Face, " " ....[SALTMINE] 13 50

Nos. 45 and 65.

Nickel, 11 Jewels, Patent Regulator, Sunk Second Dial.

No. 45. Hunting, Lever Set.......$11 00
[SALTNESS]
No. 65. Open Face, Lever Set...... 11 00
[SALTSPRING]

CHAMPION.

Gilded, 7 Jewels, Sunk Second Dial.
Hunting, Lever Set....[SALTWATER] $8 50
Open Face, " " ....[SALTWORKS] 8 50

---

16 Size New Model, Stem Wind, Bridge and Three-Quarter Plate.

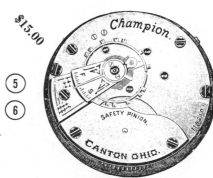

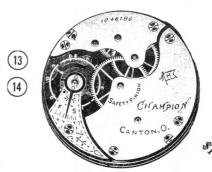

$75.00

⑨
⑩

⑦
⑧

$30.00

$30.00

$40.00

⑮

⑯

⑪
⑫

⑬
⑭

$15.00

No. 109 and Champion, Three-Quarter Plate. Fitting all Regular 16 Size, New Model, Pendant Set Cases.

WM. McKINLEY, 21 J.

Nickel, **21 Extra Fine Ruby and Sapphire Jewels,** in Solid Gold Settings, Barrel Arbor and Center Staff Jeweled with the Finest of Sapphires, Escapement Cap and Jeweled, Conical Pivots, Micrometer Regulator, Compensation Balance, Gold Screws, Breguet Hairspring, Mean Time Screws, Accurately Adjusted to Temperature, Isochronism and Positions, Patent Center Pinion, Bevel Head Gilt Screws, Highly Polished Steel Work, Polished Center Wheel, fine Double Sunk Dial, Elegantly Engraved and Damaskeened, Gold Lettering.

Hunting, Lever Set...[SALUBRIOUS] $50 00
Open Face, " " ....[SALUBRITY] 50 00

WM. McKINLEY, 17 J.

Nickel, **17 Ruby and Sapphire Jewels,** in Composition Settings, Adjusted, Breguet Hairspring, Patent Regulator, Mean Time Screws, Bright Flat Screws, Elegantly Engraved and Damaskeened Gold Lettering Arabic or Roman Dial, Red Marginal Figures.

Hunting, Lever Set...[SALVATION] $24 00
Open Face, " " ....[SALVATORY] 24 00

GEN'L STARK, 15 J.

Nickel, **17 Ruby Jewels,** in Composition Settings, Breguet Hairspring, Mean Time Screws, Patent Regulator, Bright Flat Screws, Engraved and Damaskeened, Gold Lettering Arabic or Roman Dial, Red Marginal Figures.

Hunting, Lever Set....[SALUTORY] $20 00
Open Face, " " ...[SALUTATION] 20 00

NOTICE.

Although cases are shown in illustrations of Gen'l Stark and Wm. McKinley movements, the Prices are for movements only.

No. 109.

Nickel, 15 Jewels, in Settings, Patent Regulator, Sunk Second, Hard Enamel Dial.
Hunting, Lever Set.....[SALUTER] $16 00
Open Face, " " ....[SALVABLE] 16 00

CHAMPION.

Gilt, 7 Jewels, Sunk Second, Hard Enamel Dial.
Hunting, Lever Set......[SAMBUKE] $9 50
Open Face, " " ....[SAMENESS] 9 50

Hampden Movements have Quick Trains and Compensation Balances.

Hampden Watch Co.'s Movements.

12 Size, Stem Wind, Three=Quarter Plate.

Hunting and Open Face, Stem Wind, Lever Set, Fitting Dueber Cases Only.
Quotations Are for Movements Only.

1904 SUPPLY CATALOG

23J — $130.00

$50.00

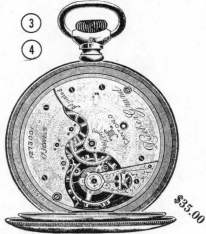

$35.00

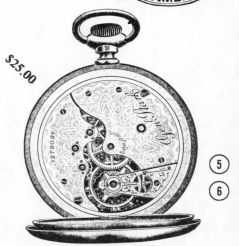

$25.00

JOHN HANCOCK.

Nickel, 21 Fine Ruby and Sapphire Jewels, Gold Settings, Escapement Cap Jeweled, Adjusted to Temperature, Isochronism and Position, Breguet Hairspring, Micrometer Regulator, Bright Bevel Head Screws, Finely Polished Steel Work, Elegantly Finished Plates with Gold Lettering, Double Sunk Glass Enamel Dial.
Hunting, Lever Set......[SAMLET] $50 00
Open Face, Lever Set..[SAMPHIRE] 50 00

DUEBER GRAND.

Nickel, 17 Ruby and Sapphire Jewels, Settings, Patent Regulator, Breguet Hairspring, Adjusted to Temperature, Elegantly Damaskeened, Gold Lettering, Sunk Second Dial.
Hunting, Lever Set.....[SAMPLER] $24 00
Open Face, Lever Set...[SANABLE] 24 00

GEN'L STARK.

Nickel, 15 Ruby Jewels, Settings, Patent Regulator, Breguet Hairspring, Engraved and Damaskeened, Gold Lettering, Sunk Second Dial.
Hunting, Lever Set..[SANABILITY] $18 00
Open Face, Lever Set.[SANAMENTE] 18 00

6 Size, Stem Wind, Three=Quarter Plate.

Hunting, Lever Set, Fitting All Regular 6 Size Pendant Set Cases.

$20.00

$15.00

$15.00

No. 213.

Nickel, 15 Jewels, Settings, Breguet Hairspring, Elegantly Engraved and Damaskeened, Gold Lettering, Sunk Second Dial...................[SANATIVE] $14 00

No. 206.

Nickel, 11 Jewels, Settings, Breguet Hairspring, Elegantly Engraved and Damaskeened, Gold Lettering, Sunk Second Dial...................[SANATORY] $12 50

No 200.

Gilded, 7 Jewels, Sunk Second Dial..$9 50
[SANCTIFIER]

The "400" 000 Size, Stem Wind, Three=Quarter Plate.

$40.00

DUEBER

"The 400."

Nickel, 16 Jewels, Raised Gold Settings, Patent Regulator, Breguet Hairspring, Sunk Second Glass Enamel or Fancy Dial, Finely Damaskeened and elegantly Finished throughout.
Hunting Only.[SANCTIFY] $24 00
Above Price is for Movement Only.

DIADEM.

Nickel, 15 Jewels, Raised Gold Settings, Patent Regulator, Breguet Hairspring, Finely Damaskeened, Sunk Second Glass Enamel Dial.
Hunting .[SANCTIMONY] $20 00
Open Face ...[SANCTION] 20 00

$15.00

MOLLY STARK.

Gilded, 7 Jewels, Breguet Hairspring, Sunk Second Dial.
Hunting...[SANCTITUDE] $13 00
Open Face.[SANCTUARY] 13 00

$30.00

$15.00

Cut showing Open Face "400" Movement with Second Hand, **in** Case.

$20.00

$15.00

Hampden 12, 6 and 000 Size Movements, in All Grades, Have Quick Trains and Compensation Balances.

Use Code Words in Brackets for All Telegraph Orders.

18 SIZE MOVEMENTS

① NEW RAILWAY
23 Jewels
Price $37.20

$130

② SPECIAL RAILWAY
21 Jewels
Price $35.40

$75

$70.00

③ JOHN HANCOCK
21 Jewels
Price $33.20

O. F. only.   Lever Sett.   Double Roller Escapement, Steel Escape Wheel, Fine Ruby and Sapphire Jewels in Solid Gold Settings and Adjusted to Temperature, Isochronism and Five Positions

Above are Railroad Grades

④ DUEBER WATCH CO.
21 Jewels
O. F. only   Lever Sett.
Double Roller Escapement
Steel Escape Wheel
Fine Ruby and Sapphire Jewels
and Adjusted to Temperature,
Isochronism and Five Positions
Price $26.60

$70

⑤ No. 64
17 Jewels
O. F. only   Pendant Sett.
Breguet Hairspring
Micrometer Regulator, Expansion
Balance
Price $11.00

$40.00

$30.00

⑥ DUEBER WATCH CO.
15 Jewels
O. F. only   Pendant Sett.
Breguet Hairspring
Patent Regulator, Expansion
Balance
Price $9.30

Movements are valued as if they were in a case but you must add the value of the case for the total value of your watch.

NUMERICAL DIAL
No Extra Charge on Railroad Grades

1917 OSKAMP—NOLTING CO.
WHOLESALE JEWELER SUPPLY
Cincinatti, Ohio

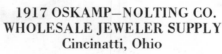

⑦ CHAMPION
$20.00
7 Jewels
Nickel, Breguet Hairspring
Expansion Balance
Price $7.20

STANDARD DIAL
Lighter Figures if Desired
No Extra Charge for Special Name on Dials

16 SIZE MOVEMENTS
RAILROAD GRADES
Sold With or Without Cases

1917 OSKAMP–NOLTING CO.

Double Roller Escapement
Steel Escape Wheel
Extra Fine Ruby and Sapphire Jewels in Solid
Gold Settings and Adjusted to Temperature,
Isochronism and Five Positions

① No. 104 $150
23 Jewels
O. F. and Htg.   Lever Sett.
Price $46.00

$70

No. 105 [Nameless] ④
WM. McKINLEY ⑤
21 Jewels
O. F. and Htg.   Lever Sett
Price $34.20

NUMERICAL
DIAL
No Extra Charge
on Railroad
Grades

STANDARD
DIAL
Heavy Arabic

Movements are valued as if they were in a case but you must add the value of the case for the total value of your watch.

Double Roller Escapement
Steel Escape Wheel
Extra Fine Ruby and Sapphire Jewels in Solid
Gold Settings and Adjusted to Temperature,
Isochronism and Five Positions

② $70

JOHN C. DUEBER
21 Jewels
O. F. Only   Lever Sett.
Price $34.20

$70

③ RAILWAY
19 Jewels
O. F. Only   Lever Sett.
Price $30.00

16 SIZE MOVEMENTS
SOLD WITH OR WITHOUT CASES

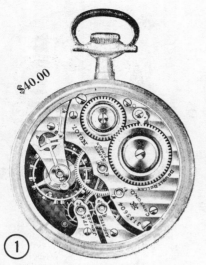

$40.00

(1)

No. 97 Htg. O. F. No. 107
17 Jewels
Adjusted, Pend. Sett.
Double Roller Escapement
Steel Escape Wheel
Ruby and Sapphire Jewels in
Composition Settings
Adjusted to Temperature
Isochronism and Three Positions and
Double Sunk Glass
Enameled Dial with
Red Marginal Figures
Price $20.00

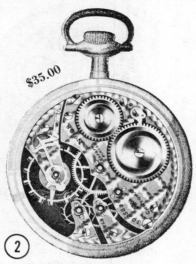

$35.00

(2)

No. 98 Htg. O. F. No. 108
17 Jewels
Pendant Sett.
Ruby Jewels in Composition Settings
Expansion Balance with Meantime
Screws
Double Sunk Glass Enameled Dial
with Red Marginal Figures
Price $15.30

$25.00

(3)

No. 99 Htg. O. F. No. 109
15 Jewels
Pendant Sett.
Jewels in Composition Settings
Expansion Balance with Meantime
Screws
Gold Lettering
Double Sunk Dial
Price $12.70

1917 OSKAMP–NOLTING CO.

$20.00

(4)

Champion
7 Jewels
O. F. and Htg. Pend. Sett.
Nickel
Breguet Hair Spring
Expansion Balance with Meantime
Screws
Sunk Second Dial
Price $8.50

Standard Dial
Stub Figures
Arabic or Roman

$15.00

(5)

No. 5
7 Jewels   Gilt
O. F. Only   Pend. Sett.
Expansion Balance with Meantime
Screws
Breguet Hairspring
Sunk Second Dial with Marginal
Figures
Price $7.00

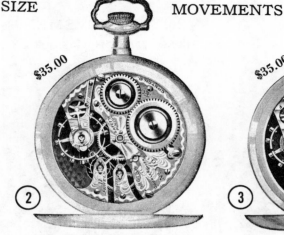

$55.00

$35.00

$35.00

No. 312 Htg. O. F. No. 314
21 Jewels
Adjusted, Pend. Sett.
Double Roller Escapement
Steel Escape Wheel
Fine Ruby and Sapphire Jewels in
Gold Settings
Sapphire Pallet Stones and Oval
Roller Jewels
Adjusted to Temperature
Isochronism and Five Positions
Price $37.50

No. 308 Htg. O. F. No. 310
17 Jewels
Adjusted, Pend. Sett.
Double Roller Escapement
Steel Escape Wheel
Ruby and Sapphire Jewels in
Composition Settings
Sapphire Pallet Stones and Oval
Roller Jewel
Price $18.80

No. 307
17 Jewels
O. F. only   Pend. Sett.
Ruby and Sapphire Jewels in
Composition Settings
Steel Escape Wheel
Patent Safety Center Pinion
Sunk Second Dial
Enamel or Gilded
Price $16.50

Movements are valued as if they were in a case but you must add the value of the case for the total value of your watch.

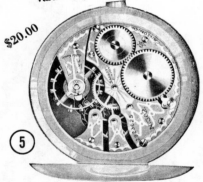

$25.00

$20.00

$15.00

No. 304 Htg. O. F. No. 306
15 Jewels
Pendant Sett.
Ruby Jewels in Composition Settings
Expansion Balance with
Meantime Screws
Double Sunk Glass Enameled Dial
Price $13.50

No. 300 Htg. O. F. No. 302
7 Jewels
Pendant Sett.
Expansion Balance with Meantime Screws
All Pivot Holes not Jeweled
Bushed with Anti-Friction Metal
Patent Safety Center Pinion
Price $9.40

No. 10
7 Jewels   Gilt
O. F. only   Pend. Sett.
Expansion Balance with
Meantime Screws
Breguet Hairspring
Sunk Second Dial with Marginal
Figures
Price $7.80

3/0 SIZE

"400"

$40.00

$20.00

$30.00

"FOUR-HUNDRED"
17 Jewels

"DIADEM"
15 Jewels

7 Jewels

"MOLLY STARK"

EXTREMELY THIN MODEL—12 SIZE
REAL AMERICAN PRODUCTS

The Paul Revere

Typically and proudly American and challenging a finer craftsmanship the world over, these Paul Revere extremely thin watches can well be termed an achievement in watch making.

AMERICA'S FINEST MEN'S WATCH
19 Jewels, Adjusted to Five Positions
17 Jewels, Adjusted to Three Positions

$200	In 19 Jewel, 18K White Gold Case, Engraved	$178.00
$180	In 19 Jewel, 14K Green Gold Case, Engraved	148.70
$160	In 19 Jewel, 14K Green Gold Case, Plain	129.30
$100	In 17 Jewel, 14K Green Gold Bass. Case, Plain	93.70
$100	In 17 Jewel, 14K Green Gold, Flat Case, Plain	104.00
$110	In 17 Jewel, 14K Green Gold Flat Case, Engraved	110.00
$120	In 17 Jewel, 14K White Gold Flat Case, Engraved	129.30
$ 70	In 17 Jewel, 25 Year Green Gold-Filled Case, Plain	67.20
$ 70	In 17 Jewel, 25 Year Green Gold-Filled Case, Engraved	69.90
$ 80	In 17 Jewel, 25 Year White Gold-Filled Case, Engraved	72.80

The Minute Man
17 Jewels Adjusted

25 Year, 14K Green Gold-Filled Case, Engraved	$60.00	$56.30
25 Year, 14K Green Gold-Filled Case, Plain	$60.00	53.70
25 Year, 14K White Gold-Filled Case, Engraved	$60.00	59.80

The dependability of the "Minute Man" manifests itself by its accurate time - keeping qualities. The delicate and pleasing designs of this model lend to it a distinctive air of individuality.

The "Nathan Hale" although not an adjusted watch in watch making parlance, is given special adjustment to the extent that we guarantee it to keep splendid time and to be thoroughly dependable.

The Nathan Hale
15 Jewels

In 25 Year, 14K Green Gold-Filled Case, Engraved		$47.90
In 25 Year, 14K Green Gold-Filled Case, Plain	$50.00	45.30
In 25 Year, 14K White Gold-Filled Case, Engraved		51.30
In 20 Year, Green Gold-Filled Case, Engraved		41.40
In 20 Year, White Gold-Filled Case, Engraved		42.70

All Above Watches Fitted with Solid Silver Hand-Carved Dials with raised figures, and excepting the 20 year 15 Jewel, Put Up in Handsome Display Boxes, with Suggested Selling Prices Attached.

18-S, 15J Hayward keywind & set gilt mvt. #164,863, Springfield, Mass. Mvt. & Dial is mint. Runs sluggish. Ex. fine 3 oz. Newport coin silver OF case. An original, good, solid attractive watch....$85.00.

18-S, gilt lettered nickel plates marked Special Railway 23J adj. Mint mvt. #1,722,741. Mint DS Montgomery dial except 1 hairline. Ex. fine heavy Fahys oresilver #1 Pat. 2-19-84, OF case with nice brass train engine inlaid in back....$155.00.

18S, 17J Special Railway. Mint 2 tone hunt Mvt. #1,017,147. Mint DS dial & hands. Duber 18Kt solid gold hunting case. Deer on back, no initial. Watch is all original and near mint throughout...$285.00.

18-S, 17J Special Railway. Near mint OF nickel and gold 2-tone full plate Mvt. #799,258. Adj., gold cups & weights, gilt regulator. A beautiful mvt. Near mint DS Arabic with red track. One minor hairline. Fine solid 14Kt YGF 25 year J. Boss screw B&B plain polish OF case. Tiny line of brass showing. A scarce watch...$90.00.

18-S, 17J New Railway (2-17-2) Mint nickel Mvt. #1,051,730, adj. Mint DS Arabic red track dial & original hands. Decorated screw B&B OF silveroid RR case...$80.00.

18-S, 17J Adj (14-17-2) near mint gilt Mvt. #783,689. Mint original DS Roman red track dial & hands. Near Mint C.W.C. Co. YGF swing ring OF case...$60.00.

16-S, 23J, Adj. near Mint nickel Mvt. #1,137,252. Plates like 1-22-2, NR in flag, gold cups, balance weights & gilt screws and lettering. LS, DR, extra fine SS Roman dial with extra hour hand. Fine YGF 20 yr. screw B&B plain polish bassine OF RR case...$170.00.

16-S, 21J, Adj. 5 pos. grade 10S. Mint gilt lettered Mvt. #2,932,926. Gold cups & weights. Mint DS Montgomery dial. Extra fine screw B&B OF 25 yr. YGF F.W.C. Co. RR case..$100.

16-S, 21J, Adj. 3 pos. Chronometer. Plates like (1-25-2). Mint Mvt. #3,544,185, DR, Fine SS Arabic red track dial & hands. Minor hairlines. Fine S.W.C. Co. 20 yr. YGF screw B&B RR case. Minor brass showing...$85.00

16-S, 17J, OF, Adj. 3 pos. Wm. McKinley, Mint nickel bridge Model. Mvt. #3,691,652. Mint decorated metal, Arabic Dueber Hampden dial & hands. Mint N.A.W. Co. Challenge white fully decorated case. A very mint dress watch...$50.00.

16-S, 17J, Model 108, fine nickel OF bridge Mvt. #3,409,420. Mint DS glass Montgomery dial, ex. fine 20 yr. YGF OF case. Birds & foliage engraved on back, watch looks original and near mint...$60.00

6-S, 14Kt. multi-color gold case. 15J nickel Mvt. #564,842. Beautiful decorated dial lever set. Mint condition..$150.00.

16-S, OF, 17J Adj. 3 pos. Wm. McKinley. Mint nickel Mvt. #3,669,295. Fine decorated Dueber Hampden metal dial & hands. Ex. fine 10Kt Dueber YGF screw B&B hand engraved back OF case..$40.00.

16-S, OF 7J mint nickel Mvt. #3,862,609. Model #10 Fine metaldial & hands. Fine I.W.C. Supreme YGP decorated case. Some brass showing. C. O. & running...$20.00.

12-S, 17J, Adj. Grade No. 310 (2-26-2). Gilt lettering. Mint DS Arabic Arabic red track dial & hands. Mint 14Kt YG 585 fine hinge OF case..$90.00.

12-S Hunting Grand Dueber. 17J, adj. Mvt. #2,365,18 25 yr. Dueber Special case. Double sunk Roman dial. Complete watch is Mint...$135.00.

12-S, 17J lever set Dueber Grand. Dueber 20 yr. GF engraved case. Watch mint condition throughout...$100.00.

12-S, 17J, adj. Paul Revere, Mint plus nickel Mvt. #3,430,328. Gold center wheel, cups & balance screws. Mint silver decorated dial, factory new 14Kt White decorated Dueber OF case..$120.00.

6-S, 15J, H.C. Grade No. 213 (7-22-2). Mint nickel Mvt. #1,177,918. Mint SS Roman dial & hands. Extra fine J. Boss 25 yr. YGF Hunting case. All over engine turned and hand engraved..$100.00.

16-S, H.C. 17J (Grade 108). Ext. fine nickel 3/4 plate Mvt. #1,214,575. Bal. Wobbles some but runs. Mint SS Roman Black Track Dial & Hands. Fine 20 yr. YGF fully decorated H.C. Shows a good bit of wear but only minor brass...$45.00

18-S, OF. 17J (Grade 64) Mint nickel full plate Mvt. #3,104,936. Pretty Damascine gold lettered plates. Ex. fine DS Arabic red track dial. Minor hairlines. Ex. find original Dueber heavy silverine screw B&B OF case. A very nice watch...$40.00.

6-S, 15J, H.C. Grade 213 (7-22-2). Ex. fine Mvt. #1,544,303. Mint gold leaf decorated dial and original hands. Beautiful 14Kt YGF multi-color case heavy raised flowers, leaves, scrolls & birds. No initial in shield...$320.00.

000-Size (400) 15J, H.C. Diadem (11-22-2). Mint gilt lettered Mvt. #2,405,247. Mint decorated dial & gold hands. Mint 25 yr. YGF Dueber Special. Beautiful engraved Hunting case...$130.00.

000-S (400) 7J, H.C. Molly Stark (13-22-2). Mint gilt Mvt. #1,340,915. Mint SS Roman dial & hands. Mint YGF Dueber Special partially decorated Hunting case...$110.00.

This page and others like it have been included to show you some actual mail order descriptions. These watches have sold during the past year. Reading these descriptions will also give you a better idea of how the case and condition of the dial can affect the value of the complete watch. The grading of the watch case, dial and movement is based on the suggested grading in my first book POCKET WATCH PRICE GUIDE published in 1972 on page 3 and 4.

HAMILTON WATCH MOVEMENT ILLUSTRATIONS

ALL PRICES AND NOTES BY THE COMPLIER OF THIS BOOK ARE IN THIS TYPE STYLE AND THE PRICES ARE <u>RETAIL</u>!!

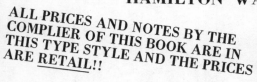

$225.00

$700.00 ③

36 Size Chrono.

$250.00

Summary Description of Movement—35 size, stem wound, safety setting movement. 21 jewels. 54-hour mainspring. Up and down winding indicator. Lever type escapement, bi-axial thermal expansion balance wheel, Elinvar-Extra hairspring, two-piece friction fit balance staff, cam type regulator. Tested for isochronism, temperature and recovery.

Movements are valued as if they were in a case but you must add the value of the case for the total value of your watch.

$40.00

④

18 Size, Model 924, Open Face
17 J, Going Barrel, Single Roller
Model 925, Hunting $40.00

⑤

$40.00

⑥

18 Size, Model 926, Open Face
17 J, Going Barrel, Single Roller
18 Size, Model 927, Hunting $40.00

⑦

$60.00

⑧

18 Size, Model 934, Open Face
17 J, Going Barrel, Single Roller
Model 935, Hunting $60.00

⑨

$40.00

⑩

18 Size, Model 936, Open Face
17 J, Going Barrel, Single Roller
Motor Barrel, Double Roller
Model 937, Hunting $40.00

⑪

$125.00

⑫

18 Size, Model 938, Open Face
17 J, Going Barrel, Single Roller
Motor Barrel, Double Roller
Model 939, Hunting $150.00

⑬

$70.00

⑭

18 Size, Model 940, Open Face
21 J, Going Barrel, Single Roller
Motor Barrel, Double Roller
Model 941, Hunting $80.00

⑮

HAMILTON WATCH MOVEMENT ILLUSTRATIONS

(1) $125.00

(1)
(2)
18 Size, Model 942, Open Face
21 J, Going Barrel, Double Roller
Model 943, Hunting $125.00

$225.00

(3)
(4)
18 Size, Model 946, Open Face
23 J. Motor Barrel, Double Roller
NO. 947 Hunting $300.00

$125.00

(5)
18 Size, Model 944, Open Face
19 J, Motor Barrel, Double Roller

$100.00

(6)
No. 948—18-size, open
face only, 17 jewels, nickel,
lever set, adjusted

950 23J $175.00
952 19J $150.00

(7) (8)
16 Size, Model 950-952
Bridge Movement, Lever Set, Open Face

Gold Train $175.00
Gilded Train $140.00

(9) GRADE 950B

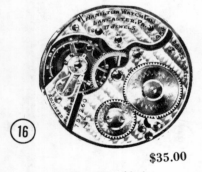

(16) $35.00

No. 954—16-size.

(17) $125.00

(18)
16 Size, Model 960, Open Face
21 J, Going Barrel, Double Roller
Model 961, Hunting $125.00

(19) $100.00

(20)
16 Size, Model 964, Open Face
17 J, Going Barrel, Single Roller
Model 965, Hunting $100.00

(10) $100.00

(11)
16 Size, Model 968, Open Face and Hunting
17 J, Going Barrel, Single Roller
Model 969, Hunting $100.00

(12) $100.00

(13)
16 Size, Model 970, Open Face
21 J, Going Barrel, Double Roller
Model 971, Hunting $100.00

(14) $100.00

(15)
16 Size, Model 972, Open Face
17 J, Going Barrel, Single and Double Roller
Model 973, Hunting

$70.00

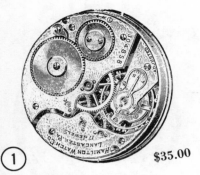

① $35.00

② $35.00

16 Size, Model 974, Open Face
17 J, Going Barrel, Single Roller
Model 975, Hunting

③ $40.00

No. 978—16-size, open face only,
nickel, ¾ plate movement, 17
extra fine jewels in settings

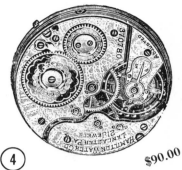

④ $90.00

⑤

16 Size, Model 990, Open Face
21 J, Going Barrel, Double Roller
Model 991, Hunting

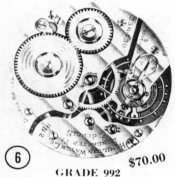

⑥ $70.00

GRADE 992

Open face, ¾ plate movt., 21 jewels,
single roller before No. 377001
double roller after No. 379000

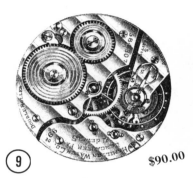

⑦ $70.00

⑧

16 Size, Model 992, Open Face
21 J, Going Barrel, Double Roller
Model 993, Hunting

$70.00

⑨ $90.00

16 Size, Model 992, Elinvar
¾ Plate, Lever Set, 21 J

⑩ $75.00

GRADE 992B

Open face, ¾ plate movt.,
21 jewels, double roller

⑪ $175.00

No. 994—16-size, open face, nickel, bridge
movement, pendant or lever set, 21 extra
fine ruby jewels in gold settings

⑫ $90.00

No. 996—16-size, open face,
lever set, nickel, ¾-plate movement, 19 fine ruby jewels in gold
settings, motor barrel, double
roller escapement

⑬ $70.00

No. 900—12-size

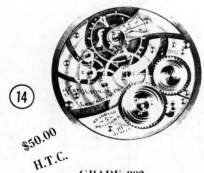

⑭ $50.00

H.T.C.

GRADE 902

Open face, bridge movt.,
19 jewels, double roller

Movements are valued as if they were in a case but you must add the value of the case for the total value of your watch.

HAMILTON WATCH MOVEMENT ILLUSTRATIONS

12 SIZE

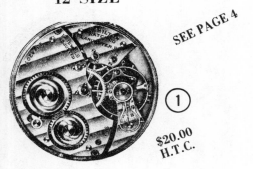

SEE PAGE 4

① 12 Size, Model 912

SEE PAGE ____ FOR 12 SIZE MODEL 400

$20.00 H.T.C.

② GRADE 912
Open face, ¾ plate movt., 17 jewels, double roller

$20.00 H.T.C.

$20.00 H.T.C.

③

No. 914—12-size

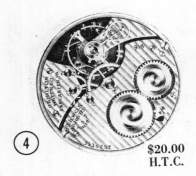

④ GRADE 918
Open face, ¾ plate movt., 19 jewels, double roller

$20.00 H.T.C.

920 Sold First As The Masterpiece

$75.00 H.T.C.

⑤

Masterpiece Grade $100.00

No. 920—12-size, open face, 23 extra fine ruby jewels

H.T.

⑥ GRADE 922
Open face, bridge movt., 23 jewels, double roller

10 SIZE

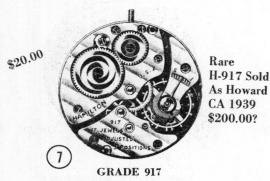

$20.00

Rare H-917 Sold As Howard CA 1939 $200.00?

⑦ GRADE 917
Open face, ¾ plate movt., 17 jewels, double roller

$30.00

⑧ GRADE 921
Open face, bridge movt., 21 jewels, double roller

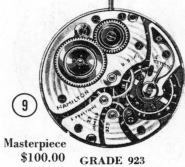

⑨

Masterpiece $100.00   GRADE 923
Open face, bridge movt., 23 jewels, double roller

Marked Masterpiece $125.00   **⑩**

O—SIZE

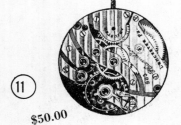

$50.00

⑪

GRADE 983
Hunting, bridge movt., 17 jewels, double roller

$75.00 **No. 985**—O-size, hunting, nickel, bridge movement, pendant set, 19 extra fine ruby jewels in gold settings, patent motor barrel, gold train, steel escape wheel, double roller escapement, sapphire pallets, micrometric regulator, Breguet hairspring, compensation balance, adjusted to temperature, isochronism and three positions.

$50.00 **No. 984**—Open face, same as above, without seconds hand.

$50.00 **No. 983**—O-size, hunting, nickel, bridge movement, pendant set, 17 extra fine ruby jewels in gold settings, steel escape wheel, double roller escapement, sapphire pallets, micrometric regulator, Breguet hairspring, compensation balance, adjusted to temperature, isochronism and three positions.

$30.00 **No. 982**—Open face, same as above, without seconds hand.

32

Hamilton Watch

① $225.00

No. 946 Open Face. Nickel, 23 Extra Fine Ruby Jewels in Gold Settings, Patent Motor Barrel, Double Roller Escapement, Steel Escape Wheel, Sapphire Pallets, Patent Micrometric Regulator, Breguet Hairspring, Compensation Balance, Double Sunk Dial, Beautifully Finished Nickel Plates, Gilt Lettering, Steel Parts Chamfered, Adjusted to Temperature, Isochronism and Five Positions.... $45.00

947 Hunting $300.00 ②

18-Size
Hamilton Movements
Lever Set Only

Movements are valued as if they were in a case but you must add the value of the case for the total value of your watch.

③ $70.00

No. 940 Open Face. Nickel, 21 Extra Fine Ruby Jewels in Gold Settings, Patent Motor Barrel, Adjusted to Temperature, Isochronism and Five Positions, Double Roller Escapement, Steel Escape Wheel, Breguet Hairspring, Compensation Balance, Patent Micrometric Regulator, Double Sunk Dial, Gilt Lettering, Beautifully and Elegantly Damaskeened $35.00

No. 941 Hunting, same as above

④ $70.00

⑤ $100.00

No. 948 Open Face. Nickel, 17 Jewels, Adjusted to Temperature, Isochronism and Three Positions, Double Roller Escapement, Steel Escape Wheel, Sapphire Pallets, Breguet Hairspring, Compensation Balance, Patent Micrometric Regulator, Double Sunk Dial, Beautifully Damaskeened $22.50

⑥ $40.00

No. 926 Open Face. Nickel, 17 Jewels, Adjusted to Temperature, Patent Micrometric Regulator, Breguet Hairspring, Compensation Balance, Single Sunk Dial..... $17.00

NO. 927 Hunting $40.00 ⑨

⑦ $40.00

No. 924 Open Face. Nickel, 17 Jewels, Breguet Hairspring, Patent Micrometric Regulator $16.00

No. 925 Hunting, same as above

⑧ $40.00

Serial No.	Date	Serial No.	Date	Serial No.	Date
50	1893	1,250,000	1910	2,350,000	1927
1,000	1894	1,290,000	1911	2,400,000	1928
5,400	1895	1,330,000	1912	2,450,000	1929
6,500	1896	1,370,000	1913	2,500,000	1930
9,500	1897	1,410,000	1914	2,520,000	1931
9,800	1898	1,450,000	1915	2,540,000	1932
12,000	1899	1,516,000	1916	2,560,000	1933
16,000	1900	1,582,000	1917	2,580,000	1934
98,000	1901	1,648,000	1918	2,600,000	1935
180,000	1902	1,714,000	1919	2,617,000	1936
262,000	1903	1,780,000	1920	2,623,000	1937
344,000	1904	1,850,000	1921	3,000,000	1939
426,000	1905	1,950,000	1922	up	1940
591,500	1906	2,050,000	1923	e,000,000up	Until
756,550	1907	2,150,000	1924	c0,000up	the
921,500	1908	2,250,000	1925	x0,000up	end of
1,086,500	1909	2,300,000	1926	and possibly others	production

**APPROXIMATE
PRODUCTION DATES**

**HAMILTON WATCH
COMPANY**

**LANCASTER, PA.
1892 to mid 1900's**

Hamilton Watch

16-Size Hamilton Movements

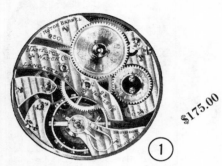

$175.00 ①

No. 950 Open Face. Nickel, Bridge Movement, Pendant or Lever Set, 23 Extra Fine Ruby Jewels in Gold Settings, Patent Motor Barrel, Gold Train, Escapement Cap Jeweled, Steel Escape Wheel, Double Roller Escapement, Sapphire Pallets, Breguet Hairspring, Micrometric Regulator, Compensation Balance, Double Sunk Dial, Adjusted to Temperature, Isochronism and Five Positions $65.00

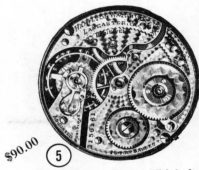

$150.00 ②

No. 952 Open Face. Nickel, Bridge Movement, Pendant or Lever Set, 19 Extra Fine Ruby Jewels in Gold Settings, Patent Motor Barrel, Steel Escape Wheel, Double Roller Escapement, Sapphire Pallets, Micrometric Regulator, Breguet Hairspring, Compensation Balance, Double Sunk Dial, Adjusted to Temperature, Isochronism and Five Positions $50.00

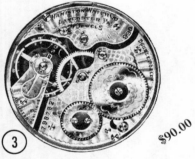

$90.00 ③

No. 990 Open Face. Nickel, ¾ Plate Movement, Lever Set only, 21 Extra Fine Ruby Jewels in Gold Settings, Steel Escape Wheel, Double Roller Escapement, Sapphire Pallets, Micrometric Regulator, Breguet Hairspring, Compensation Balance, Double Sunk Dial, Adjusted to Temperature, Isochronism and Five Positions..... $42.00

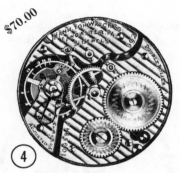

$70.00 ④

No. 992 Open Face. Nickel, ¾ Plate Movement, Lever or Pendant Set, 21 Extra Fine Ruby Jewels in Gold Settings, Double Roller Escapement, Sapphire Pallets, Gold Center Wheel, Steel Escape Wheel, Micrometric Regulator, Breguet Hairspring, Double Sunk Dial, Compensation Balance, Beautifully Damaskeened, Adjusted to Temperature, Isochronism and Five Positions $40.00
No. 993 Hunting, same as above Lever Set only ⑫

$90.00 ⑤

No. 996 Open Face. Nickel, ¾ Plate Movement, Lever Set only, 19 Fine Ruby Jewels in Gold Settings, Motor Barrel, Double Roller Escapement, Steel Escape Wheel, Sapphire Pallets, Micrometric Regulator, Breguet Hairspring, Double Sunk Dial, Compensation Balance, Adjusted to Temperature, Isochronism and Five Positions..... $36.00

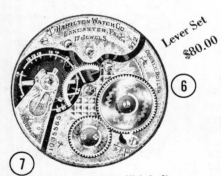

Lever Set $80.00 ⑥

⑦

No. 972 Open Face. Nickel, ¾ Plate Movement, Pendant or Lever Set, 17 Extra Fine Jewels in Gold Settings, Double Roller Escapement, Sapphire Pallets, Steel Escape Wheel, Micrometric Regulator, Breguet Hairspring, Compensation Balance, Adjusted to Temperature, Isochronism and Five Positions..... $28.00

⑪ **NO. 973 Hunting $70.00**

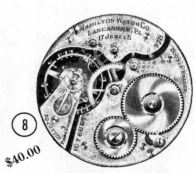

$40.00 ⑧

No. 978 Open Face. Nickel, ¾ Plate Movement, Lever Set only, 17 Extra Fine Jewels in Settings, Double Roller Escapement, Sapphire Pallets, Steel Escape Wheel, Micrometric Regulator, Breguet Hairspring, Compensation Balance, Double Sunk Dial, Adjusted to Temperature, Isochronism and Three Positions $25.00

$35.00 ⑨

No. 974 Open Face. Nickel, ¾ Plate Movement, Pendant or Lever Set, 17 Fine Jewels in Settings, Micrometric Regulator, Breguet Hairspring, Compensation Balance, Adjusted to Temperature, thoroughly well finished $20.00
No. 975 Hunting, same as above ⑩

$35.00

SEE PAGE 4

Hamilton Watch

16-Size Complete Watches

SEE PAGE 4

CASED WATCHES MUST BE MINT AND RUNNING

$300.00 ①
$275.00 ②
$200.00 ③
$200.00 ④

$325.00 ⑤
$225.00 ⑥
$225.00 ⑦

Antique Roman Dial $70.00 ⑧

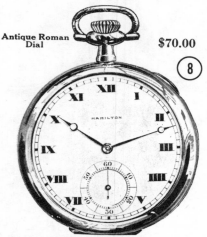

① **No. 950** in 16s Extra Heavy 14K Gold Open Face, Plain or Engine Turned Case..... $120.00
② **No. 950** in 16s Heavy 14K Gold Open Face, Plain or Engine Turned Case.. $105.00
③ **No. 950** in 16s Hamilton Permanently Guaranteed Gold Filled Open Face, Jointed, Plain or Engine Turned Case $77.00
④ **No. 950** in 16s Hamilton Permanently Guaranteed Gold Filled Open Face, Swing Ring, Plain or Engine Turned Case. (No. 950 movement can be supplied in either pendant or lever set)... $77.00
For description of movement see 16s movement page.

No. 956 Open Face Only. (Description of Movement.) Nickel, ¾ Plate Movement, Pendant Set, 17 Fine Jewels in Settings, Micrometric Regulator, Breguet Hairspring, Compensation Balance, Adjusted. (Sold Cased only.)
No. 956 in 16 size 25 year, Senior Style, Plain or Engine Turned Case........... $30.00

No. 994 Open Face Only. (Description of Movement.) Nickel, Bridge Movement, Pendant or Lever Set, 21 Extra Fine Ruby Jewels in Gold Settings, Escapement Cap Jeweled, Steel Escape Wheel, Gold Train, Double Roller Escapement, Sapphire Pallets, Micrometric Regulator, Breguet Hairspring, Compensation Balance, Adjusted to Temperature, Isochronism and Five Positions. (Sold Cased only.)
⑤ **No. 994** in 16s Heavy 14K Gold Open Face, Plain or Engine Turned Case........ $95.00
⑥ **No. 994** in 16s Hamilton Permanently Guaranteed Gold Filled Open Face, Jointed, Plain or Engine Turned Case $67.50
⑦ **No. 994** in 16s Hamilton Permanently Guaranteed Gold Filled Open Face, Swing Ring, Plain or Engine Turned Case $67.50

$300.00
$275.00
$175.00
$175.00

$260.00
$235.00
$145.00
$145.00

⑨ **No. 952** in 16s Extra Heavy 14K Gold Open Face, Plain or Engine Turned Case $107.00
⑩ **No. 952** in 16s Heavy 14K Gold Open Face, Plain or Engine Turned Case $92.00
⑪ **No. 952** in 16s Hamilton Permanently Guaranteed Gold Filled Open Face, Jointed, Plain or Engine Turned Case........ $66.00
⑫ **No. 952** in 16s Hamilton Permanently Guaranteed Gold Filled Open Face, Swing Ring, Plain or Engine Turned Case. (No. 952 movement can be supplied in either pendant or lever set)....... $66.00
For description of movement see 16s movement page.

⑬ **No. 990** in 16s Extra Heavy 14K Gold Open Face, Plain or Engine Turned Case...... $100.00
⑭ **No. 990** in 16s Heavy 14K Gold Open Face, Plain or Engine Turned Case $84.00
⑮ **No. 990** in 16s Hamilton Permanently Guaranteed Gold Filled Open Face, Jointed, Plain or Engine Turned Case....... $58.00
⑯ **No. 990** in 16s Hamilton Permanently Guaranteed Gold Filled Open Face, Swing Ring, Plain or Engine Turned Case..... $58.00
For description of movement see 16s movement page.

MOVEMENT CASE & DIAL MUST
BE MINT AND RUNNING

Hamilton Watch

Breguet Arabic Dial

Gothic Arabic Dial

12-size Complete Watches—Open Face Only

No. 920—12s Nickel, Bridge Movement, Pendant Set, 23 Extra Fine Ruby Jewels in Gold Settings, Patent Motor Barrel, Gold Train, Steel Escape Wheel, Double Roller Escapement, Sapphire Pallets, Micrometric Regulator, Breguet Hairspring, Compensation Balance, Adjusted to Temperature, Isochronism and Five Positions. Sold Cased only.

$250.00 → 18K Gold, Extra Heavy, Bassine, Open Face, Plain $155.00

14K Gold, Extra Heavy, Bassine, Open Face, Plain 130.00

14K Gold, Extra Heavy, Knurl Edge, Open Face, Plain or Engine Turned 130.00

14K Gold, Heavy, Bassine, Open Face, Plain 115.00

$200.00 → 14K Gold, Heavy, Knurl Edge, Open Face, Plain or Engine Turned 115.00

14K Gold, Open Face, Plain, Rembrandt Style Case 100.00

$150.00 → Permanently Guaranteed, Gold Filled, Bassine, Open Face, Plain or Engine Turned 85.00

Permanently Guaranteed, Gold Filled, Open Face, Plain or Engine Turned, Vandyke Style Case 85.00

Rembrandt Style Case

$220.00

$150.00 →

No. 900—12s, Nickel, Bridge Movement, Pendant Set, 19 Extra Fine Ruby Jewels in Gold Settings, Patent Motor Barrel, Gold Train, Steel Escape Wheel, Double Roller Escapement, Sapphire Pallets, Micrometric Regulator, Breguet Hairspring, Compensation Balance, Adjusted to Temperature, Isochronism and Five Positions.

14K Gold, Extra Heavy, Bassine, Plain $110.00

14K Gold, Extra Heavy, Knurl Edge, Plain or Engine Turned 110.00

14K Gold, Heavy, Bassine, Plain 95.00

14K Gold, Heavy, Knurl Edge, Plain or Engine Turned 95.00

14K Gold, Open Face, Plain, Rembrandt Style Case 83.00

Permanently Guaranteed, Gold Filled, Bassine, Plain or Engine Turned 65.00

Permanently Guaranteed, Gold Filled, Open Face, Plain or Engine Turned, Vandyke Style Case 65.00

$185.00

$165.00

$100.00

Bassine Style Case

Vandyke Style Case

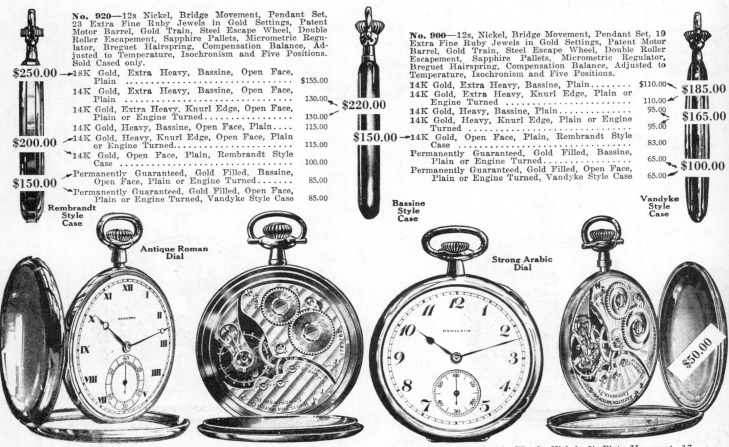

Antique Roman Dial

Strong Arabic Dial

$50.00

No. 914—12s, Nickel, ¾ Plate Movement, Pendant Set, 17 Extra Fine Ruby Jewels in Gold Settings, Steel Escape Wheel, Double Roller Escapement, Sapphire Pallets, Micrometric Regulator, Breguet Hairspring, Compensation Balance, Adjusted to Temperature, Isochronism and Three Positions. Sold Cased only.

$140.00 — 14K Gold, Extra Heavy, Bassine, Open Face, Plain...... $90.00

14K Gold, Extra Heavy, Knurl Edge, Open Face, Plain or Engine Turned 90.00

$110.00 — 14K Gold, Heavy, Bassine, Open Face, Plain.......... 75.00

14K Gold, Heavy, Knurl Edge, Open Face, Plain or Engine Turned 75.00

$100.00 — 14K Gold, Hamlet Style, Plain Case, Open Face.... 65.00

14K Gold, Open Face, Plain, Rembrandt Style Case.. 65.00

Permanently Guaranteed, Gold Filled, Bassine, Open Face, Plain or Engine Turned 45.00

$60.00 — Permanently Guaranteed, Gold Filled, Open Face, Plain or Engine Turned, Vandyke Style Case........ 45.00

No. 910—Gentleman's 12s Watch, Nickel, ¾ Plate Movement, 17 Fine Jewels in Settings, Double Roller Escapement, Micrometric Regulator, Breguet Hairspring, Compensation Balance, Adjusted, Fitted, Timed and Adjusted in a 25-Year, Gold Filled, Single Joint Case, and Mounted in a Handsome Leather Display Box. Sold Cased only.

Price $32.00

All complete watches timed and adjusted in the cases at the factory.

Our 12-size dials are interchangeable. Any style desired supplied without extra charge on new watches.

The prices given above are the established prices to the consumer

Prices furnished to Retail Jewelers upon application

36

GEO. T. BRODNAX, INC., GOLD AND SILVERSMITHS, MEMPHIS, TENN.
14 KARAT GOLD AND GOLD FILLED WATCHES FOR MEN

The cases shown here we consider the best values now being offered for the prices quoted. They were selected with care and discrimination, and we feel sure that they will appeal to conservative men.

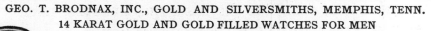

These pages from the 1924 Brodnax Catalog are included so you can compare the different watches as to their origional cost.

16—S

16—S

36140 14 kt. Engine turned to engraved shield center Hunting case, excellent weight, fitted with 15 Jewel Elgin, **$120.00**
⑲ **$50.00;** 17 Jewel Elgin, **$125.00**
⑳ **$55.00;** 19 Jewel Riverside
㉑ Waltham adjusted to 5 positions, **$90.00;** 23 Jewel Maximus Waltham adjusted to 5 **$160.00**
㉒ positions **$175.00** **$450.00**

$55.00 **12—S**

36059 25 year **gold filled** case with fancy hand-chased border and engine turned back, fitted with 17 Jewel, adjusted "G. M. Wheeler" Elgin Movement. Can be had in white or green gold filled, extra thin model case. **$60.00** ⑰
This same watch in a perfectly plain 25 year case can be had at...... **50.00** ⑱

⑥ **$115.00**
⑨ **$120.00**
⑩ **$125.00**
⑪ **$160.00**
⑫ **$450.00**

36139 14 kt. Plain polished, Hunting case, the most popular watch that we illustrate. This gives you splendid weight, and can be furnished with 7 Jewel Elgin movement for **$45.00;** 15 Jewel Elgin movement, **$50.00;** 17 Jewel Elgin, **$55.00;** 19 Jewel Riverside Waltham adjusted to 5 positions, **$90.00;** 23 Jewel Maximus Waltham adjusted to 5 positions **$175.00**

MUST BE IN MINT CONDITION AND RUNNING

① **$90.00**

36061 16 size, twenty-five year plain polished open face case, screw back and bezel, fitted with 21 jewel Bunn movement, lever set, adjusted to 5 positions, temperature and isochronism. A wonderful value, and an excellent time piece (shown reversed) **$61.00**

② **$85.00**

36062 16 size, twenty-five year open face plain polished case, with screw back and bezel, fitted with 19 jewel B. W. Raymond (Elgin) movement, lever set, adjusted to 5 positions, temperature and isochronism. A splendid watch.......... **$53.50**
Same movement in 20-year guarantee case.. **51.50**

③ **$90.00**

36063 16 size twenty-five year plain polished open face case, with screw back and bezel, fitted with 21 jewel Father Time (Elgin) movement, adjusted to 5 positions, temperature and isochronism. A splendid timekeeper. (Shown reversed).
.... **$58.50**

④ **$90.00**

36064 16 size, twenty-five year open face plain polished case, with screw back and bezel, fitted with 21 jewel Hamilton movement, lever set, adjusted to 5 positions, temperature and isochronism, fitted with plain or Montgomery dial. **$62.00**

⑤
⑥

950

36065 16 size twenty-five year open face case, plain polished, screw back and bezel, fitted with 23 jewel Hamilton movement, lever set, adjusted to 5 positions, temperature and isochronism. **$98.50**
Same movement in a heavy 14 kt. solid gold case.
.... **$130.00** **$190.00** **$300.00**

⑦ **$175.00**

36066 16 size twenty-five year open face case, plain polished, screw back and bezel, fitted with 23 jewel Sangamo special (Illinois) movement, lever set, adjusted to 6 positions, temperature and isochronism. One of the most dependable time pieces made. **$85.00**

37

1924

The watches illustrated here are fitted in heavy gold cases—the kind that will give service for a lifetime and can then be handed down to the on-coming generation. No charge is made for engraving a handsome monogram on the watch selected, and we feel confident that our artistic engravers can please you perfectly.

We show here three Patek-Philippe & Company watches for whom we are the Southern representatives. We carry a large selection of these watches in our retail store and will gladly quote prices on application. They are the finest watches in the world, and have stood every test for seventy-five years and received the highest awards since 1844.

① $400.00

PATEK-PHILIPPE

36581 First quality, 17 Ligne Size, Patek-Philippe watch, 18 karat gold case, 20 jewels, 8 adjustments.........................**$250.00** ②

Second quality, same size, 18 jewels, 8 adjustments.........................**$225.00**

$350.00

③

$450.00

PATEK-PHILIPPE

36035 18 karat heavy gold case, plain polished with chased beveled edge, inlaid with dark blue enamel, very thin model, fitted with extra quality Patek-Philippe movement, 18 Jewels, 8 adjustments, supplied with gold dial...........**$350.00**

$1500.00

④

PATEK-PHILIPPE REPEATER

36036 18 karat gold case, plain polished, extra heavy and thin model fitted with 31 jewels, extra quality Patek-Philippe movement. 8 adjustments, minute repeater, fitted with gold dial. A watch that any man would be proud to own......................**$600.00**

⑤ $175.00

36083 17 Ligne size, 14 kt. gold, plain polished, open face case, fitted with 17 Jewel International movement, adjusted to 6 positions, temperature and isochronism, extra thin model, made with platinum finished dial and raised gold numerals. A watch that will appeal to the man of discriminating taste **$125.00** ⑥
With plain dial.................... **110.00**

$150.00

⑦

$200.00

36084 17 Ligne size, polished 18 kt. gold open face case, with black enameled border and platinum finished dial, fitted with 21 jewel thin model International movement, adjusted to 6 positions, temperature and isochronism, raised gold numerals. A watch that any man would be proud to own.
....**$175.00**

⑧ ⑨ ⑩

$300.

$140.

$110.

36085 12 size heavy 14 kt. gold Hunting case, engine turned, fitted with 23 jewel Waltham Maximus movement, adjusted...... **$175.00**
Fitted with 19 jewel Riverside Waltham, 5 adjustments.........................**$90.00**
Fitted with 15 jewel Elgin movement... **50.00**

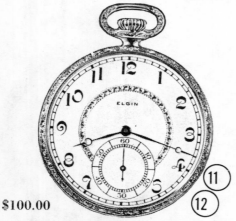

⑪ ⑫

$100.00

36060 14 karat gold, thin model Streamline Elgin with hand chased border and fancy engine turned back, fitted with 17-Jewel, G. M. Wheeler Elgin movement, with fancy dial at.........................**$100.00**
Same watch in a perfectly plain 14 karat case with plain dial can be had at..........**$75.00**

$85.00

COMPLETE WATCH MUST BE MINT AND KEEP TIME

⑬

$150.00

36058 19-Jewel "Lord Elgin" movement, in classic design, 14 karat gold case with chased border and engine turned back. This watch is ultra thin and can be had in either 14 karat white or green gold at.............**$150.00**
It has a platinum finish dial with raised gold numerals.
Be sure to specify whether white or green gold is wanted.

38

1924

① ② ③

GRUEN VERITHIN WATCHES

The Gruen Watches were among the first thin model movements ever offered, and they are produced to the point of perfection that insures satisfactory time keeping qualities, as well as beauty and convenience. The three numbers illustrated are among the most popular styles, and we highly recommend them to you. These watches, as well as any of the other numbers shown on this page, can be purchased upon one of our easy deferred payment plans that would best suit your convenience.

④ $60.00
⑤ $70.00
⑥ $85.00

$85.00
$100.00
$130.00

36074 Gruen Verithin Pentagon case of 14 karat green gold, hand chased and engraved, platinum finished dial with sunk gold lettering, fitted with 17 Jewel Precision movement, adjusted **$100.00**
19 Jewel Precision movement adjusted. **$115.00**
21 Jewel Precision movement adjusted **$140.00**

36075 Gruen Verithin Pentagon open faced case, permanently guaranteed green gold-filled hand chased and engraved, platinum finished dial and gold letters, fitted with 17 Jewel Precision movement adjusted **$70.00**
19 Jewel Precision movement adjusted **$85.00**
21 Jewel Precision movement adjusted. **$110.00**
No charge is made for engraving the watch selected with a handsome monogram.

$35.00
$40.00
$50.00

$60.00

⑦

Streamline Pendant Patented

⑪ $55.00

36076 12 size Gruen extra-thin twenty year plain polished open face case, English finish, gold dial, fitted with 15 Jewel movement adjusted to 3 positions........ **$25.00**
17 Jewel movement **30.00**
19 Jewel movement **35.00**
A sturdy and dependable time piece.

⑧
⑨
⑩

36077 17 Jewel Illinois "Autocrat" adjusted movement, in twenty-five year green gold-filled case, handsomely engraved, platinum finished dial with moire center and border, one of the finest medium priced watches made **$40.00**
This same watch with luminous hands and dial can be supplied at the same price.
Same movement in 25 year white gold-filled case.... **$43.00**

⑫ $40.00
⑬ $50.00

36800 Streamline Elgin, 20 year open face case, fitted with 17 Jewel Elgin movement, adjusted to heat, cold and Isochronism. **$35.00**

⑰ $85.00

$35.00

⑭

36079 12 size 15 Jewel Elgin movement, adjusted, in 25 year green gold-filled open face case, ribbon line engine turned and engraved and chased bezels and bow, platinum finished dial with raised gold numerals and fancy moire center..... **$25.00**
This same case, fitted with 17 Jewel Elgin movement.. **$30.00**

36080 12 size 15 Jewel Elgin movement adjusted in 25 year white gold-filled open face case, ribbon line engine turned with monogram space, complete **$30.00**
This same case, fitted with 17 Jewel adjusted Elgin movement, can be supplied for..... **$35.00**

⑮ $45.00
⑯ $50.00

36082 12 size 21 Jewel "Lincoln" (Illinois) movement, adjusted to 5 positions in 25 year white gold-filled case, with hand engraved bezel, platinum finished dial with raised gold numerals and hands **$65.00**
This same watch in 25 year green gold-filled case with luminous dial can be supplied for **$65.00**

36078 12 size 7 Jewel Elgin watch in handsomely chased gold-filled case. This can be supplied in green gold filled or white goldfilled as preferred. Unusually attractive weight and a splendid value....... **$15.00**

COMPLETE WATCH MUST BE MINT AND RUNNING

Hamilton Watches

① **MODEL 920**

$200.00

② $120.00

③ $120.00

MODEL 900

The Hamilton Watch is well and favorably known as one of the most excellent and reliable time pieces that can be secured. They are fully guaranteed by us as well as their makers. The numbers illustrated here are new designs, and while they are made along the thin model lines, the cases are of sufficient weight to give the best of service. The prices are quoted in gold and gold-filled cases of the highest quality. We make no charge for engraving handsome monogram on watch selected, where space permits. Our engravers are the most artistic that can be found, and we are sure that they can please you perfectly with their work.

④

$165.00

⑥ $120.00

⑦ $85.00

⑧ $85.00

36067 12 size, Hamilton Watch, thin model, 14 kt. green gold open face case, beautifully chased and engraved bezel and pendant, fitted with 23 jewel movement, adjusted to 5 positions...**$160.00** This same movement in permanently guaranteed green gold-filled case, can be supplied for...**$117.00** In a permanently guaranteed white gold-filled case for...**$120.00**

36069 12 size Hamilton Watch, 14 kt. green gold open face case, beautifully chased and engraved bezel and pendant, thin model, plain polished back and Platinum finished dial, fitted with 19 jewel Hamilton movement, adjusted to 5 positions. ....**$140.00** In 14 kt. white gold case of same description **140.00** In white gold-filled permanently guaranteed case. **$95.00**

⑤ $110.00

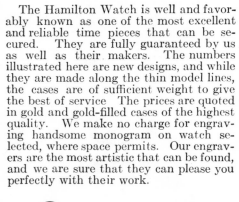

36068 12 size, Hamilton Watch, 14 kt. green gold open face case, with handsome chased bezel and pendant, fitted with 17 jewel Hamilton movement, adjusted to 5 positions (shown reversed) ..**$100.00** This same movement in permanently guaranteed green gold-filled case ....**$62.00** White gold-filled permanently guaranteed case. **$65.00**

⑥

$65.00

36070 12 size Hamilton Watch, twenty-five year green gold-filled open face case, with engraved bezel and plain polished back for monogram, engine turned dial, fitted with 17 jewel Hamilton movement...........................**$43.00** Same movement in white gold-filled case.... **46.00**

⑦

$65.00

36071 12 size Hamilton Watch, twenty-five year guaranteed gold-filled case, plain polished, English finish, fitted with 17 jewel adjusted Hamilton movement, with Platinum finish dial. One of our most popular numbers..................**$42.00**

NOTICE: DEALERS — COLLECTORS — TRADERS
If you would like more information on Hamilton than is presented in this book please read on.

40

HAMILTON WATCH

A. C. BECKEN – 1930
The Famous Hamilton 992
Railroad Models

Dependable performance combined with rugged beauty and sturdy construction have made the Hamilton 992 a favored timepiece among railroad men of America. Important dust-proof features have been incorporated into the design of these Railroad Model cases . . . they are especially constructed to meet the stern requirements and maintain the high standards of accuracy so essential in a railroad watch.

(1)

$110.00

Railroad Model No. 6
A new Hamilton Railroad watch of rugged beauty, in 14K green or white gold filled. Consumer price, $65.00.

10K gold filled yellow. Consumer price, $60.00.

H. G. Dial
No extra charge

(2)

$110.00

Railroad Model No. 5
Another Hamilton contribution to beauty in Railroad Watches, 14K gold filled green or white. Consumer price, $65.00.

10K gold filled yellow. Consumer price, $60.00.

H. A. Numerical Dial
No extra charge

16 SIZE

(3)

$110.00

Railroad Model No. 2
Featured by special pendant construction with connecting bar which makes it impossible for bow or crown to come out. 14K gold filled green or white. Consumer price, $65.00.
10K gold filled yellow. Consumer price, $60.00.

B. M. Dial. *No extra charge*

(4)

No. 950 Open Face, 16 size
Consumer price, $85.00.

White gold finish, bridge movement, lever set, 23 extra fine Ruby and Sapphire jewels in gold settings, patent motor barrel, gold train, escapement cap jeweled, steel escape wheel, double roller escapement, Sapphire pallets, Breguet hairspring, micrometric regulator, compensation balance, friction set roller jewel, double sunk dial, adjusted to temperature, isochronism, and five positions.

CASED WATCHES MUST BE MINT AND RUNNING

(6)

18 SIZE MOVEMENT
No. 940 Open Face

Consumer price, $45.00.

$70.00

Nickel, 21 extra fine Ruby and Sapphire jewels in gold settings, patent motor barrel, adjusted to temperature, isochronism, and five positions, double roller escapement, steel escape wheel, Breguet hairspring, compensation balance, patent micrometric regulator, double sunk dial, gilt lettering, beautifully and elegantly damaskeened.

(5)

$70.00

The 16 Size
Hamilton 992

is nickel, 3/4 plate, lever set, 21 extra fine Ruby and Sapphire jewels in gold settings, double roller escapement, Sapphire pallets, gold center wheel, steel escape wheel, micrometric regulator, Breguet hairspring, friction set roller jewel, double sunk dial, compensation balance, beautifully damaskeened. Adjusted to temperature, isochronism and five positions. Sold cased only.

(7)

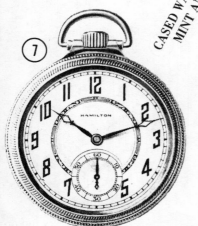

$60.00

Hamilton Traffic Special
With 6 Adjustments

The new Hamilton Traffic Special is a watch ideally suited in price and performance to the requirements of public and civil service employees, skilled and technical workers, and railroad employees not under time inspection. It is a high grade 16 size, 17 jewel movement adjusted to heat, cold, isochronism, and three positions; and embracing such refinements as a steel escape wheel and double roller escapement. Filled white or yellow gold. Available with any of the railroad dials shown above without extra charge. Consumer price, $37.50.

Dial No. 16-97. *No extra charge*

Hamilton 36 Size in Chronometer Mounting
Closely adjusted 21 jewel movement, key wind and key set. In regulation chronometer mounting, swung in gimbals. All metal fittings nickel finish. Three section mahogany box 5 in. x 5 in. x 5¼ in.

(8)

$700.00

Hamilton
The Watch of Railroad Accuracy

41

HAMILTON WATCH

The MASTERPIECE GROUP

12–SIZE

COMPLETE WATCH SHOULD BE MINT AND RUNNING

$750.00

The Hamilton Masterpiece in Platinum

There could be no finer compliment paid the graduate, the distinguished visitor, or the retiring employee—no more suitable reward for commendable services rendered—than the presentation of a Hamilton Masterpiece in platinum. It has a certain air of quality that immediately identifies it with the finer things of life. This beautiful model was designed by Hamilton in response to insistent demands for a Hamilton Masterpiece in a platinum case. The bezel is a simple circlet of platinum while the center and bow are richly carved in high relief. The dial of sterling silver has raised numerals of solid gold, the hands are also of gold.

Consumer price, $685.00

Two Hamilton Masterpiece Models in 18K Gold

Altogether worthy the name Hamilton—are these remarkable examples of the watchmaker's craft. The cases are fashioned of extra heavy 18K white or green gold, hand made throughout and richly carved. All Masterpiece models are fitted with the 23 jewel Masterpiece Hamilton, adjusted to heat, cold, isochronism and five positions. They have a patent motor barrel, gold train, steel escape wheel, double roller escapement, sapphire pallets, micrometric regulator, Breguet hairspring and compensation balance. The dials are of sterling silver, brushed or lined finish, with raised numerals of 18K gold. Models "B" or "C." Consumer price, $250.00.

Model "B" 18K Gold $300.00

Model "C" 18K Gold $300.00

Hamilton
The Watch of Railroad Accuracy

Hamilton Pocket Models
GRADE 922

The Hamilton 922 is one of America's finest timepieces. It has a white gold finish bridge, 23 extra fine Ruby and Sapphire jewels in gold settings, patent motor barrel, gold train, steel escape wheel, double roller escapement, Sapphire pallets, micrometric regulator, Breguet hairspring, compensation balance. It is pendant set and adjusted to temperature, isochronism, and five positions. Sold cased only.

A. C. BECKEN 1930

12—SIZE

H.T.C.

①

$200.00

Lafayette
In engraved case of Lafayette design, 14K gold, green or white. Consumer price, $160.00.

③

Rittenhouse **$200.00**
In engraved case of Rittenhouse design, 14K filled green or white gold. Consumer price, $120.00.

GRADE 904
Hamilton's First 21 Jewel 12 Size

The new Grade 904 Hamilton takes the place of the Grade 902 Hamilton, which has been discontinued. The Grade 904 is a white gold finish, bridge model, pendant set, 21 extra fine Ruby and Sapphire jewels in gold settings, patent motor barrel, gold train, steel escape wheel, double roller escapement, Sapphire pallets, micrometric regulator, Breguet hairspring, compensation balance, adjusted to temperature, isochronism, and five positions. Sold cased only.

12—SIZE

H.T.C.

④

$185.00

Hawthorne
In engraved case of Hawthorne design, 14K gold, green or white. Consumer price, $145.00.

⑦

$185.00

Brunswick
In engraved case of Brunswick design, 14K gold, green or white. Consumer price, $145.00.

GRADE 918

This group of thin model pocket watches is one of the most popular in the Hamilton line. The Grade 918 is nickel, ¾ plate model, pendant set, 19 extra fine Ruby and Sapphire jewels in gold settings, steel escape wheel, double roller escapement, Sapphire pallets, micrometric regulator, Breguet hairspring, compensation balance, adjusted to temperature, isochronism, and three positions. Sold cased only.

12—SIZE

$110.00

Bascine ⑨

In plain Bascine case, heavy 14K gold, yellow or green. Consumer price, $100.00.

MUST BE IN MINT CONDITION AND RUNNING

⑫ *Ramsay* **$110.00**
In case of Ramsay design, 14K gold, yellow or white. Consumer price, $100.00.

GRADE 912
Featuring New Secometer Dial

⑥

The splendid value of the 912 Hamilton has won unprecedented consumer acceptance for these attractive models. This particular grade has 17 jewels, ¾ plate, double roller escapement, micrometric regulator, Breguet hairspring, and compensation balance. The Secometer Dial adds unusual stimulus to sales opportunities and is obtainable on any 912 model at an extra cost to the consumer of $5. This new dial is an innovation in the watch industry and gives unique pocket watch convenience as well as distinctive style.

12—SIZE

$75.00

Van Buren
In engraved case of Van Buren design. 14K Gold filled, green or white. Consumer price, $55.00.

⑧ **$75.00**

Decagon
In engraved case of Decagon design. 14K Gold filled, green or white. Consumer price, $52.00.

43

HAMILTON ... THE WATCH OF RAILROAD ACCURACY

Officially Approved by Authorized Railroad Inspectors

Since 1892, Hamilton Railroad Watches have been the ultimate in dependability.

MEETING ALL TIME INSPECTION SPECIFICATIONS

DYNAVAR UNBREAKABLE LIFETIME MAINSPRING

ELINVAR-EXTRA HAIRSPRING—Self-compensating for Temperature Changes and Magnetic Influences

FULLY ADJUSTED

MICROMETRIC REGULATOR WITH 4 MEANTIME SCREWS

SAFETY SET DEVICE TO PREVENT ACCIDENTAL CHANGING OF HANDS

① $90.00

MUST BE MINT AND RUNNING

$300.00
$225.00
$190.00
$100.00

$85.00

STYLED in STEEL

⑥

RAILROAD WATCH No. 16

10K Yellow Rolled Gold Plate Case. 21 Jewels. Full Numeral, Double Sunk Dial. Available with heavy Gothic Dial **$89.50**

RAILROAD WATCH No. 17

14K Yellow Gold Case. Heavy Gothic Numerals on Double sunk Dial, or Full Numeral Dial.
② Grade 950B 23 Jewels **$375.00**
③ Grade 992B 21 Jewels **350.00**

10K Yellow Gold filled Case. Heavy Gothic Numerals on Double Sunk Dial or Full Numeral Dial.
④ Grade 950B **$125.00**
⑤ Grade 992B **99.50**

RAILROAD WATCH No. 15

Stainless Steel Case. 21 Jewels. Heavy Gothic Numerals on Double Sunk Dial. Available with Full Numeral Dial **$79.50**

TRAFFIC SPECIAL

(Traffic Specials are not railroad approved watches.)

STYLED in STEEL

⑨

$50.00

$60.00

③

TRAFFIC SPECIAL I

17 Jewels. Stainless Steel Case. Heavy Black Gothic Numerals on Single Sunk Dial. **$49.50**

TRAFFIC SPECIAL II

17 Jewels. 14K Yellow Rolled Gold Plate Case. Heavy Black Gothic Numerals on Single Sunk Dial. **$59.50**

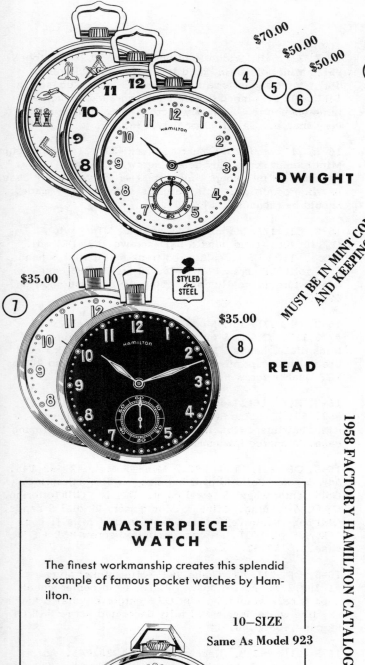

$70.00
$50.00
$50.00

④ ⑤ ⑥

$100.00

① 10-S

Model 921

BALDWIN

21 Jewels. 10K Yellow Gold-filled Case with Jointed Back and Inside Cap. Sterling Silver Dial. 14K Gold Numerals, or Numerals and Markers with Pearled Track . **$135.00**

17 Jewels. 10K Yellow Gold-filled Case with Jointed Back and Inside Cap. Sterling Silver Dial. 14K Gold Numerals with Pearled Track **$100.00**

DWIGHT

MUST BE IN MINT CONDITION AND KEEPING TIME

$150.00

TYLER

⑨

21 Jewels. 14K Yellow Gold Case with Jointed Back and Inside Cap. Sterling Silver Dial. 14K Gold Numerals, or Numerals, Markers and Squares with Pearled Track **$285.00**

$35.00

⑦

STYLED in STEEL

$35.00

⑧

READ

$150.00

Model 921

10—SIZE

HUGHES

⑩

21 Jewels. 14K Yellow Gold Case. Sterling Silver Dial. 14K Gold Numerals and Markers with Transfer Track, or Numerals with Pearled Track **$200.00**

17 Jewels. 14K Yellow Gold Case. Sterling Silver Dial. 14K Gold Numerals with Pearled Track **$175.00**

⑪

Model 917 $120.00

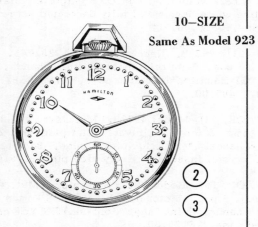

MASTERPIECE WATCH

The finest workmanship creates this splendid example of famous pocket watches by Hamilton.

10—SIZE
Same As Model 923

② ③

MASTERPIECE

23 Jewels. 18K Gold or Platinum Case. 14K Gold Numerals (Rhodium Plated for White Model) with Pearled Track on Sterling Dial.
Gold **$375.00**
Platinum **750.00**

$300.00

$500.00

Model 921 $120.00

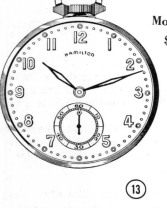

⑫

BRYAN

21 Jewels. 10K Yellow Gold Case. Sterling Silver Dial. 14K Gold Numerals and Squares with Transfer Track, or Numerals with Pearled Track **$175.00**

17 Jewels. 10K Yellow Gold Case. Sterling Silver Dial. 14K Gold Numerals and Luminous Dots with Pearled Track, or Numerals with Pearled Track **$135.00**

⑬

Model 917 $100.00

18-S, 17J, OF. Ex. fine nickel Mvt. #422,146. Model 924. Runs sluggish, needs cleaning. Mint flat SS Arabic red track dial & hands. Ex. fine 20 yr. YGF Broadway screw B&B OF case. Combination engine turned & hand engraved decoration. Some brass showing on bezel & pipe....$50.00.

18-S, H.C. 17J, Model 925. Ex. fine Mvt. #99,733. Regulator bow missing. Mint SS Arabic red track dial & hands. Fine heavy Illinois nickel swing case. Running good..$75.00.

18-S, 17J, Model 924. Ex. fine nickel full plate Mvt. #228,040. Mint flat glass enamel Roman with red track and sunk seconds dial. Ex. fine Star Watch Case. Co. Nickel screw B&B OF case...$50.00.

18-S, 15J, Model 928. Mint nickel full plate Mvt. #108,112. Mint flat Roman SS dial, fine Fahys Montauk #1 screw B&B YGF decorated OF case. Worn but solid, no brass showing. $175.00.

18-S, 17J, Adj. Model 936. Mint nickel full plate Mvt. #10,369. A very early Hamilton. Fair DS original Arabic dial 2 bad chips. Ex. fine Keystone silveroid screw B&B. Watch looks all original...$200.00.

18-S, 937 Hunting 17J mint Mvt. #12907. Scarce watch. 4,930 made. Dial mint DS Arabic with red track. Case is mint Dueber silverine with gold inside marked 20 yr. OF hinged with double back case. A mint & beautiful..$182.00.

18-S, 21J, OF, Model 940. Beautiful mint nickel Mvt. #654,542 marked adj. 5 pos, 940, DR, LS. Mint. Perfect mint DS Arabic red track dial & hands. Fine Fahys 14Kt 25 yr. YGF screw B&B OF case, showing patches of brass. Case is solid and looks good...$75.00.

18-S, 21J, OF 942 mint Mvt. #186,455. Gold letters, dial DS Montgomery. Bad crack at 7. Scarce mvt. Only 5,418 made. 20 yr. YGF decorated screw back & front. Ex. fine condition....$150.00.

18-S, OF, 19J, Model 944. Extremely fine nickel mvt. #494,353. LS, Adj. 5 pos. Mint DS glass dial with hands. Fine B.B. Royal 20 yrs. YGF OF case...$140.00.

18-S, OF, 23J, Grade 946. Mint Mvt. #439,942. Beautiful gold lettering, adj. 5 pos. Mint DS Arabic red track dial & hands. Faint crack in seconds bit. Ex. fine Phila. 20 yr. YGF screw B&B, all over decorated OF case, minor wear on back. Scarce watch...$275.00.

16-S, #950, 23J. Mint Bridge Mvt. #1,576,990. 10KT GF RR case. Dial mint...$200.00.

16-S, OF, 23J, 950-B RR. Mint nickel Mvt. #515,081, LS, DR, Adj. Temp. & 6 pos. Mint orig. DS Arabic dial & hands marked Hamilton 23 Jewels Railway Special. Ex. fine to mint Wadsworth 10KT YGF screw B&B Hamilton RR case..$175.

16-S, OF, 19J, Model 952. Mint Mvt. #752,064. Pendant set adj. 5 pos. with gold cups and balance weights. Mint DS ARABIC glass dial with hands. Mint A.W.C. Co. 14kt Y double back open case...$200.00

16-S, Model 990, 21J, Adj. Ex. fine Mvt. #350,056. Ex. fine DS glass dial with 3 small hairlines. Ex. fine white star Stellar decorated OF RR case. Fine watch...$130.00.

16-S, 21J, Adj. Bridge Hunting Mvt. #352,264. Model 961. Mint gold train, gold lettered mvt. DS Arabic dial. Mint except small hairline at 3 & 4. Recased in 14Kt solid YG hinged double back engraved & engine turned Gruen H.C. Nearly factory new. This mvt. is very scarce. Only 1100 made...$365.00.

16-S, 21J, Model 971 Hunting Mvt. #237,214. Gold cup Mint except scratch by detent screw. Original DS dial & hands. Mint except tiny chip at 4. Silverode OF case Ex. fine condition. This watch is scarce - 2497 made. Should be recased...$120.00.

16-S, OF, 17J, Model 972 RR watch. Mint Mvt. #1,140,406. Gold cups & bal. screws, LS, DR, adj. 5 pos. Mint DS porcelain red track Arabic dial & hands. Fine solid OF screw B&B Phila. 20 yr. YGF RR case, engine turning mostly gone. Tiny rim of brass showing. $90.00.

16-S, OF, 17J, adj. Model 974. Mint nickel Mvt. #778,117. C & O & running. Ex. fine DS Arabic red track dial & hands. 2 minor hairlines. J. Frank Heald Special in script on dial. Ex. fine hand engraved 20 yr. YGF Dueber screw B&B OF case...$55.00.

16-S, H.C. 16J, Model 977. Near mint nickel Mvt. #59,869. Ex. fine SS Arabic red track dial & hands. 3 minor hairlines. Ex. fine Hamilton glass back shipping case. A scarce low number watch...$85.00

16-S, OF, 21J, Grade 992. Mint RR Mvt. #2,592,145. Adj. 5 pos. Solid Elinvar balance & white hairspring. Gold center wheel & jewel cups. DR, LS, Gilt lettering. C, O, & running. Mint DS Montgomery RR dial & hands. Dial has "Sante Fe" emblem factory job. Mint J. Boss 14Kt, 25 yr. WGF, all over decorated screw B&B OF RR case...$150.00.

16-S, OF, 21J, RR, Grade 992. Mint nickel Mvt. #1,383,277. Adj. 5 pos. DR, LS, Gold center wheel, cups & bal. weights. Mint DS Montgomery dial & hands. Ex. fine white base metal fully decorated screw B&B OF RR case...$75.00.

16-S, 21J, 992-B. Near mint Mvt. #C282043. Adj. temp. 6 pos. Mint orig. bold RR dial & hands. Ex. fine 10Kt YGF Hamilton decorated edge, screw B&B, OF RR case...$85.00.

16-S, OF, 22J, Model 4992B. Mint Mvt. #40,129,268. Adj. temp. & 6 pos. Elinvar. Mint black gilt 24 hour dial & hands. Mint orig. nickel case. Back has been cut out & crystal inserted. A very nice piece...$100.00.

16-S, OF, 19J, Model 996. Mint nickel Mvt. #1157618, LS, Adj. 5 pos. Motor barrel. Mint DS Roman glass dial & hands. Mint Fahys Montauk 10KT YGF engine turned case...$125.00.

12-S, OF, 19J, Grade 900. Mint Mvt. #1751500. Adj. 5 pos. Gold cups and bal. weights. Ex. fine single sunk antique Arabic glass dial. Fine original Hamilton double back YGF, OF case. Warranted to wear permanently...$95.00.

New York Standard Watch Co.'s Movements.

Fit all American Cases of Similar Sizes. 6, 16 and 18 Size, Hunting and Open Face, Stem Wind.
Prices Guaranteed to Jobbers and Retailers, Rebating any Reductions.

1898

List Prices Each.

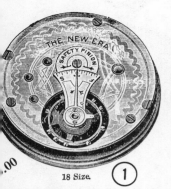

$20.00 — 18 Size. (1)

"New Era," Nickel, Damaskeened, Hunting, 7 Jewels, Lever Safety Pinion, Compensation Balance, White Enameled Dial... $4 00

(2) $20.00 — 18 Size.

"New Era," Nickel, Damaskeened, Open Face 7 Jewels, Lever Set, Safety Pinion, Compensation Balance, White Enameled Dial.... $4 00

(3) $25.00 — 18 Size.

No. 30 Nickel, Damaskeened, Hunting, 7 Jewels. Train Bearings in Metal Settings, Lever Set. Safety Pinion Compensation Balance, Superior White Enameled Dial...... $5 63

(4) $25.00 — 18 Size.

No. 31 Nickel, Damaskeened, Open Face, 7 Jewels, Train Bearings in Metal Settings Lever Set, Safety Pinion, Compensation Balance, Superior White Enameled Dial................ $5 63

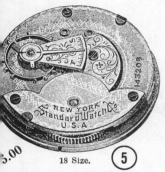   

$5.00 — 18 Size. (5)

FULL PLATE, NEW MODEL.
No. 34 Nickel, Damaskeened, Hunting, 7 Jewels. Quick Train, Lever Set, Safety Pinion, Compensation Balance......... $6 25
No. 38 Gilded, Plain, same as above......... 6 25

$25.00 — 18 Size. (6)

FULL PLATE, NEW MODEL.
No. 35 Nickel, Damaskeened, Open Face, 7 Jewels. Quick Train, Lever Set Safety Pinion, Compensation Balance......... $6 25
No. 37 Gilded, Damaskeened, same as above......... 6 25
No. 39 Gilded, Plain, same as above......... 6 25

$25.00 — 18 Size. (7)

FULL PLATE, NEW MODEL.
No. 140 Nickel, Damaskeened, Hunting. 11 Jewels in Settings, Cut Compensation Balance. Lever Set, Patent Regulator Safety Pinion, Plain or Assorted Fancy Dials.... $8 75
No. 142 Gilded, same as above. 8 75

$25.00 — 18 Size (8)

FULL PLATE, NEW MODEL.
No. 141 Nickel, Damaskeened, Open Face, 11 Jewels in Settings, Cut Compensation Balance. Lever Set. Patent Regulator. Safety Pinion. Plain or Assorted Fancy Dials, $8 75
No. 143 Gilded, same as above. 8 75

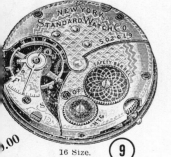 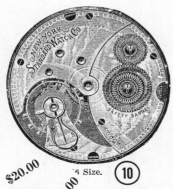  

$5.00 — 16 Size. (9)

¾ PLATE, NEW THIN MODEL.
No. 52 Nickel. Damaskeened, Hunting, 7 Jewels in Settings, Compensation Balance, Lever Set, Micrometer Regulator, Breguet Hairspring. Artistic Glass Enameled, Plain or Assorted Fancy Dials $9 38
No. 54 Gilded, Hunting, same as above......... 9 38
No. 51 Nickel, Damaskeened, Open Face, same as above, Plain or Assorted Fancy Dials......... 9 38
No. 53 Gilded, Open Face, same as above......... 9 38

$20.00 / $40.00 — 16 Size. (10)

¾ PLATE, NEW THIN MODEL
No. 56 Nickel, Damaskeened, Hunting, 11 Jewels in Settings, Compensation Balance, Lever Set, Micrometer Regulator, Breguet Hairspring. Artistic Glass Enameled, Plain or Assorted Fancy Dials $12 50
No. 58 Gilded, Hunting, same as above......... 12 50
No. 55 Nickel, Damaskeened, Open Face, same as above......... 12 50
No. 57 Gilded, Open Face, same as above......... 12 50

$15.00 — 6 Size. (11)

¾ PLATE, HUNTING.
No. 44 Nickel, Damaskeened, 7 Jewels. Quick Train, Lever Set, Safety Pinion......... $7 50
No. 46 Gilded, Plain, same as above......... 7 50

(12)

6 Size.
Showing Fancy Dial.
¾ PLATE, HUNTING.
No. 48 Nickel, Damaskeened, 11 Jewels in Settings, Cut Compensation Balance. Quick Train, Lever Set, Safety Pinion, Plain or Assorted Fancy S. S. Dials......... $10 00
No. 50 Gilded, Plain, same as above......... 10 00

New York Standard, 7 and 10 Jewel, Chronograph and Horse Timers

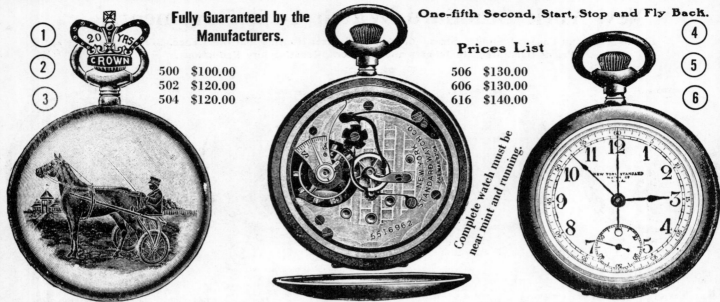

Fully Guaranteed by the Manufacturers.

500    $100.00
502    $120.00
504    $120.00

One-fifth Second, Start, Stop and Fly Back.

Prices List

506    $130.00
606    $130.00
616    $140.00

Complete watch must be near mint and running.

18-size Open Face, ¾ Plate, 7 Jewel Nickel Damaskeened, Stem Wind, Lever Set; train bearings in metal settings; quick train, one-fifth second, start, stop and fly back operated from the crown.   Cases are made in screw back and jointed bezel.

No. 500.   Nickel Silverode Case, plain polished or engine turned $10 30
No. 502.   Sterling Silver Case, plain polished or engine turned.......... 13 60
No. 504.   10-year Victory Case, plain polished, E. T. or engraved....... 14 50

No. 506.   20-year Crown Case, plain polished, E. T. or engraved........$17 30
No. 606.   20-year Boss Case, plain polished or engine turned............ 20 00
No. 616.   20-year Boss Case, fancy engraved...... 21 00

The above Crown and Boss Cases furnished with Horse Head, Horse and Jockey and Horse and Sulky engraved at engraved prices.
10-jevel Movements with Cut Expansion. Breguet Hairspring, furnished in either of the above Cases at $2.00 extra.

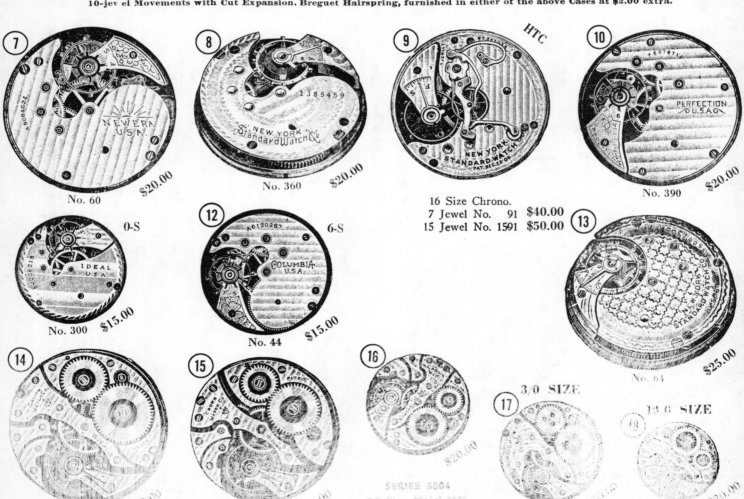

No. 60 $20.00

No. 360 $20.00

HTC

16 Size Chrono.
7 Jewel No.   91 $40.00
15 Jewel No. 1591 $50.00

No. 390 $20.00

0-S

No. 300 $15.00

6-S

No. 44 $15.00

No. 64 $25.00

No. 1516 $20.00

No. 1512 $30.00

SERIES 5004
8/0 Size, Model 1530.
Open Face & Htg.

3/0 SIZE

No. 730

10/6 SIZE

48

ALL NEW YORK STANDARD MOVEMENTS

are nickel damaskeened or gilt, train berings in metal settings, quick train, stem wind, cut expansion balance, breguet hatrspring, white enameled dial, pendant set, exccpting 18 size hunting which is lever set, made with 7 jewels only.

PRICE EACH

1909
GORDON AND MORRISON

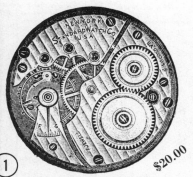

① $20.00

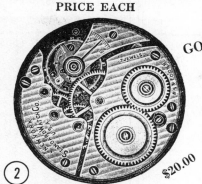

② $20.00

③ $20.00

NEW YORK STANDARD.
18-size, 7 Jewels, Nickel Damaskeened,
uick Train, Compensation Balance, Breguet
airspring, Stem Wind, White Enameled Dial.
. 68—Hunting $3.40

NEW YORK STANDARD.
18-size, 7 Jewels, Nickel Damaskeened,
Quick Train, Compensation Balance, Breguet
Hairspring, Stem Wind, White Enameled Dial.
No. 69—Open Face Pendant...........$3.40

NEW YORK STANDARD.
16-size, 7 Jewels, Nickel Damaskeened.
Quick Train, Compensation Balance, Breguet
Hairspring, Stem Wind, White Enameled or
Gilt Dial, Pendant Set.
No. 94—Hunting......................$3.80

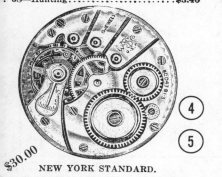

④ **⑤** $30.00

⑥ **⑦** $25.00

⑧ $20.00

NEW YORK STANDARD.
16-size Hunting or Open Face, 15 Jewels in
ttings, Nickel Damaskeened Finger Bridge
odel, Exposed Winding Wheels, Quick Train
ompensating Balance, Breguet Hairspring,
tent Regulator, White-Cream or Gilt Dials,
ound Second Dial.
. 1594—Hunting.................$5.00
. 1595—Open Face...............5.60

NEW YORK STANDARD.
12-size Hunting or Open Face, 15 Jewels in
Settings, Nickel Damaskeened Finger Bridge
Model, Exposed Winding Wheels, Quick Train.
Compensating Balance, Breguet Hairspring,
Patent Regulator, White-Cream or Gilt Dials,
Ground Second Dial.
No. 1570—Hunting $5.60
No. 1571—Open Face................5.60

NEW YORK STANDARD.
12-size Hunting, Nickel Damaskeened,
7 Jewels, Train Bearings in Metal Settings,
Quick Train, Stem Wind, Compensation Balance, Breguet Hairspring, Pendant Set.
White Enamel or Gilt Dial.
No. 170—Hunting.................$4.40

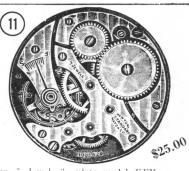

⑨ $20.00

⑩ 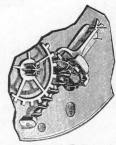 $20.00

NEW YORK STANDARD.
ize Hunting, Nickel Damaskeened,
ewels, Train Bearings in Metal
ttings, Quick Train, Stem Wind,
Compensation Balance, Breguet
airspring, Pendant Set, White
Enamel or Gilt Dial.
. 146—Hunting..........$3.80

NEW YORK STANDARD.
0-size, 7 Jewels, Nickel
Damaskeened or Gilt, Train Bear-
ings in Metal Settings. Quick Train,
Stem Wind, Cut Compensation Bal-
ance, Breguet Hairspring, White
Enameled or Gilt Dial.
No. 302—Hunting...........$6.30

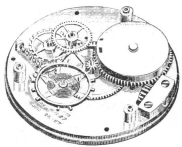
1899
VERTISEMENT

Look for this one
pretty rare.

⑫

Escapement Enlarged.

Movement with Top Plate Off.

NET PRICE LIST

AURORA

Watch Movements

GENERAL OFFICE AND FACTORY

AURORA, ILL.

SEPT. 16, 1891.

MADE WATCHES
1882 – 1892

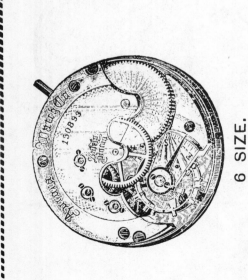

6 SIZE.

Hunting. Stem Wind.

No. 38. NICKEL.—Finely damaskeened; 15 ruby jewels, 4 pairs in settings.......$13 50 .... $50.00

No. 36. NICKEL.—Damaskeened; 13 jewels, 3 pairs in settings................ 10 00 .... $40.00

No. 35. GILT.—13 jewels; 3 pairs in settings............................. 7 75 .... $30.00

No. 33. GILT —11 jewels, 4 holes top plate in settings................. 7 25 .... $30.00

50

18 SIZE. STEM WIND.

HUNTING.

No. 10. NICKEL.—Fine train; 15 fine ruby jewels in gold settings; patent regulator; Breguet hair spring; double sunk glass enamel dial; finely finished and adjusted to heat, cold and position......$35 00 — **$95.00**

No. 8. NICKEL.—Fine train; solid nickel barrel; pat. reg.; Breguet hair spring; double sunk dial; handsomely damaskeened; adjusted......16 00 — **$70.00**

No. 113. NICKEL.—Fine train; 15 jewels, 4 pairs in composition settings; Breguet hair spring; finely damaskeened; adjusted; double sunk dial; red gold trimmings......13 75 — **$60.00**

No. 26. NICKEL.—Fine train; 15 jewels, 4 pairs in composition settings; Breguet hair spring; finely damaskeened; adjusted......12 00 — **$50.00**

No. 109. NICKEL.—15 jewels in composition settings; damaskeened, pat. reg.; adjusted......10 00 — **$40.00**

No. 22. NICKEL.—15 jewels in composition settings; damaskeened; pat. reg......8 00 — **$40.00**

No. 4½. NICKEL.—11 jewels, 4 holes top plate jeweled; pat. reg......5 50 — **$40.00**

No. 6. GILDED.—Fine train; 15 jewels; Breguet hair spring; double sunk dial; pat. reg.; adjusted......13 50 — **$50.00**

No. 3½. GILDED.—15 jewels in settings; pat. reg......7 50 — **$40.00**

No. 2. GILDED.—11 jewels; 4 holes top plate jeweled imitation settings; pat. reg......5 25 — **$40.00**

No. 1. GILDED.—7 jewels; conical pivots; sprung over polished regulator, with index; sunk seconds dial......4 00 — **$40.00**

---

18 SIZE. STEM WIND.

OPEN FACE LEVER SET.

No. 10. NICKEL.—Fine train; 15 fine ruby jewels in gold settings; patent regulator; Breguet hair spring; double sunk glass enamel dial; finely finished and adjusted to heat, cold and position......$35 00 — **$95.00**

No. 8. NICKEL.—Fine train: solid nickel barrel; pat. reg.; Breguet hair spring; double sunk dial; handsomely damaskeened; adjusted......16 00 — **$75.00**

No. 113. NICKEL.—Fine train; 15 jewels, 4 pairs in composition settings; Breguet hair spring; finely damaskeened; adjusted; double sunk dial; red gold trimmings......13 75 — **$60.00**

No. 26. NICKEL.—Fine train; 15 jewels, 4 pairs in composition settings; Bregeut hair spring; finely damaskeened: adjusted......12 00 — **$50.00**

No. 109. NICKEL.—15 jewels in composition settings; damaskeened; pat. reg.; adjusted......10 00 — **$40.00**

No. 22. NICKEL.—15 jewels in composition settings; damaskeened; pat. reg......8 00 — **$40.00**

No. 4½. NICKEL.—11 jewels, 4 holes top plate jeweled; pat. reg......5 50 — **$40.00**

No. 6. GILDED.—Fine train; 15 jewels; Breguet hair spring; double sunk dial; pat. reg.; adjusted......13 50 — **$50.00**

No. 3½. GILDED.—15 jewels in settings; pat. reg......7 50 — **$40.00**

No. 2. GILDED.—11 jewels; 4 holes top plate jeweled imitation settings; pat. reg......5 25 — **$40.00**

No. 1. GILDED.—7 jewels; conical pivots; sprung over polished regulator, with index; sunk seconds dial......4 00 — **$40.00**

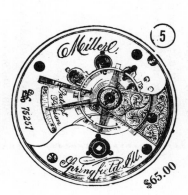
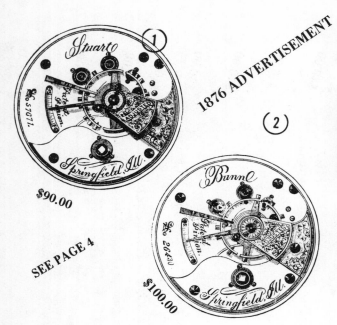
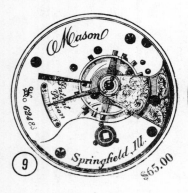
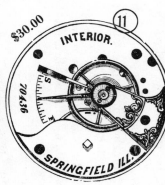
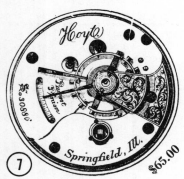

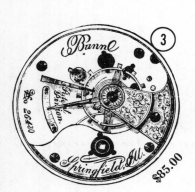

ILLINOIS
Springfield Watch Comp'y,

MANUFACTURERS OF

KEY AND STEM-WINDING MOVEMENTS.

SEE PAGE 4   Stem-Winders Fit Waltham Style Cases without change.

Patent Setting Bar on Stem-winders.

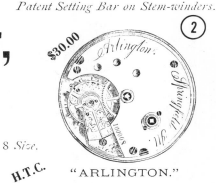

② $30.00

8 Size.

H.T.C.   "ARLINGTON."

18 SIZE,

FULL PLATE,

CUT

EXPANSION BALANCES.

① $40.00

No. 1

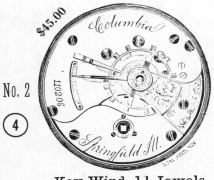

Key Wind, 7 Jewels.

$35.00

No. 1

③

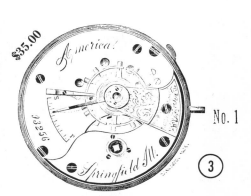

Stem Wind, 7 Jewels.

$45.00

No. 2

④

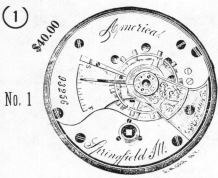

Key Wind, 11 Jewels.

⑤

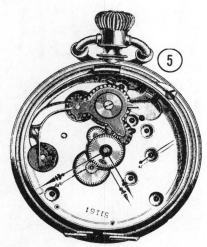

$35.00

No. 2

⑥

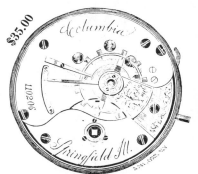

Stem Wind, 11 Jewels.

All Grades are Gilded without Softening the plates.

LOW PRICED MOVEMENTS

THIS PAGE IS A COMPOSIT
OF 1878 AND 1879 ADVERTISEMENTS

$30.00   DIURNAL   ⑦

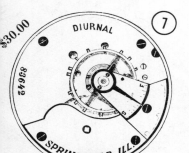

For Sale by Wholesale Dealers
in the United States and Canada.

$30.00   S.W.Co.   ⑧

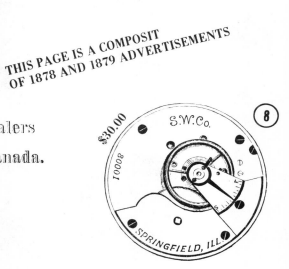

OFFICES:

No. 11 Maiden Lane, New York.   No. 172 State Street, Chicago.

Springfield, Illinois.   53

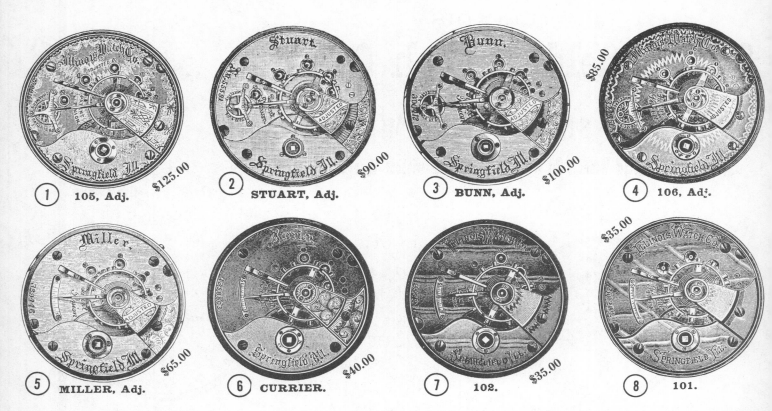

① 105, Adj. $125.00
② STUART, Adj. $90.00
③ BUNN, Adj. $100.00
④ 106, Adj. $85.00
⑤ MILLER, Adj. $65.00
⑥ CURRIER. $40.00
⑦ 102. $35.00
⑧ 101. $35.00

ILLINOIS WATCH COMPANY,
❧ SPRINGFIELD, ILLS. ❧

New York Office, 21 Maiden Lane.   1884 ADVERTISEMENT   Chicago Office, 71 Washington Street.

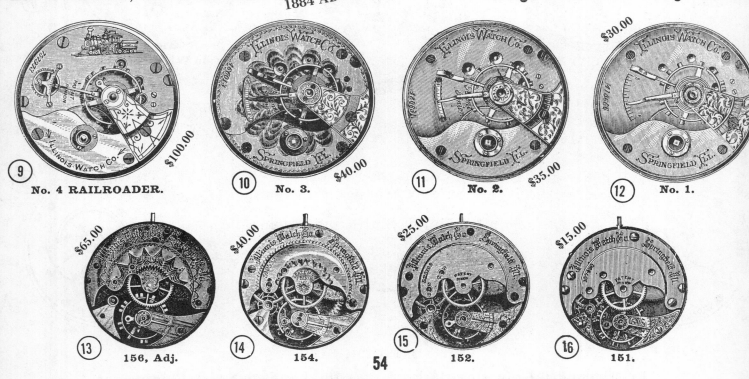

⑨ No. 4 RAILROADER. $100.00
⑩ No. 3. $40.00
⑪ No. 2. $35.00
⑫ No. 1. $30.00
⑬ 156, Adj. $65.00
⑭ 154. $40.00
⑮ 152. $25.00
⑯ 151. $15.00

54

FOR SALE BY ALL JOBBERS.

ILLINOIS WATCH CO. MOVEMENTS.

1888 SUPPLY CATALOG   **18 Size Movements.**

SEE PAGE 4

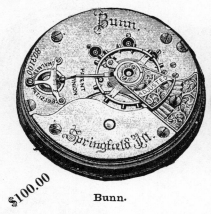

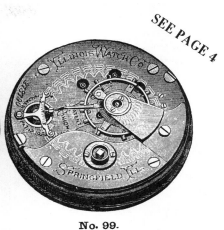

$100.00

Bunn.   No. 60.   No. 99.

18 Size, Full Plate, Hunting or Open Face Lever Set—Gilt.

		Key Wind.	Stem Wind.	
BUNN.	15 jewels, 4 pairs in settings, adjusted, patent regulator		$35.00	$100.00
MILLER.	15 " 4 " " " $65.00	$20.50	26.50	65.00
No. 107.	Nameless, same as Bunn		35.00	70.00
" 5.	15 jewels, 4 pairs in settings, patent regulator, adjusted $65.00	19.00	25.00	40.00
" 60.	15 " 4 " " " "		17.00	30.00
" 6.	11 " 4 upper holes, silver index $40.00	10.00		
" 2.	11 " 4 " "		12.50	$20.00
I. W. Co. 7	" plain, sunk second dial $35.00	7.00	10.00	20.00

18 Size, Full Plate—Nickel.

		Key Wind.	Stem Wind.	
No. 105.	15 jewels, 4 pairs in settings, adjusted, patent regulator, Breguet hair spring		$100.00	$125.00
" 65.	15 " 4 " " " " "		30.00	90.00
" 99.	11 " 4 upper holes, patent regulator $40.00	$11.50	15.50	30.00
" 101.	11 " 4 " "		14.00	40.00

Ladies' ¾ Plate Movements.

H.T.C.

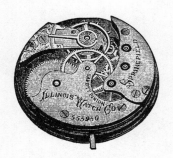

No 141.   No. 130.   No 144.

				6 Size.		4 Size	
$80.00	No. 146.	Nickel, 16 jewels, 4½ pairs settings, adjusted	$60.00		No. 136	$60.00	$80.00
35.00	" 144.	" 15 " 4 " "	27.00		" 134	27.00	35.00
30.00	" 142.	" 11 " 4 upper holes	18.50		" 132	18.50	30.00
30.00	" 143.	Gilded, 15 " 4 pairs settings	24.00		" 133	24.00	30.00
25.00	" 141.	" 11 " 4 upper holes	14.50		" 131	14.50	25.00
25.00	" 140	" 7 " plain			" 130	12.00	25.00

FACTORY and GENERAL OFFICE:
Springfield, Illinois

NEW YORK OFFICE:
Corner Broadway and John Streets

No 120. 14 Size.

No. 146. 6 Size.

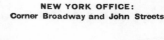

No. 143. 6 Size.

No. 121. 14 Size.

No. 60. 18 Size, O. F.,
Pendant Setting.

No. 99. 18 Size, O. F.
Pendant Setting.

To the
Retail Watch Dealers:

We have tendered our resignation as co-operating manufacturers with the National Association of Jobbers in American Watches, and we beg to advise the Trade that they can now be supplied with our movements through our special jobbers. If dealers who have heretofore been unable to obtain our goods through Association Jobbers will write to any of our offices, we will see that your orders are promptly filled.

Your particular attention is directed to our present production of

18 S. Accurately Adjusted Movements.

Hunting, Open Face and Key-Winders in Gilt and Nickel.

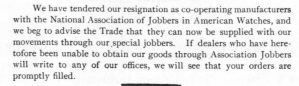

ILLINOIS WATCH COMPANY

Our New Model,
18 s. Open Face Movements
IN
Pendant Setting, with Straight Line Escapement

are now on the market, and the great demand for them is the best criterion of their merit, and of the judgment of the Trade concerning them.

THE ILLINOIS WATCH COMPANY

Guarantee all movements made by them to be equal in every respect to those of any other manufacture, and solicit a comparison of similar grades.

No. 116. 16 Size.

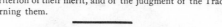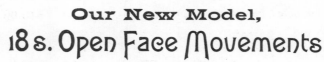

No. 115. 16 Size.

No. 113. 16 Size.

No. 114. 16 Size.

No. 99. 18 Size, O. F.
Pendant Setting.

No. 144. 6 Size.

I. W. Co. 18 Size O. F.
Pendant Setting.

No. 141. 6 Size.

No. 60. 18 Size, O. F.
Pendant Setting.

CHICAGO OFFICE:
104 State Street

SAN FRANCISCO OFFICE:
220 Sutter Street

ILLINOIS WATCH COMPANY'S MOVEMENTS, SPRINGFIELD, ILL.

18 Size, Stem-Wind, Hunting and Open Face. Open Face are Lever Set.
A. C. BECKEN — 1896

SEE PAGE 4

Bunn Hunting or Open Face.

$125.00
100.00
80.00
90.00

Nickel, adjusted to temperature, isochronism and positions, 21 fine ruby jewels in gold settings, compensation balance with gold screws, patent regulator, Breguet hair spring, double sunk glass enamel dial.
Bunn Special............(1)....$46 00

Nickel, adjusted to temperature, isochronism and positions, 17 ruby jewels in gold settings, compensation balance with gold screws, patent regulator, Breguet hair spring, double sunk glass enamel dial.
Bunn. Nickel.................$32 00
Bunn. Gilt, same as above..(3).. 28 00

Nickel, adjusted to temperature, isochronism and positions, 17 jewels (5 pairs in settings), compensation balance, patent regulator, Breguet hair spring, double sunk dial.
No. 65............(4)....$24 00

$40.00
30.00
30.00
25.00

No. 50.

Half nickel, 17 jewels (5 pairs in settings), compensation balance, patent regulator, Breguet hair spring, double sunk dial.
No. 61..............(5)...$16 00

Gilt, 17 jewels (5 pairs in settings), compensation balance, patent regulator, Breguet hair spring, double sunk dial.
No. 60..............(6)...$15 00

Half nickel, 15 jewels (4 pairs in settings), compensation balance, patent regulator, Breguet hair spring.
No. 51..............(7)......$12 50

Gilt, 15 jewels (4 pairs in settings), compensation balance, patent regulator, Breguet hair spring.
No. 50..............(8)...$11 50

$30.00
25.00
25.00
20.00
35.00

I. W. Co.

Half nickel, 11 jewels, compensation balance, patent regulator.
No. 99....................(9)....$10 50

Half nickel, 11 jewels, compensation balance.
No. 101....................(10)...$10 00

Gilt, 11 jewels, compensation balance.
No. 2....................(11)....$9 50

Gilt, 7 jewels, compensation balance.
I. W. Co....................(12)....$8 00

Same as above, key winding.
I. W. Co....................(13)....$7 00

16 Size, Stem-Wind, Hunting and Open Face. Open Face are Lever Set.

$35.00
30.00
30.00

$80.00
$35.00

Nickel, adjusted to heat, cold and positions, 16 jewels (4½ pairs in gold settings), compensation balance, Breguet hair spring, micrometer regulator, double sunk glass enamel dial.
No. 116....................$36 00

Gilt, adjusted, 15 jewels (4 pairs in settings), compensation balance, Breguet hair spring, micrometer regulator, double sunk dial.
No. 115....................(15)....$19 00

Nickel, 15 jewels (4 pairs in settings), compensation balance, Breguet hair spring, micrometer regulator, sunk second, inside circle dial.
No. 114. Nickel...........(16)....$16 00
No. 113. Gilt.............(17)... 15 00

Nickel, 11 jewels (2 pairs in settings), compensation balance, sunk second, inside circle dial.
No. 112....................(18)...$12 50

$25.00
20.00

Gilt, 11 jewels (2 pairs in settings), compensation balance, sunk second, inside circle dial.
No. 111....................(19)....$10 50

Gilt, 7 jewels, compensation balance, sunk second dial.
No. 110....................(20)....$8 00

Ladies' 6 Size, Stem-Wind and Lever Set, Hunting.

$80.00
35.00
30.00

Nickel, adjusted, 16 jewels (4½ pairs in gold settings), compensation balance, double sunk glass enamel dial.
No. 146....................$36 00

Nickel, 15 jewels (4 pairs in settings), compensation balance, S. S., inside circle dial.
No. 144. Nickel...........(22)....$20 00
No. 143. Gilt.............(23).... 18 00

$30.00
25.00

Nickel, 11 jewels, compensation balance, S. S. dial.
No. 142....................(24)....$12 50

Gilt, 11 jewels, compensation balance, S. S. dial.
No. 141....57....(25)....$11 50

$25.00
25.00

Nickel, 7 jewels, compensation balance, S. S. dial.
No. 149....................(26)....$10 0

Gilt, 7 jewels, compensation balance, S. S. dial.
No. 140....................(27)....$0

18 Size Illinois Watch Co. Movements Stem Wind, Lever Set

NOTICE: The Illinois Watches are very high class and are considered to be equal to all other makes. They are finely finished throughout and are accurately timed before leaving the factory.

The Prices are for Watch Movements Without Cases. They will fit any 18 Size Case

1

Guaranteed to Pass Railroad Inspection.
"Bunn Special," 24 Jewels, $77.34.

18 size, 24 ruby and sapphire jewels, gold settings, adjusted to temperature, 6 positions and isochronism, compensating balance, gold screws, including timing screws, double roller, steel escape wheel, Juergensen mainspring, double sunk dial.

1911 R. T. & CO.

FAMOUS RAILROAD WATCHES

Notice the low prices on these railroad grades; also read the specifications telling of their perfect construction. The Illinois Watches are very popular with Railroad Men because they give perfect service and are low priced. If for any reason any one of these movements does not give perfect satisfaction, it can be returned to us and the purchase price will be refunded.

SEE PAGE 4

2

Guaranteed to Pass Railroad Inspection.
"Bunn Special," 21 Jewels, $58.00.

18 size, 21 ruby and sapphire jewels, gold settings, adjusted to temperature, 6 positions and isochronism, compensating balance, gold screws, including timing screws, double roller, steel escape wheel, Juergensen mainspring, double sunk dial.

3 $35.00

"No. 79," $21.34.

18 size, 17 jewels in polished settings, accurately adjusted to temperature, compensation balance with gilt timing screws, Breguet hair spring, patent micrometer regulator. This movement is finely finished throughout, has fine enameled dial and damaskeened nickel movement plates.

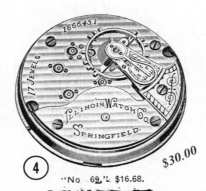

4 $30.00

"No. 69," $16.68.

Read the description.

18 size, 17 jewels in polished settings, beautifully damaskeened nickel movement plates, compensation balance wheel, patent micrometer regulator, Breguet hair spring, carefully regulated before leaving the factory. Guaranteed to be a perfect timekeeper.

5 $25.00

"No. 59," $14.00.

The Most Popular 15 Jeweled Watch Movement on the Market.

18 size, 15 jewels in polished settings, damaskeened nickel movement plates, compensation balance wheel, patent micrometric regulator, Breguet hair spring. Guaranteed to give satisfaction to the wearer.

Illinois Watch Co. O Size Watch Movements

6 $30.00

Illinois.

0-size, 17 jewels, polished settings, compensating balance, with timing screws, steel escape wheel, polished gold center wheel, Breguet hairspring, patent micrometric screw regulator, exposed concaved and polished winding wheels.
No. 37 .... $28.68

7 $25.00

Illinois.

0-size, 15 jewels in settings, Breguet hairspring, damaskeened nickel movement plates, patent center pinion, fine enameled dial. A high-grade watch movement, guaranteed to keep perfect time.
No. 35. 15 jewels ...... **58** $21.34

8 $25.00

Illinois.

0-size, 11 jewels in settings, Breguet hairspring, damaskeened nickel movement plates, patent center pinion, straight regulator, fine enameled dial. A high-grade movement, guaranteed to keep perfect time.
No. 33. 11 jewels $18.00

16 Size Illinois Watch Co. Movements. Stem Wind, Lever Set

The prices are for watch movements without cases.   They will fit any 16 Size cases

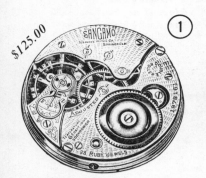

$125.00 ① ②

$100.00

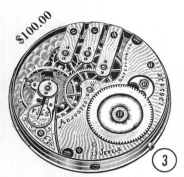

$100.00

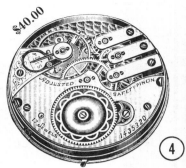

$40.00 ④

Guaranteed to Pass Railroad Inspection.
"Sangamo" 21 Jewels, $65.34.
16 size, 21 ruby and sapphire jewels; gold settings; adj. to temp., 6 pos. and isochronism; comp. bal., gold screws including timing screws; double roller; steel escape wheel; gold train; breg. hairspring; pat. reg.; Juergensen mainspring; double sunk dial.

Guaranteed to Pass Railroad Inspection.
"A. Lincoln," $56.00.
16 size, 21 ruby and sapphire jewels; gold settings; adj. to temp., 5 pos. and isochronism; compensating balance with timing screws; double roller; steel escape wheel; gold center wheel; breg. hairspring; pat. reg.; Juergensen mainspring; double sunk dial.

Guaranteed to Pass Railroad Inspection.
"No. 187" Bridge, $50.68.
16 size, 17 ruby and sapphire jewels; gold settings; adj. to temp., 5 pos. isochronism; comp. bal., gold screws, including timing screws; double roller; steel escape wheel; beveled gold train; patent regulator; Juergensen mainspring; double sunk dial.

"No. 186" Bridge, $36.68.
16 size, 17 ruby jewels; adj. to temp., four pos. compensating balance with timing screws; gold center wheel; breg. hairspring; pat. reg.; gilt engraved double sunk dial.

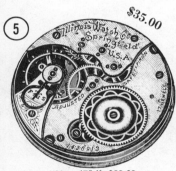

⑤ $35.00

⑥ $30.00

⑦ $25.00

⑧ $20.00

"No. 175," $28.68.
16 size, 17 jewels in polished settings; adjusted to temperature, compensation balance, timing screws; breguet hairspring, patent regulator, double sunk dial.

"No. 174," $24.00.
16 size, 17 jewels in polished settings; compensation balance; breguet hairspring, patent regulator; gilt engraved double sunk dial.

"No. 173," $19.34.
16 size, 15 jewels in polished settings; breguet hairspring, patent regulator, compensation balance, double sunk dial.

"No. 172," $15.34.
16 size, 11 jewels in polished settings; breguet hairspring, patent regulator, white enameled dial.

12 Size Illinois Watch Co. Movements.   Stem Wind, Pendant Set

These movements will fit any 12 Size cases

⑨

⑩ $35.00 $30.00

⑪ $20.00

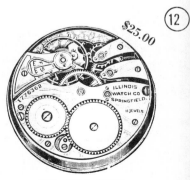

⑫ $25.00

"No. 273," $32.00.
12 size, 17 jewels; polished settings; adjusted to temperature; compensating balance, with setting screws; steel escape wheel; beveled and polished gold center wheel; breg. hairspring; pat. regulator; exposed concaved and polished winding wheels.

"No. 255," $24.00.
12 size, 17 jewels; polished settings; compensating balance, with timing screws; beveled and gold center wheel; breguet hairspring; pat. regulator; exposed, concaved and polished winding wheels.

"No. 228," $19.34.
12 size, 15 jewels; polished settings; compensating balance, with timing screws; beveled center wheel; breguet hairspring; patent regulator; exposed winding wheel.

"No. 219," $16.68.
12 size, 11 jewels; polished settings; compensating balance, with timing screws; breguet hairspring; patent regulator; exposed winding wheels.

THESE WATCHES WERE MADE BY ILLINOIS WATCH CO.

The Quality Question

The Quality Question is the first and most important to be considered in the purchase of any of these articles. : : : : :

Every order placed with us indicates unlimited confidence in our integrity and ability to furnish the best possible value for the money, and our sales are larger each succeeding year because of unfailing efforts to justify the people's confidence. Our aim is to give each purchaser a better value than he expected.

Nobody but an expert JEWELER can tell from ordinary examination much about the quality of any article of jewelry, and even an expert cannot be sure on many points. It remains for time to show the wearing qualities and durability.

We fully realize these facts, and there is no division in our store where goods are more carefully examined for defects in quality than here. Every article which does not prove satisfactory after test is put aside.

In fact, there are many articles of jewelry and many kinds of watches which we do not sell at all, in spite of a considerable popular demand, simply because they do not give satisfaction in the long run, and the purchaser is eventually dissatisfied with his or her purchase.

A large proportion of the articles sold in a jewelry store are intended for gifts, and it is our policy to sell only articles of which the giver may not be ashamed.

The descriptions are not exaggerated in any way. If we quote an article as solid gold, we mean that every bit of metal used in its construction is solid gold; if such is not the case, the fact is stated in the catalogue.

If the settings are imitation gems, the fact is always set forth, so that you can tell exactly what you are getting every time.

SPECIALLY GUARANTEED
WASHINGTON WATCHES

SEE PAGE 4

Prices complete in cases are given on the following pages.

If you want to own a distinctively American watch, built on honor and not to sell cheap, buy a "Washington."

You can show it in any part of the world and truthfully say "This is the best American watch made," and consequently the best watch in the world.

Washington watches are long established and well known. We have sold them for many years with unvarying satisfaction to the users.

We control the factory output of Washington watches, and we use our control to keep the quality high and the price low. The descriptions of Washington watches in our catalogue are positively accurate and truthful.

If we say that a Washington watch is adjusted to position, we mean just what we say. You will find each position adjusted Washington movement stamped accordingly, and if you care to test the watch by running it for 24 hours, each in different positions, face up, face down, stem up, stem down, etc., you will find only the slightest variation in each position.

The majority of watches advertised as adjusted to temperature and position have only the ordinary temperature adjustment, and if tested will show a great variation in different positions.

The manufacturer does not sell such a watch as "position adjusted," but simply as "adjusted to heat and cold" and the position adjustment exists only in the advertiser's mind.

September 16th 1911

We hereby guarantee the accompanying watch movement No. 1615391 made by the Washington Watch Co. to be in first-class, accurate time keeping order, and to remain so for three years from date. There are no "ifs" to this guarantee, we rely on your honor not to abuse your watch, and we will make any necessary repairs, including cleaning, free of charge for three years from this date.

MONTGOMERY WARD & CO

Do not return guarantee when watch needs repairs. Our records show date of purchase.

ONE OF THE MANY LETTERS FROM SATISFIED PURCHASERS OF "WASHINGTON WATCHES"

Montgomery Ward & Co., Dear Sirs:—The Washington watch that I purchased of you several months ago has proven highly satisfactory in every respect, and would recommend them to anybody who wants a good, durable and perfect timepiece and the best value for the money.

Above all I can vouch for the faithfulness of the unconditional guarantee which goes with it, as I broke my watch on its arrival in trying to open it and returned it the next day, charges collect, as per guarantee, and within a few days received it again, repaired and in perfect condition, all charges prepaid and not a question asked.

This I consider one of the most remarkable guarantees I have ever heard of, and should of itself remove any doubt which might exist in the mind of anybody as to the quality of the watches.

Yours truly,
Fallbrook, Pa.   W. L. Waughn.

---

16 Size Thin Model "Monroe"

①

12 Size "Liberty Bell"
② $30.00

Our guarantee on higher grades of Washington watches is the most liberal that was ever known.

It does not balk at anything, but agrees to keep your watch in order for three years NO MATTER WHAT HAPPENS TO IT. If the watch requires cleaning and re-oiling, we do the work free. If it is dropped and damaged we repair it free and don't ask any questions, also we pay the express charges BOTH WAYS. A printed guarantee to this effect goes with every "Lafayette," "Army and Navy" and "Senate" watch (see sample guarantee above). The lower price Washington watches are guaranteed for one year. This does not mean that they will only last for a year, indeed every Washington watch made will last an ordinary lifetime, with proper usage.

12 Size "Senate"
③ $30.00

12 Size "Army and Navy"
④ $85.00

Is made for a boy's watch, but it is really good enough for anyone to carry. The "Monroe" is a fine nickel movement, exactly the same as the "Liberty Bell" except that it has 11 jewels and plain dial, not double-sunk. 11 jewels in burnished settings, double expansion balance, compensating for heat and cold, safety pinion, stemwind and lever set, against all odds the finest 11 jewel watch made in America. **$20.00**

17 jewels in burnished settings, double cut expansion balance, compensating for heat and cold, safety pinion, gold center wheel, exposed train and winding wheel, Breguet hairspring, patent regulator, quick train, enameled dial with red marginal figures, stemwind and pendant set. The "Liberty Bell" is one of the most popular watches ever made. In fact, it looks and runs too well for the price and folks buy it instead of a higher priced watch. **$30.00**

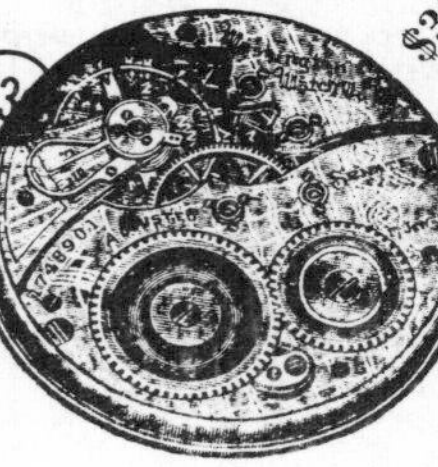

17 ruby jewels in burnished settings, adjusted to heat and cold, gold center wheel, compensation balance, safety pinion, exposed escapement, steel escape wheel, patent silver damaskeened finish, fine glass enamel dial with red marginal figures quicktrain, stemwind and pendant set. The "Senate" is the cheapest adjusted Washington, and is a great timekeeper, and guaranteed unconditionally for three years.

21 ruby jewels in polished cup settings adjusted to temperature, three positions, isochronism, gold center wheel, compensation balance, with timing screws, safety pinion, exposed escapement, steel escape wheel, train and winding wheels, patent regulator, Breguet hairspring, beautiful silver damaskeen finish, finest glass enameled dial with red marginal figures, quick train, stemwind and pendant set. Warranted unconditionally for three years.

---

16 Size Thin Model "Army & Navy"

⑤ $85.00

16 Size Thin Model "Senate"
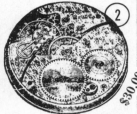
⑥ $35.00

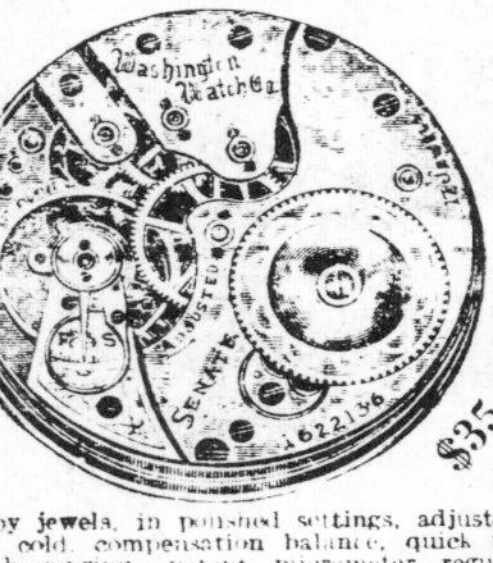

16 Size Thin Model "Liberty Bell"
⑦ $35.00

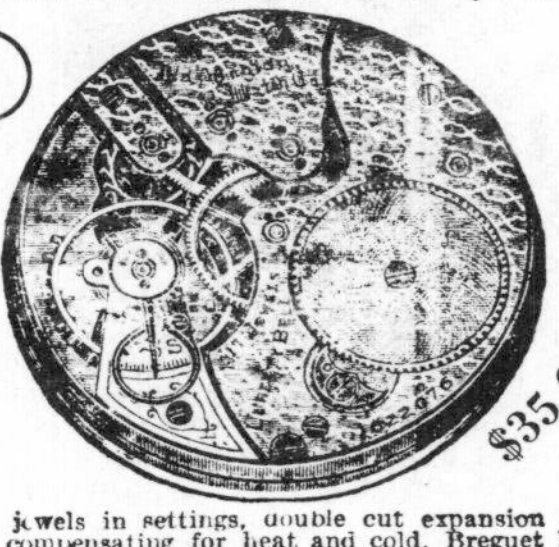

16 Size Thin Model "La Fayette"

⑧ $110.00

21 extra fine ruby and sapphire jewels in burnished gold settings, adjusted to heat, cold, positions and isochronism, compensation balance, entire escapement cap jeweled, solid gold timing screws, sapphire roller and pallet jewels, exposed train and escapement, exposed polished steel winding wheels, Breguet hairspring, patent micrometer regulator, beveled steel escape wheel, rich silver damaskeening, quick train, fine double sunk dial with red marginal figures, stemwind and lever set. It is unconditionally guaranteed for three years.

17 ruby jewels, in polished settings, adjusted to heat and cold, compensation balance, quick train, Breguet hairspring, patent micrometer regulator, fine double sunk dial, beautiful silver damaskeen finish, stemwind and lever set. You cannot equal the "Senate" for beauty and time-keeping at anything like the same price. Being a popular priced watch and unconditionally guaranteed for three years, the sale of this grade is very large.

17 jewels in settings, double cut expansion balance, compensating for heat and cold, Breguet hairspring, patent regulator, fine double sunk dial with red marginal figures, silver damaskeen finish, exposed polished steel winding wheels, stemwind and lever set, quick train. The "Liberty Bell" is a perfect beauty in appearance and is as well finished as many $25.00 watches. Its timekeeping qualities are remarkable for a medium price watch.

23 finest ruby and sapphire jewels, solid gold settings, accurately adjusted to heat, cold, 6 positions and isochronism, compensation balance with gold timing screws, beveled solid gold train wheels, beveled steel escape wheel, quick train, double roller escapement, exposed polished concave winding wheel, train and escapement, Breguet hairspring, patent micrometer regulator, rich silver damaskeen finish, glass enamel double sunk dial with red marginal figures, stemwind and lever set. This is the best 16 size watch made, and is guaranteed unconditionally for three years.

---

18 Size "Army and Navy"

⑩ $90.00

18 Size "La Fayette"

⑪ $400.00

18 Size "Liberty Bell"

⑨ $40.00

18 Size "Senate"

⑫ $40.00

The Washington Watch Co. never made anything cheaper than this "Senate." 17 jewel watches till the "Liberty Bell" and "Monroe" were produced to meet the demand for lower priced movements of this make. The "Liberty Bell" is a handsome nickel movement, 17 jewels in settings, patent regulator, Breguet hairspring, compensation balance, enameled dial with red marginal figures, and specially hardened balance staff, quick train, stemwind and lever set. Every watch of this grade is as carefully regulated before shipping as the finest grade, and the result is that they run well enough for anyone.

Cost considered, this is the best all around watch made. It has the accurate timekeeping qualities of the finest watches, and is sold at a moderate price. For timekeeping and immunity from breakage, we will not except the "Army and Navy" against any watch made except the "La Fayette." It has 21 selected ruby jewels in settings, is accurately adjusted to heat, cold, five positions and isochronism, hardened balance staff resisting breakage, compensation balance, steel escape wheel, patent micrometer regulator, Breguet hairspring, patent safety pinion, handsome silver damaskeened nickel plates, with gold lettering and double sunk dial with red marginal figures, quick train, stemwind and lever set. These watches have been carried in the Philippines, Cuba, South America and all over this country. They are not affected by climatic changes and rarely require any repairs. They carry our three year unconditional guarantee.

24 selected ruby and sapphire jewels in highly burnished solid gold settings, accurately adjusted to heat and cold, 6 positions and isochronism. The timing screws used to adjust the balance wheel are solid gold. The adjustment of a "La Fayette" watch occupies a skilled workman a part of each day for several weeks, sometimes for months; the method being the same as used in adjusting the ships' chronometers. The balance staff is hardened purposely to withstand severe jars, this being the most easily broken part of a watch. Escape wheels are highly polished steel with beveled teeth, conical pivots, compensation balance, Breguet hairspring, patent micrometer regulator, double sunk glass enameled dial, with heavy Roman or Arabic figures and red marginal figures, solid nickel plates finished in silver damaskeen, quick train, stemwind and lever set, double roller escapement. The "La Fayette" is the highest grade 18 size watch made in America. We guarantee it unconditionally for 3 years.

This is the best popular priced watch in the world. Though made with 17 jewels, it will run closer than most 21 jewel watches. The "Senate" is a handsomely damaskeened nickel movement with 17 selected jewels in settings, patent regulator, Breguet hairspring, adjusted to heat and cold, patent safety pinion, double sunk dial with red marginal figures, quick train, stemwind and lever set. Balance staff is hardened so that an ordinary jar or fall will not break it or throw the balance out of poise. Although we sell the "Senate" at as low a price as other 17 jewel watches, it carries our unconditional 3 year guarantee.

ILLINOIS-SPRINGFIELD WATCHES

SEE PAGE 4

1917 OSKAMP—NOLTING CO.

Illinois-Springfield Watches

卍

18 Size
Full Plate
Lever Setting

23J $165.00

21J $100.00

(1)
(2)

Bunn Special

21 and 23 Jewels, Hunting and Open Face

Nickel; extra quality ruby and sapphire jewels, solid gold settings; accurately adjusted to temperature, six positions and isochronism; carefully rated and timed; double roller escapement; sapphire roller and pallet jewels; poised fork and pallet; entire escapement cap jeweled, hand finished conical pivots; beveled steel escape wheel; special quality hardened and tempered compensating balance, with gold screws including mean time screw; patent micrometric screw regulator, best quality Swiss Breguet hairspring, Phillipe coil; safety screw center pinion; first quality mainspring, all steel parts highly polished; double sunk glass enamel dial; damaskeened in bright spotted pattern.

The 23 jewel Bunn Special contains the Illinois Jeweled Barrel.

The highest grade 18 size watches made and guaranteed to give satisfaction under the most trying conditions of railway service.

23 Jewel Bunn Special.... **$53.00**

21 Jewel Bunn Special ...**$42.00**

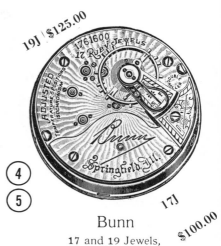

19J $125.00

17J $100.00

(4)
(5)

Bunn

17 and 19 Jewels, Open Face Only

Nickel; fine ruby and sapphire jewels, solid gold settings; accurately adjusted to temperature, five positions and isochronism; carefully rated and timed; double roller escapement, sapphire roller and pallet jewels; hardened, polished and beveled steel escape wheel; poised fork and pallet; compensating hard balance with gold screws, including timing screws; best quality Swiss Breguet hairspring, Phillipe coil; safety screw center pinion; first quality mainspring; all steel parts highly polished; double sunk glass enamel dial; handsomely damaskeened in bright sunburst pattern.

The 19 jewel Bunn contains Illinois Jeweled Barrel.

The Standard Watches in 17 and 19 Jewels for Railway Service.

19 Jewel Bunn Special.... **$36.50**

17 Jewel Bunn Special....**$33.00**

$125.00

(3)

A. Lincoln

21 Jewels, Open Face Only

Nickel; 21 ruby and sapphire jewels, gold settings; adjusted to temperature, five positions and isochronism; compensating hard balance, having gold screws, including timing screws; double roller escapement; sapphire roller and pallet jewels; entire escapement cap jeweled and conical pivots; beveled, polished steel escape wheel; best quality Breguet hairspring; first quality mainspring; safety screw center pinion; patent micrometric screw regulator; friction fitted dust band; double sunk dial, heavy Arabic figures; damaskeened in attractive bright striped pattern; black enameled lettering.

A most satisfactory watch for railroad service **$37.00**

(6)

$50.00

No. 89

17 Jewels, Hunting and Open Face

17 jewels, polished settings; adjusted to heat and cold; hardened compensating balance, with timing screws; Breguet hairspring; micrometric screw regulator; double sunk dial; heavy Arabic figures; gilded screws and regulator; damaskeened in beautiful gilt and nickel pattern.................**$17.25**

Illinois-Springfield Watches

$30.00

(7)

No. 69

17 Jewels, Hunting and Open Face

17 jewels, composition settings; compensating hard balance with timing screws; best quality Swiss Breguet hairspring; patent safety center pinion; patent micrometric screw regulator.................**$12.00**

ILLINOIS-SPRINGFIELD WATCHES

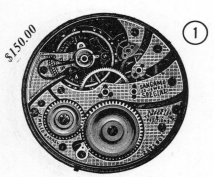

$150.00 ①

Sangamo Special
23 Jewels, Open Face Only

23 extra quality ruby and sapphire jewels, raised gold settings; accurately adjusted to temperature, six positions and isochronism; very carefully rated and timed; special quality hardened and tempered compensating balance, with gold screws including mean time screws; rounded polished gold train wheels; double roller escapement; beveled and polished steel escape wheel; one piece polished and cornered pallet and fork; gold guard pin staked in fork; selected quality red ruby jewels, oval top and bottom; ruby jeweled pin; entire escapement cap jeweled, hand finished, conical pivots; best quality Breguet hairspring; safety screw center pinion; Illinois superior mainspring; Illinois friction reducing sapphire jeweled barrel; recoiling click; screws are chamfered and slots cornered; double sunk glass enamel dial; plates and bridges have chamfered edges; are nicely finished and artistically damaskeened; engraving inlaid with gold.

The highest grade 16 size 23 jeweled watch made............ **$66.00**

WATCHES ON THIS PAGE NOT 60 HOUR

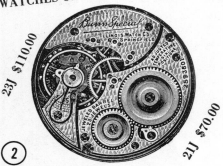

23J $110.00   21J $70.00

② ③

Bunn Special
21 and 23 Jewels, Hunting and Open Face

Extra quality ruby and sapphire jewels, raised gold settings; accurately adjusted to temperature, six positions and isochronism; very carefully rated and timed; special quality hardened and tempered compensating balance, with gold screws including mean time screw; rounded arm polished gold train wheels; double roller escapement; entire escapement cap jeweled, conical pivots; beveled and polished steel escape wheel; best quality Breguet hairspring; safety screw center pinion; Illinois superior mainspring; patent micrometric screw regulator; recoiling safety click; concaved, polished and rayed winding wheels; screws are chamfered and slots cornered; double sunk glass enamel dial; plates and bridges have chamfered edges, are nicely finished and artistically damaskeened.

The 23 Bunn Special contains the Illinois Jeweled Barrel.

Exceptionally high grade 16 size watches for railroad or any severe service.

23 Jeweled Bunn Special........ **$55.00**

21 Jeweled Bunn Special........ **$47.50**

Illinois-Springfield Watches

16 Size Bridge and Three-Quarter Plate Lever Setting

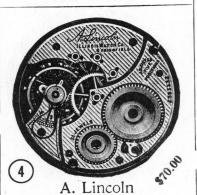

④

$70.00

A. Lincoln
21 Jewels, Hunting and Open Face

Nickel; 21 ruby and sapphire jewels, gold settings; adjusted to temperature, five positions and isochronism; special quality hardened and tempered compensating balance, with gold screws including mean time screws; exposed double roller escapement; sapphire roller and pallet jewels; beveled steel escape wheel; entire escapement cap jeweled; conical pivots; beveled and polished gold center wheel; patent micrometric screw regulator; best quality Breguet hairspring; patent safety screw center pinion; concaved, polished visible winding wheels; friction fitted dust band; double sunk dial, damaskeened in bright striped pattern; black enamel lettering.

A most satisfactory watch for railroad service.

21 Jewels, hunting or open face **$43.00**

Illinois-Springfield Watches

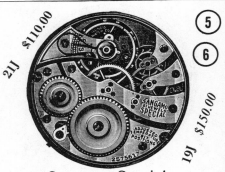

21J $110.00 ⑤ ⑥ 19J $150.00

Sangamo Special
19 and 21 Jewels, Open Face Only

Extra quality ruby and sapphire jewels; raised gold settings; accurately adjusted to temperature, six positions and isochronism; very carefully rated and timed; special quality hardened and tempered compensating balance, with gold screws including mean time screws; rounded arm polished gold train wheels; double roller escapement; beveled and polished steel escape wheel; one piece polished and cornered pallet and fork; gold guard pin staked in fork; selected quality red ruby pallet jewels, oval top and bottom; ruby jewel pin; best quality Breguet hairspring; safety screw center pinion; entire escapement of the 21 jewel is cap jeweled, hand finished conical pivots; Illinois superior mainspring; recoiling click; screws are chamfered and slots cornered; double sunk glass enamel dial; plates and bridges have chamfered edges, are nicely finished and artistically damaskeened; engraving inlaid with gold.

The highest grade 16 size 19 and 21 jeweled watches made.

The 19 jewel Sangamo Special contains the Illinois Jeweled Barrel.

21 Jewel Sangamo **$55.00**

19 Jewel Sangamo **$50.00**

19J $85.00 ⑦ ⑧ 17J $85.00

Bunn
17 and 19 Jewels, Hunting and Open Face

Extra quality ruby and sapphire jewels; raised gold settings; accurately adjusted to temperature, five positions and isochronism; very carefully rated and timed; special quality hardened and tempered compensating balance, with gold screws including mean time screws; rounded arm polished gold train wheels; double roller escapement; beveled and polished steel escape wheel; one piece polished pallet and fork; sapphire pallet jewels and jewel pin; best quality Breguet hairspring; safety screw center pinion; Illinois superior mainspring; patent micrometric screw regulator; recoiling click; concaved, polished and rayed winding wheels; screws are chamfered and slots cornered; double sunk glass enamel dial; plates and bridges have chamfered edges, are nicely finished and artistically damaskeened.

The 19 jewel Bunn contains the Illinois Jeweled Barrel.

The Standard Watches in 17 and 19 jewels for railway service.

19 Jewel Bunn Special........ **$42.00**

17 Jewel Bunn Special........ **$36.50**

ILLINOIS-SPRINGFIELD WATCHES

SEE PAGE 4

Illinois-Springfield Watches

1917 OSKAMP—NOLTING CO.

**16 and 0 Sizes
Bridge Model
Pendant Setting**

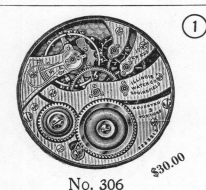

① $30.00

No. 306

17 Jewels, Hunting and Open Face

17 jewels; polished settings; adjusted to temperature, three positions; hardened compensating balance with timing screws; rounded arm train wheels; polished gold top center wheel; tempered and polished steel escape wheel; best quality Breguet hairspring; safety screw center pinion; micrometric screw regulator; concaved winding wheels; recoil safety click; double sunk dial; gilded screws and regulator; beautifully damaskeened in narrow striped pattern.

A watch that is an exceptionally durable and accurate timekeeper............**$24.50**

④ $30.00

No. 305

17 Jewels, Hunting and Open Face

17 jewels; polished settings; adjusted to temperature; hardened compensating balance with timing screws; steel escape wheel; rounded arm train wheels; gold top center wheel; Breguet hairspring; patent micrometric screw regulator; safety screw center pinion; concaved and polished winding wheels; recoil safety click; double sunk dial; striped rayed pattern damaskeening; black enamel lettering. A watch that can be conscientiously recommended,...........**$22.00**

② $30.00

No. 304

17 Jewels, Hunting and Open Face

17 jewels; hardened compensating balance with timing service; rounded arm train wheels; safety screw center pinion; Breguet hairspring; patent micrometric screw regulator; safety recoil click; perfect self-locking setting device; double sunk dial.

Finish and timekeeping qualities of this watch far better than expected of one of this grade. **$19.00**

③

No. 204

17 Jewels
Hunting and Open Face

17 jewels; hardened compensating balance with timing screws; exposed escapement; hardened polished steel escape wheel; patent micrometric screw regulator; best quality Swiss Breguet hairspring; patent center safety pinion; perfect self-locking setting device; Swiss mainspring; highly polished, concaved visible winding wheels; sunk second dial set in recess of plate; friction fitted dust band; beautifully damaskeened in a striped rayed pattern. See illustration below.. **$21.00**

$40.00

⑤ $25.00

No. 303

15 Jewels, Hunting and Open Face

15 jewels; hardened compensating balance with timing screws; Breguet hairspring; rounded arm train wheels; safety screw center pinion; patent micrometric screw regulator; safety recoil click; perfect self-locking setting device; double sunk dial. The most attractive and best finished watch made in 15 jewels.............. **$15.50**

⑥

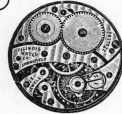
$25.00

No. 203

15 Jewels
Hunting and Open Face

15 jewels; hardened compensating balance with timing screws; steel escape wheel; exposed escapement; best quality Swiss Breguet hairspring; patent safety center pinion; perfect self-locking setting device; Swiss mainspring; sunk second dial set in recess of plate; friction fitted dust band; handsomely damaskeened........**$17.00**

⑦

No. 201

11 Jewels
Hunting and Open Face

11 jewels; hardened compensating balance with timing screws; exposed escapement; best quality Swiss Breguet hairspring; patent safety center pinion; perfect self-locking setting device; Swiss mainspring; exposed winding wheels; sunk second dial set in recess of plate; friction fitted dust band; handsomely damaskeened........**$13.25**

$20.00

ILLINOIS-SPRINGFIELD WATCHES

SEE PAGE 4

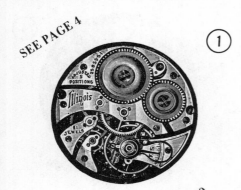

① No. 409 $85.00

21 Jewels,
Hunting and Open Face

21 extra quality diamond, ruby and sapphire jewels, raised gold settings; accurately adjusted to temperature, five positions and isochronism; very carefully rated and timed; special quality hardened and tempered compensating balance, with gold screws, including mean time screws; rounded arm polished gold train wheels; double roller escapement; beveled and polished steel escape wheel; one piece polished and cornered pallet and fork; gold guard pin staked in fork; selected quality red ruby pallet jewels, oval top and bottom; ruby jewel pin; best quality Breguet hair-spring; safety screw center pinion; entire escapement cap jeweled, hand finished, conical pivots; Illinois superior mainspring; patent micrometric screw regulator; recoiling click; concaved and polished winding wheels; screws are chamfered and slots cornered; double sunk glass enamel dial; plates and bridges have chamfered edges, are nicely finished and artistically damaskeened; engraving inlaid with gold....**$55.00**

Illinois-Springfield Watches

1917 OSKAMP–NOLTING CO.

12 Size
Bridge Model
Pendant Setting

$55.00

③

A. Lincoln
21 Jewels
Hunting and Open Face

21 ruby and sapphire jewels, gold settings; adjusted to temperature, five positions and isochronism; special quality hardened and tempered compensating balance, with gold screws including mean time screws; exposed double roller escapement; sapphire roller and pallet jewels; beveled steel escape wheel; entire escapement cap jeweled; conical pivots; beveled and polished gold center wheel; patent micrometric screw regulator; best quality Breguet hairspring; patent safety screw center pinion; concaved, polished visible winding wheels; double sunk dial; damaskeened in bright striped pattern; black enamel lettering.

Price of
Movement only **$43.00**

HIGH GRADE 12-SIZE ILLINOIS

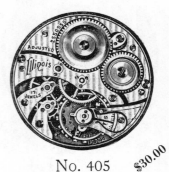

$200.00

② No. 410

23 Jewels, Hunting and Open Face
12 Size

23 extra quality ruby and sapphire jewels; gold settings; adjusted to temperature, six positions and isochronism; spring tempered compensating balance; gold screws including timing screws; steel escape wheel; double roller; gold train wheels; Breguet hairspring; patent regulator; safety screw center pinion; safety recoil click; Illinois Superior Motor Barrel; double sunk dial; is accurately constructed and highly finished in every detail.

W2166. ....$90.00

④ No. 405 $30.00

17 Jewels
Hunting and Open Face

17 jewels, oreide settings, adjusted to temperature; spring tempered compensating balance with timing screws; double roller escapement; hardened and polished steel escape wheel; sapphire pallets; sapphire jewel pins, gold, beveled and polished center wheel; Breguet hairspring; patent micrometric screw regulator; safety screw center pinion; perfect self-locking setting device; concaved and polished winding wheels; safety recoil click; damaskeened in bright striped pattern. A very attractive, well finished and thoroughly dependable movement.. **$23.25**

⑤

No. 403 $25.00

15 Jewels
Hunting and Open Face

15 jewels, polished settings; spring tempered compensating balance with timing screws; rounded arm center wheel; Breguet hairspring; patent micrometric screw regulator; safety screw center pinion; perfect self-locking setting device; recoil safety click; damaskeened in bright, broad striped pattern. An unusually well designed and constructed watch................**$15.00**

Illinois-Springfield Watches

ILLINOIS-SPRINGFIELD WATCHES

SEE PAGE 4

1917 OSKAMP–NOLTING CO.

Bridge Model   3-0 Size   Pendant Setting

HC $25
OF $15

No. 24
17 Jewels
Hunting and Open Face

17 jewels; hardened compensating balance with timing screws; exposed escapement; hardened polished steel escape wheel; patent micrometric screw regulator; best quality Swiss Breguet hairspring; patent center safety pinion; perfect self-locking setting device; Swiss mainspring; highly polished, concaved, visible winding wheels; sunk second dial set in recess of plate; beautifully damaskeened in a striped rayed pattern ... **$21.00**

HC $25
OF $15

No. 23
15 Jewels
Hunting and Open Face

15 jewels; hardened compensating balance with timing screws; steel escape wheel; exposed escapement; best quality Swiss Breguet hairspring; patent safety center pinion; perfect self-locking setting device; Swiss mainspring; sunk second dial set in recess of plate; handsomely damaskeened **$17.00**

HC $20
OF $15

No. 21
11 Jewels
Hunting and Open Face

11 jewels; hardened compensating balance with timing screws; exposed escapement; best quality Swiss Breguet hairspring; patent safety center pinion; perfect self-locking setting device; Swiss mainspring; exposed winding wheels; sunk second dial, set in recess of plate; handsomely damaskeened .. **$13.25**

ILLINOIS WATCH COMPANY

ILLINOIS SPRINGFIELD WATCH CO. 1869–1879
SPRINGFIELD ILLINOIS WATCH CO. 1879–1885
ILLINOIS WATCH CO.   1885–1927

Made watches in Springfield, Illinois from 1869 to 1927 when sold to HAMILTON who assembled remaining movements until 1939.

APPROXIMATE PRODUCTION DATES

SERIAL NO.	DATE	SERIAL NO.	DATE
15,000	1872	1,000,000	1900
37,000	1873	1,280,000	1901
59,000	1874	1,560,000	1902
81,000	1875	1,840,000	1903
103,000	1876	2,120,000	1904
125,000	1877	2,460,000	1905
147,000	1878	2,600,000	1906
169,000	1879	2,940,000	1907
191,000	1880	3,220,000	1908
210,000	1881	3,502,000	1909
230,000	1882	3,800,000	1910
250,000	1883	3,900,000	1911
270,000	1884	4,000,000	1912
285,000	1885	4,070,000	1913
300,000	1886	4,150,000	1914
333,000	1887	4,220,000	1915
366,000	1888	4,230,000	1916
399,000	1889	4,240,000	1917
432,000	1890	4,250,000	1918
465,000	1891	4,300,000	1919
478,000	1892	4,400,000	1920
531,000	1893	4,500,000	1921
570,000	1894	4,683,000	1922
600,000	1895	4,866,000	1923
680,000	1896	5,049,000	1924
760,000	1897	5,232,000	1925
840,000	1898	5,415,000	1926
920,000	1899	5,600,000	1927

No. 907
19 Jewels
Open Face
14-k Gold Case
Without Bracelet

$52.00

$45.00

$75.00

No. 903
15 Jewels, Open Face
Convertible
14k-Gold Case
Without Bracelet

$36.50

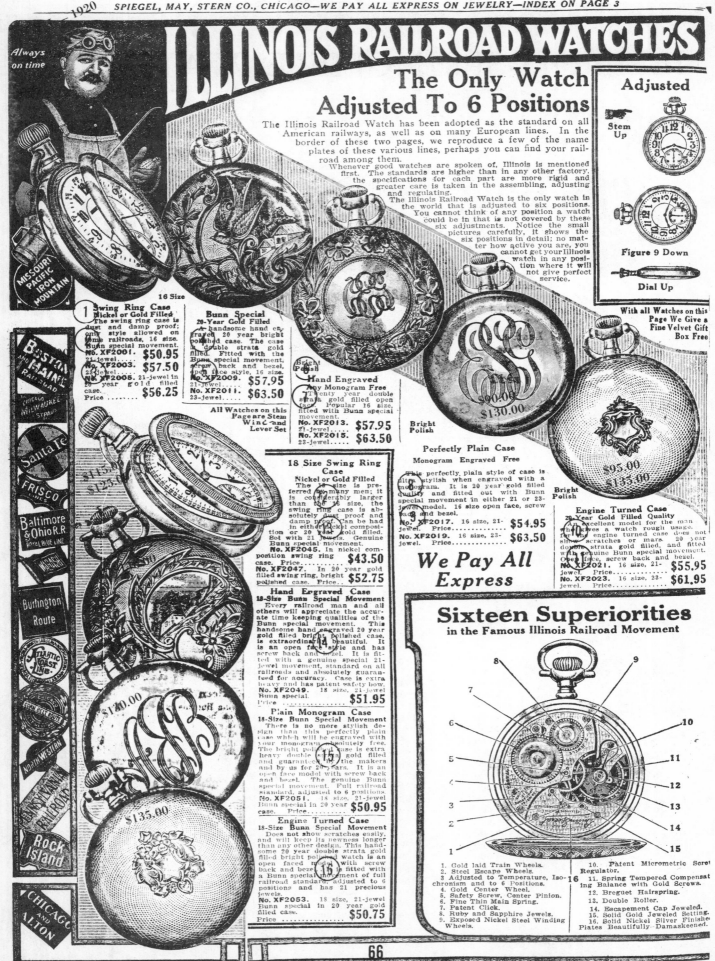

STANDARD ON ALL RAILROADS

The Watch That Passes Inspection Every Time

In order to be adapted by a railroad, a watch must be built according to certain standards which have been laid down by various roads as the very least that they expect a watch carried by their employees to be.

But there are various grades of railroad watches just the same as there are different kinds of automobiles. All railroads require good watches. Any watch that just barely passes railroad inspection must be a very good watch, but in the Illinois the railroad specifications are just a beginning. There are hundreds of little superiorities and refinements that no railroad would think of demanding.

That is why the Illinois watch is a joy to the heart of every railroad man. All railroads require inspection at regular intervals and at any one of these inspections if a watch does not pass it means expensive and costly repairs.

To 6 Positions

Stem Down

Figure 9 Up

Dial Down

With all Watches on This Page We Give a Fine Velvet Gift Box Free

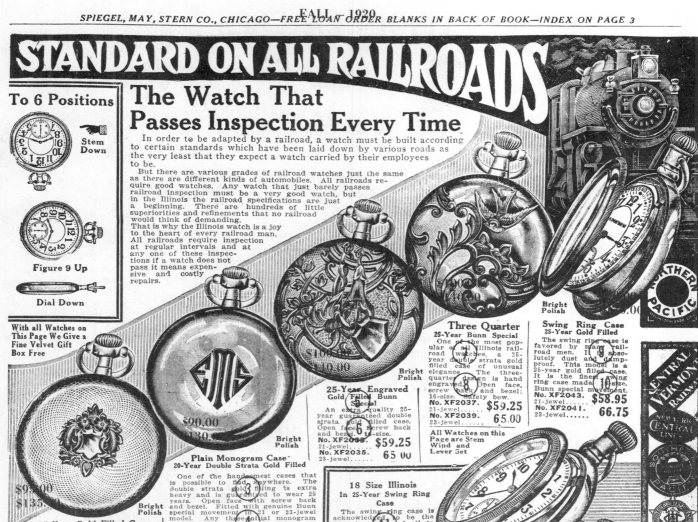

Three Quarter
25-Year Bunn Special
One of the most popular of all Illinois railroad watches, a 25-year double strata gold filled case of unusual elegance. The three-quarter design is hand engraved. Open face, screw back and bezel; 16-size; safety bow.
No. XF2037. 21-jewel...... $59.25
No. XF2039. 23-jewel...... 65.00

Swing Ring Case
25-Year Gold Filled
The swing ring case is favored by many railroad men. It is absolutely dust and damp-proof. This model is a 25-year gold filled case. It is the finest swing ring case made. 16-size. Bunn special movement.
No. XF2043. 21-jewel...... $58.95
No. XF2041. 23-jewel...... 66.75

25-Year Engraved
Gold Filled Bunn Special
An extra quality 25-year guaranteed double strata gold filled case. Open face, screw back and bezel. 16-size.
No. XF2033. 21-jewel...... $59.25
No. XF2035. 23-jewel...... 65.00

All Watches on this Page are Stem Wind and Lever Set

Plain Monogram Case
20-Year Double Strata Gold Filled
One of the handsomest cases that is possible to find anywhere. The double strata gold filling is extra heavy and is guaranteed to wear 25 years. Open face with screw back and bezel. Fitted with genuine Bunn special movement in 21 or 23-jewel model. Any three-initial monogram engraved free.
No. XF2029. 16-size, 21-jewel. Price.......... $58.95
No. XF2031. 16-size, 23-jewel. Price.......... 64.50

25-Year Gold Filled Case
Handsome Engine Turned Design
The 25-year case is extra durable and well worth the additional cost. The special engine turned design withstands hard usage to a great degree. Fitted with genuine Bunn special movement. Open face model. Screw back and bezel.
No. XF2025. 16-size, 21-jewel. Price.......... $58.95
No. XF2027. 16-size, 23-jewel. Price.......... 65.00

About A Year to Pay

18 Size Illinois
In 25-Year Swing Ring Case
The swing ring case is acknowledged to be the very best of all to protect the movement from dust and dampness. In the 25-year quality bright polished double strata gold filled you have the finest swing ring case that is made. We will engrave your monogram free if you will mention your initials. Movement is genuine Bunn special 18-size, fitted with 21 precious jewels.
No. XF2057. 18-size, 21-jewel. Price........ $54.95

Three Quarter Engraved
18 Size Bunn Special
Here is one of the most handsome cases we show, produced in a genuine 25-year bright polished double-strata gold filled quality. It is an open face style with screw back and bezel and is fitted with a 21-jewel Bunn special movement of safety bow.
No. XF2059. 18-size, 21-jewel Bunn special. Price...... $54.95

Plain Monogram Case
18 Size Bunn Special
Here is a perfectly plain, bright polished case of extra heavy weight, being guaranteed for 25 years. It is a very stylish case when engraved with an initial similar to the illustration. We will do this work free on request. This case is fitted with an 18-size Bunn special movement. Is a 21-jewel model and is full railroad standard. Safety bow. Open face, screw back and bezel.
No. XF2061. 18-size, 21-jewel, Bunn special. Price................... $52.95

Engine Turned Case
25-Year—18 Size 21 Jewel
You cannot buy a better engine turned case than this unless you would pay several times as much for one of solid gold. It is genuine 25-year quality bright polished double-strata gold filled. It is an open face model with screw back and bezel. Has safety box and pinion. Fitted with a 21-jewel Bunn special movement of guaranteed accuracy and reliability. Will pass inspection on every railroad in the United States. Order on 30 Days' Free Loan.
No. XF2063. 18-size, 21-jewel, Bunn special. Price................. $52.25

Montgomery or Plain Dial

Plain Dial

Pure Ivory White

Montgomery Dial

Any Watch On These 2 Pages Furnished in Choice Of Montgomery Or Plain Dial

The 18 Size Movement
The 18-size movement comes in a 21-jewel model only. These jewels are high quality rubies and sapphires in gold settings. Each movement is adjusted to 6 positions, temperature and isochronism. It has double roller escapement, hardened, polished steel escape wheel. Compensating balance.

The 16 Size Movement
This 16-size movement comes in a choice of 21 or 23 genuine ruby or sapphire jewels in gold settings. It is adjusted to six positions, temperature and isochronism. Compensating balance has solid gold screws. Highly finished, hardened, beveled steel escape wheel; double roller, cap jewel escape

18 Size

16 Size

WATCH MUST BE MINT
AND RUNNING

The Illini

12 SIZE   **21 JEWELS**

ADJUSTED TO FIVE POSITIONS

An extremely thin watch of the most exclusive design, made especially for the business or professional man desiring an attractive, durable, accurate and high grade timekeeper for a lifetime of service.

21 extra quality ruby and sapphire jewels; special tempered compensating center arm balance, having gold screws including timing screws; adjusted to temperature, five positions and isochronism; Breguet hairspring; double roller escapement; hardened and polished steel escape wheel; patent Illinois superior motor barrel, both pivots of barrel staff operating in sapphire jewels; patent recoil bar and pinion click; concaved and polished winding wheels; perfect pendant setting mechanism of exceptional simplicity entirely in movement; snap bezel dial.

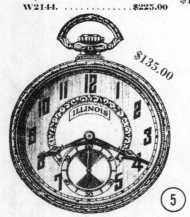

(1)
(2)

ENGRAVED EMPIRE

Raised figure dial. White or green gold.

14K Solid engraved, with cap.
W2143. ....**$240.00** $155.00
14K Solid plain, with cap.
W2144. ....**$225.00** $150.00

(3)
(4)

Engraved Empire 18K white gold, special raised gold figure dial.
W2139. Complete....**$297.00** $175.00
14K special raised gold figure dial.
W2140. Complete....**$264.00** $160.00

$135.00

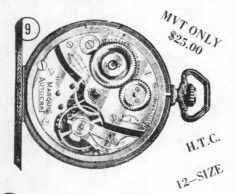

(5)

14K green gold, engraved Empire, etched raised figure dial.

W2137. ....**$240.00**

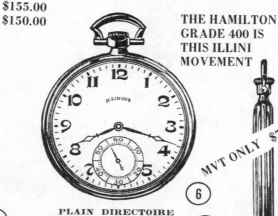

THE HAMILTON
GRADE 400 IS
THIS ILLINI
MOVEMENT

MVT ONLY $75.00

(6)
(7)

PLAIN DIRECTOIRE

Inlaid enamel figure dial.
14K green gold plain, no cap.
W2141. ....**$218.40** $140.00
14K green gold engraved, no cap.
W2142. ....**$233.20** $130.00

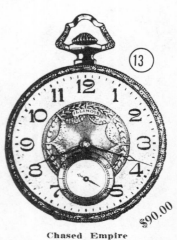

"Illini"

(8)

H.T.C.

Movement and Side Views

THE MARQUIS-AUTOCRAT

The Aristocrat of Watches

17 Jewels, Adjusted to Three Positions.

MVT ONLY
$25.00

(9)

H.T.C.

12–SIZE

(10)

CAMBRIDGE MODEL

14K green or white solid gold Queen case. Special etched, lined or butler back. Sterling silver inlaid figure, etched center dial.

W2151. No cap . $90.00 .. $108.00
W2152. Cap case. $100.00 . 122.40

The Autocrat

17 Jewels; Adjusted to Temperature and Isochronism   12–SIZE

MVT ONLY
$25.00

(12)

(13)

Chased Empire

$90.00

Chased Empire

Green or white gold Moire dial.
W2163. 14K Solid gold...**$88.80**

23 JEWEL RAILROAD WATCHES

60 Hour . . . 6 Position . . . Motor Barrel

SEE PAGE 4

GF
SG $350.00

① ②

MVT ONLY $150.00

③

Sangamo Special

ONE of the most important improvements in the history of watchmaking is the 60 hour Illinois motor barrel enclosed mainspring. This feature safeguards the railroad man against any failure to wind his watch at the end of the 24 hour period. But, its greatest advantage lies in furnishing that reserve power which makes possible an even distribution of tension with the resulting reduction of error in the first 24 hour period and the minimizing of any error for the full 48 hours.

The adjustment to six positions provides a further guard against possibility of error in that the sixth adjustment, the most difficult of all, corrects those tendencies to error which might not have been discovered in the adjustments to the first five positions.

The Sangamo Special is the finest railroad watch made by Illinois. Wadsworth has provided an especially designed case with an extra heavy and durable stationary bow. The dial is furnished as shown with double sunk center, glass enameled surface and heavy Gothic figures. Case in 14 karat white, green or yellow gold filled or 14 karat white, green or yellow solid gold. Hinged back is standard. Screw back and bezel cases if desired are furnished in 14K white or yellow gold filled.

14K gold filled, Consumer price, $90
14K solid gold, Consumer price, $150

SPECIFICATIONS — Sangamo Special

23 jewels-adjusted to six positions, heat, cold and isochronism; solid gold raised jewel settings; hardened and tempered compensating balance; Breguet hairspring; double roller escapement; hardened tempered beveled and polished steel escape wheel; positive micrometric screw regulator; safety recoil click; Illinois Superior Jeweled Motor Barrel with 60 hour mainspring.

Extra heavy and durable case with a non-pull-out bow and dust-proof pendant.

The Bunn Special

60 Hour . . 6 Position . . Motor Barrel

FOR the man who really desires a Superior quality 23 jeweled watch and does not feel warranted in buying a Sangamo Special; the Bunn Special 23 Jeweled watch is recommended. In it are incorporated all the advantages of Illinois experience and utmost inventive skill. The superior motor barrel, the 6 position adjustment and the 60 hour running mainspring help to make the 23 jewel Bunn Special exceed all railroad watch requirements . . The extra quality sapphire jewels in which both pivots of the going arbor operate add to the perfection and the fine quality of workmanship with which the 23 jewel Bunn Special is made.

$200.00

④

Above model furnished in 14K white or green gold filled; also green center with white back and bezel keystone case fitted in a double sunk glass enamel dial with heavy arabic figures, also furnished with Montgomery double sunk glass enamel dial with heavy arabic figures or Butler center silvered dial with railroad figures.

The case may be furnished with either plain or engraved back.

Consumer price, $75.00
Engraved Back
Consumer price, $77.00

$150.00

⑤

SPECIFICATIONS — 23 Jewel Bunn Special

16 Size 23 Jewels Three-Quarter Plate Model Adjusted to 6 positions and heat, cold and isochronism; raised gold jewel settings; spring tempered compensating balance with solid gold screws; polished gold beveled train wheels; double roller escapement and entire escapement cap jeweled; steel escape wheel; Breguet hairspring; concaved and polished steel winding wheels; positive micrometric screw regulator; safety recoiling click.

Illinois Superior Jeweled Motor Barrel.

1930 — A. C. BECKEN

$200.00

⑥

Above model furnished in 10K yellow gold filled case. With double sunk glass enamel dial heavy arabic figures, also furnished with Montgomery double sunk glass enamel dial, heavy arabic figures or Butler center silvered dial.

This case may be furnished with either plain or engraved back.

Consumer price, $70.00
Engraved Back
Consumer price, $72.00

Prices quoted are consumer prices. For cost to dealer see current Illinois Price List.

SINCE 1870 AT
SPRINGFIELD, ILLINOIS

21 JEWEL RAILROAD WATCHES

60 Hour .. 6 Position .. Motor Barrel

SEE PAGE 4
$135.00

The Bunn Special

$135.00

Movement Specifications

16 size   21 Jewel   Three-Quarter Plate Model
21 selected ruby and sapphire jewels; adjusted to 6 positions heat, cold and isochronism; solid gold raised jewel settings; hardened and tempered compensating balance with Breguet hairspring; double roller escapement; hardened and tempered beveled and polished steel escape wheel; positive micrometric screw regulator; safety recoil click; Illinois Superior Motor Barrel with 60 Hour mainspring. Fitted, timed and rated in cases at the factory.

Special Design Case

THE cases, designed by the leading manufacturers, are the result of their years of experience in the making of fine watch cases. These movements are fitted, timed and rated in their cases at the factory. Both styles of cases are made with screw back and bezel, the metal used being much thicker than is usually found in standard 16 size cases. The bows are absolutely non-pull-out, and pendant contains a special dust-proof feature, making it impossible for dust or dirt to work through into the movement.

①

First Model in 14K white or green gold filled Wadsworth case, showing heavy Arabic figure dial, furnished in double sunk glass enamel or with Butler silvered center.

Consumer price, $65.00
Engraved Back
Consumer price, $67.00

②

First Model in 14K white or green gold filled Wadsworth case, showing Montgomery numerical dial.

Consumer price, $65.00
Engraved Back
Consumer price, $67.00

$130.00

③

First Model in 10K yellow gold filled Wadsworth case, showing heavy Arabic figure dial, furnished in double sunk glass enamel dial, or with Butler silvered center. Also with Montgomery numerical dial, if desired.

Consumer price, $60.00
Engraved Back
Consumer price, $62.00

1930 — A. C. BECKEN

The Bunn Special 21 jewel movement in all cases illustrated on this page.

See movement specifications above

Six-Sixty   Model 29

Bunn Special

Model shown furnished in 14K filled white or green gold, and 10K filled natural gold. Dial shown to the left is heavy railroad Arabic figure dial; dial to right is Montgomery numerical dial. Either furnished in double sunk glass enamel, or silvered dial with Butler center.

10K gold filled, Consumer price, $60.00   **④**
14K gold filled, Consumer price, $65.00   **⑤**
Engraved Back
10K gold filled, Consumer price, $62.00   **⑥**
14K gold filled, Consumer price, $67.00   **⑦**

$130.00
130.00
140.00
140.00

MODEL 29

MODEL 29

Prices quoted are consumer prices.
For cost to dealer see current Illinois Price List.

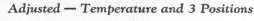

THE 19 JEWEL DISPATCHER

1930 — A. C. BECKEN

SEE PAGE 4

Adjusted — Temperature and 3 Positions

IN THE more strenuous occupations of the commercial world there is a very apparent and recognized need for a durable, dependable and accurate timepiece. Illinois to provide for this watch has builded into the Dispatcher, the sturdiness and appearance of railroad grades. Though it will not pass time inspection its 19 jeweled adjusted movement will give that accurate time-keeping service so essential to the men of our modern industry. It is supplied in cases of either 14K white or 10K natural gold filled. A very rugged and sturdy effect is given to the case by a knurled bezel and back also by the sweep of the bow which is absolutely non-pull-out. The pendant is also dust-proof protecting the movement from dirt and grit.

10K yellow gold filled. Consumer price, $40.00
14K white gold filled. Consumer price, $45.00

Furnished with plain or engraved backs.

① ② $65.00 $60.00

$40.00

③

19 jewels; adjusted to temperature and three positions; spring tempered compensating balance; double roller escapement; sapphire jewels; steel escape wheel; rounded arm train wheels; gold center wheel; Breguet hairspring; patent regulator; safety recoil click.

COMMERCIAL MOVEMENTS

WATCH MUST BE EXTRA FINE OR BETTER AND RUNNING

The movements illustrated and described below are all high-grade accurate and dependable timepieces. They are not sold as complete watches but may be readily fitted in standard make cases of any design by wholesalers or retailers, thus affording an unlimited assortment of cases to choose from.

16 Size Movements

④ $40.00

No. 169 19 Jewels 16 Size
Open face   Lever Set
Consumer price, $32.50

19 jewels; adjusted to temperature and three positions; spring tempered compensating balance; double roller escapement; sapphire jewels; steel escape wheel; rounded arm train wheels; gold center wheel; Breguet hairspring; patent regulator; recoil click; double sunk or silvered dial.

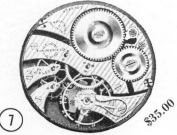

$30.00 ⑤

No. 167 17 Jewels 16 Size
Open face
Consumer price, $24.00

17 jewels; polished settings; adjusted to temperature; hardened compensating balance; double roller escapement; steel escape wheel; rayed center wheel; Breguet hairspring; patent micrometric screw regulator; safety pinion; rayed winding wheels; safety recoil click; white enamel or silvered dial.

12 Size Movements

⑥ $40.00

21 Jewel   No. 121   Open Face
Consumer price, $38.00

21 jewels; adjusted to temperature and 3 positions; compensating balance; double roller escapement; steel escape wheel; sapphire jewels; gold strata beveled and polished center wheel; Breguet hairspring; patent regulator; safety pinion; concaved and polished winding wheels; recoil click; damaskeened in a striped pattern.

⑦ $35.00

19 Jewel   No. 129   O. F.
Consumer price, $32.50

19 jewels; adjusted to temperature and three positions; spring tempered compensating balance; double roller escapement; sapphire jewels; steel escape wheel; rounded arm train wheels; gold center wheel; Breguet hairspring; recoil click.

⑧ $30.00

17 Jewel   No. 127   Open Face
Consumer price, $24.00

17 jewels; oreide settings; adjusted to temperature; spring tempered compensating balance; double roller escapement; steel escape wheel; sapphire jewels; rayed center wheel; Breguet hairspring; patent micrometric screw regulator; safety pinion; rayed winding wheels; safety recoil click; damaskeened in a striped pattern.

Prices quoted are consumer prices. For cost to dealer see current Illinois Price List.

12 Size, Special 19-Jewel Illinois 14k Gold Filled

COMPLETE IN FINE DISPLAY BOX. RETAILS FOR $40.00

White 14k Filled Design No. 15

①

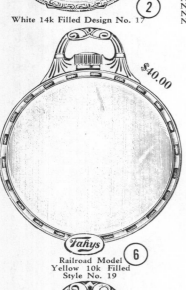

White 14k Filled Design No. 17

②

PRICE $40.00

Illinois Special

A. C. BECKEN — 1930

CASES SHOULD BE EXTRA FINE OR BETTER

③

SPECIAL

Nineteen jewels. Adjusted to temperature, three positions and isochronism; compensating balance; double roller escapement; sapphire pallets and roller-jewel; steel escape wheel; gold center wheel, Brequet hair spring; patent regulator; safety screw center pinion; safety recoil click; concaved and polished winding wheels. Complete in 14k filled assorted engraved cases.

No. 5000   12 size, 19-jewel Illinois, with case design No. 15 . . . . $48.30
No. 5001   12 size, 19-jewel Illinois, with case design No. 16 . . . . 48.30
No. 5002   12 size, 19-jewel Illinois, with case design No. 17 . . . . $55.00 . . . 48.30
No. 5003   12 size, 19-jewel Illinois, with case design No. 18 . . . . 46.30

White or Green 14k Filled Design No. 16

④

White or Green 14k Filled Design No. 18
Specify White or Green when ordering.

⑤

16 Size, Special, 19 and 21-Jewel Illinois Movements and Complete Watches

PRICES EACH
WHITE AND GREEN GOLD FILLED
Where Watches are Illustrated with White and Green Cases, Specify Style Wanted When Ordering

$40.00

Railroad Model Yellow 10k Filled Style No. 19

⑥

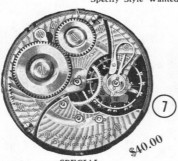

$40.00   ⑦ $30.00   ⑧

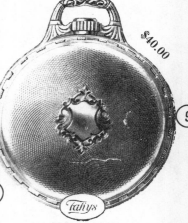

$40.00

Railroad Model Yellow 10k Filled Style No. 20

⑨

SPECIAL
21 Jewels, Adjusted 3 Positions
21 jewels; adjusted to temperature and three positions; spring tempered compensating balance with timing screws; double roller escapement; sapphire pallets and roller jewel; steel escape wheel; rounded arm train wheels; gold center wheel; Breguet hairspring; patent regulator; recoil click; double sunk dial.
Prices for Movements Only.
No. 5004   21 jewel, 16 size. O. F.
Each $39.00

SPECIAL
19 Jewels, Adjusted 3 Position
19 jewels; adjusted to temperature and three positions; spring tempered compensating balance with timing screws; double roller escapement; sapphire pallets and roller jewel; steel escape wheel; rounded arm train wheels; gold center wheel; Breguet hairspring; patent regulator; recoil click; double sunk dial.
Prices for Movements Only.
No. 5005   19 jewel, 16 size. O. F.
Each $33.00

ABOVE MOVEMENTS COMPLETE IN 10K FILLED FAHYS CASES AS ILLUSTRATED

No. 5006   21-jewel Illinois, yellow 10k filled, Railroad model, open face, case No. 19 . . . . $50.70
No. 5007   21-jewel Illinois, yellow 10k filled, Railroad model, open face, case No. 20 . . . . $80.00 . . . . 52.00
No. 5008   21-jewel Illinois, yellow 10k filled, Railroad model, open face, case No. 21 . . . . 52.70
No. 5009   21-jewel Illinois, yellow 10k filled, Railroad model, open face, case No. 22 . . . . 52.70
No. 5010   19-jewel Illinois, yellow 10k filled, Railroad model, open face, case No. 19 . . . . 44.70
No. 5011   19-jewel Illinois, yellow 10k filled, Railroad model, open face, case No. 20 . . . . $70.00 . . . . 46.00
No. 5012   19-jewel Illinois, yellow 10k filled, Railroad model, open face, case No. 21 . . . . 46.70
No. 5013   19-jewel Illinois, yellow 10k filled, Railroad model, open face, case No. 22 . . . . 46.70

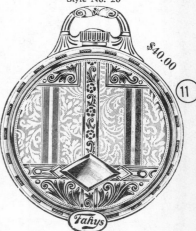

$40.00

Railroad Model Yellow 10k Filled Style No. 21

⑩

$40.00

Railroad Model Yellow 10k Filled Style No. 22

⑪

SEE PAGE 4

THE MARQUIS-AUTOCRAT

12 SIZE THIN MODEL

17 Jewels.   Adjusted 3 Positions

$60.00

$60.00

SMARTLY attractive, modern design, dependable accuracy, Illinois workmanship at its best --- all at a reasonable price. This well describes the Marquis-Autocrat line.

Of course, this fine watch has all the advantages of Illinois design; the Illinois Motor Barrel, the adjustments to three positions, heat, cold and isochronism. Nowhere can be found such value as in the Marquis-Autocrat.

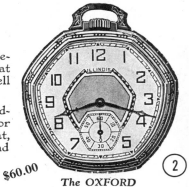

① The CUSHION

Furnished in engraved or plain bezel, 14K white gold filled case. Silvered finish dial with etched Roman polished gilded numerals. Fitted with Marquis-Autocrat movement.
Consumer price, $55.00

SPECIFICATIONS—MARQUIS-AUTOCRAT

The Marquis-Autocrat contains 17 selected ruby and sapphire jewels. Adjusted to three positions, heat, cold and isochronism; has special quality tempered and hardened compensating balance; double roller escapement; steel escape wheel; gold center wheel; Breguet hairspring; patent regulator adjustment; concaved and polished winding wheels; Illinois Superior Motor Barrel and safety recoil click.

② The OXFORD

Furnished in engraved oxidized 14K white or green gold filled case with plain back. The dial is Butler center with etched raised polished gilded figures. Fitted with Marquis-Autocrat movement.
Consumer price, $50.00

$55.00

$60.00

$ 90.00
$100.00

③ The ETON

14K filled white gold chased case. The dependable Illinois Marquis-Autocrat movement fitted with an engraved center dial with inlaid enamel figures insures accurate and dependable time.

Consumer price, $50.00

④ The TRUSTEE

14K white or yellow gold filled case; plain back with beautiful inlaid enamel design. Fitted with the Marquis-Autocrat movement; white finish silver dial with black outline enamel figures.

Consumer price, $55.00

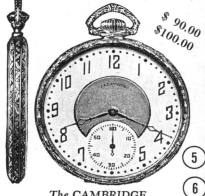

⑤ ⑥ The CAMBRIDGE

14K green solid gold case fitted with the Marquis-Autocrat movement. Special etched, lined or Butler back. Sterling silver inlaid enamel figure, raised figure or etched center dial.
Consumer price, Queen case, $75.00
Consumer price, Cap case, .. $85.00

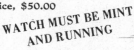

WATCH MUST BE MINT AND RUNNING

REGULAR 12 SIZE WATCHES

$45.00

$80.00
$60.00

The Autocrat
17 Jewels

Produced to meet the exacting taste of those who desire a medium priced watch that may be depended upon for accuracy and durability. It is fully guaranteed to be reliable and give the high standard service which brings enduring satisfaction. The Autocrat is equipped with compensating balance, Breguet hairspring, micrometric screw regulator and has 17 sapphire jewels, all of which have been included with the usual care which characterizes all Illinois watches.

The Dorian
19 Jewels

The Illinois Dorian initiates a new line of Illinois cased watches. The excellence of the 19 jeweled movement which is enclosed in the Dorian has long been well known to those who know fine watches. It has 19 sapphire jewels; adjusted to temperature and 3 positions; spring tempered compensating balance; double roller escapement; steel escape wheel; rounded arm train wheels; gold center wheel; Breguet hairspring; patent regulator; recoil click.

⑦ The AUTOCRAT

Fitted in chased green or white 14K gold filled case. Raised figure, luminous, engraved or special Moire dial.
Consumer price, $43.50

⑧ The DORIAN

In 14K filled white or natural gold, with the new "Rotor-Second" Dial.
Consumer price, $55.00
With regular dial.
Consumer price, $50.00

Prices quoted are consumer prices. For cost to dealer see current Illinois Price List.

1930 A. C. BECKEN — SEE PAGE 4

THE A. LINCOLN
12 Size Thin Watch
19 Jewels. Adjusted 5 Positions

BEAUTIFUL -- are these Illinois A. Lincolns. Their luxurious simplicity, their perfection in every detail, their life and color, portray the hand of a master artist in case design . . . . These qualities are carried deeper than the beautiful A. Lincoln case. Within is another luxurious simplicity, another perfection of detail, that betrays the hand of master watch technicians.

(1) $125.00

The DICTATOR
Fine 19 jewel movement fitted with 14K solid white lined back, white Butler back or Butler bezel and back. Gold case with inside cap. Sterling silver dial, applied 18K gold figures.
Consumer price, $110.00

(2) $90.00

The TRUSTEE
14K white or yellow gold filled case; plain back with beautiful inlaid enamel design. Fitted with the fine A. Lincoln movement; white finish silver dial with black outline enamel figures.
Consumer price, $75.00

MVT Only H.T.C.

(3) $135.00

The BARRISTER
Fine 19 jewel movement. 14K green Butler, lined back. Solid gold case with inside cap. Sterling silver dial with applied 18K gold figures.
Consumer price, $110.00

SPECIFICATIONS—A. LINCOLN

19 ruby and sapphire jewels, raised settings; adjusted to temperature, five positions and isochronism; special quality hardened and tempered center arm compensating balance; double roller escapement; sapphire roller and pallet jewels; beveled steel escape wheel; gold center wheel; conical pivots; patent micrometric screw regulator; best quality Breguet hairspring; recoil click; Illinois Superior Jeweled Motor Barrel; concaved and polished winding wheels damaskeened in bright striped pattern; black enameled lettering

(4) $135.00

The BARRISTER
14K green solid gold, full chased center and bezels, inside cap case with plain or lined back. A 19 jeweled movement with new process etched dial with Roman figures.
Consumer price, $100.00

(5) $125.00

The PIONEER
14K green or white gold, full chased inside cap case with lined back. The movement is a 19 jewel Illinois with special etched center dial.
Consumer price, $75.00

(6) $120.00

The ACORN
14K filled green gold inside cap case, silver etched or embossed raised figure dials. The 19 jewel movement assures dependable accuracy.
Consumer price, $75.00

Prices quoted are consumer prices. For cost to dealer see current Illinois Price List.

(7) $125.00

The PIONEER
14K filled green or white gold, full chased inside cap case with plain back, fitted with a 19 jeweled movement. Special etched center dial.
Consumer price, $75.00

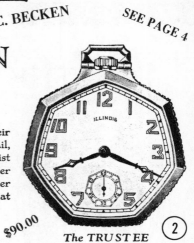

1937 OSKAMP–NOLTING CO.

Movement: 23 Jewels, Rubies and Sapphires, Inner-terminal Hairspring, Winding Indicator, Jeweled Main-wheel, Steel Safety Barrel, Adjusted to Temperature and Six Positions.

MONTGOMERY DIALS

Can Be Had on All Makes of Railroad Watches Illustrated at No Extra Cost.

COMPLETE WATCH MUST BE MINT CONDITION & RUNNING

$250.00

① **WALTHAM "VANGUARD"**

No. 17266 . . . . $79.50
16 Size, 23 Jewel Waltham Vanguard Movement. Winding Indicator. Adjusted to 6 Positions. 10k Yellow Gold Filled Case. Butler Finish.

$135.00

② **WALTHAM "VANGUARD"**

No. 17267 . . . . $69.00
16 Size, 23 Jewel Waltham Vanguard Movement. Winding Indicator. Adjusted to 6 Positions. 10k Yellow Rolled Gold Plate Case, Engraved Border. Plain Back.

14th Model—21J Open Face, 60 Hour Bunn Special—Grade 161
23J Open Face, 60 Hour Bunn Special—Grade 163
15th Model—21J Open Face, 60 Hour Bunn Special, Elinvar—Grade 161A
23J Open Face, 60 Hour Bunn Special, Elinvar—Grade 163A

BUNN SPECIAL
ELINVAR RAILROAD WATCHES

Illinois Bunn Special Elinvar Railroad Watches are acknowledged to have the greatest improvements in history of watch-making to insure more dependable time under adverse conditions. A watch with rustless hairspring and balance and not disturbed by magnetic influences or temperature variations. These improvements supplement the famous 60-hour mainspring, which is an exclusive feature of Illinois Railroad Watches.

"Exclusive license under U. S. Patents No. 1,313,291, dated August 19, 1919, and No. 1,454,473, dated May 8, 1923."

SIXTY HOURS
SIX POSITIONS

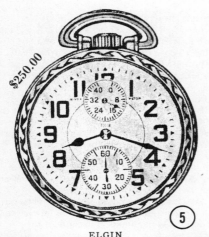

163
163-A
$275.00

③ **ILLINOIS**

No. 17268 . . . . $86.00
16 Size, 23 Jewel Illinois Bunn Special Elinvar Movement. 10k Yellow Gold Filled, Railroad Model Case. Butler Finish.

THESE 2 ILLINOIS WATCHES WERE BEING FINISHED AND SOLD BY HAMILTON AT THIS TIME.

161
161-A
$200.00

④ **ILLINOIS**

No. 17269 . . . . $79.50
16 Size, 21 Jewel Illinois Bunn Special Elinvar Movement. 10k Yellow Gold Filled, Railroad Model Case. Butler Finish.

WATCHES ON THIS PAGE ARE IN FACTORY CASES

On the "Crack" Trains of America's Leading Railroads — Where Seconds Mean Safety — You Will Find Engineers Depend on ELGIN RAILROAD WATCHES. Elgin's Have Special Features Found in No Other Make of Railroad Watch.

$250.00

⑤ **ELGIN**

No. 17270 . . . . $92.00
16 Size, 23 Jewel B. W. Raymond Movement. 9 Adjustments, 6 to Positions. 14k White Gold Filled Case. Butler Finish. Winding Indicator.

$100.00

⑥ **ELGIN**

No. 17271 . . . . $85.00
16 Size, 21 Jewel B. W. Raymond Movement. 8 Adjustments, 5 to Positions. 10k Yellow Gold Filled Case. Butler Finish.

18-S, 24 ruby jewels, adj. BUNN Special. Mint mvt. 1,605,963. DS antique style arabic RR. Mint dial, mint Naw Co. 20 yr. YGF, OF decorated case. Watch is mint. $450.00

18-S, 24 ruby jewels, mint nickel full plate Mvt. 1,538,737. Marked adjusted Bunn Special, Springfield, Ill. Mint DS glass enamel bold antique arabic dial except chip at center hole. Mint plus 14 K solid YG double backed, fully hinged, heavy weight, engine turned, OF case. Beautiful watch and case looks original. $550.00

18-S OF 21 ruby jewels, Bunn Special. Mint nickel mvt. 17,424,92. LS adj. temp. 6 pos. Isochronism. Gold cups and balance screws. Mint DS. arabic antique glass dial with hands. Extra fine Philadelphia YGF OF case. Guaranteed 20 years. $140.00

18-S, 21-J, OF. A Lincoln. Mint nickel mvt. 2,203,826. LS. Adj. 5 pos. DR. Extra fine DS arabic red track RR dial and hands. 2 minor hairlines. Extra fine SWC Co. 25 yr. YGF screw B&B case. Light wear on light hand engraved back. $155.00

18-S 17-J, OF. Mint 2 tone nickel full plate, adj., mvt. 1,415,613. Gold cups and balance weights. Slight discoloration on 1 corner of barrel bridge but a beautiful mvt. Fine orig. DS Porc. arabic black track RR dial and hands. Minor hairlines. Dial originally fastened to mvt. with screws at 3 and 8. CO & R Fine excelsior silverode. Screw B&B orig. looking case. $135.00

18-S 15-J OF (model 4 Railroader) Mint gilded mvt. 701,644. CA 1896. Transition key wind, chalmers pat. 12-19-82. Regulator, train engine engraved on plate. Running fine. Mint SS original Roman outside 13 to 24 inside (Canadian RR) dial and hands. Fine Fahys No . 1 screw B&B oresilver OF case. $150.00

18-S 15-J 2nd model, fine nickel full plate Hunting Mvt. 140,294,1877, marked Brunswick Watch Co., Mo., Adj. Standard mint DS glass roman dial with black outside track marked American & Bowman in script. Fine Keystone Star YGF box hinge, hand engraven decorated, hunting case. Solid case with light wear. $100.00

18-S OF 17-J (Grade 89). Mint plus beautiful 2 tone nickel full plate mvt. 1,241,228 CA 1900. adjusted LS gilt trim and antique letters. Gold filled. Mint orig. DS Porc. arabic red track dial and hands. Extra fine Wadsworth Referee, 20 yr. YGF, screw B&B plain polish OF RR case. $110.00

16-S Sangamo 23-J mtr. barrel 60 hr. Mvt. 4,736,825. Sangamo Special 14 K solid gold Wadsworth case. Mint condition. $225.00

16-S, 23-J Sangamo, Mint ¾ nickel plate with gilt letters and gold train mvt. 2,307,928. Almost mint old style DS dial, fine B&B Royal 20 yr. case. $140.00

16-S OF 23-J 60 Hour Bunn Special mint nickel mvt. 5,182,157. LS adj. temp. 6 pos. Mint DS Illinois glass RR dial marked "Bunn Special 23 Jewel 60 Hour." Fine Star Watch Case Co. Slettar 10 K Y RGP. OF case. $200.00

16-S 23-J 60 HOUR BUNN SPECIAL 6 pos LS Mint RR mvt. 5456734. Finished by Hamilton & marked 163 A ELINVAR. Perfect orig. DS dial and hands marked ILLINOIS 23 J BUNN SPECIL. Extra fine J Boss 10 K YGF lightly decorated RR case. $225.00

16-S OF 21-J Elinvar Bunn Special 161A. Mint nickel mvt. 5481486. LS adj. temp. 6 pos. 60 Hour motor barre. Mint DS glass RR dial and hands Extremely fine Keystone 14 K white GF. Illinois Bunn Special Model 206 OF case. $200.00

16-S 21-J Sangamo Special. Mint plus nickel bridge mvt. 2,575,591. Adj. temp., six positions. Gold train, cups and weights. Gilt lettering. Mint plus original DS Montgomery dial. Factory new Keystone J. Boss 10 K YGF screw B&B heavy RR OF case. $140.00

16-S 21-J Sangamo. ¾ 2 tone nickel plates, Mvt. 1,523,207. Small hairline and chip in original dial, 10 K YGF J. Boss OF RR case in find condition. $85.00

16-S Sante Fe Special 21-J, adj. DR. LS, mvt. 4,809,731. Mint. Dial DS Montgomery, in a new 10 K YGF J. Boss case. $150.00

16-S 21-J BUNN Special. Mint nickel Mvt. 3,581,339. Double rachet, adj. temp. and 6 pos. DR, LS, gold train. Near mint DS, bold glass RR dial. Extra fine snap B&B Keystone base metal white RR case. Cln, oiled, adj.. $90.00

16-S, 21-J Adj. 5 pos. A. Lincoln. Mint nickel ¾ plate mvt. 3,782,461. DR LS. Gold center wheel, cups and weights. Mint bold RR dial. 10 K YGF star case. Watch looks all original and mint. $135.00

16-S OF 21-J A. Lincoln. Mint single rachet mvt. 2,081,833. DR LS Adj. 5 pos. gold center wheel, cups and balance screws. 2 rust spots on barrel. Fine solid Keystone base metal screw B&B RR OF case. $75.00

16-S OF 17-J Model 305. Extra fine bridge mvt. 3,648,743. Fine arabic DS red track dial. Hairling. Fine B&B favorite 25 yr. green GF screw B&B OF case. Some brass showing. $40.00

16-S OF 17 Ruby Jewel. Grade 187. Extremely fine nickel bar type mvt. 1572531. LS adj. temp 6 pos. Isochronism. Extra fine DS glass dial with two small hairlines. Extra fine Keystone J. Boss 10 K YGF OF case. $125.00

12-S 23-J 5 pos Beautiful special Grade 410. Mint mvt. 2589651. Mint DS porc dial. Mint heavy AWC CO. 14 K SYG. Double back case. Dial case & mvt. marked BRENNER WATCH CO. YOUNGSTOWN OHIO. $250.

12-S 23-J OF Grade 410. Mint high grade nickel mvt. 4206999; Gold train cups balance secres, motor barrel DR Adj. 5 pos. Beautiful Damaskeened. Mint orig. decorated dial and hands. Mint 10 K RG Illinois snap B&B OF case. $210.00

12-S 17-J "The Marquis". Mint nickel ¾ plates marked adj. 3 pos. 17-J motor barrel. Mvt. 4082728. Beautiful near mint brushed silver dial with raised gold numberals and hands. Mint plus all over. Engraved Marquis Model 25 yr. WGF case. $80.00

12-S OF 19-J Mint nickel mvt. 1901575. Pendent set adj 3 pos. Marked "Ariston USA" on mvt. Ard dial. Manufactured for "Marshall Field & Co. Mint DS glass dial with hands. Mint double backed Ariston 14 K M. F. Ard Co. OF case with presentation in back. $150.00

12-S OF 21-J A. Lincoln. Extra fine nickel mvt. 3586345. Pendent set adj. 5 pos. Fine single sunk Illinois metal dial with hands. Fine Wadsworth YGF double back OF case. Warranted 25 yr. $65.00

12-S 21-J Mint ¾ same as Model 121, nickel plates marked Santa Fe Special adj. temp. & pos. 21-J Illinois Watch Co. Springfield. Double roller. 4298559. Mint flat porcelain Montgomery, sunk seconds dial marked Santa Fe Special in script and Illinois. Near mint plain polish bassine screw B&B original 20 yr. YGF OF Santa Fe Case. $110.00

6-S, 0, etc. will value about the same as Elgin or Waltham, Similar grades and cases.

Illinois Watch Company made watches for many watch companies. Illinois collectors will sometimes pay a little extra for the same grade watch with another company name on it. You can usually identify the grade either by the Damasceening pattern or plates or both.

I have in my files advertising sheets showing watches made by Illinois with the following company names. BURLINGTON WATCH CO. Chicago, Ill., value 25% less than Illinois. IOWA WATCH CO., value same or 25% better than Illinois. MONARCH 16-S by Illinois same value. MARSHALL FIELD AND CO. same value. WASHINGTON WATCH CO. higher grades 25% or more. BENJAMIN FRANKLIN. These are very good and scarce. Look for 25 jewel single rachet in 16-size, value $1000.00 and 26 jewel 18-size, full plate, value $1000.00. SANTA FE WATCH CO., 25% to 50% more. PAILLARD NON MAGNETIC WATCH CO OF AMERICA, 25% more. SEARS ROEBUCK & CO. same value. BALL WATCH CO., Cleveland, Ohio, PENNSYLVANIA SPECIALS, PLYMOUTH WATCH CO. (sears), ILLINOIS CENTRAL WATCH CO. I'm sure there are others.

A word of caution here! Some of these companies also had other companies make watches for them, so not all watches with these names will be Illinois.

The Illinois Watch Co. was a great company to advertise. They put dozens of names on their watch movements. I doubt if you could ever complete a collection and is very popular with collectors because of this.

$100.00

Buck Rogers Pocket Watch. Heres a watch every youngster will want. America's adventurous faforites, Buck Rogers and Wilma are shown in action on the brilliant colored dial. The hands are shaped like cosmic rays. Ruggedly built like Buck's Rocket ship,

NEW HAVEN 1935

$100.00

Moon Mullins and Kayo. Those well known comical characters reproduced in colors on the dial.

$100.00

Skeezix, reproduced in colors on the dial. A watch that will appeal to the youngsters. Nickel plated plain polished case. Unbreakable crystal. Guaranteed movement.
No. 1W15. Each............. .75

BY — 1934
Ingersoll

Already 1½ million children are learning punctuality with Mickey Mouse Watches—and parents are as happy about it as the children. The movements are standard Ingersoll make—dependable and sturdy. Pocket watch and fob, $1.50 in a gift box.

"I KEEP TIME FOR 1½ MILLION HAPPY CHILDREN"

$150.00

MICKEY MOUSE WATCHES

$60.00 **$60.00** **$60.00**

NEW THIN 1935 MODELS
New Haven Wrist Watches, with Orphan Annie, Smitty, or Dick Tracy in bright snappy colors on the dial. Real timekeepers, thin models, curved backs to fit the wrist, unbreakable crystals, detachable real leather bands, in colors to match the watch. Each in a handsome display box.
No. 11W30. Orphan Annie. Each............. 2.25
No. 11W31. Smitty. Each 2.25
No. 11W36. Dick Tracy. Each 2.25

$125.00

MICKEY MOUSE WRIST WATCH, complete with bracelet, now only $2.95. The demand is so heavy that there is often a scarcity. Buy for Christmas now.

$100.00

MICKEY MOUSE ALARM CLOCK, $1.50. Teaches early rising to children. Standard Ingersoll clock and alarm mechanisms.

$100.00 **$75.00** **$100.00**

"THREE LITTLE PIGS". As delightful as Mickey. Pocket watch and fob, $1.50. Wrist watch, $2.95. Alarm clock, $1.50.

Comic character watches are very hard to place a value on. The pocket models are more hard to find than the wrist. I have had all kinds of figures quoted to me up to $350.00 on a Mickey Mouse pocket at a California auction. I'm not to well versed on the values of this type watch collectible. I find that people who collect these usually do not collect other watches. I have shown the date of these catalogs to give you a chance to see how old your watch is. I personally feel this is an area where you should watch your step. The original dials will fit any watch of the same model movement made by the same company. There is at this time a company or companies reproducing both pocket and wrist character dials and they are being put on old movements. I would seem to me that $125.00 for Mickey Mouse wrist and $150.00 or better for a pocket watch that is all original, running and fine or better condition is what I will suggest. Always keep in mind that they have been produced continually since they were first introduced and new ones are still a big seller. Other comic characters are valued less.

ELGIN NATIONAL WATCH CO.'S MOVEMENTS.

K–$35.00
10 Size
Class 46
15 Jewels
Gilded

K–$25.00
10 Size
Class 47
15 Jewels
Gilded

K–$20.00
10 Size
Class 48
7 Jewels
Gilded

K–$20.00
10 Size
Class 48
11 Jewels
Gilded

CUTS OF

ELGIN MOVEMENTS

———

HOW TO BUY AN ELGIN
WATCH.

———

The top 4 movements on this page are 10 size and very
hard to find a case for. This limits their value unless you
have a case or need a part. Add $100.00 if cased in 20 year
hunting case in extra fine or better.

I feel key wind American watches are
sleepers and should bring more than
they do. They are the antique American
watches.

For the purpose of guarding the public against the worthless imitations of our goods that are sometimes sold, we herewith present *fac simile* representations of the upper plates of the various grades of Elgin Watches manufactured by the National Watch Company now in market. Purchasers will please note that no movement purporting to be of Elgin manufacture is genuine unless the trade mark upon it corresponds with some one of the cuts shown upon these pages.

Each trade mark represents a distinct grade and quality of watch, and all watches of the *same trade mark* are of the *same general quality* and of the *same price*, with the exception of movements marked "Adjusted." These constitute a distinct grade, and are of higher price than the *unadjusted* movements. *The prices of the various movements in cases the Company cannot furnish*, as the prices vary with weight and style of case selected, and *the Company do not engage in the manufacture or supplying of cases*, but movements simply, *sold only to Dealers*, who case, regulate and otherwise prepare them for their customers. Purchasers are advised to call upon the dealer known or recommended to them nearest their place of residence. Deception will be less likely to be practiced in style of movement and quality of case, and greater interest will be taken in putting the watch in good condition before purchase, and in keeping it in good condition after purchase, than would be done by a dealer living at a distance, who cannot be held personally accountable for his sales. Watch buyers, as a rule, should *avoid unknown dealers, traders and C. O. D. advertisers.* The lower their prices, and the more plausible their advertisements, the greater the risk of the purchaser. *Brass Watches*, called *Oroide, Swiss imitation of American Watches*, worthless as timekeepers, or, in some instances, *genuine American Watches in plated or pewter cases*, are sold by hundreds to people in all parts of the country, who are being duped by unscrupulous advertisers, and led by them to purchase by the offer of *low prices;* a sorry comfort for the possession of a worthless article. Parties who buy *Watches of known trade marks* and *established reputation* upon the recommendation of dealers who have a character to sustain, are saved from swindles of the nature referred to, and, as a rule, will be satisfied with their purchases.

Dealers throughout the country are now supplied with the Elgin Watches, and are offering them to the public in genuine Gold and Silver Cases at very low prices.

Call on your Jeweler and ask to see them.

**ELGIN WATCH GRADES ARE SHOWN EITHER
BY A NAME ON THE PLATE OR A NUMBER, OR
WHERE THE GRADE IS NOT SHOWN ON THE
MOVEMENT, THE NAME OR NUMBER AT THE
BEGINNING OF THE DESCRIPTION IS THE
GRADE.**

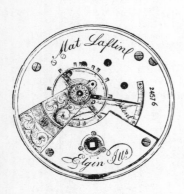

S–$30.00
K–$30.00
Size 18
Class 4
7 Jewels
Gilded

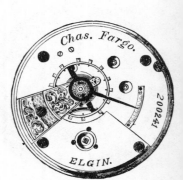

K–$30.00
Class 5
7 Jewels
Gilded

K–$30.00
Size 18
Class 4
7 Jewels
Gilded

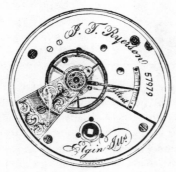

K–$40.00
18 Size
Class – 4
15 Jewels
Gilded

K= Keywind, S= Stem wind
Add $10.00 to $20.00 if MVT is Nickel.

78

READ PAGE 4 TO 7

ALL PRICES AND NOTES BY THE COMPLIER OF THIS BOOK ARE IN THIS TYPE STYLE AND THE PRICES ARE RETAIL!!

Size 18
Class 1
Gilded
K—15 Jewels $50.00
K—17 Jewels $50.00
add $20.00 if nickel

Size 18
Class 1
Gilded
K—15 Jewels $50.00
K—17 Jewels $50.00
add $20.00 if nickel

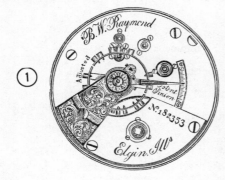

Of the movements represented we desire to call especial attention to the two grades of the "B. W. Raymond" movement, also to the "H. Z. Culver" and "H. H. Taylor" adjusted. Particular attention is given in the manufacture of these movements to their adjustment and regulation, and it is believed that they are, without exception, *the best full plate watches made in this country.* They have been subjected to every known test in their use upon land and water, upon the rail and in shops, and as a result they rank to-day, with the dealers who have sold them, and the purchasers who are wearing them, as among the finest time-keepers in the market. Testimonials could be printed from hundreds of disinterested dealers, and from thousands of leading citizens, as to the truth of the above, if considered necessary. To railroad men, who may be considering as to the watch most reliable for their use, we would say that the *Elgin Watches* are purchased by the Pennsylvania Railroad Co., and placed in the hands of their Engineers as a part of their engine equipment. Also, that over twenty of the leading Superintendents of the largest Railroad Companies in the United States have given written testimonials that they consider the Elgin Watch the best Railroad time-keeper in use. So far as *anything* short of actual personal testing of the watch can be satisfactory, these facts should be so. Please note the word *adjusted* engraved upon the plates of all adjusted movements.

———

THE ENTIRE LIST OF

Full Plate Movements

Will be upon the market

At the date of this Almanac

JAN'Y 1, 1875,

AS STEM WINDERS

OR AS

KEY WINDERS.

———

Elgin National Watch Co.,

CHICAGO.

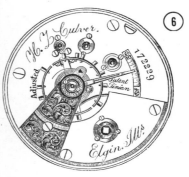

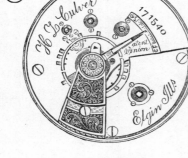
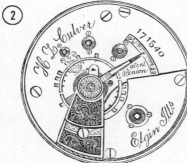

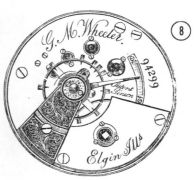

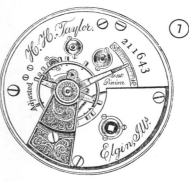

S—$50.00
K—$50.00
Size 18
Class 2
15 Jewels
Gilded

K—$40.00
Size 17
Class 15
7 Jewels
Gilded

S—$30.00
K—$30.00
18 Size
Class 5
11 Jewels
Gilded

S—$50.00
K—$50.00
Size 18
Class 2
15 Jewels
Gilded

S—$50.00
K—$50.00
Size 18
Class 3
15 Jewels
Gilded
Add $20.00 if
Nickel

S—$45.00
K—$45.00
Size 18
Class 4
15 Jewels
Gilded

79

ELGIN NATIONAL WATCH CO'S MOVEMENTS.

18 Size, Full Plate Movements.

1888 SUPPLY CATALOG

18 Size, Full Plate, Key Wind.

No. 97. Nameless, 7 jewels, quick train, patent safety pinion _____ $ 7.00 $20.00

18 Size, Full Plate, Hunting, Stem Wind.

B. W. RAYMOND. Nickel, 15 jewels, 4 pairs in settings, patent regulator, adjusted, Breguet hair spring _____ $40.00 $50.00
B. W. RAYMOND. Gilded, 15 jewels, 4 pairs in settings, patent regulator, adjusted, Breguet hair spring _____ 35.00 $50.00
H. H. TAYLOR. Nickel, 15 jewels, 4 pairs in settings, patent regulator, adjusted, Rreguet hair spring _____ 30.00 $50.00
H. H. TAYLOR. Gilded, 15 jewels, 4 pairs in settings, patent regulator, adjusted Breguet hair spring _____ 25.00 $50.00
G. M. WHEELER. Nickel, 15 jewels, 4 pairs in settings, patent regulator _____ 18.00 $25.00
G. M. WHEELER. Gilded, 15 "   4   "   "   "   " _____ 17.00 $20.00
No. 80. Nameless. Gilded (same as H. H. Taylor)_____ 25.00 $40.00
 " 82.   "   "   "   G. M. Wheeler)_____ 17.00 $20.00
 " 10.   "   "   11 jewels, 4 upper holes_____ 12.50 $20.00
 " 96.   "   "   7   "   quick train, patent safety pinion _____ 10.00 $10.00
 " 33.   "   Nickel, (same as H. H. Taylor)_____ 30.00 $40.00
 " 103.   "   "   15 jewels, 4 pairs in settings, patent regulator ___ 18.00 $20.00
 " 102.   "   "   11   "   4 upper holes_____ 14.00 $15.00

18 Size, Full Plate, Open Face, Pendant Set, Stem Wind.

B. W. RAYMOND. Gilded (description above)_____ $35.00 $40.00
H. H. TAYLOR.   "   "   "   _____ 25.00 $40.00
G. M. WHEELER.   "   "   "   _____ 17.00 $20.00
No. 76. Nameless.   "   (same as H. H. Taylor)_____ 25.00 $35.00
 " 75.   "   "   "   G. M. Wheeler)_____ 17.00 $20.00
 " 74.   "   "   "   No. 10)_____ 12.50 $15.00
 " 73.   "   "   "   "   96)_____ 16.00 $10.00
G. M. WHEELER. Nickel, 15 jewels, 4 pairs in settings, patent regulator _____ 18.00 $25.00
No. 44. Nameless.   "   (same as G. M. Wheeler, Nickel) _____ 18.00 $20.00
 " 43.   "   "   11 jewels, 4 upper holes_____ 14.00 $15.00

16 Size, ¾ Plate, Stem Wind.

No. 104. Gilt Movement, 7 jewels (open face pendant set) _____ $10.00 $15.00
 " 92.   "   11   "   _____ 13.50 $15.00
 "   2.   "   13   "   3 pairs in settings, patent regulator ___ 20.00 $15.00
 "   3.   "   15   "   4   "   "   "   "   adjusted, Breguet hair spring 31.00 $20.00
 "   4. Nickel movement, 15 jewels, 4 pairs in settings, patent regulator, adjusted, Breguet hair spring _____ 40.00 $30.00
                                                                                              $40.00

16 Size, Interchangeable, ¾ Plate, Stem Wind and Set.

No. 50. Nickel movement, 15 jewels, 4 pairs in settings, patent regulator, adjusted, Breguet hair spring _____ $55.00 $50.00
 " 72. Nickel movement, 21 ruby jewels in raised gold settings, patent regulator, adjusted, Breguet hair spring _____ 170.00 $250.00

16 Size, Interchangeable, ¾ Plate, Bridge Movement.

No. 86. Nickel movement, 15 jewels, 4 pairs in settings, patent regulator, adjusted, Breguet hair spring _____ $64.00 $75.00

Ladies' 6 Size, Stem Wind, Lever Set Movements.

No. 95. Gilt movement, 7 jewels _____ $12.00 $15.00
 " 94.   "   "   11   "   _____ 14.50 $15.00
 " 65.   "   "   13   "   3 pairs in settings_____ 18.00 $15.00
 " 101. Nickel   "   11   "   _____ 15.50 $20.00
 " 45.   "   "   13   "   3 pairs in settings_____ 20.00 $20.00
 " 67.   "   "   15   "   4   "   "   _____ 27.00 $20.00
 " 71.   "   "   17 fine ruby jewels, 5 pairs in settings, adjusted _____ 60.00 $25.00
                                                                                              $140.00

ELGIN NATIONAL WATCH CO.'S MOVEMENTS.

18 Size Movements.

READ PAGE 4 TO 7

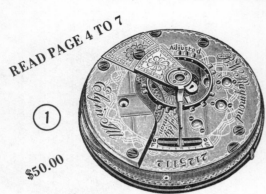 $50.00

 $50.00

$50.00

$25.00

B. W. RAYMOND. NICKEL.   **H. H. TAYLOR. NICKEL.**   **G. M. WHEELER. NICKEL.**

Corresponding Grades in Nameless, Open Face and Gilt.

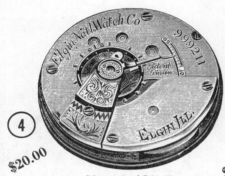 $20.00

 $10.00

 $15.00

No. 10. GILT.   **No. 96. GILT.**   **No. 102. HALF NICKEL.**

Corresponding Grades in Open Face.

16 Size Movements.

 $10.00

 $40.00

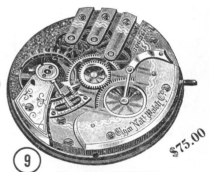 $75.00

No. 92. GILT.   **No. 4. NICKEL.**   **No. 86. NICKEL.**

Quotations of Full Line on Opposite Page.

6 Size Movements.

 $15.00

 $15.00

 $15.00

No. 94. GILT.   **No. 45. NICKEL.**   **No. 67. NICKEL.**

Quotations of Full Line on Opposite Page.

ELGIN NATIONAL WATCH COMPANY'S MOVEMENTS.

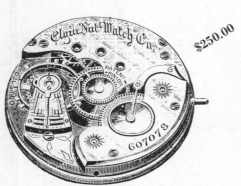

$100.00

$250.00

Nickel, 20 ruby jewels, adjusted to temperature, isochronism and positions, escapement cap jeweled, gold settings, patent regulator, Breguet hair spring, glass enameled double sunk dial.

No. 149. Hunting........ ....$45 00
No. 150. Open Face................... 45 00

Nickel, compensation balance, adjusted to heat, cold, isochronism and position, 21 extra fine red ruby jewels, raised gold settings, Breguet hair spring, patent micrometer regulator, double sunk dial, finely finished throughout, bridge interchangeable.

No. 91. 16 size...................$170 00

$250.00

$50.00

$75.00

Nickel, compensation balance, adjusted to heat, cold, isochronism and position, 21 extra fine red ruby jewels, raised gold settings, Breguet hair spring, patent micrometer regulator, double sunk dial, finely finished throughout, ¾ plate, interchangeable

No. 72 ....$170 00

Nickel, compensation balance, Breguet hair spring, adjusted, patent regulator, 15 jewels (4 pairs settings), ¾ plate, interchangeable, Hunting or Open Face.

No. 50 ....$36 00

Nickel, compensation balance, Breguet hair spring, adjusted, patent regulator, 15 jewels (4 pairs settings), bridge, interchangeable, Hunting or Open Face.

No. 86 ....$36 00

ELGIN 16-SIZE

ELGIN 10-SIZE

H.T.C.

21J—$40.00
19J—$40.00
17J—$30.00
17J—$20.00
15J—$20.00

H.T.C.

21J—$10.00
17J—$10.00
15J—$10.00

Train side of movement

LEVER SETTING			PENDANT SETTING	
21 Jewels Grade 571	19 Jewels Grade 572	17 Jewels Grade 573	17 Jewels Grade 574	15 Jewels Grade 575

15 JEWEL Grade 546	17 JEWEL Grade 542	21 JEWEL Grade 543

82

Elgin National Watch Co.'s Movements.

WILL FIT ANY AMERICAN CASE OF SIMILAR SIZE. 0, 6, 16 AND 18 SIZE, HUNTING AND OPEN FACE, STEM WIND.

LIST PRICES EACH.

18 SIZE, STEM WIND, HUNTING OR OPEN FACE, PENDANT SET, NAMED.

B. W. Raymond, Nickel, 17 Jewels, Adjusted Patent Regulator, D. S. Dial......$46 25
G. M. Wheeler, Nickel, 17 " " " " " 23 75
" " Gilded, 17 " " " " " 20 63

18 SIZE, STEM WIND, HUNTING, NAMELESS.

No. 149 Nickel, 20 Ruby Jewels, Adjusted to Temperature, Isochronism and
    Position, Patent Regulator, D. S. D......$62 50
No. 144 Nickel (same as G. M. Wheeler)......23 75
No. 143 Gilt " " " 20 63
No. 169 Hunting. Nickel, 15 Jewels (4 P. Set), Pat. Reg., Com. Bal......18 13
No. 141 Gilt, 15 Jewels (4 pairs in Setting)......15 63
No. 171 Nickel, 7 Jewels, Comp. Bal., Breg. Hair-Spring......10 00
No. 96 Gilt, 7 Jewels, Compensation Balance......10 00

18 SIZE, NAMELESS, STEM WIND, PENDANT SET, OPEN FACE ONLY.

No. 150 Nickel, same as No. 149......$62 50
No. 148 " " " 144......23 75
No. 147 Gilt, " " 143......20 63
No. 170 Nickel, " " 169......18 13
No. 145 Gilt, " " 141......15 63
No. 172 Nickel, " " 171......10 00
No. 73 Gilt, " " 96......10 00

NEW MODEL.

16 SIZE, THREE-QUARTER PLATE, STEM WIND, HUNTING AND OPEN FACE, PENDANT SETTING.

Nameless, Engraved, Elgin National Watch Co.

No. 156 Hunting, Nickel, Bridge, Adjusted to Temperature and Positions, Compensation-Balance, 21 Extra Fine Red Ruby Jewels, 6 pairs Raised Gold Settings, Escapement Cap Jeweled, Cone Pivots, Micrometer Regulator, Breguet Hair-Spring, Double Sunk Soft Enamel Dial, First Quality Moon Hands, Dust Band, Thoroughly First Quality Finish......$112 50

No. 155 Nickel, ¾ plate, Adjusted to Temperature and Positions, Compensation-Balance 17 Rosy Ruby Jewels, 5 pairs Gold Settings, Micrometer Regulator, Breguet Hair Spring, Double Sunk Soft Enamel Dial, Dust Band, First Quality Moon Hands Finely Finished Throughout......50 00

No. 154 Nickel, ¾-plate, Adjusted to Temperature, Compensation-Balance, 17 Jewels, 5 pairs Settings, Micrometer Regulator, Breguet Hair-Spring, Sunk Second Soft Enamel Dial, First Quality Moon Hands, Dust Band, Thoroughly Well Finished......40 00

No. 153 Nickel, ¾-plate, Adjusted, Compensation-Balance, 17 Jewels. 5 pairs Settings, Micrometer Regulator, Breguet Hair-Spring, Sunk Second Soft Enamel Dial, First Quality Spade Hands, Dust Band......26 75

No. 152 Nickel, ¾-plate, 15 Jewels, 4 pairs Settings, Micrometer Regulator, Compensation-Balance. Breguet Hair-Spring, Sunk Second Soft Enamel Dial, Medium Spade Hands, Dust Band......19 38

No. 185 Gilt, 15 Jewels, 4 pairs Settings, Compensation-Balance, Breguet Hair-Spring, Sunk Second Soft Enamel Dial......19 38

No. 151 Gilded, ¾-plate, 7 Jewels, Breguet Hair-Spring, Compensation-Balance, Sunk Second Soft Enamel Dial, Spade Hands, Dust Band......10 63

16 SIZE, OPEN FACE, NAMELESS, PENDANT SET.

No. 162 Same as No. 156......$112 50
No. 161 " " 155......50 00
No. 160 " " 154......40 00
No. 159 " " 153......26 75
No. 158 " " 152......19 38
No. 186 " " 185......19 38
No. 157 " " 151......10 63

6 SIZE, STEM WIND, NAMELESS.

No. 176 Nickel, 17 Ruby Jewels, Adjusted, 5 pairs Raised Gold Settings, Micrometer Regulator. Polished Steel Index, Compensation Balance, Breguet Hair-Spring, Glass Enameled Dial, Finely Finished Throughout......$40 00

No. 168 Nickel, 16 Ruby Jewels, 4½ pairs Raised Setting, Micrometer Regulator, Gold Index, Compensation-Balance, Breguet Hair-Spring, Soft Enamel Dial 27 50
No. 133 Nickel, 15 Jewels, 4 pairs Settings......20 00
No. 175 Nickel, 7 Jewels, Compensation-Balance, Breguet Hair-Spring......12 50
No. 117 Gilt, 7 Jewels, Compensation-Balance......12 50

0 SIZE, ¾-PLATE.

No. 174 Nickel, same as No. 176......$40 00
No. 167 " " " 168......27 50
No. 130 " " " 121......20 00
No. 173 " " " 175......12 50
No. 109 Gilt, " " 117......12 50

6 Size.
No. 176 Hunting. Nickel, Adjusted, Compensation-Balance; 17 Fine Ruby Jewels (5 pairs Raised Gold Settings), B. H. Spring, Finely Finished Throughout......$40 00

6 Size.
No. 168 Hunting, Nickel, Compensation-Balance, Adjusted; 16 Jewels, 4½ pairs Settings......$27 50

6 Size.
No. 133 Hunting, Nickel, 15 Jewels, 4 pairs Settings......$20 00

No. 117 Hunting, Compensation-Balance, 7 Jewels, Gilt......$12 50
No. 175 Same as above, Nickel..12 50

18 Size.
Hunting or Open Face.
B. W. Raymond Nickel, 17 Jewels..$46 25 Adjusted Patent Regulator, Breguet Hair-Spring, Double Sunk Dial.

16 Size, Nameless, New Model.
No. 153 Hunting, Nickel, ¾ plate, Adjusted, Compensation-Balance, 17 Jewels 5 pairs Settings, Micrometer Regulator, Breguet Hair-Spring, Sunk Second Soft Enamel Dial. First Quality......$26 25
No. 159 Open Face, same as above......26 25

16 Size, Nameless, New Model.
No. 152 Hunting. Nickel, ¾-plate, 15 Jewels, 4 pairs Settings Micrometer Regulator, Compensation Balance, Sunk Second Soft Enamel Dial......$19 38
No. 158 Open Face, same as above......19 38

0 Size.
No. 174 Hunting, Nickel, Adjusted, Compensation-Balance, 17 Fine Ruby Jewels (5 pairs Raised Gold Settings), Breguet Hair-Spring, Finely Finished Throughout......$40 00

0 Size.
No. 167 Hunting, Nickel, Compensation-Balance, 16 Jewels (4½ pairs Settings)......$27 50

0 Size.
No. 130 Hunting, Nickel, 15 Jewels (4 pairs Settings)......$21 25

0 Size.
No. 109 Hunting, Gilt, Compensation-Balance, 7 Jewels......$14 38
No. 173 Same as above, Nickel..14 38

18 Size.
Hunting or Open Face.
G. M. Wheeler, Nickel, 17 Jewels..$23 75 Adjusted Patent Regulator, Breguet Hair-Spring.
G. M. Wheeler, Gilded, same as above......$20 63

Elgin National Watch Co.'s Movements.

16 Size, Three-Quarter Plate and Bridge Model.

Fitting All Regular New Model Pendant Set Cases.

Veritas $120.00

Nos. 156 and 162.

Nickel, 21 Extra Fine Red Ruby Jewels in Raised Gold Settings, Adjusted to Temperature. Isochronism and Positions, Gold Train Wheels, Steel Escape Wheel, Breguet Hair Spring, Micrometric Regulator, Patent Recoiling Click, Patent Self-Locking Setting Device, Double Sunk Glass Enamel Dial, Beautifully Damaskeened Plates, Closely Timed and Thoroughly First Quality Finish Throughout.

No. 156. Hunting, Pendant Set...$100 00
[RUNNET]
No. 162. Open Face, Pendant Set. 100 00
[RUPTURED]

$200.00

No. 270. (Open Face only.)

Nickel, 21 Fine Ruby Jewels in Gold Settings, Adjusted to Temperature, Isochronism and Positions, Gold Train Wheels, Steel Escape Wheel, Breguet Hair Spring, Micrometric Regulator, Patent Recoiling Click, Patent Self-Locking Setting Device, Double Sunk Glass Enamel Dial, Engraving Gold Inlaid. Closely Timed and Finely Finished Throughout.

No. 270. Open Face, Lever Set....$50 00
[RURAL]

$100.00

Nos. 243 and 246.

Nickel, 17 Ruby Jewels in Gold Settings, Adjusted to Temperature, Isochronism and Positions, Gold Train Wheels, Steel Escape Wheel, Breguet Hair Spring, Micrometric Regulator, Patent Recoiling Click, Patent Self-Locking Setting Device, Double Sunk Glass Enamel Dial, Engraving Gold Inlaid. Closely Timed and Finely Finished Throughout.

No. 243. Hunting, Pendant Set....$44 00
[RURALNESS]
No. 246. Open Face, Pendant Set.. 44 00
[RURALITY]

$40.00

1904 SUPPLY CATALOG

No. 280. (Open Face Only.)

Nickel, 17 Ruby Jewels in Gold Settings, Adjusted to Temperature, Isochronism and Positions, Gold Center Wheel, Steel Escape Wheel, Breguet Hair Spring, Micrometric Regulator, Patent Recoiling Click, Patent Self-Locking Setting Device, Double Sunk Glass Enamel Dial, Engraving Gold Inlaid. Closely Timed and Finely Finished Throughout.

No. 280. Open Face, Lever Set....$40 0
[RURALIZE]

$75.00

No. 242. (Hunting only.)

Nickel, 17 Jewels in Gilded Settings, Adjusted to Temperature, Gold Center Wheel, Breguet Hair Spring, Micrometric Regulator, Patent Recoiling Click, Patent Self-Locking Setting Device, Sunk Second Glass Enamel Dial. Thoroughly Well Finished.

No. 242. Hunting, Pendant Set...$35 00
[RUSHING]

$35.00

Nos. 241 and 244.

Nickel, 17 Jewels in Gilded Settings, Adjusted to Temperature, Gold Center Wheel, Breguet Hair Spring, Micrometric Regulator, Patent Recoiling Click, Patent Self-Locking Setting Device, Sunk Second Glass Enamel Dial.

No. 241. Hunting, Pendant Set....$23 00
[RUSHLIGHT]
No. 244. Open Face, Pendant Set.. 23 00
[RUSSETING]

$30.00

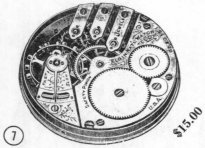 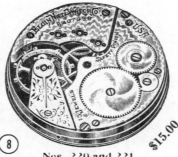 

Nos. 247 and 248.

Nickel, 15 Jewels in Settings, Breguet Hair Spring, Micrometric Regulator, Patent Recoiling Click, Patent Self-Locking Setting Device, Sunk Second Glass Enamel Dial.

No. 247. Hunting, Pendant Set....$17 00
[RUSTICMAN]
No. 248. Open Face, Pendant Set.. 17 00
[RUSTICATED]

$15.00

Nos. 220 and 221.

Nickel, 15 Jewels in Settings, Breguet Hair Spring, Polished Regulator, Patent Self Locking Setting Device, Sunk Second Dial.

No. 220. Hunting, Pendant Set....$15 00
[RUSTICITY]
No. 221. Open Face, Pendant Set.. 15 00
[RUSTLING]

$15.00

FATHER TIME.

Nickel, 21 Fine Ruby Jewels, Gold Settings, Adjusted to Temperature, Isochronism and Positions. Steel Escape Wheel, Breguet Hairspring, Micrometric Regulator, Patent Recoiling Click, Double Sunk Dial.

Hunting, Lever Set..[RUGGEDNESS] $40 00
Open Face, " .....[RUGOSITY] 40 00

$120.00

Fancy Dials—An extra charge of $1 00 will be made for Fancy Dials on Elgin movements in all sizes and all grades.

BUSIEST HOUSE IN AMERICA

Elgin National Watch Co.'s Movements.

12 Size, Stem Wind, Three-Quarter Plate.   Fitting Regular 12 Size Pendant Set Cases.

(1) $150.00

(2) $100.00

(3) $40.00

Nos. 190 and 194.
Nickel, 23 Extra Fine Red Ruby Jewels, Escapement Cap Jeweled, Raised Gold Settings, Adjusted to Temperature, Isochronism and Position, Breguet Hairspring, Steel Escape Wheel, Patent Regulator, Gold Train Wheels, Patent Safety Barrel, Patent Recoiling Click, Patent Self-Locking Setting Device, Glass Enamel Dial, Plates Beautifully Damaskeened and parts finely finished.
No. 190. **Hunting,** Pendant Set...$100 00
[RYEGRASS]
No. 194. **Open Face,** Pendant Set.. 100 00
[SABAISM]

Nos. 236 and 237.
Nickel, 21 Extra Fine Red Ruby Jewels, Raised Gold Settings, Adjusted to Temperature, Isochronism and Position, Breguet Hairspring, Steel Escape Wheel, Patent Regulator, Gold Train Wheels, Patent Safety Barrel, Patent Recoiling Click, Patent Self-Locking Setting Device, Glass Enamel Dial, Plates Beautifully Damaskeened and parts finely finished throughout.
No. 236. **Hunting,** Pendant Set....$77 00
[SABALERA]
No. 237. **Hunting,** Pendant Set 77 00
[SABANERO]

Nos. 189 and 193.
Nickel, 19 Fine Ruby Jewels, Raised Gold Settings, Adjusted to Temperature, Isochronism and Position, Breguet Hairspring, Steel Escape Wheel, Patent Regulator, Gold Train Wheels, Patent Safety Barrel, Patent Recoiling Click, Patent Self-Locking Setting Device, Glass Enamel Dial, Plates Beautifully Damaskeened, Gold Inlaid Engraving.
No. 189. **Hunting,** Pendant Set $49 00
[SABBATH]
No. 193. **Open Face,** Pendant Set .. 49 00
[SABBATICAL]

(4) $30.00

(5) $20.00

(6) $20.00

(7) $10.00

Nos. 275 and 276.
Nickel, 17 Jewels, Raised Gilded Settings, Adjusted, Breguet Hairspring, Patent Regulator Gold Center Wheel, Patent Safety Barrel, Patent Recoiling Click, Patent Self-Locking Setting Device, Glass Enamel Dial, Damaskeened Plates.
No. 275. **Hunting,** Pendant Set......[SABIAMENTE] $27 50
No. 276. **Open Face,** Pendant Set ...[SABIANAL] 27 50

Nos. 259 and 260.
Nickel, 15 Jewels, Settings, Breguet Hairspring, Patent Regulator, Gold Center Wheel, Patent Safety Barrel, Patent Recoiling Click, Patent Self-Locking Setting Device, Glass Enamel Dial, Damaskeened Plates.
No. 259. **Hunting,** Pendant Set......[SABLE] $18 00
No. 260. **Open Face,** Pendant Set...[SABLIERE] 18 00

Nos. 233 and 235.
Nickel, 15 Jewels, Settings, Breguet Hairspring, Polished Regulator, Patent Recoiling Click, Patent Self-Locking Setting Device, Sunk Second Glass Enamel Dial.
No. 233. **Hunting,** Pendant Set.[SABLONNER] $16 00
No. 235. **Open Face,** Pendant Set...[SABOTIER] 16 00

Nos. 232 and 234.
Nickel, 7 Jewels, Breguet Hairspring, Polished Regulator, Patent Recoiling Click, Patent Self-Locking Setting Device, Sunk Second Glass Enamel Dial.
No. 232. **Hunting,** Pendant Set ....[SABOULER] $12 50
No. 234. **Open Face,** Pendant Set...[SABRENAS] 12 50

6 Size, Stem Wind, Pendant Set.
Fitting All Regular 6 Size Pendant Set Cases.

No. 216.
Nickel, 15 Jewels, in Settings, Breguet Hairspring, Polished Regulator, Sunk Second Dial.
Hunting, Pendant Set............................[SABRETACHE] $13 50

No. 286.
Nickel, 7 Jewels, Breguet Hairspring. Polished Regulator, Sunk Second Dial.
Hunting, Pendant Set........................[SABULOUS] $10 00

(8) $20.00

No. 216.

(9) $15.00

No. 286.

0 Size, Stem Wind, Pendant Set.   Fitting All Regular 0 Size Pendant Set Cases.

(10) (11) (12) $50.00

(13) (14) $40.00

(15) (16) $20.00

(17) (18) $15.00

Nos. 201 and 205.
Nickel, 19 Fine Ruby Jewels, Raised Gold Settings, Adjusted to Temperature, Gold Train Wheels, Steel Escape Wheel, Breguet Hairspring, Micrometric Regulator, Patent Safety Barrel, Patent Recoiling Click, Patent Self-Locking Setting Device, Sunk Second Glass Enamel Dial, Beautifully Damaskeened Plates, finely finished throughout.
No. 201. **Hunting,** Pendant Set ...[SACABALA] $44 00
No. 205. **Open Face,** Pendant Set ....[SACCADE] 44 00

Nos. 263 and 264.
Nickel, 17 Ruby Jewels, Raised Gilded Settings, Adjusted to Temperature, Gold Train Wheels, Gold Escape Wheel, Breguet Hairspring, Micrometric Regulator, Patent Safety Barrel, Patent Recoiling Click, Patent Self-Locking Setting Device, Sunk Second Glass Enamel Dial, Engraving Gold Inlaid.
No. 263. **Hunting,** Pendant Set..[SACCHRINE] $26 00
No. 264. **Open Face,** Pendant Set[SACCIFORME] 26 00

Nos. 267 and 268.
Nickel, 15 Jewels, Settings, Gold Center Wheel, Breguet Hairspring, Polished Regulator, Patent Recoiling Click, Patent Self-Locking Setting Device, Sunk Second Dial.
No. 267. **Hunting,** Pendant Set [SACERDING]. $20 00
No. 268. **Open Face,** Pendant Set [SACERDOTAL] 20 00

Nos. 269 and 281.
No. 269. Nickel, 7 Jewels, Breguet Hairspring, Polished Regulator, Patent Recoiling Click, Patent Self-Locking Setting Device, Sunk Second Dial.
Hunting, Pendant Set.....$13 00
[SACHELER]
No. 281. Nickel, 11 Jewels, Settings, Breguet Hairspring, Polished Regulator, Patent Recoiling Click, Patent Self-Locking Setting Device, Sunk Second Dial.
Hunting, Pendant Set $16 00
[SACKAGE]

1904 SUPPLY CATALOG

18 SIZE, ELGIN NATIONAL WATCH COMPANY'S MOVEMENTS.
Prices are for Movements Only Without Cases.

$60.00

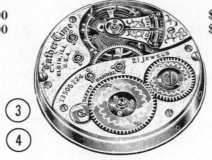

$160.00
$100.00

$95.00
$65.00

18 Size.

No. 10. Elgin Veritas, nickel, 23 fine ruby jewels in raised gold settings, adjusted to temperature, isochronism and positions, gold train wheels. Double roller escapement steel escape wheel, pallet arbor and escape pinion, cone pivoted and cap jeweled compensating balance, Breguet hairspring, micrometric regulator, barrel arbor pivots running in jewels, double sunk dial, stem winder and lever set, made only in open face....... **$106.66**

No. 11. Elgin Veritas, nickel, 21 fine ruby jewels. Hunting or open face, lever set. Price **$96.00**

18 Size.

No. 12. Elgin Father Time, nickel, 21 fine ruby jewels, gilded settings, adjusted to temperature, isochronism and positions, quick train straight line escapement, steel escape wheel, exposed pallets, compensating balance, Breguet hairspring, micrometric regulator, patent double sunk dial, damaskeened plates. Hunting or open face. **$82.64**

No. 14. Elgin, No. 348, nickel, 21 jewel, adjusted. Hunting or open face. **$74.66**

18 Size.

No. 15. Elgin, B. W. Raymond, nickel, 19 fine ruby jewels in raised gold settings, adjusted to temperature, isochronism and positions, gold train wheels, steel escape wheels, compensating balance, Breguet hairspring, micrometric regulator, patent safety barrel, barrel arbor pivots running in jewels, double sunk dial, dust ring, damaskeened plates, stem winder and lever set, made only in open face.. **$72.00**

$30.00

M & M 1912 SUPPLY CATALOG

$25.00
$20.00

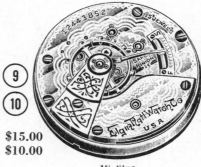

$15.00
$10.00

18 Size.

No. 16. 18 size Elgin. G. M. Wheeler, ¾ plate, nickel, bridge model. 17 jewels, gilded settings, adjusted to temperature, compensating balance. Breguet hairspring, micrometric regulator, sunk second dial, dust ring, damaskeened plates, stem wind and set. Hunting or open face. **$45.33**

18 Size.

No. 17. 18 size Elgin, nickel, No. 378, 17 jewels, adjusted, exposed pallet stones, compensating balance, Breguet hairspring, micrometric regulator, depressed center, sunk second dial, dust ring, damaskeened plates. Hunting or open face. Price **$25.30**

No. 18. Same as above, but unadjusted, Elgin, No. 335, nickel, 17 jewels. Hunting or open face...................... **$19.00**

18 Size.

No. 19. Elgin, No. 316, nickel, 15 jewels. (setting), nickel compensating balance, Breguet hairspring, oval regulator, nickel index. Hunting or open face....... **$16.00**

No. 20. Elgin, No. 287, nickel, 7 jewel, nickel compensating balance, Breguet hairspring, oval steel regulator, nickel index, damaskeened, stem winder and stem setter Hunting or open face.. **$10.80**

16 Size, Elgin National Watch Company's Movements.

$350.00

$160.00
$100.00

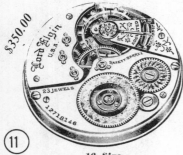

$75.00

16 Size.

No. 21. Lord Elgin, open face only, three-quarter plate model, pendant set, 23 ruby and sapphire jewels, gold jewel settings, barrel arbor pivots running in jewels; double roller escapement, with steel escape wheel; exposed sapphire pallet stones; pallet arbor cone-pivoted and cap-jeweled; compensating balance; Breguet hairspring, with micrometric regulator adjusted to temperature, isochronism and positions; safety barrel with spring rigidly mounted on bridge; exposed wheels; patent recoiling click f-locking device; dust ring. **$213.33**

16 Size.

No. 22. Veritas, 23 diamond, ruby and sapphire jewels, gold jewel settings, barrel arbor pivots running in jewels, double roller escapement, steel escape wheel, exposed sapphire pallet stones, pallet arbor cone-pivoted and cap-jeweled, escape pinion cone-pivoted and cap-jeweled, compensating balance with pivots running on diamonds, Breguet hairspring, micrometric regulator, adjusted to temperature, isochronism and five positions, safety barrel with spring box rigidly mounted on bridge, patent recoiling click and self-locking setting device, double sunk glass enamel dial, finely finished, engraving inlaid with gold...................... **$106.66**

No. 23. Elgin, Veritas, 21 jewels (only in open face), lever set............. **$96.00**
Guaranteed to pass railroad inspection.

16 Size.

No. 24. Father Time, nickel, 21 ruby and sapphire jewels, gold jewel settings, double roller escapement with steel escape wheel, exposed sapphire pallet stones, pallet arbor cone-pivoted and cap-jeweled, escape pinion cone-pivoted and cap-jeweled, compensating balance, Breguet hairspring with micrometric regulator, adjusted to temperature, isochronism and five positions; safety barrel, with spring box rigidly mounted on bridge; exposed winding wheels; patent recoiling click and self-locking setting device; dust ring, double-sunk glass enamel dial, plates beautifully damaskeened and finely finished; engraving inlaid with gold. Established retail selling price........ **$82.66**

16 SIZE, ELGIN NATIONAL WATCH COMPANY'S MOVEMENTS.
Prices are for Movements Only Without Cases.

$55.00

$30.00

$25.00

$65.00

$15.00

$10.00

16 Size.

16 Size.

16 Size.

No. 25. Elgin. B. W. -Raymond, 19 jewels, ¾ plate, nickel, bridge model, gilded settings, adjusted to temperature, compensating balance, Breguet hairspring, micrometric regulator, sunk second dial, dust ring, damaskeened plates, stem wind and set. Hunting or open face. Price $72.00

No. 26. Elgin. B. W. Raymond, 17 jewels, ¾ plate, nickel, bridge model, gilded settings, adjusted to temperature, compensating balance, Breguet hairspring, micrometric regulator, sunk second dial, dust ring, damaskeened plates, stem wind and set. Hunting or open face. Price $66.64

No. 27. Elgin, G. M. Wheeler, nickel. 17 jewels, gilded settings, adjusted to temperature, gold center wheel, compensating balance, Breguet hair-spring. micrometric regulator, sunk second dial, dust ring, damaskeened plates, stem winder and pendant setter. Hunting or open face $45.28

No. 28. Elgin, No. 381, adjusted, nickel, 17 jewel. Hunting or open face .. $30.26

No. 29. Elgin, No. 312, nickel, 15 jewel settings, quick train, straight line escapement, exposed pallets, compensating balance, Breguet hairspring, micrometric regulator, display winding work, patent recoiling click, self-locking setting device, dust ring, damaskeened plates, stem winder and pendant setter. Hunting or open face $21.60

No. 30. Elgin, No. 290, nickel, 7 jewels, quick train, exposed pallets, compensating balance, Breguet hairspring, polished steel regulator, stem winder and pendant setter. Hunting or open face .. $12.68

12 Size, Elgin National Watch Company's Movements.

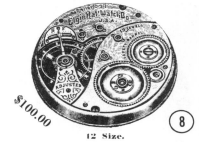

$250.00

$100.00

12 Size.

12 Size.

No. 31. Elgin, No. 190, nickel, 23 extra fine red ruby jewels (raised gold settings), adjusted to temperature, isochronism and positions, gold train wheels, steel escape wheel, pallet arbor and escape pinion, cap-jeweled, exposed pallets, compensating balance, Breguet hairspring, micrometric regulator, patent safety barrels, barrel arbor pivots running in jewels, sunk second glass, enameled dial, stem winder and pendant setter. Hunting or open face. $186.66

No. 32. Elgin. No. 189, nickel, 19 rosy ruby jewels (raised gold settings), adjusted to temperature, isochronism and positions, gold train wheels, steel escape wheel, exposed pallets, compensating balance, Breguet hairspring, micrometric regulator, patent safety barrel, barrel arbor pivots running, stem winder and pendant setter. Hunting or open face. Price $80.00

If you are a serious Elgin collector, trader or investor, read the following paragraph. I have for sale copies of additional material on Elgins that I have collected for my own use. It is spiral bound on 8½ x 11 pages. It contains the following: Complete serial number up to 50 million and the grade for each. Complete descriptions for 523 grades, showing for each grade the class, size, style, model, setting, train and number of jewels for each watch of the 523 grades. There are 51 line drawings of movements showing size, model, plate, hunting, openface, key or stem wind, lever or pendant setting and winding indicator. This book will give you positive identification. Some production figures on the early movements and other information that the serious Elgin fan needs to get the most enjoyment and profit on watches he buys or sells. Ask for "Elgin Serial Number Book". This book is not available to wholesalers and can be obtained only by sending $10.00 to Roy Ehrhardt, P. O. box 9808, Kansas City, Missouri 64134. It has not been professionally printed because of the limited demand for this type of research material but I assure you the quality is acceptable and you will be pleased.

$35.00

$30.00

$20.00

$10.00

12 Size.

12 Size.

No. 33. Elgin, G. M. Wheeler, nickel. 17 jewels (raised gilded settings), adjusted to temperature, gold center wheel, exposed pallets, compensating balance, Breguet hairspring, micrometric regulator, sunk second glass, enameled dial, stem winder and pendant setter. Hunting or open face $45.28

No. 34. Elgin 383, hunting style or open face, 12 size, nickel, 17 jewels (raised gilded settings), adjusted to temperature, gold center wheel, exposed pallets, compensating balance, Breguet hair-spring, micrometric regulator, patent safety barrel, sunk second glass enamel dial, pendant set $36.00

No. 36. Elgin, No. 314, nickel, 15 jewels (settings), gold center wheel, exposed pallets, compensating balance, Breguet hair-spring, micrometric regulator, sunk second glass, enameled dial stem winder and pendant setter. Hunting or open face $21.60

No. 37. Elgin. No. 301, nickel, 7 jewels (setting), nickel compensating balance, Breguet hairspring, nickel index. Hunting or open face $14.00

These movements will fit any American made case. We quote prices of cases separately. For prices of cases refer to pages following. When selecting a watch be sure that case and movement are of the same size.

1917 OSKAMP–NOLTING CO.

Eighteen-Size Elgin Movements

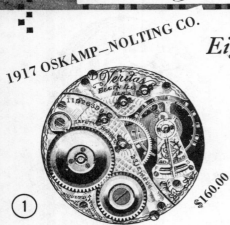

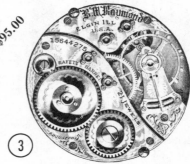

$160.00

(2) $100.00

$95.00

VERITAS, O. F., Nickel, ¾ Plate

LEVER Setting for Railroad Service. Twenty-three diamond, ruby and sapphire jewels. Gold jewel settings. Barrel arbor pivots running in jewels. *Double-roller escapement.* Steel escape wheel. Poised pallet and fork. Exposed sapphire pallet stones. Balance, pivots running on diamonds. Micrometric regulator. Adjusted to temperature, isochronism, five positions. Safety barrel. Patent recoiling click and self-locking setting device. Double-sunk glass enamel dial. Engraving inlaid with gold. Plates beautifully damaskeened and finely finished.

23 Jewels   Price $60.00

VERITAS, O. F., Nickel, ¾ Plate

LEVER Setting for Railroad Service. Twenty-one diamond, ruby and sapphire jewels. Gold jewel settings. *Double-roller escapement.* Steel escape wheel. Exposed sapphire pallet stones. Balance, pivots running on diamonds. Micrometric regulator. Adjusted to temperature, isochronism, five positions. Safety barrel. Patent recoiling click and self-locking setting device. Double-sunk glass enamel dial. Plates beautifully damaskeened and finely finished.

21 Jewels   Price $56.50

B. W. RAYMOND, O. F., Nickel, ¾ Plate

LEVER Setting for Railroad Service. Twenty-one diamond, ruby and sapphire jewels. Gold jewel settings. *Double-roller escapement.* Steel escape wheel. Exposed sapphire pallet stones. Balance, pivots running on diamonds. Micrometric regulator. Adjusted to temperature, isochronism, five positions. Patent recoiling click and self-locking setting device. Double-sunk glass enamel dial. Engraving inlaid with gold. Plates damaskeened and finely finished.

21 Jewels   Price $50.00

$95.00

$60.00

$60.00

FATHER TIME, O. F., Nickel, ¾ Plate

LEVER Setting for Railroad Service. Twenty-one diamond, ruby and sapphire jewels. Gold jewel settings. *Double-roller escapement.* Steel escape wheel. Exposed sapphire pallet stones. Balance, pivots running on diamonds. Micrometric regulator. Adjusted to temperature, isochronism, five positions. Patent recoiling click and self-locking setting device. Double-sunk glass enamel dial. Engraving inlaid with gold. Plates damaskeened and finely finished.

21 Jewels   Price $46.50

B. W. RAYMOND, O. F., Nickel, ¾ Plate

LEVER Setting for Railroad Service. Nineteen diamond, ruby and sapphire jewels. Gold jewel settings. Barrel arbor pivots running in jewels. *Double-roller escapement.* Steel escape wheel. Exposed sapphire pallet stones. Balance, pivots running on diamonds. Micrometric regulator. Adjusted to temperature, isochronism, five positions. Safety barrel. Patent recoiling click and self-locking setting device. Double-sunk glass enamel dial. Engraving inlaid with gold. Plates damaskeened and finely finished.

19 Jewels   Price $42.00

No. 349, O. F., Nickel

LEVER Setting for Railroad Service. Twenty-one ruby and sapphire jewels. Gold jewel settings. *Double-roller escapement.* Steel escape wheel. Exposed sapphire pallet stones. Compensating balance. Micrometric regulator. Adjusted to temperature, isochronism, five positions. Patent recoiling click. Double-sunk glass enamel dial. Engraving inlaid with gold. Plates damaskeened and finely finished.

21 Jewels   Price $40.00

$65.00

(8) $30.00

$25.00

B. W. RAYMOND, O. F., Nickel, ¾ Plate

LEVER Setting for Railroad Service. Seventeen ruby and sapphire jewels. Gold jewel settings. *Double-roller escapement.* Steel escape wheel. Exposed sapphire pallet stones. Compensating balance. Micrometric regulator. Adjusted to temperature, isochronism, five positions. Patent recoiling click and self-locking setting device. Double-sunk glass enamel dial. Engraving inlaid with gold. Plates damaskeened and finely finished.

17 Jewels   Price $38.00

G. M. WHEELER, Htg.,) Nickel,
G. M. WHEELER, O. F., } ¾ Plate

LEVER Setting. Seventeen jewels (settings). Ruby and sapphire balance and center jewels. *Double-roller escapement.* Steel escape wheel. Exposed pallet stones. Compensating balance. Micrometric regulator. Adjusted to temperature, isochronism, three positions. Patent recoiling click and self-locking setting device. Double-sunk glass enamel dial. Plates damaskeened. Engraving inlaid with gold.

17 Jewels   Price $27.00

No. 379, O. F., Nickel, Full Plate

LEVER Setting. Seventeen jewels (settings). Ruby and sapphire balance and center jewels. Double roller escapement. Steel escape wheel. Exposed pallet stones. Compensating balance. Micrometric regulator. Adjusted to temperature, isochronism. Double-sunk dial. Plates damaskeened.

17 Jewels   Price $17.00

Elgin High grade Watches

Eighteen-Size Elgin Movements

No. 335, Htg., Lever Set, } Nickel,
No. 336, O. F., Pendant Set, } Full Plate

SEVENTEEN jewels (settings). Ruby and sapphire balance and center jewels. Exposed pallet stones. Cut expansion balance. Micrometric regulator. Depressed center sunk-second dial. Plates damaskeened.

17 Jewels .... Price $13.00

No. 316, Htg., Lever Set, } Nickel,
No. 317, O. F., Pendant Set, } Full Plate

FIFTEEN jewels (settings). Ruby balance jewels. Exposed pallet stones. Cut expansion balance. Micrometric regulator. Sunk-second dial. Plates damaskeened.

15 Jewels .... Price $11.00

No. 287, Htg., Lever Set, } Nickel,
No. 288, O. F., Pendant Set, } Full Plate

SEVEN jewels (settings). Ruby balance jewels. Exposed pallet stones. Cut expansion balance. Polished oval regulator. Sunk-second dial. Plates damaskeened.

7 Jewels .... Price $8.00
No. 294, O. F., seven jewels, gilt Price $7.20

Elgin Complete Railroad Watches

COMPLETE WATCH MUST BE EXTRA FINE AND RUNNING

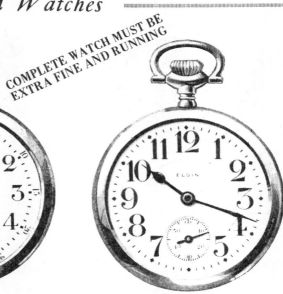

Minute Numeral Dial

Winding Indicator

Forty-Nine Dial

Elgin Railroad Dials:
Above are pictured the popular railroad dials. Decorated dials and Louis XV hands on all grades and sizes, $1.10 extra. Metal dials, 90 cents extra. The minute numeral dial and the 49 dial are supplied without extra charge on railroad grades.

Elgin Winding Indicators:
Elgin railroad watches are supplied with winding indicator if so desired. This feature is of great importance, and no jeweler should be without an indicator watch in stock. The convenience to Railroad Men is apparent, for this is an almost absolute safeguard against "run-downs" the most common and disastrous cause of trouble. The indicator will help you sell watches to men who already have standard time pieces but who want to have the finest most up-to-date mechanism on the market.

Extra for winding indicator, $7.80.

Prices of Elgin Complete Railroad Watches:
Fitted in special thin model 20 year cases

$195.00	Veritas, 23 Jewels	$67.80
$110.00	Veritas, 21 Jewels	64.35
$100.00	Father Time 21, Jewels	54.35
$100.00		
$90.00	B. W. Raymond, 21 Jewels	57.80
$55.00	B. W. Raymond, 19 Jewels	49.80
$65.00	B. W. Raymond, 17 Jewels	45.80
	G. M. Wheeler (not a railroad watch)	34.80

ADD *$150.00* FOR WINDING INDICATOR ON EITHER 18 SIZE OR 16 SIZE.

89

Sixteen-Size Elgin Movements

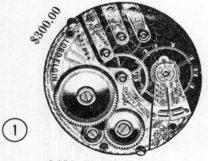

$300.00

① LORD ELGIN, Htg.,
LORD ELGIN, O. F., } Nickel

PENDANT Winding and Setting. Twenty-one ruby and sapphire jewels. Gold jewel settings. *Double-roller escapement.* Steel escape wheel. Exposed ruby pallet stones. Compensating balance. Micrometric regulator. Adjusted to temperature, isochronism, five positions. Patent recoiling click and self-locking setting device. Dust ring. Double-sunk glass enamel dial. Plates beautifully damaskeened and finely finished.

21 Jewels   Price $110.00

Elgin Watches are in Demand

ELGIN Watches are known and advertised the world over. They have a reputation for quality of many years standing. For this reason they are easy to sell and you can be sure they will give your customers complete satisfaction. Concentrate on a complete stock of Elgins and get a quick turnover with its consequent profits.

$160.00
$100.00

② ③ VERITAS, O. F., Nickel

LEVER Setting for Railroad Service. Pendant Winding. Twenty-three ruby and sapphire jewels. Gold jewel settings. Barrel arbor pivots running in jewels. *Double-roller escapement.* Steel escape wheel. Exposed sapphire pallet stones. Compensating balance. Micrometric regulator. Adjusted to temperature, isochronism, five positions. Safety barrel. Patent recoiling click and self-locking setting device. Double-sunk glass enamel dial. Engraving inlaid with gold. Plates beautifully damaskeened. Closely timed and finely finished throughout.

23 Jewels   Price $60.00
21 Jewels   Price $56.50

$75.00

④ B. W. RAYMOND, O. F., Nickel

LEVER Setting for Railroad Service. Pendant Winding. Twenty-one ruby and sapphire jewels. Gold jewel settings. *Double-roller escapement.* Steel escape wheel. Exposed sapphire pallet stones. Compensating balance. Micrometric regulator. Adjusted to temperature, isochronism, five positions. Safety barrel. Patent recoiling click and self-locking setting device. Dust ring. Double-sunk glass enamel dial. Engraving inlaid with gold. Plates damaskeened and finely finished.

21 Jewels   Price $50.00

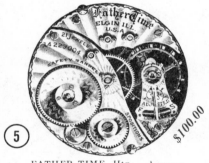

$100.00

⑤ FATHER TIME, Htg.,
FATHER TIME, O. F., } Nickel

LEVER Setting for Railroad Service. Pendant Winding. Twenty-one ruby and sapphire jewels. Gold jewel settings. *Double-roller escapement.* Steel escape wheel. Exposed sapphire pallet stones. Compensating balance. Micrometric regulator. Adjusted to temperature, isochronism, five positions. Safety barrel. Patent recoiling click and self-locking setting device. Dust ring. Double-sunk glass enamel dial. Engraving inlaid with gold. Plates damaskeened and finely finished.

21 Jewels   Price $46.50

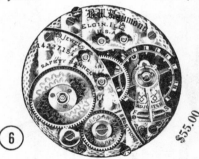

$55.00

⑥ B. W. RAYMOND, Htg.,
B. W. RAYMOND, O. F., } Nickel

LEVER Setting for Railroad Service. Pendant Winding. Nineteen ruby and sapphire jewels. Gold jewel settings. *Double-roller escapement.* Steel escape wheel. Exposed sapphire pallet stones. Compensating balance. Micrometric regulator. Adjusted to temperature, isochronism, five positions. Safety barrel. Patent recoiling click and self-locking setting device. Dust ring. Double-sunk glass enamel dial. Engraving inlaid with gold. Plates damaskeened and finely finished.

19 Jewels   Price $42.00

$65.00

⑦ B. W. RAYMOND, O. F., Nickel

LEVER Setting for Railroad Service. Pendant Winding. Seventeen ruby and sapphire jewels. Gold jewel settings. *Double-roller escapement.* Steel escape wheel. Exposed sapphire pallet stones. Compensating balance. Micrometric regulator. Adjusted to temperature, isochronism, five positions. Safety barrel. Patent recoiling click and self-locking setting device. Dust ring. Double-sunk glass enamel dial. Engraving inlaid with gold. Plates damaskeened and finely finished.

17 Jewels   Price $38.00

$30.00

⑧ G. M. WHEELER, Htg.,
G. M. WHEELER, O. F., } Nickel

PENDANT Winding and Setting. Seventeen jewels (settings). Ruby and sapphire balance and center jewels. Exposed pallet stones. *Double-roller escapement.* Compensating balance. Micrometric regulator. Adjusted to temperature, isochronism, three positions. Patent recoiling click and self-locking setting device. Dust ring. Double-sunk glass enamel dial. Plates damaskeened. Engraving inlaid with gold.

17 Jewels   Price $27.00

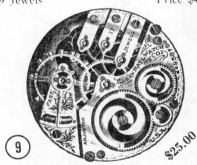

$25.00

⑨ No. 381, Htg.,
No. 382, O. F., } Nickel

PENDANT Winding and Setting. Seventeen jewels (settings). Ruby and sapphire balance and center jewels. Adjusted to temperature. Exposed pallet stones. *Double-roller escapement.* Compensating balance. Micrometric regulator. Patent recoiling click and self-locking setting device. Depressed center sunk-second dial. Dust ring. Damaskeened plates.

17 Jewels   Price $21.00

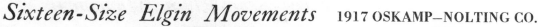
Sixteen-Size Elgin Movements   1917 OSKAMP–NOLTING CO.

$20.00

①

No. 386, Htg. } Nickel
No. 387, O. F.,

PENDANT Winding and Setting. Seventeen jewels (settings). Ruby and sapphire balance and center jewels. Exposed pallet stones. *Double-roller escapement.* Cut expansion balance. Micrometric regulator. Patent recoiling click and self-locking setting device. Depressed center sunk-second dial. Dust ring. Damaskeened plates.

17 Jewels   Price $19.70

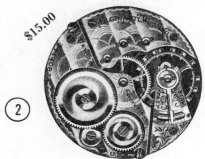

$15.00

②

No. 312, Htg., } Nickel
No. 313, O. F.,

PENDANT Winding and Setting. Fifteen jewels (settings). Ruby balance jewels. Exposed pallet stones. *Double-roller escapement.* Cut expansion balance. Micrometric regulator. Patent recoiling click and self-locking setting device. Dust ring. Sunk-second dial. Plates damaskeened.

15 Jewels   Price $15.50

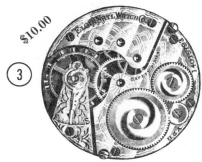

$10.00

③

No. 290, Htg., } Nickel
No. 291, O. F.,

PENDANT Winding and Setting. Seven jewels (settings). Ruby jewels. Exposed pallet stones. Cut expansion balance. Breguet hair spring, with polished regulator. Patent recoiling click and self-locking setting device. Dust ring. Sunk-second dial. Plates damaskeened.

7 Jewels   Price $9.80

④

$60.00
in a box

Sixteen-Size Elgin Watch

(G. M. Wheeler Model)

DOUBLE roller escapement. Adjusted to temperature, isochronism and three positions. Finely finished throughout. Special gold-filled case without cap. Jointed back. Guaranteed 20 years.

17 Jewels   **Price $37.10**

Complete in Mahogany Box

Lord Elgin — Twelve-Size   Extra Thin Model

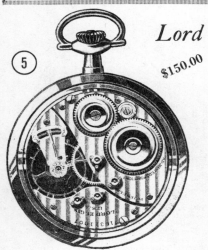

⑤

$150.00

LORD ELGIN, O F., Nickel, Pendant Setting

SEVENTEEN finest ruby and sapphire jewels. Raised gold jewel settings. Gold cock dome. Carefully adjusted to temperature, isochronism, five positions. *Double-roller escapement.* Steel escape wheel. Exposed sapphire pallet stones. Sapphire jewel pin. Compensating balance with gold screws. Breguet hair-spring with micrometric regulator. Exposed winding wheels, cupped and finely glossed. Bevel head screws. Patent recoiling click and self-locking setting device. Dust ring. Artistic glass enamel or metal dial, of most exclusive and original design. Plates beautifully damaskeened in narrow straight line flutes. Cased at the factory, closely timed and regulated in the case.

14K Solid Gold Case   **$132.00**

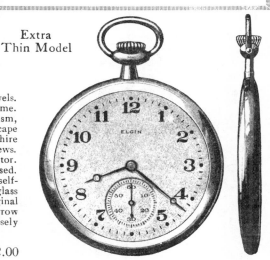

Lord Elgin is sold only as a complete watch

Elgin High Grade Watches

Twelve-Size Elgin Movements

$250.00

① LORD ELGIN, Htg., } Nickel
LORD ELGIN, O. F.,

PENDANT Winding and Setting. Twenty-three sapphire and ruby jewels. Gold jewel settings. Barrel arbor pivots running in jewels. *Double-roller escapement.* Steel escape wheel. Exposed ruby pallet stones. Compensating balance. Micrometric regulator. Adjusted to temperature, isochronism, five positions. Safety barrel, with spring box rigidly mounted on bridge. Exposed winding wheels. Patent recoiling click and self-locking setting device. Dust ring. Sunk-second glass enamel dial. Plates beautifully damaskeened and finely finished.

23 Jewels ...... Price $110.00

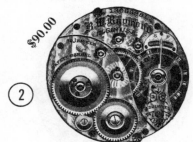

$90.00

② B. W. RAYMOND, Htg., } Nickel
B. W. RAYMOND, O. F.,

PENDANT Set, Nineteen fine ruby and sapphire jewels (raised gold settings). Adjusted to temperature, isochronism, five positions. *Double-roller escapement.* Steel escape wheel. Exposed pallet stones. Compensating balance. Breguet hair spring. Micrometric regulator. Patent safety barrel, with spring box rigidly mounted on bridge. Barrel arbor pivots running in jewels. Exposed winding wheels. Patent recoiling click. Patent self-locking setting device. Sunk-second glass enamel dial. Dust ring. Frosted and damaskeened plates. Engraving inlaid with gold. Carefully timed and finely finished throughout.

19 Jewels ...... Price $50.00

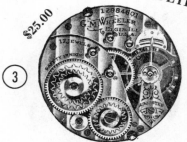

$25.00

③ G. M. WHEELER, Htg., } Nickel
G. M. WHEELER, O. F.,

PENDANT Set. Seventeen jewels (settings). Adjusted to temperature, isochronism and three positions. *Double-roller escapement.* Steel escape wheel. Exposed pallet stones. Compensating balance. Breguet hair spring. Micrometric regulator. Exposed winding wheels. Patent recoiling click. Patent self-locking setting device. Sunk-second glass enamel dial. Dust ring. Engraving inlaid with gold. Damaskeened plates.

17 Jewels ...... Price $27.00

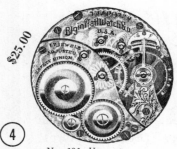

$25.00

④ No. 383, Htg., } Nickel
No. 384, O. F.,

PENDANT Winding and Setting. Seventeen jewels (settings). Ruby and sapphire balance and center jewels. Adjusted to temperature. Exposed pallet stones. *Double-roller escapement.* Compensating balance. Micrometric regulator. Exposed winding wheels. Patent recoiling click and self-locking setting device. Sunk-second dial. Dust ring. Damaskeened plates.

17 Jewels ...... Price $21.00

Twelve-Size Elgin Complete Watches

⑤ $115.00

B. W. Raymond Model
19 Jewels

Complete in special Gold Filled Case with Cap; jointed back and bezel, flush joints; Guaranteed 25 years.
Price $61.10

⑧ $50.00

G. M. Wheeler Model
17 Jewels

Complete in special Gold Filled Case with Cap; jointed back and bezel, flush joints; Guaranteed 25 years.
Price $39.80

Each model is fitted in a handsome presentation box

92

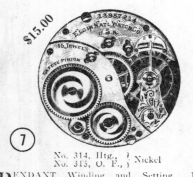

$15.00

⑦ No. 314, Htg., } Nickel
No. 315, O. F.,

PENDANT Winding and Setting. Fifteen jewels (settings). Ruby balance jewels. Exposed pallet stones. *Double-roller escapement,* with micrometric regulator. Exposed winding wheels. Patent recoiling click and self-locking setting device. Dust ring. Sunk-second dial. Plates damaskeened.

15 Jewels ...... Price $15.50

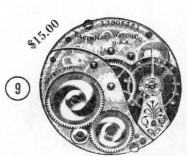

$20.00

⑥ No. 344, Htg., } Nickel
No. 345, O. F.,

PENDANT Winding and Setting. Seventeen jewels (settings). Ruby and sapphire balance and center jewels. *Double-roller escapement.* Exposed pallet stones. Cut expansion balance. Breguet hair spring, with micrometric regulator. Exposed winding wheels. Patent recoiling click and self-locking setting device. Dust ring. Sunk-second dial. Plates damaskeened.

17 Jewels ...... Price $19.70

$15.00

⑨ No. 301, Htg., } Nickel
No. 303, O. F.,

PENDANT Winding and Setting. Seven jewels (settings). Ruby balance jewels. Exposed pallet stones. *Double-roller escapement.* Cut expansion balance. Breguet hair spring, with polished regulator. Exposed winding wheels. Patent recoiling click and self-locking setting device. Dust ring. Sunk-second dial. Plates damaskeened.

7 Jewels ...... Price $10.90

Elgin Movements—Six-Size and Smaller

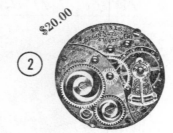

(1) $20.00

No. 295, Htg., Nickel   **15 Jewels**
PENDANT Winding and Setting. Fifteen jewels (settings). Ruby balance jewels. Exposed pallet stones. Cut expansion balance. Breguet hair spring, with polished regulator. Sunk-second dial. Plates damaskeened.
6 Size   Price $12.30

No. 286, Htg., Nickel
7 Jewels (settings)   Price $8.70

(2) $20.00

No. 419., Htg. } Nickel   **15 Jewels**
No. 420, O. F.,
PENDANT Winding and Setting. Fifteen jewels (settings). Ruby balance jewels. *Double-roller escapement.* Exposed pallet stones. Cut expansion balance. Breguet hair spring, with micrometric regulator. Exposed winding wheels. Patent recoiling click and self-locking setting device. Sunk-second dial. Plates damaskeened.
3/O-Size   Price $18.40

(3) $15.00

No. 417, Htg., } Nickel   **7 Jewels**
No. 418, O. F.,
PENDANT Winding and Setting. Seven jewels (settings). Ruby balance jewels. *Double-roller escapement.* Exposed pallet stones. Cut expansion balance. Breguet hair spring, with polished regulator. Exposed winding wheels. Patent recoiling click and self-locking setting device. Sunk-second dial. Plates damaskeened.
3/O-Size   Price $12.30

1917 OSKAMP—NOLTING CO.

(4) $10.00

LADY RAYMOND, Htg., Nickel   **15 Jewels**
PENDANT Winding and Setting. Fifteen jewels (settings). Ruby balance jewels. *Double-roller escapement.* Exposed pallet stones. Cut expansion balance. Breguet hair spring, with polished regulator. Exposed winding wheels. Sunk-second glass enamel dial. Damaskeened plates.

5/O-Size { 15 Jewels   Price $24.10
          { 7 Jewels   Price $17.30

(5) $10.00

LADY ELGIN, O. F., Nickel   **17 Jewels**
PENDANT Winding and Setting. Seventeen ruby and sapphire jewels. Gold jewel settings. Exposed pallet stones. Steel escape wheel. *Double-roller escapement.* Breguet hair spring, with polished regulator. Sunk-second glass enamel dial. Plates damaskeened and finely finished. Open-face with seconds; Hunting without seconds.
10/O-Size   Price $42.50

(6) $10.00

LADY ELGIN, O. F., Nickel   **15 Jewels**
PENDANT Winding and Setting. Fifteen jewels (settings). Ruby balance jewels. *Double-roller escapement.* Exposed pallet stones. Breguet hair spring, with polished regulator. Sunk-second glass enamel dial. Plates damaskeened. Open-face with seconds; Hunting without seconds.
10/O-Size   Price $35.20

ELGIN MILITARY WATCHES

With Plain or Luminous Dials

ELGIN Military Watches have nickel movements and are equipped with double roller escapements. They are especially adapted to hard outdoor use.

Complete i... ..dy, compact case of special design. Strong, mannish looking, silvered dial with heavy figures and hands. Heavy cowboy-style strap of battleship gray, perforated for ventilation.
3, O-Size   7 jewels

Selling Price: With plain dial and hands
        Extra for luminous hands and dots   - -
        Extra for luminous hands and figures

Luminous Dial
(Night View)

Sportsmen, motorists, golfers, athletes and army and navy men instantly appreciate the features which make this the handy "extra watch" for outdoor service.

Luminous Dial
Day View

(7) $15.00 Running

With Plain Dial

How the Elgin Movements shown on previous page case up as <u>*Bracelet*</u> *Watches*

① $20.00 GF

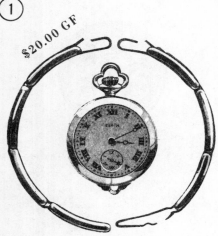

② $20.00 GF

③ $20.00 GF

10/O-Size Lady Elgin   10/O-Size Lady Elgin   10/O-Size Lady Elgin

The *Lady Elgin* is a 9½ ligne movement, 17 or 15-jewels, and cases up very beautifully. It is made with a second hand — a special feature in so small a watch. An attractive assortment of dials is offered, suitable for full open face, three-quarter or skylight casing.

④ 15J GF $20.00

⑤ 15J GF $30.00

⑥ 7J GF $25.00

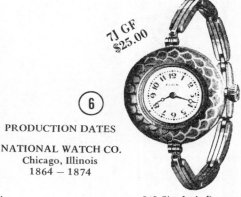

5/O-Size Lady Raymond   5/O-Size Lady Raymond   5/O-Size Lady Raymond

PRODUCTION DATES

NATIONAL WATCH CO.
Chicago, Illinois
1864 — 1874

The 5/O-size *Lady Raymond* is a 15-jewel movement. A 7-jewel movement is also made in this size. Both these Elgin movements may be had in full open face, three-quarter opening or skylight cases, of various designs.

THE ELGIN NATIONAL WATCH CO.
1874 — Mid 1900's

⑦ 15J GF $30.00

⑧ 15J GF $30.00

3/O-Size Elgin   3/O-Size Elgin

The 3/O-size can be furnished convertible or non-convertible, full open face, three-quarter or skylight casing, enamel or metal dials without extra charge.

101	1867	14,000,000	1909
100,000	1870	15,000,000	1910
200,000	1874	16,000,000	1911
400,000	1875	17,000,000	1912
500,000	1877	18,000,000	1914
600,000	1879	19,000,000	1916
700,000	1880	20,000,000	1917
800,000	1881	21,000,000	1918
1,000,000	1882	22,000,000	1919
2,000,000	1886	23,000,000	1920
3,000,000	1888	26,000,000	1923
4,000,000	1890	29,000,000	1926
5,000,000	1893	33,000,000	1929
6,000,000	1895	34,000,000	1933
7,000,000	1897	36,000,000	1936
8,000,000	1899	38,000,000	1939
9,000,000	1900	41,000,000	1942
10,000,000	1903	43,000,000	1945
11,000,000	1904	45,000,000	1948
13,000,000	1907	50,000,000	1953

The Smallest Elgin and Waltham Bracelet Watches

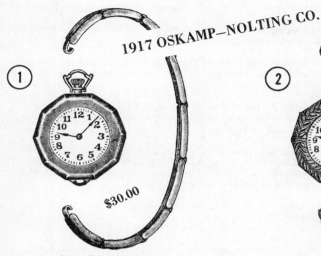

1917 OSKAMP—NOLTING CO.

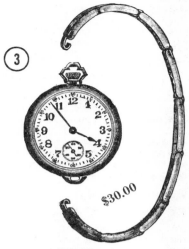

(1) $30.00

(2) $35.00

(3) $30.00

Elgin Bracelet Watch.
10x0-Size, 14k Solid Gold Polygon, ¾ Skylight
Plain Case and Bracelet.
Fitted with 15-Jewel Lady Elgin Movement.
No. 481 ....$62.40

Elgin Bracelet Watch.
10x0-Size, 14k Solid Gold Polygon, ¾ Skylight
Engraved Case and Bracelet.
Fitted with 15-Jewel Elgin Movement.
No. 482 ....$61.60

Elgin Bracelet Watch.
10x0-Size, 14k Solid Gold, Plain, Full Dial
Case and Bracelet.
Fitted with 15-Jewel Lady Elgin Movement.
No. 483 ....$58.00

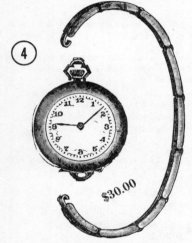

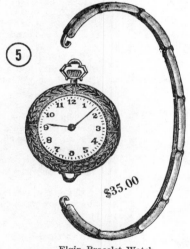

(4) $30.00

(5) $35.00

(6) EYE OPENED FOR ATTACHING BRACELET PATENTED MAY 11 1915 $40.00

Elgin Bracelet Watch.
10x0-Size, 14k Solid Gold, ¾ Skylight,
Plain Case and Bracelet.
Fitted with 15-Jewel Lady Elgin Movement.
No. 484 ....$58.50

Elgin Bracelet Watch.
10x0-Size, 14k Solid Gold, ¾ Skylight,
Engraved Case and Bracelet.
Fitted with 15-Jewel Elgin Movement.
No. 485 ....$60.75

The "Waltham Bracelet" Watch.
Disappearing Eye.
Special 10 Ligne Solid 14k, Gold Case
and Bracelet.
Fitted with 17-Jewel Riverside Waltham
Movement.
No. 486 ....$87.50

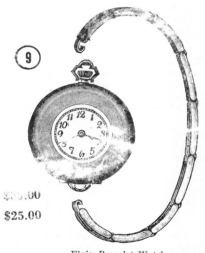

(7) $30.00

(8) $30.00 $25.00

(9) $30.00 $25.00

The "Waltham Bracelet" Watch.
Disappearing Eye.
Special 10 Ligne Solid 14k Gold Case
and Bracelet.
Fitted with 15-Jewel Sapphire Waltham.
No. 487 ....$69.50

Elgin Bracelet Watch.
5x0-Size, Solid 14k Gold, Skylight Engraved
Case and Bracelet.
Fitted with 15-Jewel Lady Raymond Elgin.
No. 488 ....$49.80
Fitted with 7-Jewel Elgin Works.
No. 489 ....$44.00

Elgin Bracelet Watch.
5x0-Size, Solid 14k Gold Skylight
Plain Case and Bracelet.
Fitted with 15-Jewel Lady Raymond Elgin.
No. 490 ....$47.60
Fitted with 7-Jewel Elgin Works.
No. 491 ....$41.80

18-S Hunting HH Taylor Grade 15-J Adj. mvt. 1,378,796. Mint Double sunk Roman dial Fancy hands cased in extra heavy yellow 14 K solid gold. Fancy engraved with horse and scene. Watch and case near mint. $300.00

18-S 21-J Grade 348. Mint mvt 11,185,637. Heavy Roy 14 K Solid Gold Hunting case flat lids engine turned. Mint condition. $300.00

18-S 23-J Veritas. Mint mvt. 13,121,685. ¾ plate diamond cap jewels. Mint 14 K Solid Gold Hand Engraved. open face case. $275.00

18-S Hunting Case 15-J. Extra fine nickel mvt. 2,421,326. Extra fine single sunk Elgin National Roman Numeral glass dial with almost invisible hairline cracks. Extra fine 14 K Yellow Gold Hunting Case. $175.00

18-S Hunting Case 15-J B.W. Raymond Grade 70. Extremely fine gilt, low serial 571,337. LS adj. gold balance weights. Extremely fine DS Roman Numeral glass dial with butterfly hands. Extremely fine yellow 18 K solid gold. Engine turned Hunting Case. $375.00

18-S Full plate open face 17-J adj. mvt. 10,325,733. Grade 249 Gilted mvt. Blaver coin silver 3 oz. case. Dial mint. Watch in extra fine condition. $55.00

18-S HC keywind and set. Fine gilted mvt. 655,974. Running but needs cleaning. Extra fine original hand lettered flat Roman dial and hands. Faint hairlines. Fine solid gold engin hunting case. Marked 18 K No. 572 with an eagle and lion. Looks like 8 or 10 K to me. Case is solid gold with about ½ of the engine turning worn off. Looks old, original and handsome. $170.00

18-S 15-J Keywind Grade HL Culver mint gilded RR mvt. 171,273. CA 1872 CO & running fine. Near mint SS hand lettered Roman dial. 3 small chips at 6,7 & 10. No case plastic mvt. holder. $45.00

18-S Standard on dial and movement 17-J adj. Gold cups and weights. Grade 116, mvt. 5,842,903. Mint DS dial. Mint silver OF case. Engraved scene. $110.00

18-S 21-J Grade 349. Full plate gold letters, Keystone 10 K GF case (mint) DS dial. $90.00

18-S Father Time 21-J Full plate open face. Mvt. 8,778,160. Case elg. 20 yr. double stock. Dial mint. $100.00

18-S 21-J Full plate. Grade 150. Gold letters mint DS dial, Mvt. 6,363,550. 20 yr. case GF. Near mint. $120.00

16-S ¾ plate 15-J adj. mvt. 747,010. Fancy nickel mvt. Hunting case heavy 14 K solid gold. Fancy engraved. Mint condition. Flat lid case. $250.00

16-S OF 23-J Veritass. Mvt. 25,271,994. Elgin Fiant Watch Case Co. 14 K solid gold. Mint condition. $225.00

16-S 21-J Father Time ¾ plate mvt. 24,627,220. Dueber Special. 25 yr. OF case. Up and down indicator. Mint condition. $270.00

16-S Grade 4. ¾ plate. 15-J adj. Mvt. 809,687. Cased in extra heavy 18-K solid gold hunters case. Hand engraved. Mint condition. $265.00

Elgin 16-S Hunting Bridge model Grade 243. Gold train. Fancy gold writing, decor... ...ing wheel, double sunk Roman perf. dial. Watch mint. 17-J adj. presentation. Keystone 14 K solid gold engraved case. Mint watch. $225.00

16-S 23-J Lord Elgin. Beautiful mint mvt. 12,718,386. Gold Train and Trim. Mint perfect DS dial and hands. Mint 14 K solid yellow gold OF case. $525.00

16-S OF 23-J Lord Elgin Grade 351. Mint nickel mvt. 12,718,290. Pendant set adj. 5 pos. Mint double sunk Elgin glass dial with original hands. Mint yellow gold filled crescent OF case warrented 25 yr. $475.00

16-S OF 23-J Veritas Up and Down indicator. Mint nickel Railroad mvt. 22,554,052. Lever Set adj, 5 pos. Mint Elgin single sunk indicator, glass dial with hands. Mint keystone J. Boss 14 K white gold filled OF case. $350.00

16-S OF 21-J Veritas. Grade 360. Mint nickel mvt. 13,482,006. Lever set, adj. 5 pos. Gold cups and balance weights. Extra fine single sunk Montgomery glass dial with hands. Extra fine Wadsworth 20 yr. yellow gold filled OF case. $125.00

16-S 21-J Bridge mvt. 10,814,589. Grade 270. Gold Train, gold letters. Mint DS dial B&B Royal 20 yr. yellow gold filled RR case. Watch is mint condition. $120.00

16-S 17-J Grade 280. Bridge model RR Grade mvt. 10,247,567. Gold letters, gold center wheel. Mint Dueber, 20 yr. gold filled RR case. Mint DS dial. $100

16-S 21-J B W Raymont. Mint ¾ plate RR mvt. 42,282,157. Flat Montgomery dial. Star GF case. Mint condition. $90.00

16-S 21-J Grade 91. Bridge model Convertible mvt. Black letters, gold train, gold escape wheel and reg. screw. Philadelphia GF 20 yr. case. Eng. DS Roman dial, Watch mint. $385.00

16-S 17-J Bridge model GM Wheeler mvt. 15,637,911. 20 yr. Engraved Philadelphia case. Mint green and gold decorated dial with gold fern hands. All over mint watch. $80.00

14-S Key Wind. Winds and sets in back 15-J adj. ¾ plate made for foreign markets. mvt. 474,264. Grade 46. 18 K Solid Gold Engraved pair case. Deal 18 K Gold with multi colored gold decoration and numbers. Mint case. Hand engraved and very pretty. $350.00

12-S 23-J Grade 190. Mint mvt. 8,503,004. Gold mtr. barrel. Gold Train. Perfect double sunk Montgomery dial. 14 K solid gold hunting case. Embossed with high relief. Beautiful mint gentlemans watch. $375.00

12-S Grade 237. ¾ plate black letters. 21-J Gold train Mtr. barrel. mvt. 8,540,553. 14 K solid gold Keystone case open face. Flat hand painted glass dial. Engraved monogram back lid. Mint. $250.00

12-S Lord Elgin Grade 543. 21-J adj. 5 position m vt. L 468,824. Keystone 14 K. solid gold case OF plain polished fancy bow C hands and numerals. Excellent condition $110.00

12-S 21-J ¾ plate mvt. 8,540,009. Grade 237. Motor barrel. 14 K solid gold case. Dial and hands mint. Watch mint. $235.00

12-S B W Raymond 19-J with jeweled mtr. barrel. Pink and white decorated dial trimmed with gold and gold hands. Perfect ¾ plate. 25 yr. Yellow Gold Filled. Engraved case. Mint mvt. 15,123,076. $150.00

12-S 15-J hunting ¾ nickel plate mvt. 14,040,570. Grade 314, mint and running. Extra fine flat porcelain Arabic dial sunk seconds, red track, mint hands engraved pilot 20 yr. yellow gold filled double back hunting case. A nice carrying watch. $75.00

10-S Keywind Hunting 7-J mvt. 450,080. 14 K solid gold hunting case, flat lids. Mint condition. $150.00

8-S Hunting 11-J Gilt mvt. 2,163,917. Dueber 18 K Solid Gold case. Very fancy hand engraved. Mint condition. $165.00

6-S 14 K solid gold hunting case. 11-J gilt mvt. 2,861,094. Flat lids with scalloped edge. Engraved case. $135.00

6-S Dueber 14 K solid gold case. 11-J gilt mvt. 2,705,733. Fancy silver and yellow dial. Watch is mint. $150.00

6-S Fahys permanent hunting case. Case paper still in back lik. 17-J very high grade with gold trim and raised gold cups. Mvt. 7,938,165. Case fancy engraved. Mint condition. Gradt 176. Class 53. $125.00

6-S Solid gold hunting case. 11-J Gilted mvt. 3,848,210. Hand entraved case. Mint condition. $150.00

0-S 15-J Philadelphia 14 K solid gold hunting case. Beautiful multi colored gold raised flowers, ribbons and leaves. 1-10 point diamond Mvt. 10,850,137. Mint condition. $350.00

0-S Fancy pink decorated dial. Fern hands. J Boss 25 yr. case. 15-J mvt. 14,359,095. Hand engraved. Small diamond in lid. Mint. Fancy bow. $210.00

0-S 14 K solid gold hunting case by Beaver. 15-J Gilt mvt. 3,913,601. Hand engraved case. Mint condition watch. $150.00

OS, 15J hunter. Near mint nickel mvt. 17,536,582. C & O Mint SS Arabic red trach dial and hands. Mint plus hand engraved, double back full hinged 20 yr. YGF SWC Co. Hunting case. A dandy little lady's watch. $100.00

96

ELGINS AND OTHER COMPANIES

This is all of the Elgin movement pictures that I could come up with. There are others, and many with other trade names. These shown are basically the ones marketed by Elgin. Elgin's high grade watches and models, of which a limited number were made, are very collectible. I have shown most of the high grade movements.

I am sure there are other movements that are scarce I am not sure uf. A thorough study would have to be made of the Elgin serial number list. On the other hand, even though numbers were assigned to a specific movement, it doesn't mean they were all manufactured. And no one knows or probably will ever know how many have survived. I think watches will eventually be collected like coins and the same rules will apply. I believe that watches are a very good investment, as well as providing many hours of enjoyment to the collector.

I have not attempted to set the price on any watch movement. I have tried to follow past sales that I know of, and opinions of collectors that are old timers and have some of these watches in their collections. The Elgins that will increase most rapidly are the ones that are high grade and the sleepers that only a few collectors (or no one yet) knows about.

As collectors and investors become more and more knowledgeable about watches, prices will increase faster on the high grade and scarce movements. A most important thing to consider in the value of a watch is that the lowest serial number of that model movement is the most desirable and therefore the most valuable.

I you are a serious Elgin collector, trader or investor, and if you are to realize the most from your finds, you will need in addition to this book, a copy of the Elgin serial numbers.

All the things I have written here about Elgins will also apply to other companies, such as Waltham, Hamilton, Illinois, Hampden, Rockford, Columbus, South Bend, etc.

Watch collecting is a most challangeing and rewarding hobby. I think if you studied the rest of your life on American watches and makers there would still be watches and information turn up that would be new to you.

The pages of this book will work for you in many ways. A study of the pages will show you which years certain models were offered for saie. The factory descriptions will teach you what to look for in the high grade watches, whether they are pictured or not. By high grade I mean the top four or five watches in each size, the most expensive, the highest. I have tried to leave the advertising sheets in as near original form as I could to show how they sold their watches. I seems to me the Damasceened patterns was almost always the same on a particular grade so you can figure out the grade even when it was made for a jewelry store, etc. By comparing a watch not pictured with a similar one pictured will give you a close idea of its value. When watch prices have varied from what I have shown it will still be a valuable reference book.

How much is a watch worth or how much can I get for my watch. My experience has shown that you really don't ever know what something is worth until you sell it or try to sell it and then if you do you may feel you have sold it to low.

Watch prices have increased at an amazing rate in the past four years with the sharpest rise in solid gold, 21 jewel or better and the scarce or rare older American watches. Foreign watches are not considered in this book. Many new collectors have started collecting watches inthe past two years. I joined the NAWCC in 1969. My number is 23096. Recently two of my friends joined and received numbers over 40,000 and being a week apart there is over 100 numbers between them.

For many years American watches were completely overlooked by wealthy collectors. Now we have investment minded collectors who buy mostly American and want mostly the high grades and the oldest in original cases.

Getting the highest price for a watch is mainly finding somone with the money who wants the watch you have for sale. A watch may change hands five or ten times before it reaches a collector who will keep it. A dealer in simple terms knows what they will pay and then looks for watches to sell them A dealer most times will be your best buyer because they are collectors first themselves or with a fair profit knows someone who will buy your watch. A little extra time looking for a collector who wants your watch will usually get you more money.

97   ROY EHRHARDT   *Roy Ehrhardt*

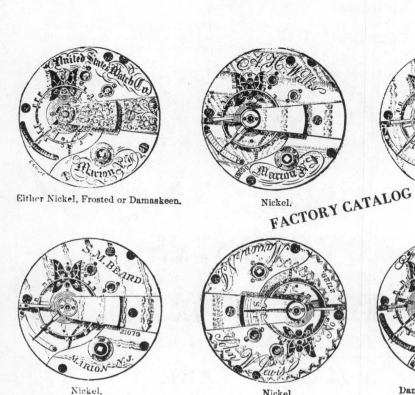

Either Nickel, Frosted or Damaskeen.

Nickel.

FACTORY CATALOG

Nickel.

Nickel.

Nickel.

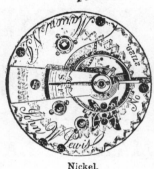

Nickel.

Damaskeen or Frosted.

Damaskeen or Frosted.

Damaskeen or Frosted.

Damaskeen or Frosted.

Either Frosted or Damaskeen.

Frosted.

Damaskeen or Frosted.

Damaskeen or Frosted.

Damaskeen or Frosted.

Damaskeen or Frosted.

BEWARE of worthless imitations with which the country is flooded. To avoid imposition, purchase only of responsible dealers, and *Insist* on a certificate of genuineness from those of whom you purchase, and see that the words, "*Marion, N. J.,*" are engraved on the plate over the Main-Spring Barrel. ☞All others are spurious.

UNITED STATES WATCH CO.
1864 to 1872
MARION WATCH CO.
1872 to 1874

I don't have enough actual knowledge to place a retail value on United States Watch Co. and these later Marion Watches. Watch dealers always ask $175.00 and up for watches in any kind of case.

99

Newark Watch Co.   1864 to 1870   N.Y. & N.J.
Cornell Watch Co.   1870 to 1874   Chicago
Cornell Watch Co.   1874 to 1876   San Fransisco
California Watch Co. 1876 to 1862   Berkley

Magazine Ad.

November, 1871.

These Cornell Watches range from $200.00 in a fine silver case ip to $500.00, for the California Cornell.

WATCH MOVEMENTS
MANUFACTURED BY THE
CORNELL WATCH COMPANY,
OF CHICAGO, ILL.

New York Office, 21 MAIDEN LANE.

PAUL CORNELL, Pres't.   J. C. ADAMS, Gen'l. Agent.

 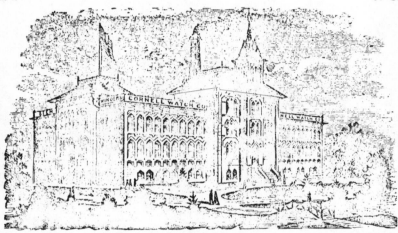 

STEM WINDERS.

No. 1. Named Paul Cornell, Chicago, Ills.
Jeweled in 19 Actions, Genuine Ruby, Gold Settings, Expansion Balance adjusted to Heat, Cold and Position, with Screw Regulator.

No. 2. Named C. M. Cady, Chicago, Ills.
Jeweled in 15 Actions, Expansion Balance with Screw Regulator.

KEY WINDERS.

No. 3. Named H. N. Hibbard, Chicago Ills.
Five Pairs Extra Jewels, Expansion Balance, Adjusted.

No. 4. Named Geo. F. Root, Chicago Ills.
Jewelled in 15 Actions, Expansion Balance, Set Jewels.

No. 5. Named John Evans, Chicago, Ills.
Jewelled in 15 Actions, Expansion Balance

No. 6. Named J. C. Adams, Chicago, Ills.
Jewelled in 11 Actions Expansion Balance.

No. 7. Named E. S. Williams, Chicago, Ills.
Expansion Balance, Jewelled in 7 Actions.

No. 8. Named Geo. W. Waite, Hyde Park.
Gold Balance, Jewelled in 7 Actions.

No. 9. Named Geo. W. Waite, Hyde Park
Steel Balance, Jewelled in 7 Actions.

The above movements are quick beat, (18,000 per hour,) and especially adapted for R. R. time keepers.
An Illustrated Catalogue giving full description of movements, with cuts and prices, will be ready for the trade shortly.

J. C. ADAMS, General Agent, 21 Maiden Lane.

100

United States Watch Co.'s Movements

NEW YORK OFFICE, 187 Broadway.   **CHICAGO OFFICE, Venetian Building.**   **BOSTON OFFICE, 421 Washington St.**

1894

To The Trade

(1) $70.00

No. 42, Fine Nickel Movement, 15 Ruby Jewels in Gold Settings, Safety Pinion, Hardened and Tempered Breguet Hairspring, Compensation-Balance, Patent Regulator, Double Sunk Dial, Adjusted.

(2) $45.00

No. 49, Nickel, 11 Jewels, Safety Pinion, Compensation-Balance, Hardened and Tempered Breguet Hairspring, Patent Regulator, Top Plate Jeweled in Settings, Sunk Second Dial.

(3) $40.00

No. 46, Nickel, 11 Jewels, Safety Pinion, Compensation-Balance, Top Plate Jeweled in Settings.

(4) $35.00

No. 47, Gilded, 11 Jewels, Safety Pinion, Compensation-Balance, Top Plate Jeweled in Settings,

(5) $60.00

No. 84, Adjusted, Nickel, 15 Jewels in Gold Settings, Safety Pinion, Compensation-Balance, Patent Regulator, Double Sunk Dial, Hardened and Tempered Breguet Hairspring.

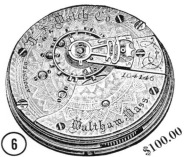

(6) $100.00

No. 79, First Quality Nickel Movement, 17 Ruby Jewels in Gold Settings, Safety Pinion, Hardened and Tempered Breguet Hairspring, Compensation-Balance, Adjusted to Heat, Cold, Positions and Isochronism, Patent Regulator, Double Sunk Dial. This movement is especially adapted for Railway Service.

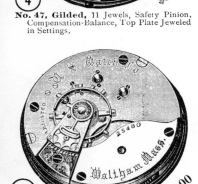

(7) $40.00

No. 43, Fine Gilded Movement, 15 Ruby Jewels in Gold Settings, Safety Pinion, Hardened and Tempered Breguet Hairspring, Compensation-Balance, Patent Regulator, Double Sunk Dial, Adjusted.

(9) $150.00

"The President."

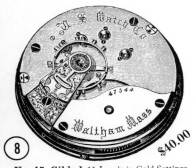

(8) $40.00

No. 45, Gilded, 15 Jewels in Gold Settings, Safety Pinion, Compensation-Balance, Patent Regulator, Double Sunk Dial, Hardened and Tempered Breguet Hairspring.

OFFICE OF
THE UNITED STATES WATCH CO.
WALTHAM, MASS.

This is to Certify, that Watch Movement No.........................., called **"The President,"** is First Quality Nickel, 18 Size, Full Plate, Stem Winding and Lever Setting. It has a **Double Roller Escapement, 17 Jewels** in Gold Settings, Safety Pinion, Hardened and Tempered Breguet Hairspring, Compensation Balance, Adjusted to **Heat, Cold, Isochronism,** and **All Positions,** Matheson's Patent Regulator, Double Sunk Dial, and is highly finished in all its parts.

This movement is made in both Open-Face and Hunting, and is **the only 18 Size Double Roller,** Lever-Setting Movement on the market.

Having all the advantages of this form of Escapement, it recommends itself at once, especially for Railroad Service and all conditions where the watch is subjected to violent external motion.

The Company **guarantees that this movement** will vary less than **six sec= onds in a calendar month,** and fully warrants and defends each and every representation above made.

T. B. EATON, Pres't.   A. E. HAMMER, Treas.

"The President" can be had only of
JOHN J. McGRANE, No. 187 Broadway, New York City,
to whom all orders should be addressed.

The United States Watch Co., Waltham, Mass., offers its full line of 6 Size Hunting and 18 Size Hunting and Open-Face Movements, to the trade with the WARRANTY that in the principles of construction, honesty of workmanship and timekeeping qualities they are UNSURPASSED by any watch on the market. ☞ If your jobber does not carry our movements, write to the factory, WALTHAM, MASS., and your order will be honored.

PRICE-LIST ON APPLICATION.

United States Watch Co.'s Movements, Waltham, Mass.

1898 SUPPLY CATALOG

Named and Nameless. 18 Size Quick Train Hunting and Open Face and Stem Wind are Lever Set. Fit all American Cases of Similar Size

18 Size, Stem Wind, Full Plate, Hunting.

List Prices Each.

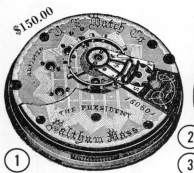

$150.00

(1)

THE PRESIDENT. 18 Size, Nickel, Hunting Open Face and Stem Wind. Lever Set 17 Extra Fine Ruby Jewels (5 Pairs in Gold Settings) Matheson's Patent Regulator, Bregue Hair-Spring, Accurately Adjusted to Temperature, Isochronism and Positions Double Roller Escapement, Double Sunk, Glass Enamel Dial with Marginal Figures..................... $68 75

$100.00

(2) (3)

No. 39 Hunting, First Quality Nickel. 17 Ruby Jewels in Gold Settings, Safety Pinion, Hardened and Tempered Breguet Hair-Spring. Compensation Balance, Adjusted to Heat, Cold Position and Isochronism, Patent Regulator, Double Sunk Dial This Movement is Especially Adapted for Railway Service.... .... $50 00

No. 79 Open Face, Same as above, 50 00

$80.00

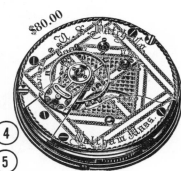

(4) (5)

No. 40 Hunting, Fine Nickel, 17 Ruby Jewels in Gold Settings, Safety Pinion, Hardened and Tempered Breguet Hair-Spring, Compensation-Balance. Adjusted to Heat, Cold and Position, Patent Regulator, Double Sunk Dial.. $37 50

No. 80 Open Face, Same as above, 37 50

$70.00

(6) (7)

No. 52 Hunting, Fine Nickel, 17 Jewels in Gold Settings, Double Roller Escapement, Nickel Train Wheels, Safety Pinion, Hardened and Tempered Breguet Hair-Spring, Compensation-Balance Adjusted. Patent Regulator, Double Sunk Dial................. $32

No. 92 Open Face, Same as above, 23 3

$70.00

(8) (9)

No. 53 Hunting, Nickel, 15 Jewels in Settings, Safety Pinion, Compensation Balance, Patent Regulator, Double Sunk Dial, Hardened and Tempered Breguet Hair-Spring................. $17 50

No. 93 Open Face, Same as above, 17 50

$60.00

(10) (11)

No. 54 Hunting, Nickel, 15 Jewels in Settings, Safety Pinion, Compensation Balance, Plain Regulator, Hardened and Tempered Hair-Spring..................... $15 63

No. 94 Open face, Same as above.. 15 63

$45.00

(12) (13)

No. 56 Hunting, Nickel, 11 Jewels, Safety Pinion, Compensation-Balance. Hardened and Tempered Breguet Hair-Spring, Patent Regulator, Top Plate Jeweled in Settings................. $14 38

No. 96 Open Face, Same as above, 14 38

$40.00

(14) (15)

No 57 Hunting, Gilded, 15 Jewels in Settings Safety Pinion, Compensation - Balance, Patent Regulator, Hardened and Tempered Hair-Spring. $14 3

No. 97 Open Face, Same as above, 14 3

MADE WATCHES 1884 to 1903

SOLD TO E. HOWARD

Watches are as yet not popular with collectors. You will see these same movements marked "A new Watch Co. at Waltham" because of a lawsuit with Waltham, they could be valued about the same. The high grades seem to be scarce expecially "The President"

$45.00

(16) (17)

No. 58 Hunting, Nickel, 11 Jewels, Safety Pinion, Compensation-Balance, Plain Regulator, Top Plate Jeweled in Settings...... $13 75

No. 98 Open Face, Same as above, 13 75

$30.00

No. 48 Hunting, Gilded, 7 Jewels, Safety Pinion, Compensation Balance, Plain Regulator..... $10 00

No. 88 Open Face, Same as above. 10 00

United States Watch Co.'s Movements.

Waltham, Mass.

6 and 16 Size, 3-4 Plate, Stem Wind, Hunting and Open Face.

List Prices Each.

16 Size, Hunting, Stem Wind, Lever Set, Thin Model.

$75.00 ①

No. 103 Nickel; 17 Ruby Jewels, Pairs in Settings; Breguet Hairspring; Micrometer Regulator; Double Sun Dial; Adjusted to Heat, Cold and Positions; Safety Center Pinion, Compensation Balance..... $37 50

$65.00 ②

No. 104 Nickel; 17 Jewels, 5 Pairs in Settings; Breguet Hair-Spring; Micrometer Regulator; Double Sunk Dial; Safety Center Pinion, Compensation Balance..... $22 50

$50.00 ③

No. 105 Nickel; 15 Jewels, 4 Pairs in Settings; Breguet Hair-Spring; Micrometer Regulator; Sunk Second Dial; Safety Center Pinion, Compensation Balance.... $18 75

$50.00 ④

No. 106 Nickel; 15 Jewels, 4 Pairs in Settings; Plain Regulator; Sunk Second Dial; Safety Center Pinion, Compensation Balance..... $16 25

$40.00 ⑤

No. 107 Gilded; 15 Jewels, 4 Pairs in Settings; Plain Regulator; Sunk Second Dial; Safety Center Pinion, Compensation Balance $15 00

$35.00 ⑥

No. 108 Nickel; 11 Jewels in Settings; Plain Regulator; Sunk Second Dial; Safety Center Pinion, Compensation Balance $14 38

$35.00 ⑦

No. 109 Nickeled; Damaskeened; 7 Jewels; Safety Center Pinion, Compensation Balance............. $10 63

$30.00 ⑧

No. 110 Gilded; 7 Jewels; Safety Center Pinion, Compensation Balance............. $10 63

6 Size, Hunting, Stem Winding and Lever Setting, Quick Train.

$75.00 ⑨

No. 60 First Quality Nickel; 17 Ruby Jewels in Gold Settings; Safety Pinion; Compensation Balance; Hardened and Tempered Breguet Hair-Spring; Fully Adjusted; Double Sunk Dial....................... $37 50

$50.00 ⑩

No. 68 Fine Nickel; 16 Jewels in Gold Settings; Safety Pinion; Compensation Balance; Hardened and Tempered Breguet Hair-Spring; Adjusted; Double Sunk Dial.......... $25 00

$40.00 ⑪

No. 62 Nickel; 15 Jewels in Settings; Safety Pinion; Compensation Balance, Sunk Second Dial. $17 50

$30.00 ⑫

No. 63 Gilded; 15 Jewels in Settings; Safety Pinion; Compensation Balance; Sunk Second Dial. $16 25

$30.00 ⑬

No. 61 Nickel; 11 Jewels; Safety Pinion; Compensation Balance; Top Plate Jeweled in Settings........ $15 63

$25.00 ⑭

No. 65 Gilded; 11 Jewels; Safety Pinion; Compensation Balance; Top Plate Jeweled in Settings.... ..... $14 38

103

$25.00 ⑮

No. 66 Gilded; 7 Jewels; Safety Pinion; Compensation Balance.... $12 50

$25.00 ⑯

No. 69 Nickeled; Damaskeened; 7 Jewels; Safety Pinion; Compensation Balance..................... $12 50

COLUMBUS WATCH CO

Columbus, Ohio.

PARTS OF THREE 1899 &
1890 ADVERTISEMENTS

$200

18 SIZE. RAILWAY KING.

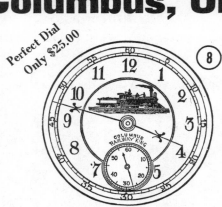

Perfect Dial
Only $25.00

RAILWAY KING DIAL.

$200

No. 18 and 98.
No. 18 is for Hunting case, winds at III.
No. 98 is Open Face, same grade,
winds at XII.   Pendant Set.

$85

No. 28. Htg., 16 Jewels, Nickel,
D. S. dial.
No. 98. O. F. adj. Breg. hairspring,
Damaskeened, P. R.

$85

No. 27. Htg., Nickel, 16 Jewels.
D. S. dial.
No. 97. O. F. adj. Breg. hairspring,
P. Reg.

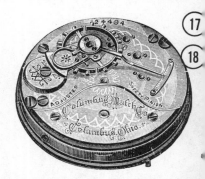

No. 34. Htg., Nickel, 15 Jewels.
No. 95. O. F., adj. Pat. Reg.

$65.00

No. 33. Htg., Nickel, 15 Jewels.
No. 94. O. F., Breg. hairspring,
Pat. Reg.

$50.00

No. 32. Htg., Gilt, 15 Jewels.
No. 93. O. F., Breg. hairspring, P.
Reg.

$50

No. 21. Htg., Gilt, 11 Jewels.
No. 91. O. F., Ex. Bal.

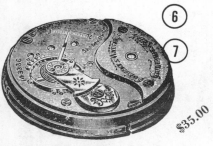

$35.00

No. 20. Htg., Gilt, 7 Jewels.
No. 90. O. F., Ex. Bal.

$60.00

$45.00

NORTH STAR NICKEL.
NORTH STAR GILT.

$40.0

No. 22. Htg. } Gilt, 11 Jewels.
No. 92. O. F. } Pat. Reg.

COLUMBUS WATCH CO.

PARTS OF THREE 1889 & 1890 ADVERTISEMENTS

3-4 PLATE, 16 SIZE MOVEMENTS.

① ②

$110

No. 47. Htg., Nickel, 16 Jewels, adj.
No. 87. O. F., D. S. dial, Breg. hair-spring, P. R.

③ ④

$90

No. 46. Htg., Nickel, 15 Jewels, Breg. hairspring.
No. 86. O. F., adj. D. S. dial, P. R.

⑤ ⑥

$70.00

No. 41. Htg., Gilt, 11 Jewels.
No. 81. O. F.

The Higher Grades of the Columbus Watches are centre jeweled and beautifully finished. Our Nos. 43 and 83 are the lowest in price of any 16 size Nickel Movement in the market.

$140

⑦

For the Finest Retail Trade we particularly recommend our new

Nos. 48 and 57

Sixteen and Six Sizes.

16 SIZE. NO. 48.

$100.00

⑧ ⑨

No. 43 and 83.
No. 43 is for Htg. case, winds at III.
No. 83 for O. F., winds at XII.

No. 48. 16 size Hunting Movement. Damaskeened in gold, jeweled with the finest rubies and extra centre jewel in raised gold settings, with red polished train and micrometer regulator. Movement has full adjustment.

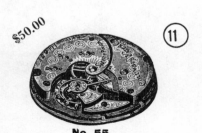

$90.00

6 SIZE. NO. 57.

$50.00 ⑪

No. 55.
15 Jewels set in red gold settings. Can be furnished with dbl. sunk dials if preferred, at difference in cost of dials.

$40.00 ⑫

No. 53.
11 Jewel Nickel. Jewels in red gold settings. The cheapest Nickel movement in the market with set jewels.

$35.00 ⑬

No. 51.
11 Jewel, Gilt.

6 size No. 57. Damaskeened in gold, full jeweled with extra centre jewel in raised gold settings, is without exception the handsomest movement for ladies' use ever placed on the market.

ASK YOUR JOBBER FOR THEM.

18 Size, 21 Jewels.
NEW COLUMBUS TIME KING.

21J	$160.00
23J	$225.00
17J	$115.00
25J	$800.00

① **Hunting and Open Face.**

Nickel, 21 Genuine Ruby Jewels, set in red, Solid Gold Raised Settings, Escapement Cap Jeweled, Adjusted to Temperature, Positions and Isochronism, Breguet Hair Spring, Patent Center Pinion, Patent Regulator, Polished Dust Band and Stem Wind, Beveled Steel Work, Pearled Plates; fine, white, cut, and beveled edge, hard enameled, double sunk, Red marginal figured Roman or Arabic Dial; handsomely damaskeened in Gold on Nickel _____ $25 00

I don't have any factory pictures of Columbus Key Wind Movements. They could be valued about the same grade for grade with the Illinois or Rockford's shown on the other pages of this book.

18 Size, Full Plate, Stem Wind.
NUMBERED MOVEMENTS.

$80.00

② **Hunting, No. 203.**   **Open Face, No. 204.**

Nickel, 17 Jewels, set in red Gold Settings, Adjusted to Temperature and Positions, Breguet Hair Spring, Patent Center Pinion, Patent Regulator, Dust Band and Polished Stem Wind, Pearled Plates, double sunk black marginal figured Dial, Damaskeened in Gold on Nickel _____ $13 00

1895 FACTORY PRICE LIST

$100.00

③ **Hunting, No. 1.**   **Open Face, No. 2**

Nickel, 17 Ruby Jewels, set in red solid Gold Raised Settings, Adjusted to Temperature, Positions and Isochronism, Breguet Hair Spring, Patent Center Pinion, Patent Regulator, Polished Dust Band and Stem Wind, Beveled Edge Steel Work, Pearled Plates; fine, white, hard enameled, double sunk, beveled edge, red marginal figured Dial; nicely damaskeened in Gold on Nickel _____ $16

$70.00

④ **Hunting, No. 3.**   **Open Face, No. 4.**

Nickel, 16 Jewels, set in red Gold Settings, Adjusted to Temperature and Positions, Breguet Hair Spring, Patent Center Pinion, Patent Regulator, Dust Band and Polished Stem Wind, Pearled Plates, double sunk black marginal figured Dial, Damaskeened in Gold on Nickel _____ $ 9 50

18 Size, Full Plate, Stem Wind.   18 Size, Full Plate, Stem Wind.

NUMBERED MOVEMENTS.   NUMBERED MOVEMENTS.

1895 FACTORY PRICE LIST

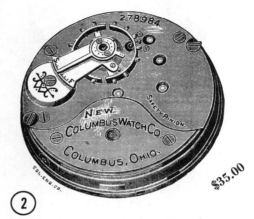

① $50.00

Hunting, No. 5.   Open Face, No 6.

② $35.00

Hunting, No. 9.   Open Face No. 10.

Nickel, 16 Jewels set in red Gold Settings, Breguet Hair Spring, Patent Regulator, Patent Center Pinion, sunk Seconds, black marginal Figured Dial and nicely Damaskeened__ $6 50

Gilt, 7 Jewels, Tempered Hair Spring, Patent Center Pinion, Dust Band, and fine, white, hard enameled Dial _ _ _ _ _ $4 00

All 18 and 16 Size Open Face, also all 6 size Movements manufactured by the New Columbus Watch Company are **LEVER SET**.

Movements are valued as if they were in a case but you must add the value of the case for the total value of your watch.

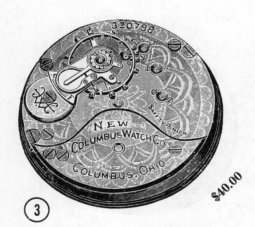

③ $40.00

Hunting, No. 7.   Open Face, No. 8

$150

Nickel, 11 Jewels in red Gold Settings, Patent Regulator, Patent Center Pinion, Dust Band; fine, white, hard enameled, sunk Seconds, black marginal figured Dial, and nicely Damaskeened _ _ _ _ _ _ _ _ _ _ _ _ _ _ $5 00

R. W. K. Special H't'g and O. F.

16 Size, Twenty=one Jewels.
NEW COLUMBUS RUBY.

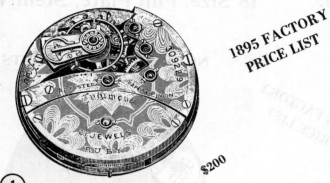

1895 FACTORY PRICE LIST

① **Hunting and Open Face.** $200

Nickel, 21 Genuine Ruby Jewels, set in red Solid Gold Raised Settings, Escapement Cap Jeweled, Adjusted to Temperature, Beveled Steel Work, Positions and Isochronism, Breguet Hair Spring, Patent Center Pinion, Patent Regulator, Polished Stem Wind, Beveled Edge Steel Work, Pearled Plates; fine, white, cut and beveled edge, hard enameled, double sunk, red marginal figured Roman or Arabic Dial; handsomely Damaskee:ed in Gold on Nickel.............$30 00

We recommend this Watch wherever accurate time is required and a medium size watch is desired. We fully guarantee same in every respect.

16 Size, 3=4 Plate, Stem Wind.

Numbered Movements.

② $120

Hunting, No. 11.   Open Face, No. 12.

Nickel, 17 Genuine Ruby Jewels, set in red Solid Gold Raised Settings, Adjusted to Temperature, Positions and Isochronism, Breguet Hair Spring, Patent Center Pinion, Patent Regulator, Pearled Plates, Beveled Steel Work; fine, white, hard enameled, double sunk, beveled edge, red marginal figured Dial, handsomely Damaskeened in Gold on Nickel............$20 00

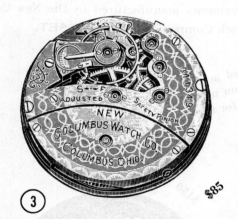

③ $85

Hunting, No. 13.   Open Face, No 14.

Nickel, 16 Jewels, set in red Gold Settings, Adjusted to Temperature and Positions, double sunk black marginal figured Dial, Breguet Hair Spring, Patent Regulator, Patent Center Pinion, Pearled Plates, nicely Damaskeened in Gold on Nickel $10

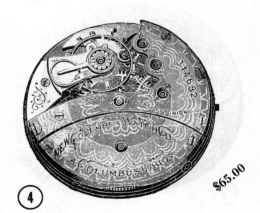

④ $65.00

Hunting, No. 315.   Open Face, No 316.

Nickel, 16 Jewels, set in red Settings, Breguet Hair Spring, Patent Regulator, Patent Center Pinion, Seconds sunk, black marginal figured Dial, and nicely Damaskeened...............$6 50

16 Size, 3=4 Plate, Stem Wind.

Numbered Movements.

1895 FACTORY PRICE LIST

(1) $60.00

Hunting, No. 17.   Open Face, No. 18.

Nickel, 11 Jewels, set in red Settings, Patent Regulator, Patent Center Pinion, fine, white, hard enameled black marginal figured Dial, and nicely Damaskeened ----------------------------- $ 5 00

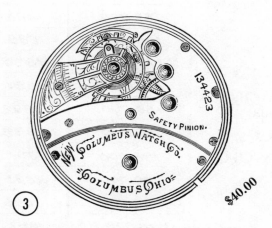

(3) $40.00

Hunting, No. 19.   Open Face, No. 20.

Gilt, 7 Jewels, Tempered Hair Spring, Patent Center Pinion, fine, white, hard enameled Dial ----------------------------- $ 4 00

6 Size, 3=4 Plate, Stem Wind.

Numbered Movements.

(2) $85.00   **No. 100.**

Nickel, Adjusted, 16 Ruby Jewels set in red Gold Raised Settings, Patent Center Pinion, Pearled Plates, double sunk red marginal figured Dial, handsomely Damaskeened in Gold on Nickel ----------------------------- $10 00

(4) $70.00   **No. 104.**

Nickel, 16 Jewels, in red Gold Settings, Adjusted, Patent Center Pinion, fine, white, hard enameled, double sunk, black marginal figured Dial, nicely Damaskeened in Nickel ----------- $ 8 00

6 Size, 3=4 Plate, Stem Wind.

Numbered Movement.

1895 FACTORY PRICE LIST

①

No. 103.

$65.00

Nickel, 16 Jewels, in red Gold Settings, Patent Center Pinion, fine, white, hard enameled, Seconds sunk, black marginal Dial, nicely Damaskeened.. $6 75

6 Size, 3=4 Plate, Stem Wind.

②

No. 102.

$40.00

Gilt, 7 Jewels, Tempered Hair Spring, Patent Center Pinion, fine, white, hard enameled Dial_____ __ _____ $4 50

COLUMBUS WATCH CO.

APPROXIMATE PRODUCTION DATES

SERIAL NO.	DATE
40,000	1883
80,000	1884
121,000	1885
130,000	1886
141,000	1887
152,000	1888
163,000	1889
174,000	1890
180,000	1891
184,000	1892
189,000	1893
195,000	1894
200,000	1895
205,000	1896
210,000	1897
215,000	1898
220,000	1899
225,000	1900
245,000	1901
265,000	1902
288,000	1903

③

$50.00

No. 101.

COLUMBUS WATCH CO.
1886 to 1903
Sold To
SOUTH BEND WATCH CO.
In 1903

All Columbus watches are good collector items. They are old and not many made.

Nickel, 11 Jewels, set in red settings, Patent Center Pinion, fine, white, hard enameled, black marginal figured Dial, and nicely Damaskeened_____ $5 25

SETH THOMAS WATCH MOVEMENTS.

FIT ALL STYLES STANDARD CASES.

Quick Train, 3-4 Plate, Safety Pinion, Expansion Balance, Stem-
Winding and Setting, Sunk (Cut) Seconds Dial.

(18) $50.00
No. 33. O. F. Gilded.
18 SIZE. 7 JEWELS. PLAIN REGULATOR

(7) $60.00
No. 34. Hunting, Gilded.
18 SIZE. 7 JEWELS. PLAIN REGULATOR

(13) $70.00
No. 170. O. F. Nickel.
18 SIZE. 15 JEWELS. MICROMETER REGULATOR

(3) $150.00
No. 171. Hunting, Nickel.
18 SIZE. 15 JEWELS. MICROMETER REGULATOR

(17) $50.00
No. 55. O. F. Gilded.
18 SIZE. 11 JEWELS. MICROMETER REGULATOR

(8) $70.00
No. 56. Hunting, Gilded.
18 SIZE. 11 JEWELS. MICROMETER REGULATOR

(10) $75.00
No. 201. O. F. Nickel.
18 SIZE. 15 JEWELS. ADJUSTED.
MICROMETER REGULATOR.

(2) $164.00
No. 202. Hunting, Nickel.
18 SIZE. 15 JEWELS. ADJUSTED.
MICROMETER REGULATOR.

(14) $50.00
No. 70. O. F. Gilded.
18 SIZE. 15 JEWELS. MICROMETER REGULATOR
OR
(15) **No. 101. O. F. Gilded.**
18 SIZE. 15 JEWELS. ADJUSTED. MICROMETER
REGULATOR.

(6) $100.00
No. 71. Hunting, Gilded.
18 SIZE. 15 JEWELS. MICROMETER REGULATOR
OR
(16) **No. 102. Hunting, Gilded.**
18 SIZE. 15 JEWELS. ADJUSTED. MICROMETER
REGULATOR.

(9) $175.00
Henry Molineux. O. F. Nickel.
18 SIZE. 17 RUBY JEWELS IN GOLD SETTINGS.
ADJUSTED. MICROMETER REGULATOR.
BREGUET H. S., D. S. DIAL.

(1) $200.00
Henry Molineux. Hunting, Nickel.
18 SIZE. 17 RUBY JEWELS IN GOLD SETTINGS.
ADJUSTED. MICROMETER REGULATOR.
BREGUET H. S., D. S. DIAL.

(19) $40.00
No. 46. Gilded.
6 SIZE. 7 JEWELS.

(20) $75.00 (21) $55.00
No. 119. Nickel. **No. 122. Nickel.**
6 SIZE. 15 JEWELS. 6 SIZE. 11 JEWELS.

(11) $75.00
No. 196. O. F. Nickel.
18 SIZE. 15 JEWELS. ADJUSTED.
MICROMETER REGULATOR.

(4) $175.00
No. 197. Hunting, Nickel.
18 SIZE. 15 JEWELS. ADJUSTED.
MICROMETER REGULATOR.

(12) $60.00
No. 96. O. F. Gilded.
18 SIZE. 15 JEWELS. ADJUSTED
MICROMETER REGULATOR.

(5) $100.00
No. 97. Hunting, Gilded.
18 SIZE. 15 JEWELS. ADJUSTED.
MICROMETER REGULATOR.

This page is a result of combining 3 pages from a 1893 Seth Thomas Factory Catalog. I placed the numbers (1) (2) (3) etc. in the order I thought the grades were. With (1) in the cut away plate being the highest and (9) in the ¾ plate being also the highest. The high grade early Seth Thomas watches make a beautiful and fine collection Some of these movements are probably rare and are under priced. The 25 Jewel Maiden Lane is worth at this time about $1000.00 and the 28 Jewel Maiden Lane about $3000.00 to the right buyer. Neither of these movements are pictured.

111

Maiden Lane.

18 size, full plate, Open Face model.

21 ruby jewels in gold settings, patent regulator. Breguet hair spring, double sunk dial, adjusted, nickel .... $50 00 ... $200.00

No. 510. 17 jewels, Breguet hair spring, patent regulator, adjusted, double sunk dial, nickel 28 00 $175.00

No. 182. 17 jewels, Breguet hair spring, patent regulator, adjusted, nickel .. 18 00 $150.00

No. 82. 17 jewels, Breguet hair spring, patent regulator, adjusted, gilt ... 16 00 $80.00

No. 159. 15 jewels, nickel 12 00 80.00

No. 59. 15 jewels, gilt 11 00 60.00

No. 58. 11 jewels, gilt 10 00 60.00

Movements are valued as if they were in a case but you must add the value of the case for the total value of your watch.

Henry Molineux.

Hunting and Open Face, 18 size, ¾ plate Hunting model.

20 ruby jewels in gold settings, patent regulator, Breguet hair spring, double sunk dial, adjusted, nickel $50 00

$250.00

A. C. BECKEN 1896

No. 56. 11 jewels, Hunting, gilt $10 00 $70.00

No. 55. 11 jewels, Open Face, gilt 10 00 70.00

No. 34. 7 jewels, Hunting, gilt.... 8 00 60.00

No. 33. 7 jewels, Open Face, gilt....... 8 00 60.00

No. 34.

18 Size,

18 Size,

No. 506.

¾ plate model.

No. 508. 17 jewels, patent regulator, adjusted, double sunk dial, Hunting, nickel $28 00 $100.00

No. 506. 17 jewels, patent regulator, adjusted, double sunk dial, Open Face, nickel 28 00 $100.00

No. 408. 17 jewels, patent regulator, adjusted, double sunk dial, Hunting, gilt 26 00 $80.00

No. 406. 17 jewels, patent regulator, adjusted, double sunk dial, Open Face, gilt 26 00 $80.00

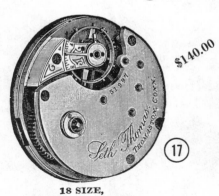

$140.00

18 SIZE,
3/4 PLATE, KEY WIND.

No. 180.

18 size,

¾ plate model.

$80.00 **No. 180.** 17 jewels, patent regulator, adjusted, Hunting, nickel $18 00

$80.00 **No. 179.** 17 jewels, patent regulator, adjusted, Open Face, nickel 18 00

$80.00 **No. 80.** 17 jewels, patent regulator, adjusted, Hunting, gilt.......... 16 00

$80.00 **No. 79.** 17 jewels, patent regulator, adjusted, Open Face, gilt....... 16 00

$60.00 **No. 152.** 15 jewels, Hunting, nickel ... $12 00

$60.00 **No. 52.** 15 jewels, Hunting, gilt....... 11 00

SETH THOMAS
WATCH MOVEMENTS

CENTENNIAL EDITION

TRADE PRICE LIST

September 1, 1913

Seth Thomas Clock Company

Established 1813

**Manufacturers of High-Grade Timepieces
for 100 Years**

15 Maiden Lane
New York

215 W. Randolph St.
Chicago

RAILROAD GRADES.

$200.00

(1)

**MAIDEN
LANE**

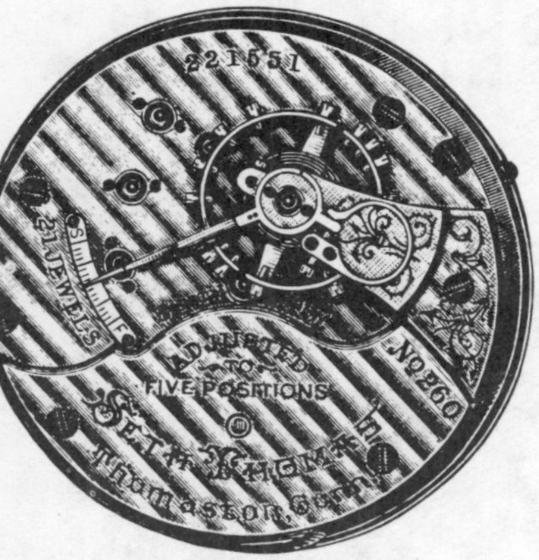

$175.00

(2)

No. 260

$150.00

(3)

No. 382

RAILROAD MOVEMENTS.

**18-SIZE FULL PLATE, OPEN FACE, IN 17 AND
21 JEWELS.**

**DOUBLE ROLLER ESCAPEMENT AND
RECESSED BALANCE.**

Breguet Hairspring, Cut Compensation Balance
with Timing Screws, Banking Screws, Safety
Pinion and Patent Micrometer Regulator.

Maiden Lane. Nickel, 21 Jewels in Gold Settings, Diamond Balance End Stones, Double Roller Escapement and Recessed Balance Wheel, Adjusted to Temperature, Isochronism and five positions. Steel Escape Wheel, Gold Balance Screws, D. S. Railroad Dial and Hands. The Pallet Arbor and Escape Pinion are cone-pivoted and cap-jeweled. Polished dust band. Movement is closely timed and beautifully finished in gold on solid nickel. Lever Set $50.00

No. 260. Nickel, 21 Jewels, Double Roller Escapement and Recessed Balance Wheel, Adjusted to Temperature, Isochronism and five positions. Steel Escape Wheel, D. S. Railroad Dial and Hands. The Pallet Arbor and Escape Pinion are cone-pivoted and cap-jeweled. Polished dust band. Movement is closely timed and finely finished throughout, and is recommended for the most exacting service. Lever Set $40.00

No. 382. Nickel, 17 Jewels, Double Roller Escapement and Recessed Balance Wheel. Adjusted to Temperature, Isochronism and five positions. Steel Escape Wheel, D. S. Railroad Dial and Hands. Polished dust band. Lever Set $30.00

These Railroad Grades are guaranteed to be up to the standard required for railway service and to be reliable timepieces.

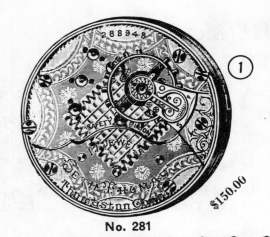

288948

$150.00

No. 281

SPECIAL 17-JEWEL, 18-SIZE, FULL PLATE, OPEN-FACE MOVEMENT.

No. 281. Nickel, 17 Jewels, Adjusted to Temperature, Breguet Hairspring, Patent Center Pinion, Patent Micrometer Regulator and Cut Compensation Balance with Fine Double Depressed Railroad Dial and Hands. Pendant Set ....

This movement is finely finished throughout and beautifully Damaskeened in gold and nickel.

1913 FACTORY CATALOG

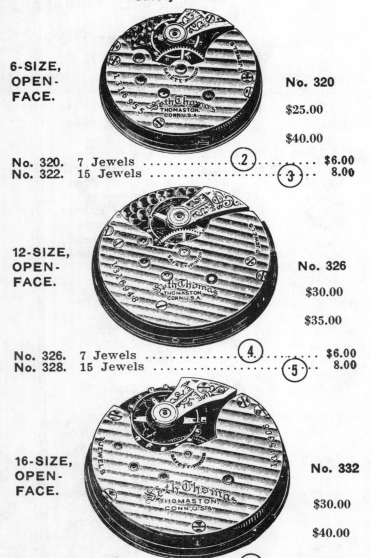

SETH THOMAS OPEN-FACE, PENDANT SET MOVEMENTS.

Nickel, Fancy Damaskeening. Cut Compensation Balance Wheel with Timing Screws. Banking Screws. Breguet Hairspring. Safety Pinion.

6-SIZE, OPEN-FACE.

No. 320

$25.00

$40.00

No. 320. 7 Jewels .... ②.......... $6.00
No. 322. 15 Jewels .... ③.... 8.00

12-SIZE, OPEN-FACE.

No. 326

$30.00

$35.00

No. 326. 7 Jewels .... ④ $6.00
No. 328. 15 Jewels .... ⑤. 8.00

16-SIZE, OPEN-FACE.

No. 332

$30.00

$40.00

No. 332. 7 Jewels .... ⑥ $6.00
No. 334. 15 Jewels .... ⑦ 8.00

SETH THOMAS HUNTING, LEVER SET MOVEMENTS.

Nickel, Fancy Damaskeening. Cut Compensation Balance Wheel with Timing Screws. Banking Screws. Breguet Hairspring. Safety Pinion.

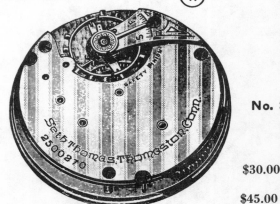

No. 205

$25.00

$40.00

6-SIZE, HUNTING.
Gilt and Nickel Damaskeening.
No. 35. 7 Jewels ... ⑧ $6.30
No. 205. 15 Jewels .... ⑨ 8.30

12 x 6 SIZE, HUNTING. $20.00
Gilt and Nickel Damaskeening. $30.00
12-Size Spread Dials fitted to 6-Size Movements.
No. 15. 7 Jewels ... ⑩ 6.30
No. 19. 15 Jewels .... ⑪ 8.30

No. 37

$30.00

$45.00

18-SIZE, ¾ PLATE, HUNTING.
No. 37. 7 Jewels .... ⑫ $5.40
No. 207. 15 Jewels, Patent Regulator . ⑬ 8.50

114

BRACELET (WRIST) WATCHES.

① List, $14.00   **$35.00**

0-SIZE.

Movement has 7 Jewels, Steel Escape Wheel, Exposed Pallets, Cut Compensation Balance with Timing Screws and Banking Screws. Patent Safety Pinion, Breguet Hairspring, Polished Regulator. Finely finished plates. Pendant Set.

In Solid Nickel Case with Black Morocco or Pig Skin Wrist Straps.

See Page 4

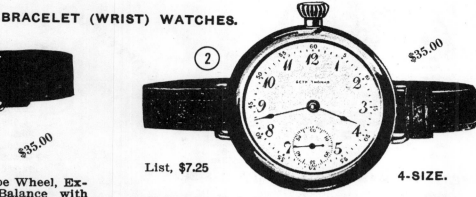

② $35.00

List, $7.25   **4-SIZE.**

Seven-Jeweled Movement, Breguet Hairspring, Banking Screws, Safety Pinion and fitted with Fine White Porcelain Dial with Red Marginal Figures, Pendant Set.

A refined, practical, and reliable article for both men and women; fitted in Solid Nickel Case with Wrist Strap in Black Morocco or Pig Skin; 4-size watch in special snug model case, but a trifle larger than the 0-size case.

1913 FACTORY CATALOG

No. 27

12-SIZE, OPEN-FACE MOVEMENTS IN 7, 15 AND 17 JEWELS. BRIDGE MODEL.

No. 28. Nickel, 17-Ruby and Sapphire Jewels in Raised Gold Settings, Adjusted to Temperature and three positions, Patent Micrometer Regulator, Compensating Balance with Timing Screws and Banking Screws, Breguet Hairspring, Exposed Winding Wheels, Polished Gold-Plated Center Wheel and Train Wheels and finely finished throughout, fitted with Fine White Porcelain Dial. Pendant Set **③ $50.00** **$25.00**

No. 27. Nickel, 17 Ruby Jewels in Raised Gold Settings, fitted with Patent Micrometer Regulator, Compensating Balance with Timing Screws and Banking Screws, Breguet Hairspring, Exposed Winding Wheels, Polished Center Wheel, fitted with Fine White Porcelain Dial. Pendant Set **④ $45.00** **$17.00**

No. 26. Nickel, 15 Ruby Jewels in Gold Settings, fitted with Patent Micrometer Regulator, Compensating Balance with Timing Screws and Banking Screws, Breguet Hairspring, Exposed Winding Wheels, Polished Center Wheel, fitted with Fine White Porcelain Dial. Pendant Set **⑤ $35.00** **$13.50**

No. 25. Nickel, 7 Jewels, fitted with Patent Micrometer Regulator, Compensating Balance with Timing Screws and Banking Screws, Breguet Hairspring, Exposed Winding Wheels, Polished Center Wheel, fitted with Fine White Porcelain Dial. Pendant Set **⑥ $25.00** **$10.00**

We can supply our 12-size Movements in 20 and 25-year Open-Face Cases of very thin special models.

Silver and Gilt dials for above movements can be had $1.00 list extra.

No. 9

O SIZE HUNTING MOVEMENTS.

No. 9. Nickel, 17 Ruby Jewels, Gold Settings, Steel Escape Wheel, Exposed Pallets, Cut Compensation Balance with Timing Screws and Banking Screws, Patent Safety Pinion, Breguet Hairspring, Beautifully Damaskeened Plates. Finely finished throughout. Pendant Set **⑦ $75.00** **$20.00**

No. 3. Nickel 15 Jewels, Raised Gold Settings, Steel Escape Wheel, Exposed Pallets, Cut Compensation Balance with Timing Screws and Banking Screws, Patent Safety Pinion, Breguet Hairspring. Finely finished. Pendant Set **⑧ $50.00** **$15.00**

No. 1. Nickel, 7 Jewels, Steel Escape Wheel, Exposed Pallets, Cut Compensation Balance with Timing Screws and Banking Screws, Patent Safety Pinion, Breguet Hairspring, Polished Regulator. Finely finished plates. Pendant Set **⑨ $20.00** **$10.00**

These movements can be had fitted with Open-Face (no seconds) Dial, same price.

115   **No. 1**   **No. 3**

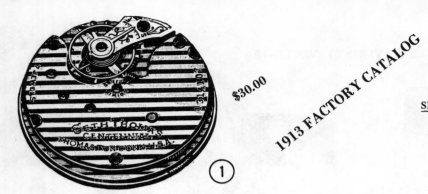

$30.00

(1)

SETH THOMAS "CENTENNIAL," 16-SIZE.

Movement made in 3 sizes, only for cases illustrated on page 8.

Movements are Nickel-Damaskeened and have 7 Jewels, Breguet Hairsprings, Safety Pinions, Banking Screws, etc.; Fine Porcelain Dials with Red Marginal Figures and Pressed Seconds.

SETH THOMAS WATCH CO.
Made watches 1884 to 1914
Thomaston, Conn.

APPROXIMATE PRODUCTION DATES

SERIAL NO.	DATE	SERIAL NO.	DATE
4,000	1885	500,000	1900
9,000	1886	552,000	1901
20,000	1887	604,000	1902
50,000	1888	657,000	1903
80,000	1889	710,000	1904
110,000	1890	763,000	1905
150,000	1891	817,000	1906
176,000	1892	937,000	1907
204,000	1893	1,057,000	1908
246,000	1894	1,177,000	1909
288,000	1895	1,325,000	1910
334,000	1896	1,835,000	1911
376,000	1897	2,355,000	1912
418,000	1898	3,000,000	1913
460,000	1899	3,600,000	1914

See Page 4

$25.00

(2)

$30.00

(3)

(4) $35.00

**Ladies' and Girls' 4-Size.
Jointed Back.**

**Men's and Boys' Small 12-Size.
Screw Front and Back.**

**Men's and Boys' Regular 16-Size.
Screw Front and Back.**

SETH THOMAS "CENTENNIAL" OPEN-FACE WATCHES.
7-JEWEL HIGH-GRADE MOVEMENTS.
RED MARGINAL DIALS.

		List
All the above 3 sizes in Solid Nickel, Plain Polished Cases		$5.30
4-Size, 10-Year in Plain, Engine-Turned or Die-Engraved ⑤		7.00
12-Size, 10-Year in Plain, Engine-Turned or Die-Engraved ⑥	$35.00	7.70
16-Size, 10-Year in Plain, Engine-Turned or Die-Engraved ⑦	40.00	8.00
4-Size, 20-Year in Plain, Engine-Turned or Die-Engraved ⑧	45.00	9.10
12-Size, 20-Year in Plain, Engine-Turned or Die-Engraved ⑨	40.00	9.50
16-Size, 20-Year in Plain, Engine-Turned or Die-Engraved ⑩	45.00	9.80
4-Size, 20-Year, Fine Hand-Engraved Patterns ⑪	50.00	9.50
12-Size, 20-Year, Fine Hand-Engraved Patterns ⑫	45.00	10.00
16-Size, 20-Year, Fine Hand-Engraved Patterns ⑬	50.00	10.30
	55.00	

All these cases are open-face, fitted with French bows and elliptical pendants; latest models, except the 4-size 10-year which has snap back and regular antique pendant and bow.

These patterns offer the jeweler an opportunity of carrying a complete line of popular sizes to meet the average need. Our unusual facilities for many years enable us to make, at this time, this "Centennial" line, which we believe represents the greatest value ever offered the trade and public at the prices these watches will be sold for.

These watches are cased and timed at the factory and are sold complete only.

THE TRUMP MOVEMENT SERIES "I"

Manufactured by
The Waterbury
Watch Company
Waterbury,
Connecticut

THE CHARLES BENEDICT MOVEMENT SERIES "K"

LONG WIND MOVEMENT SERIES "E"
Discontinued 1890.

$150.00 plus
in extra fine
complete watch

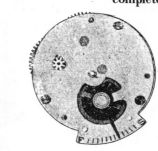

VIEW OF SERIES "E" MOVEMENT.

THE ELFIN MOVEMENT SERIES S

TUXEDO MOVEMENT SERIES "R"

THE OLD ADDISON MOVEMENT SERIES "N"

117

THE
COLUMBIAN
MOVEMENT
SERIES "H" *Hunting Case*

THE
AMERICUS
MOVEMENT
SERIES "J"

Manufactured by
The Waterbury
Watch Company
Waterbury,
Connecticut

I have not tried to value these Waterbury movements. They are mostly duplex escapements and not many of them survive. Most movements take a special case. Some came cased in beautiful enamel, gold and highly decorated cases. The movements are hard to fix. Be careful when buying one not running. The long winds are very desirable collector watches.

THE
ADDISON
MOVEMENT
SERIES "W"

1907-8.

"O" size

The new straight line lever 17 jewels—Series T-M.

THE
RUGBY
MOVEMENT
SERIES "P"

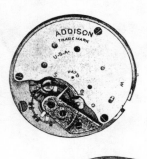

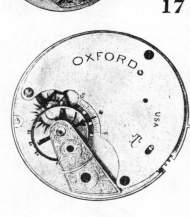

THE
OXFORD
MOVEMENT
SERIES "T"

THE
WATERBURY
MOVEMENT
SERIES "L"

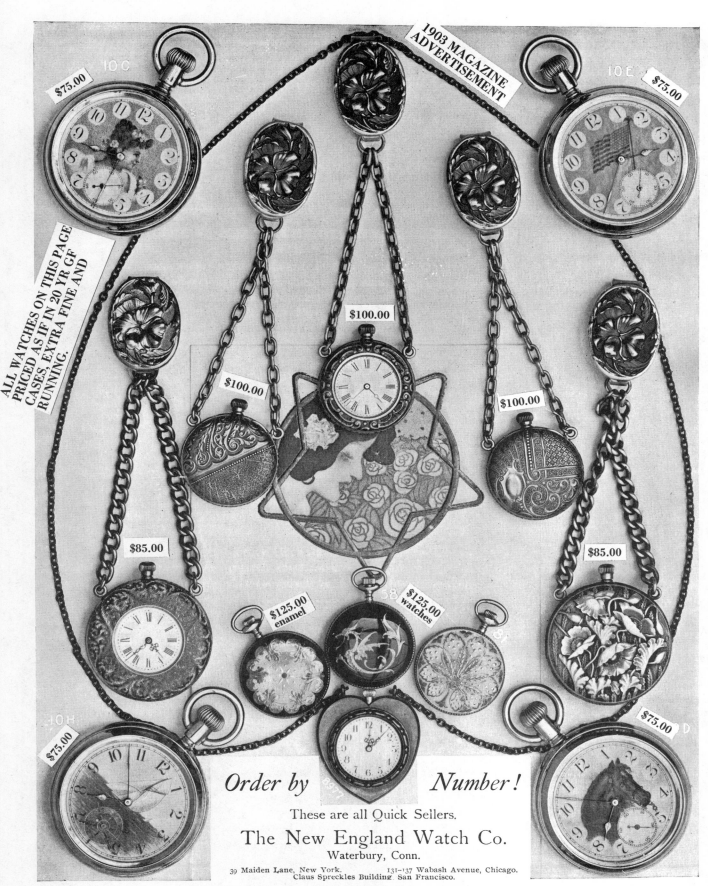

1903 MAGAZINE ADVERTISEMENT

$75.00

$75.00

ALL WATCHES ON THIS PAGE PRICED AS IF IN 20 YR GF CASES, EXTRA FINE AND RUNNING.

$100.00

$100.00

$100.00

$85.00

$85.00

$125.00 enamel

$125.00 watches

$75.00

$75.00

Order by *Number!*

These are all Quick Sellers.

The New England Watch Co.
Waterbury, Conn.

39 Maiden Lane, New York.   131-137 Wabash Avenue, Chicago.
Claus Spreckles Building, San Francisco.

119

$75.00

$85.00

$25.00

$125.00

$75.00

JANUARY 1904 ADVERTISEMENT

$75.00

$60.00

$60.00

$60.00

$75.00

$75.00

$75.00

Don't let your stock run low— these **Watches** are *staples* for every day of every month of every year. They are better *after-Christmas sellers* than anything the dealer ever has to sell. Keep up a good window or show case display and they will sell themselves.

Happy New Year!

New England Watch Co.,
Waterbury, Conn.

New York, 37-39 Maiden Lane.   Chicago, 131-137 Wabash Ave.
San Francisco, Claus Spreckels Bldg.

NON-MAGNETIC CHRONOGRAPHS.

HUNTING OR OPEN FACE.

1-5 Seconds—Start, Stop and Fly Back.

	14k. Gold Case.	18k. Gold Case.
No. 101. Extra Quality Finest Nickel Movement ; Full Ruby Jeweled ; Double Roller and Cap Jeweled Escapement ; Exposed Pallets ; **Paillard's Patent Non-Magnetic Inoxydable Compensation-Balance and Breguet Hair-Spring**; Adjusted to Temperature, Isochronism and to all positions ; finely finished throughout; **Cased in 18k. Gold**	$367.50	$397.50
No. 110. Extra Quality Finest Nickel Movement, same as above, with Split-Seconds, **Cased in 18k. Gold**	450.00	480.00
No. 102. Fine Nickel Movement; Full Ruby Jeweled; Double Roller and Cap Jeweled Escapement; Exposed Pallets ; **Paillard's Patent Non-Magnetic Inoxydable Compensation-Balance and Breguet Hair-Spring**; Adjusted to Temperature, Isochronism and six positions; **Cased in 18k. Gold**	292.50	322.50
No. 112. Fine Nickel Movement, same as above, with Split-Seconds; **Cased in 18k. Gold**	367.50	397.50
No. 103. Nickel Movement; Ruby Jewels; Double Roller Escapement; Exposed Pallets ; **Paillard's Patent Non-Magnetic Inoxydable Compensation-Balance and Breguet Hair-Spring**; Adjusted to Temperature, Isochronism and positions; **Cased in 18k. Gold**	247.50	277.50

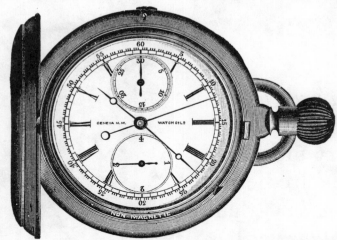

Chronograph, Quarter-Seconds and Minute Register.

	14k. Gold Case.	18k. Gold Case.
No. 120. Extra Quality Finest Nickel Movement; Full Ruby Jeweled; Double Roller and Cap Jeweled Escapement; Exposed Pallets ; **Paillard's Patent Non-Magnetic Inoxydable Compensation-Balance and Breguet Hair-Spring**; Accurately Adjusted to Temperature, Isochronism and all positions; finely finished throughout, Heavy 18k. Case	$457.50	$487.50
No. 125. Extra Quality Finest Nickel Movement, same as above, with Split-Seconds; Heavy 18k. Case	532.50	562.50

Minute Repeaters.

No. 130. Extra Quality Finest Nickel Movement; Heavy 18k. Case	535.00	585.00
No. 135. Fine Quality Nickel Movement ; Heavy 18k. Case	517.50	547.50

Five-Minute Repeaters.

No. 140. Extra Quality Finest Nickel Movement; Heavy 18k. Case	435.00	465.00
No. 145. Fine Quality Nickel Movement; Heavy 18k. Case	397.50	427.50

Quarter Repeaters.

No. 150. Extra Quality Finest Nickel Movement; Heavy 18k. Case	412.50	442.50
No. 155. Fine Quality Nickel Movement; Heavy 18k. Case	382.50	412.50

Combined Repeaters and Chronographs.

No. 210. Minute Repeater and Chronograph, Heavy 18k. Case	690.00	720.00
No. 215. Quarter " " " " " "	607.50	637.50

The above we do not carry in stock, but can furnish at a week's notice.

122

There is not enough details given above and I don't have much good information on relent sales to try to value this page. I think they would be worth at least as much as original cost and the repeaters much more.

PAILLARD NON-MAGNETIC WATCHES.

18 SIZE HUNTING AND OPEN FACE

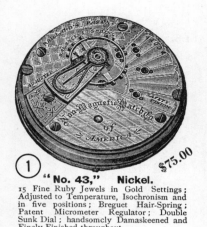

1890 ADVERTISEMENT

All of the watches on this page were made by Peoria Watch Co.

① **"No. 43,"** **Nickel.** $75.00
15 Fine Ruby Jewels in Gold Settings; Adjusted to Temperature, Isochronism and in five positions; Breguet Hair-Spring; Patent Micrometer Regulator; Double Sunk Dial; handsomcly Damaskeened and Finely Finished throughout.

② **"No. 45,"** **Nickel.** $70.00
15 Ruby Jewels in Gold Settings; Adjusted to Temperature, Isochronism and in three positions; Breguet Hair-Spring; Patent Micrometer Regulator; Double Sunk Dial.

③ **"No. 47,"** **Gilded.** $60.00
15 Ruby Jewels in Gold Settings; Adjusted to Temperature, Isochronism and in three positions; Breguet Hair-Spring; Patent Micrometer Regulator; Double Sunk Dial.

The above movements are accurately "Adjusted" and timed, and are especially adapted for Railroad uses, or wherever fine and accurate time is required.

④ **"No. 34,"** **Nickel.** $50.00
15 Jewels, in Settings; Exposed Pallets; Breguet Hair-Spring; Patent Micrometer Regulator.

⑤ **"No. 32,"** **Gilded.** $40.00
15 Jewels, in Settings; Exposed Pallets; Breguet Hair-Spring; Patent Micrometer Regulator.

⑥ **"No. 25,"** **Nickel.** $40.00
11 Jewels (top plate) in Settings; Breguet Hair-Spring; Patent Micrometer Regulator.

⑦ **"No. 21,"** **Gilded.** $40.00
11 Jewels (top ptate) in Settings; Breguet Hair-Spring; Patent Micrometer Regulator.

The attention of the trade is directed to the descriptions of these movements and to their HIGH ORDER OF MERIT. Every grade has Breguet Hair-Spring; Patent Regulator and Jewels in Settings, held by screws. They are Quick Train; Straight Line Lever Escapements; Exposed Pallets; Safety Centre Pinion, and are the only watch movements made in America containing the celebrated PAILLARD NON-MAGNETIC COMPENSATION BALANCE and HAIR-SPRING, and for intrinsic value are

UNEXCELLED BY ANY OTHER MAKE.

A. C. SMITH, General Agent,

177 Broadway, - - New York.

Paillard

A. C. SMITH, Gen'l Manager.

16-Size; Stem-Wind; Open-Face and Hunting, Lever-Set.

FITTING STANDARD MAKES OF THIN-MODEL ELGIN 16-SIZE CASES.

No. "71," . . **Nickel** — $70.00
20 Finest Quality Red Ruby Jewels in Gold Settings; Jeweled Center; Full Cap Jeweled Escapement; Breguet Hair Spring; Accurately Adjusted to Temperature, Isochronism and all Positions; Micrometer Regulator; Double Sunk Dial; Finely Damaskeened and finished throughout.

No. "72," . . **Nickel** — $60.00
18 Fine Ruby Jewels in Gold Settings; Center Jeweled; Cap Jeweled Escape Wheel; Breguet Hair Spring; Accurately Adjusted to Temperature, Isochronism and Six Positions; Micrometer Regulator; Double Sunk Dial.

No. "73," . . **Nickel** — $50.00
16 Ruby Jewels in Gold Settings; Jeweled Center; Breguet Hair Spring; Adjusted to Temperature, Isochronism and Four Positions; Micrometer Regulator.

No. "74," . . **Nickel** — $45.00
15 Ruby Jewels in Settings; Breguet Hair Spring; Adjusted to Temperature, Isochronism and Three Positions; Micrometer Regulator.

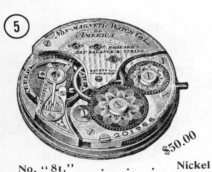

No. "81," . . . **Nickel** — $50.00
15 Jewels in Settings; Adjusted to Heat and Cold; Breguet Hair Spring; Patent Micrometer Regulator.

This attractive Electrotype furnished upon application.

No. "82," . . . **Gilded** — $40.00
15 Jewels in Settings; Adjusted to Heat and Cold; Breguet Hair Spring; Patent Micrometer Regulator.

No. "83," . . . **Gilded** — $35.00
11 Jewels (top plate) in Settings. Exposed Pallets; Flat Spring; Straight Regulator.

No. "84," . . . **Gilded** — $30.00
7 Jewels; Exposed Pallets; Flat Spring; Straight Regulator.

FOR SALE BY ALL LEADING JOBBERS.

DESCRIPTIVE PRICE-LISTS FURNISHED UPON APPLICATION.

Non=Magnetic Watch Compy,

177 Broadway, New York.

Non=Magnetic Charmilles Watches.

16 Size Open-Face, Stem-Winding, Pendant-Setting, Solid Nickel, Non-Magnetic, Accurate Timekeepers, High Quality, Low Price.

No. 4. Nickel case, open-face, embossed designs, old silver finish.

Price $3.76

Old silver finish is a gray oxidization, finished in imitation of old silver and with the embossed design brought out in relief, gives it a very rich appearance and wears well.

These designs are made in a great variety, representing hunting scenes, jockey, sulky, bicycle, racing, stag, horses, locomotives, etc.

JUST THE THING FOR SPORTSMEN.

Prices Quoted

Are Net Cash.

No. 1. Nickel case, open-face, plain polished, or satin finished; "Arabic" or "Roman" dial.

Price $3.29

The greatest value for the money of any watch ever made.

DESIRABLE "BOYS" WATCH.

These are not rolled plate, but are two plates of 14 K. gold with plate of composition between, and offer greatest economy in casing and greatest value. Made in engine-turned, plain polished Juergensen, plain polished half-bascine and engraved. Engraving extra, according to design. A world beater.

No. 5. Nickel case, open-face, embossed border, old silver finish, raised silver designs.

Price $4.23

A very attractive watch; the heavy embossed border and raised design gives it a rich, clean-cut appearance. Made in a large variety of designs.

New

Novel in Construction.
Quick Sellers. High Quality.
Low Price.
Wonder of the Age.

JANUARY 1899 ADVERTISEMENT

Absolutely
Non=
Magnetic.

Complete watch in extra fine to mint to mint condition. $50.00 to $75.00 depending on design of case and appearance. (Swiss made).

THE "CHARMILLES" MOVEMENT

is made of Solid Nickel, handsomely damaskeened. The center of the case is a part of the movement, thus insuring greater strength and reducing cost. It is 16 size, ¾ plate, open-face, stem-winding and pendant hand-setting; straight-line lever escapement; 7 jewels; non-magnetic balance, hairspring and escapement; is non-magnetic and non-oxidizable. The wheels and pinions as well as all parts are better finished than in higher-priced movements. Fully warranted and guaranteed perfect timekeepers.

No. 6. Steel case, open-face, plain polished, black oxidized, fancy dial.

Price $3.76

No. 7. Steel case, open-face, plain polished, black oxidized, raised silver designs, fancy dial.

Price $4.70

These are very neat appearing watches. The black oxidization is done by a secret process and is guaranteed to wear.

"Charmilles" Watches are machine-made watches. All parts are interchangeable, and any portion can be readily duplicated at a small cost from leading material dealers. Send in your orders early to insure prompt execution.

A. C. BECKEN, 103 State Street, CHICAGO, ILL.

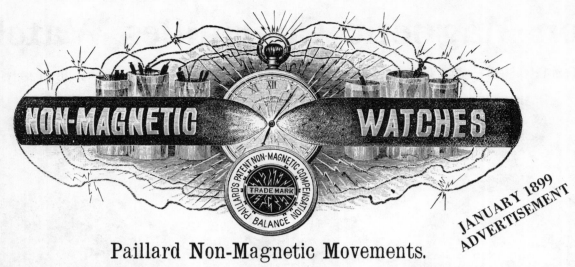

NON-MAGNETIC WATCHES

TRADE MARK

PAILLARDS PATENT NON-MAGNETIC COMPENSATION BALANCE No. 1

JANUARY 1899 ADVERTISEMENT

Paillard Non-Magnetic Movements.

These Celebrated Movements contain Paillard's Patent Non-Magnetic Compensation Balance and Hair-Spring, and are Guaranteed to be Exempt from the influence of MAGNETISM or HUMIDITY, and to HOLD THEIR RATE.

18 Size Hunting and Open-Face.

$100.00

24 Jewels $400.00

G. Nickel, adjusted to temperature and positions, 17 jewels, compensation balance, patent regulator, Breguet hairspring, double sunk dial, handsomely damaskeened in gold lettering and gilded steel works. ②

$50.00

H. Nickel, 17 jewels, compensation balance, patent regulator, Breguet hairspring, double sunk dial. ③

$45.00

I. Nickel, 15 jewels, compensation balance, patent regulator, Breguet hairspring, double sunk dial. ④

$35.00

K. Gilded, 15 jewels, compensation balance, patent regulator, Breguet hairspring, double sunk dial. ⑤

① **F.** Nickel, adjusted to temperature, isochronism and positions, 21 extra fine ruby jewels in gold settings, compensation balance with gold screws, patent regulator, Breguet hairspring, double sunk glass enamel dial, elaborately damaskeened in gold, with black enamel lettering.

16 Size Hunting and Open-Face (fit new model Elgin cases).

The movements on this page were all made by the Illinois Watch Co.

New No. 72. Nickel, adjusted to temperature and positions, 17 jewels, compensation balance, patent regulator, Breguet hairspring, double sunk dial, dust band, handsomely damaskeened in gold with gold lettering and gilded steel work. ⑦ $70.00

New No. 73. Nickel, 17 jewels, compensation balance, patent regulator, Breguet hairspring, double sunk dial, dust band, handsomely damaskeened with gold lettering. ⑧ $40.00

New No. 74. Nickel, 15 jewels, compensation balance, patent regulator, Breguet hairspring, dust band. ⑨ $30.00

No. 75. Gilt, 15 jewels, compensation balance, patent regulator, Breguet hairspring, dust band. ⑩ $25.00

No. 76. Gilt, 11 jewels in settings, compensation balance, patent regulator, Breguet hairspring, dust band. ⑪ $25.00

$85.00

⑥ **New No. 71.** Nickel, adjusted to temperature, isochronism and position, 21 extra fine ruby jewels in gold settings, compensation balance with gold screws, patent regulator, Breguet hairspring, double sunk glass enamel dial, dust band, elaborately damaskeened in gold with black enameled lettering.

Write for Confidential Price-List on the New Improved 18 and 16 Size Paillard Non-Magnetic Movements.

A. C. BECKEN, 103 State Street, CHICAGO, ILL.

South Bend Watch Co.'s Movements. See Page 4

Made by the New Watch Company at South Bend, Ind.

Movements Are Latest Models, Made With New Machinery in a Strictly Modern, Up-to-date Factory. The Chief Aim Being to Build up a Reputation, by Making a Watch of Superior Quality and Second to None.

18 Size, Full Plate.

No. 340 and 341.

Nickel, 17 Jewels in Settings. Adjusted to Temperature and Position, Polished Steel Micrometric Regulator, Breguet Hairspring. Finely Finished Train, Plates Handsomely Damaskeened, Double Sunk Glass Enameled Dial.

No. 340. **Hunting**, Lever Set......$20 00
[SAPLESS]
No. 341. **Open Face**, Lever Set..... 20 00
[SAPLING]

$40.00

Nos. 330 and 331.

Nickel, 15 Jewels in Settings, Polished Steel Micrometric Regulator, Breguet Hairspring, Plates Finely Damaskeened, Sunk Second Glass Enamel Dial.

No. 330. **Hunting**, Lever Set......$12 00
[SAPORINE]
No. 331. **Open Face**, Lever Set..... 12 00
[SAPORUS]

$30.00

The South Bend Movements All Have Compensation Balance, Quick Train, Straight Line Escapement and Safety Pinion.

6 Size, Three-Quarter Plate.

$40.00

No. 180.

Nickel, 17 Jewels in Settings, Raised Center Jewel, Breguet Hairspring, Steel Parts Highly Finished and Nickel Plates Elaborately Damaskeened, Sunk Second Glass Enamel Dial, Very Accurately Timed.

No. 180. **Hunting**, Lever Set..... $20 00
[SAPOSTER]

No. 170.

Nickel, 15 Jewels in Settings, Breguet Hairspring, Plates Handsomely Damaskeened, Sunk Second Glass Enamel or Fancy Dial with Gilt Hands.

No. 170. **Hunting**, Lever Set.......$13 50
[SAPONACE]

$30.00

1904 SUPPLY CATALOG

No. 160.

Nickel, 11 Jewels in Settings, Breguet Hairspring, Plates Finely Damaskeened, Sunk Second Glass Enamel Dial.

No. 160. **Hunting**, Lever Set.......$11 00
[SAPOT]

$20.00

16 Size, Three-Quarter Plate.

Nos. 290 and 291.

Nickel, 17 Jewels in Settings. Adjusted to Temperature and Position, Polished Steel Micrometric Regulator, Breguet Hairspring, Finely Finished Train, Gold Center Wheel, Exposed Winding Wheels Highly Polished, Plates Handsomely Damaskeened, Double Sunk Glass Enamel Dial.

No. 290. **Hunting**, Lever Set $23 00
[SAPONARY]
No. 291. **Open Face**, Lever Set..... 23 00
[SAPONIFY]

$40.00

Nos. 280 and 281.

Nickel, 15 Jewels in Settings, Polished Steel Micrometric Regulator, Breguet Hairspring, Highly Finished Train, Round Arm Gilt Center Wheel, Exposed Winding Wheels Finely Polished, Damaskeened Plates, Fine Double Sunk Glass Enamel Dial. Movement Carefully Timed.

No. 280. **Hunting**, Lever Set......$17 00
[SAPPER]
No. 281. **Open Face**, Lever Set..... 17 00
[SAPPINESS]

$35.00

SOUTH BEND WATCH CO.
South Bend, Indiana

Made watches from 1903 to about 1930. Serial numbers start at or near 370,000 up to around 1,400,000. The high grade watches are very good collector watches, especially the 16-size and 18-size Studebakers and the 16-size Polaris.

SOUTH BEND WATCHES AND CASES

1911

SOUTH BEND WATCH CO.
SOUTH BEND, INDIANA

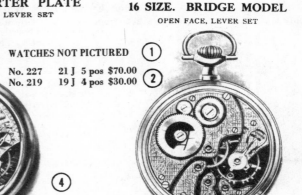

16 SIZE. THREE-QUARTER PLATE
HUNTING OR OPEN FACE. LEVER SET

Read Page 4-7

WATCHES NOT PICTURED

No. 227 21 J 5 pos $70.00
No. 219 19 J 4 pos $30.00

$70.00 $70.00

21 JEWELS
NO. 294, HUNTING. NO. 295, OPEN FACE

DESCRIPTION

Jewels—21 ruby and sapphire jewels. Gold settings. Olive hole balance jewels.

Plates—Nickel. Richly damaskeened. Pearl finish under dial and on under side of plates. Gilt lettering. Extra highly polished, cupped and beveled visible winding wheels. Recoiling click. Dust band.

Balance—Chamfered and extra highly polished compensating balance with gold balance screws. Meantime screws. Breguet hair spring. New stationary hair spring stud. Patent regulator.

Escapement—Double roller escapement, cone pivoted and cap jeweled. Exposed sapphire pallets. Sapphire jewel pin. Steel escape wheel, highly finished and beveled with all acting surfaces ground and polished. Tested on half time without hair spring.

Adjustments—Adjusted to temperature, five positions and isochronism. Most accurately rated.

Dial—Double sunk or fancy, glass enamel, ground edge dial.

Finish—Bevel head screws throughout. Highly polished round arm gold center wheel and train.

A most highly finished and accurately constructed movement. A movement that meets the most exacting requirements of railroad service. Certificate of rating furnished upon application.

16 SIZE. BRIDGE MODEL
OPEN FACE, LEVER SET

$80.00

17 JEWELS
NO. 223, OPEN FACE

Jewels—17 Ruby and sapphire jewels. Gold settings. Olive hole balance jewels.

Plates—Genuine nickel. Richly damaskeened. Pearl finish under dial and on under side of plates. Gilt lettering. Extra highly polished, cupped and beveled visible winding wheels. Recoiling click. Dust band.

Balance—Chamfered and extra highly polished compensating balance with gold balance screws. Meantime screws. Breguet hair spring. Self-locating hair spring stud. Micrometer nut and screw anti-backlash regulator.

Escapement—Double roller escapement. Exposed Synthetic ruby pallets. Sapphire jewel pin. Steel escape wheel, highly finished and beveled with all acting surfaces ground and polished. Tested on half time without hair spring.

Adjustments—Adjusted to temperature, five positions and isochronism. Most accurately rated.

Dial—Double sunk, fancy, or Montgomery Numerical glass enamel, ground edge dial.

Finish—Cornered screws throughout. Highly polished round arm gold center wheel and train.

A movement of the highest finish, especially designed for railroad service. Passed by all chief time inspectors and accompanied by certificate insuring purchaser against any changes whatsoever in railroad requirements for five years from date of purchase. Certificate of rating furnished upon application. Shipped in nickel, glass front and back, skeleton display case.

16 SIZE. BRIDGE MODEL
OPEN FACE LEVER SET

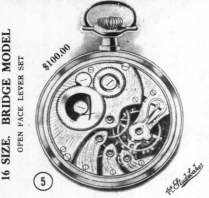

$100.00

21 JEWELS
NO. 229, OPEN FACE

Jewels—21 Ruby and sapphire jewels. Gold settings. Olive hole balance jewels.

Plates—Genuine nickel. Richly damaskeened. Pearl finish under dial and on under side of plates. Gilt lettering. Extra highly polished, cupped and beveled visible winding wheels. Recoiling click. Dust band.

Balance—Chamfered and extra highly polished compensating balance with gold balance screws. Meantime screws. Breguet hair spring. Self-locating hair spring stud. Micrometer nut and screw anti-backlash regulator.

Escapement—Double roller escapement. Cone pivoted and cap jeweled. Exposed Synthetic ruby pallets. Sapphire jewel pin. Steel escape wheel, highly finished and beveled with all acting surfaces ground and polished. Tested on half time without hair spring.

Adjustments—Adjusted to temperature, five positions and isochronism. Most accurately rated.

Dial—Double sunk, fancy, or Montgomery Numerica glass enamel, ground edge dial.

Finish—Cornered screws throughout. Highly polished round arm gold center wheel and train.

A movement of the highest finish, especially designed for railroad service. Passed by all chief time inspectors and accompanied by certificate insuring purchaser against any changes whatsoever in railroad requirements for five years from date of purchase. Certificate of rating furnished upon application. Shipped in nickel, glass front and back, skeleton display case.

16 SIZE. THREE-QUARTER PLATE

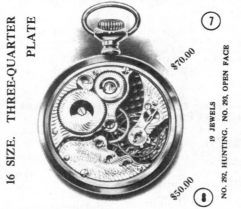

$70.00 $50.00

19 JEWELS
NO. 292, HUNTING. NO. 293, OPEN FACE

Jewels—19 ruby and sapphire jewels. Gold settings. Olive hole balance jewels.

Plates—Nickel. Handsomely damaskeened. Pearl finish under dial and on under side of plates. Gilt lettering. Highly polished and damaskeened, cupped and beveled visible winding wheels. Recoiling click. Dust band.

Balance—Chamfered and extra highly polished compensating balance with gold balance screws. Meantime screws. Breguet hair spring. New stationary hair spring stud. Patent regulator.

Escapement—Double roller escapement. Exposed sapphire pallets. Sapphire jewel pin. Steel escape wheel, highly finished with all acting surfaces ground and polished. Tested on half time without hair spring.

Adjustments—Adjusted to temperature, five positions and isochronism. Very accurately rated.

Dial—Double sunk or fancy, glass enamel, ground edge dial.

Finish—Bevel head screws. Gold round arm center wheel; train wheels swaged, round arm, gold train effect.

A highly finished, high grade movement in every particular. One that meets every requirement for railroad service. Certificate of rating furnished upon application.

Shipped in nickel, glass front and back, skeleton display case.

16 SIZE. THREE-QUARTER PLATE

$40.00 $40.00

17 JEWELS
NO. 298, HUNTING. NO. 299, OPEN FACE

Jewels—17 ruby and sapphire jewels. Composition settings. Olive hole balance jewels.

Plates—Nickel. Handsomely damaskeened. Gilt lettering. Highly polished, cupped and beveled visible winding wheels. Recoiling click. Dust band.

Balance—Chamfered and polished compensating balance. Meantime screws. Breguet hair spring. New stationary hairspring stud. Patent regulator.

Escapement—Double roller escapement. Steel escape wheel. Tested on half time without hair spring.

Adjustments—Adjusted to temperature and three positions. Accurately rated.

Dial—Double sunk or fancy, glass enamel, ground edge dial.

Finish—Bevel head jewel, plate and case screws. Gold round arm center wheel; train wheels swaged round arm, with gold effect.

A high grade movement that will give exceptionally accurate service under all conditions.

Shipped in nickel, glass front and back, skeleton display case.

16 SIZE. BRIDGE MODEL
OPEN FACE, LEVER SET

(1) See Page 4 $35.00

17 JEWELS, OPEN FACE
NO. 217, OPEN FACE

Jewels—17 Ruby and sapphire jewels. Composition settings. Olive hole balance jewels.

Plates—Genuine nickel. Handsomely damaskeened. Gilt lettering. Highly polished, cupped and beveled visible winding wheels. Recoiling click. Dust band.

Balance—Chamfered and polished compensating balance. Meantime screws. Breguet hair spring. Self-locating hair spring stud. Micrometer nut and screw anti-backlash regulator.

Escapement—Double roller escapement. Steel escape wheels. Tested on half time without hair spring.

Adjustments—Adjusted to temperature and three positions. Accurately rated.

Dial—Double sunk or fancy, glass enamel, ground edge dial.

Finish—Bevel head jewel, plate, and case screws. Gold round arm center wheel, round arm train wheels with gold effect.

16 SIZE. THREE-QUARTER PLATE

1911 FACTORY CATALOG

(3) $30.00
(2) $30.00

17 JEWELS
NO. 212, HUNTING. NO. 215, OPEN FACE
HUNTING, LEVER SET. OPEN FACE, PENDANT SET

Jewels—17 Jewels. Composition settings. Olive hole balance jewels.

Plates—Genuine nickel. Tastily damaskeened. Ray beveled visible winding wheels. Recoiling click. Dust band.

Balance—Polished compensating balance. Meantime screws. Breguet hair spring. Self-locating hair spring stud. Micrometer nut and screw anti-backlash regulator.

Escapement—Double roller escapement. Steel escape wheel.

Tested on half time without hair spring.

Very closely timed.

Adjustments—Adjusted to temperature only.

Dial—Double sunk or fancy, glass enamel, ground edge dial.

Finish—Bevel head jewel, plate, and case screws. Round arm center and train wheels with gold effect.

16 SIZE. THREE-QUARTER PLATE
OPEN FACE ONLY. PENDANT SET

(4) $30.00

17 JEWELS, OPEN FACE
NO. 211, OPEN FACE

Jewels—17 Jewels. Composition settings. Olive hole balance jewels.

Plates—Genuine nickel. Nicely damaskeened. Polished and damaskeened visible winding wheels. Recoiling click. Dust band.

Balance—Polished compensating balance. Meantime screws. Breguet hair spring. Self-locating hair spring stud. Micrometer nut and screw anti-backlash regulator.

Escapement—Steel escape wheel.

Tested on half time without hair spring.

Very closely timed.

Dial—Single sunk, glass enamel, ground edge dial.

Finish—Bevel head jewel, plate, and case screws. Round arm center wheel.

16 SIZE. THREE-QUARTER PLATE

(5) $25.00
(6) $25.00

15 JEWELS
NO. 204, HUNTING. NO. 207, OPEN FACE
HUNTING, LEVER SET. OPEN FACE, PENDANT SET

Jewels—15 Jewels in settings. Composition settings. Olive hole balance jewels.

Plates—Genuine nickel. Nicely damaskeened. Polished and damaskeened visible winding wheels. Recoiling click. Dust band.

Balance—Polished compensating balance. Meantime screws. Breguet hair spring. Self-locating hair spring stud. Micrometer nut and screw anti-backlash regulator.

Tested on half time without hair spring.

Very closely timed.

Dial—Double sunk or fancy, glass enamel, ground edge dial.

16 SIZE. THREE-QUARTER PLATE
LEVER SET

(7)
(8) $25.00

15 JEWELS
NO. 280, HUNTING. NO. 281, OPEN FACE

Jewels—15 jewels in settings. Olive hole balance jewels.

Plates—Nickel. Nicely damaskeened. Polished and damaskeened visible winding wheels. Recoiling click. Dust band.

Balance—Polished compensating balance. Meantime screws. Breguet hair spring. Patent regulator.

Tested on half time without hair spring.

Very closely timed. Round arm center wheel.

Dial—Double sunk or fancy, glass enamel, ground edge dial.

16 SIZE. THREE-QUARTER PLATE
LEVER SET

(9)
(10) $20.00

7 JEWELS
NO. 260, HUNTING. NO. 261, OPEN FACE

Jewels—7 jewels. Olive hole balance jewels.

Plates—Nickel. Nicely damaskeened. Ray visible winding wheels. Recoiling click. Dust band.

Balance—Cut expansion balance. Meantime screws. Breguet hair spring.

Tested on half time without hair spring.

Closely timed.

(11) $20.00

7 JEWELS, OPEN FACE
NO. 203, OPEN FACE

16 SIZE. THREE-QUARTER PLATE
OPEN FACE. PENDANT SET

Jewels—7 Jewels. Composition settings. Olive hole balance jewels.

Plates—Genuine nickel. Nicely damaskeened. Ray visible winding wheels. Recoiling click. Dust band.

Balance—Cut expansion balance. Meantime screws. Breguet hair spring. Self-locating hair spring stud.

Tested on half time without hair spring.

Closely timed.

Dial—Single sunk, glass enamel, ground edge dial. **129**

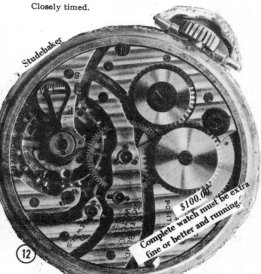

Studebaker

(12) $100.00
Complete watch must be extra fine or better and running

18 SIZE. FULL PLATE
HUNTING OR OPEN FACE. LEVER SET

See Page 4

① $150.00 ② $150.00

21 JEWELS
NO. 328, HUNTING. NO. 329, OPEN FACE

The Studebaker

Jewels—21 extra fine ruby and sapphire jewels. Gold settings. Olive hole balance jewels.
Plates—Richly damaskeened in a handsome pattern. Pearl finish under dial and on under side of plates. Gilt lettering. Stem winding work all highly polished and finished. Recoiling click. Dust band.
Setting—Lever. Self-locking setting device.
Balance—Chamfered and extra highly polished compensating balance with gold balance screws. Meantime screws. Breguet hair spring. New stationary hair spring stud. "Precision" nut and screw regulator.
Escapement—Double roller escapement, cone pivoted and cap jeweled. Sapphire pallets and jewel pin. Steel escape wheel, highly finished and beveled with all acting surfaces ground and polished. Tested on half time without hair spring.
Adjustments—Adjusted to temperature, five positions and isochronism. Most accurately rated.
Dial—Special, high-grade glass enamel, ground edge dial.
Finish—All visible steel work, plate and case screws, highly polished and cornered.

18 SIZE. FULL PLATE
OPEN FACE *ONLY.* LEVER SET

③ $130.00

17 JEWELS
NO. 323, OPEN FACE

The Studebaker

Jewels—17 extra fine ruby and sapphire jewels. Gold settings. Olive hole balance jewels.
Plates—Richly damaskeened in a handsome pattern. Pearl-finish under dial and on under side of plates. Gilt lettering. Stem winding work all highly polished and finished. Recoiling click. Dust band.
Setting—Lever. Self-locking setting device.
Balance—Chamfered and extra highly polished compensating balance with gold balance screws. Meantime screws. Breguet hair spring. New stationary hair spring stud. "Precision" nut and screw regulator.
Escapement—Double roller escapement. Sapphire pallets and jewel pin. Steel escape wheel, highly finished and beveled with all acting surfaces ground and polished. Tested on half time without hair spring.
Adjustments—Adjusted to temperature, five positions and isochronism. Most accurately rated.
Dial—Special, high-grade glass enamel, ground edge dial.
Finish—All visible steel work, plate and case screws, highly polished and cornered.

18 SIZE. FULL PLATE
HUNTING OR OPEN FACE. LEVER SET

④ $40.00 ⑤ $40.00

17 JEWELS
NO, 344, HUNTING. NO. 345, OPEN FACE

DESCRIPTION

Jewels—17 ruby and sapphire jewels. Composition settings. Olive hole balance jewels.
Plates—Nickel. Handsomely damaskeened. Gilt lettering. Recoiling click. Dust band.
Setting—Lever. Self-locking setting device.
Balance—Chamfered and highly polished compensating balance. Meantime screws. Breguet hair spring. New stationary hair spring stud. "Precision" nut and screw regulator.
Escapement—Double roller escapement. Steel escape wheel. Tested on half time without hair spring.
Adjustments—Adjusted to temperature and three positions. Accurately rated.
Dial—Double sunk or fancy, glass enamel, ground edge dial.
Finish—Bevel head plate and jewel screws. Visible steel work nicely polished.

1911 FACTORY CATALOG

⑥ $35.00 ⑦ $35.00

17 JEWELS
NO. 312, HUNTING. NO. 313, OPEN FACE

DESCRIPTION

Jewels—17 ruby and sapphire jewels. Composition settings. Olive hole balance jewels.
Plates—Nickel. A most attractive pattern of damaskeening. Recoiling click. Dust band.
Setting—Lever. Self-locking setting device.
Balance—Chamfered and polished compensating balance. Meantime screws. Breguet hair spring. New stationary hair spring stud. "Precision" nut and screw regulator.
Escapement—Double roller escapement. Steel escape wheel. Tested on half time without hair spring.
Adjustments—Adjusted to temperature. Very closely timed.
Dial—Single sunk, glass enamel, ground edge dial.
Finish—Bevel head plate and jewel screws. All visible steel work polished.

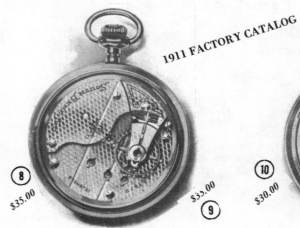

⑧ $35.00 ⑨ $35.00

17 JEWELS
NO. 346, HUNTING. NO. 347, OPEN FACE

DESCRIPTION

Jewels—17 ruby and sapphire jewels. Composition settings. Olive hole balance jewels.
Plates—Nickel. A most attractive pattern of damaskeening. Recoiling click. Dust band.
Setting—Lever. Self-locking setting device.
Balance—Chamfered and polished compensating balance. Meantime screws. Breguet hair spring. New stationary hair spring stud. "Precision" nut and screw regulator.
Escapement—Steel escape wheel. Tested on half time without hair spring.

Very closely timed.

Dial—Single sunk, glass enamel, ground edge dial.
Finish—Bevel head plate and jewel screws. All visible steel work polished.

A well finished movement throughout.

130

⑩ $30.00 ⑪ $30.00

15 JEWELS
NO. 332, HUNTING. NO. 333, OPEN FACE

DESCRIPTION

Jewels—15 jewels in settings. Olive hole balance jewels.
Plates—Nickel. Nicely damaskeened. Recoiling click. Dust band.
Setting—Lever. Self-locking setting device.
Balance—Polished compensating balance. Meantime screws. Breguet hair spring. New stationary hair spring stud. "Precision" nut and screw regulator.

Tested on half time without hair spring.

Very closely timed.

Dial—Single sunk, glass enamel, ground edge dial.

A serviceable, well-finished movement throughout.

0 SIZE
OPEN FACE. PENDANT SET

0 SIZE. BRIDGE MODEL
HUNTING. PENDANT SET

1911 FACTORY CATALOG

17 JEWELS   **$20.00**
NO. 121, OPEN FACE   ①

Same movement identically as grade No. 120 except furnished without second hand.

15 JEWELS   **$15.00**
NO. 111, OPEN FACE   ②

Same movement identically as grade No. 110 except furnished without second hand.

7 JEWELS   **$15.00**
NO. 101, OPEN FACE   ③

Same movement identically as grade No. 100 except furnished without second hand.

17 JEWELS
NO. 120, HUNTING

$40.00   ④

DESCRIPTION

Jewels—17 ruby and sapphire jewels in settings. Olive hole balance jewels.

Plates—Nickel. Handsomely damaskeened. Gilt lettering. Highly polished and damaskeened visible winding wheels. Dust band.

Balance—Chamfered and highly polished compensating balance. Meantime screws. Breguet hair spring.

Very closely timed. Gold round arm center wheel.

Dial—Single sunk, plain or fancy, glass enamel, ground edge dial.

0 SIZE. BRIDGE MODEL
HUNTING. PENDANT SET

15 JEWELS   **$30.00**
NO. 110, HUNTING   ⑤

DESCRIPTION

Jewels—15 ruby and sapphire jewels in settings. Olive hole balance jewels.

Plates—Nickel. Finely damaskeened. Polished and damaskeened visible winding wheels. Dust band.

Balance—Highly polished compensating balance. Meantime screws. Breguet hair spring.

Closely timed.

Dial—Single sunk, plain or fancy, glass enamel, ground edge dial.

0 SIZE. THREE-QUARTER PLATE
HUNTING. PENDANT SET

7 JEWELS   **$20.00**
NO. 100, HUNTING   ⑥

DESCRIPTION

Jewels—7 jewels. Olive hole balance jewels.

Plates—Nickel. Nicely damaskeened. Ray visible winding wheels. Dust band.

Balance—Polished compensating balance. Meantime screws. Breguet hair spring.

Dial—Single sunk, plain, glass enamel, ground edge dial.

Trenton Watch Co.'s Movements, Trenton, N. J.

W.ll Fit any American Cases of Similar Sizes.   List Prices Each.

6, 16 and 18 Size, Hunting and Open Face, Stem Wind, Lever Set.

$25.00

$30.00

$30.00

$30.00

6 Size.
No. 52 Nickel Damaskeened, 7 Jewels Cut Expansion Balance. $6 50
No. 50 Nickel Damaskeened, 7 Jewels. Cut Expansion Balance, Hard Enameled Dial.......... 7 50

6 Size.
No. 55 Nickel Damaskeened, 11 Jewels in Raised Settings, Hard Enameled Dial............... $10 00

18 Size.
HUNTING OR OPEN FACE.
No. 5 "Peerless" Nickel, 7 Jewels, ¾ Plate, Screw Balance, Patent Safety Pinion............... $4 38

18 Size.
HUNTING OR OPEN FACE.
No. 70 Nickel Damaskeened, 7 Jewels, Cut Expansion Balance, Safety Pinion, Right Angle, Lever Escapement, Screw Bankings, Quick Train............... $5 00
No. 71 Gilt, Same as Above........ 5 63

$30.00

$30.00

$25.00

HTC $50.00

HUNTING OR OPEN FACE.
No. 80 Nickel Damaskeened, 11 Jewels in Settings, Cut Expansion Balance Safety Pinion, Right Angle, Lever Escapement, Screw Bankings, Quick Train... $6 88
No. 81 Gilt, Same as Above....... 7 50

18 Size.
HUNTING OR OPEN FACE.
No. 85 Nickel Damaskeened, 11 Jewels in Settings, Micrometer Regulator, Cut Expansion Balance, Safety Pinion, Right Angle, Lever Escapement, Screw Bankings, Quick Train.......... $8 75
No. 86 Gilt, Same as Above....... 8 75

16 Size.
HUNTING OR OPEN FACE.
No. 30 Nickel Damaskeened, 7 Jewels, Cut Expansion Balance, Safety Pinion, Straight Line Lever Escapement, Screw Bankings, Quick Train............... $7 50
No. 31 Plain Gilt, Same as Above. 8 13

18 Size.
OPEN FACE ONLY.
No. 90 Gilt, 9 Jewels, Cut Compensation Balance, with Stop, Start and Flyback (Flyback Attachment working from the Pendant) Plain or Fancy Dial........... $25 00

15 jewels in settings, solid nickel plates, beautifully damaskeened in gold, handsome white or fancy dial.
No. 100. Hunting or Open Face... ....$11 00

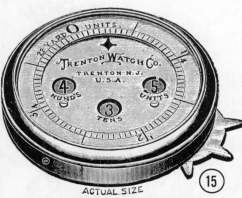

No. 35. Hunting or Open Face $9 00 $30.00

No. 36. Same as above, plain gilt.. 9 00

Solid nickel plates, 11 jewels, handsomely damaskeened in gold, handsome white or fancy dial.
No. 38. Hunting or Open Face.... ...$10 00

Solid nickel plates, beautifully damaskeened in gold, 16 jewels in raised settings, handsome white or fancy dial. $50.00
No. 45. Hunting or Open Face ...$12 00

The Peerless Cyclometer.
Registers 1,000 miles and repeats. Weight is only 2¼ ounces. Made of aluminum.
Price $2 40

16 size, 11 jewels in raised settings, stem winding, lever setting, thin model, nickel damaskeened, cut expansion balance, micrometer regulator, safety pinion, straight-line lever escapement, screw bankings, quick train, Breguet hair spring, handsome white or fancy dial, and fits all regular 16 size lever or pendant set cases.

The Monogram

Trenton Watch

16-S 17J $50.00
16-S 19J $75.00

Decorated Dials and Louis XV Hands for all grades and sizes

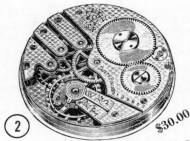 $20.00

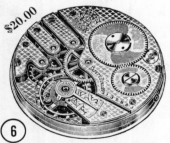 $20.00

No. 130. Bridge Model, 16 Size, 7 Jewel, Hunting and Open-Face, Pendant Setting

Nickel damaskeened, quick train, straight line lever escapement, exposed pallets, cut expansion balance, hardened and tempered breguet hairspring, safety pinion, screw bankings, exposed polished steel winding wheels, dust band, roman or arabic white enamel dial with monogram "T. W. Co."

$20.00

No. 100. Bridge Model, 0 Size, 7 Jewel, Hunting and Open-Face, Pendant Setting

Nickel damaskeened, quick train, straight line lever escapement, exposed pallets, cut expansion balance, hardened and tempered breguet hairspring, safety pinion, screw bankings, exposed polished steel winding wheels, dust band, roman or arabic white enamel dial and red marginal figures. Open-face, without seconds.

$30.00

No. 135. Bridge Model, 16 Size, 11 Jewel, Hunting and Open-Face, Pendant Setting

Nickel damaskeened, quick train, straight line escapement, exposed pallets, cut expansion balance, hardened and tempered breguet hairspring, safety pinion, screw bankings, exposed polished steel winding wheels, dust band, depressed center and seconds white enamel dial with monogram "T. W. Co."

 $20.00

No. 310. FORTUNA." 6 Size, 7 Jewel, Hunting and Open Face, Pendant Setting

Nickel damaskeened, cut expansion balance, safety pinion, screw bankings, straight line lever escapement, hardened and tempered breguet hairspring, quick train, exposed winding wheels, handsome white enamel dial with depressed seconds and red marginal figures. Open-face, without seconds.

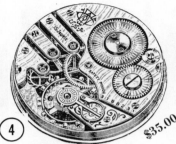 $35.00

No. 140. Bridge Model, 16 Size, 15 Jewel, Hunting and Open-Face, Pendant Setting

4 pairs in settings, micrometer regulator, nickel damaskeened, quick train, straight line lever escapement, exposed pallets, cut expansion balance, hardened and tempered breguet hairspring, safety pinion screw bankings, exposed polished steel winding wheels, dust band, roman or arabic depressed center and seconds white enamel dial and red marginal figures.

 $20.00

No. 320. "FORTUNA." 12 Size, 7 Jewel, Hunting and Open-Face, Pendant Setting

Nickel damaskeened, cut expansion balance, safety pinions, screw bankings, straight line lever escapement, hardened and tempered breguet hairspring, quick train, exposed winding wheels, handsome white enamel dial with depressed seconds and red marginal figures. Open-face, without seconds.

No. 200. "RELIANCE." 16 Size, 7 Jewels. ARE TO BE HAD IN HUNTING ONLY.

Nickel damaskeened, cut expansion balance, safety pinion, screw bankings, straight line lever escapement, hardened and tempered breguet hairspring, quick train, exposed winding wheels, dust band, handsome white enamel dial with depressed seconds. Hunting lever set.
Price, $6.00.

PARTS OF JANUARY 1902, JULY 1904 AND OCTOBER 1905 MAGAZINE ADS'

TRENTON WATCHES

are reliable timekeepers and peerless for their price. You will find them easy sellers.

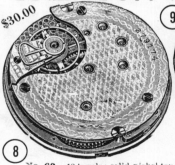 $30.00

 $20.00

 $30.00

No. 62. 12 jewels ; solid nickel top plate, handsomely damaskeened in gold ; comp. balance ; screw bankings ; straight line lever escapement ; micrometer regulator ; Breguet hairspring ; handsome white enamel dial ; fits regular lever or pendant set cases.
Price, $7.00.

No. 52. 7 jewels, nickel damaskeened comp. balance, screw bankings, straight line lever escapement, hardened and tempered hairspring, quick train ; and fits regular lever or pendant set cases.
Price, $5.00.

PRICES ACCORDING TO KEYSTONE KEY.

No. 7. 7 jewels, nickel damaskeened comp. balance, screw bankings, straight line lever escapement, hardened and tempered hairspring, handsome white enamel dial ; fits regular lever or pendant set cases.
Price, $4.00.

ASK YOUR JOBBER FOR THEM.

Trenton Watch Co.
TRENTON, N. J.

J. T. SCOTT & CO.,
No. 11 MAIDEN LANE, NEW YORK.
SOLE EASTERN WHOLESALE AGENTS FOR THE
Rockford Watch

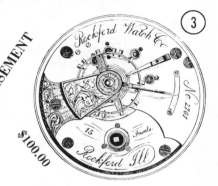

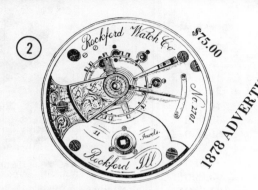

Nine grades of Key and Stem-Winding, Quick Train Movements

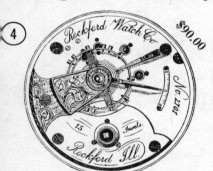

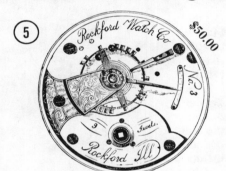

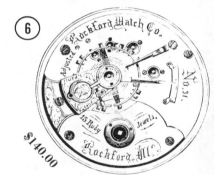

Superior Full Plate, 18 Size, Railway Watches!

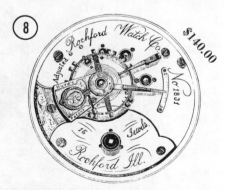

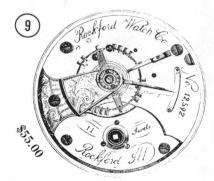

☞ A special feature of these Movements, and one which has greatly commended them to Railroad Men, by whom they are now largely used, is the fact that the cheaper as well as the finer grades all have the QUICK TRAINS.

EVERY MOVEMENT WARRANTED BY SPECIAL CERTIFICATE.

Rockford key winds do not appear very frequent. They tend to float from one collector or trader to the next. It is my opinion that there is not that many of them. I may not have them valued properly as I don't have many actual sales recorded. They are antique and very collectible and I believe worth more than they are now selling for. The values I have assigned to these movements do not take into account the low serial numbers. These numbers especially No.3 and No.31 would be worth much more.

ROCKFORD WATCH COMPANY'S MOVEMENTS.

18 Size, Stem Wind, Full Plate, Hunting and Open Face.   Open Face is Lever Set only.   The Best Watches on the Market for the Money.

No. 60.   17 Ruby Jewels.

Nickel, 17 ruby jewels in red gold settings, extra large ruby center jewels, elaborate fancy dial and gold hands, Breguet hair spring, patent micrometer regulator, fully and finely adjusted, gold damaskeening on nickel. The best watch in the world for the money.

$100.00	No. 80.	Hunting	$50 00
100.00	No. 60.	Open Face	50 00

Nickel, 17 jewels, fully adjusted, double sunk glass enamel dial, Breguet hair spring, patent micrometer regulator, damaskeened on nickel

$90.00	No. 81.	Hunting	$40 00
90.00	No. 61.	Open Face	40 00

Nickel, 17 jewels, adjusted to heat, cold and position, Breguet hair spring, patent micrometer regulator, red settings, finely damaskeened, sunk second dial, red marginal figures.

$70.00	No. 82.	Hunting	$20 00
70.00	No. 62.	Open Face	20 00

Approximate Production Dates

Serial No.	Date
8,000	1876
18,000	1877
30,000	1878
40,000	1879
50,000	1880
60,000	1881
70,000	1882
80,000	1883
90,000	1884
104,000	1885
116,000	1886
128,000	1887
140,000	1888
152,000	1889
164,000	1890
176,000	1891
198,000	1892
234,000	1894
294,000	1896
324,000	1897
354,000	1898
384,000	1899
414,000	1900
448,000	1901
482,000	1902
550,000	1904
655,000	1907
730,000	1909
815,000	1911
850,000	1912
880,000	1913
930,000	1914
936,000	1915

No. 70.   16 Jewels.

Nickel, 16 jewels in red gold settings, extra large ruby center jewel, double sunk dial, Breguet hair spring, patent micrometer regulator, fully and finely adjusted and gold damaskeened.

No. 70.	Hunting	$30 00	$80.00
No. 88.	Open Face	30 00	80.00

Nickel, 15 jewels, finely adjusted, double sunk dial, Breguet hair spring, patent micrometer regulator, damaskeened in gold on nickel. Unquestionably the best watch on the market to-day for the price.

No. 84.	Hunting	$25 00	$75.00
No. 87.	Open Face	25 00	75.00

Nickel, 15 jewels, adjusted, Breguet hair spring, double sunk dial, patent micrometer regulator, red settings finely damaskeened.

No. 77.	Hunting	$25 00	$75.00
No. 76.	Open Face	25 00	75.00

Gilt, same description as No. 77 and No. 76.

No. 79.	Hunting	$20 00	$50.00
No. 78.	Open Face	20 00	50.00

No. 83.   15 Jewels.

Nickel, 15 jewels, adjusted to heat and cold, Breguet hair spring, sunk second dial, red marginal figures, either Arabic or Roman, patent micrometer regulator red settings

No. 83x.	Hunting	$18 00	$50.00
No. 86x.	Open Face	18 00	50.00

Gilt, same description as No 83x and No. 86x.

No. 85x.	Hunting	$16 00	$40.00
No. 89x.	Open Face	16 00	40.00

Nickel, 15 jewels, Breguet hair spring, patent regulator, fine glass enamel sunk second dial, red settings.

No. 83.	Hunting	$14 00	$50.00
No. 86.	Open Face	14 00	50.00

No. 69x.   11 Jewels.

11 jewels in settings, sunk second, glass enamel dial, compensation balance, tempered hair spring.

$45.00	No. 69x.	Nickel, pat. reg., Hunting	$13 50
45.00	No. 66x.	Nickel, pat. reg., Open Face	13 50
$40.00	No. 68x.	Gilt, pat. reg., Hunting	12 50
40.00	No. 67x.	Gilt, pat. reg., Open Face	12 50

ROCKFORD WATCH COMPANY'S MOVEMENTS.

18 Size. Stem Wind. Full Plate. Hunting and Open Face. Open Face is Lever Set only. The Best Watches on the Market for the Money.

1896 A. C. BECKEN
SUPPLY CATALOG

No. 69. 11 Jewels.

① Gilt, same description as No. 83 and No. 86
② **No. 85.** Hunting.............. $13 00 $40.00
No. 89. Open Face.............. 13 00 40.00

③ Nickel, 11 jewels in settings, sunk second, glass enamel dial, compensation balance, tempered hair spring
④ **No. 69.** Hunting.............. $11 50 $45.00
No. 66. Open Face.......... 11 50 45.00

⑤ Gilt, same description as No 69 and No. 66.
⑥ **No. 68.** Hunting.............. $10 50 $40.00
No. 67. Open Face............. 10 50 40.00

No. 94. 9 Jewels.

9 jewels in settings, compensation balance, tempered hair spring. These movements have the same dial as the 11 jewel.

⑦ **No. 93.** Gilt, Hunting.......... $9 50 $30.00
⑧ **No. 94.** Gilt, Open Face........ 9 50 30.00

ROCKFORD WATCH CO.'S MOVEMENTS.

New 16 Size. 3-4 Plate, Hunting and Open Face—Open Face is Lever Set only.

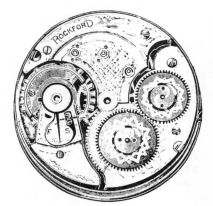

$65.00
65.00

Nickel, 15 jewels, adjusted, Breguet hair spring, double sunk dial, patent micrometer regulator, finely damaskeened.
No. 102. Hunting............ ⑪ ...$30 00
No. 123. Open Face........ ⑫ 30 00

Nickel, 16 jewels, finely and fully adjusted, rubies in raised settings, extra large center jewel, Breguet hair spring, double sunk dial, patent micrometer regulator, gold damaskeened on nickel. Acknowledged the most showy and best movement offered to the trade to-day.
No. 100. Hunting.........⑨....$45 00 $125.00
No. 121. Open Face ......⑩.... 45 00   125.00

$55.00
55.00

Nickel, 15 jewels, fully adjusted, Breguet hair spring, double sunk dial, patent micrometer regulator, gold damaskeened on nickel.
No. 101. Hunting.........⑬....$30 00
No. 122. Open Face......⑭....$30 00

ROCKFORD WATCH CO.'S MOVEMENTS.

New 16 Size. 3-4 Plate, Hunting and Open Face—Open Face is Lever Set only.

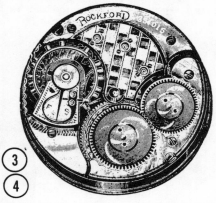

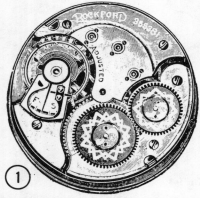

Nickel, 15 jewels, red settings, Breguet hair spring, sunk second dial with red marginal figures, patent micrometer regulator, damaskeened.

No. 103. Hunting ...... $40.00 ...... $14 00
No. 124. Open Face ..... 40.00 ...... 14 00

Gilt, same description as Nos 103 and 124
No. 112. Hunting $13 00
No. 132. Open Face ..... $35.00 ...... 13 00
35.00

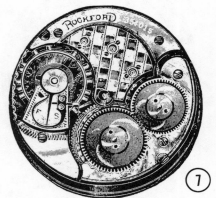

Nickel, 11 jewels, upper holes jeweled, tempered hair spring, sunk second dial, either Roman or Arabic.

No. 104. Hunting $11 50
No. 125. Open Face ..... $40.00 ...... 11 50
40.00

Gilt, 15 jewels, adjusted, Breguet hair spring, double sunk dial, patent micrometer regulator, finely damaskeened.

No. 111. Hunting $20 00
No. 131. Open Face 20 00 $40.00
40.00

Gilt, 11 jewels, upper holes jeweled, tempered hair spring, sunk second dial, either Roman or Arabic.

No. 113. Hunting $10 50
No. 133. Open Face ..... $30.00 ...... 10 50
30.00

Rockford Watch Company's 6 Size, Hunting, Stem-Wind Movements.

No. 152.

No. 150.

Gilt, 9 jewels, tempered hair spring, jewels in settings, glass enamel dial.

No. 114. Hunting $9 50
No. 134. Open Face ..... $30.00 ...... 9 50
30.00

Rockford Watch Company's 6 Size, Hunting, Stem-Wind Movements.

Nickel, 16 jewels in raised gold settings, extra center jewel, finely adjusted, double sunk dial, Breguet hair spring, patent regulator, gold damaskeened on nickel.
No. 150 ...... $100.00 ...... $40 00

Nickel, 15 jewels, adjusted, gold damaskeened on nickel, double sunk dial.
No. 151 ...... $75.00 ...... $30 00

Nickel, 15 jewels, finely damaskeened, sunk second dial with red marginal figures, tempered hair spring.
No. 152 ...... $75.00 ...... $20 00
$50.00

Rockford Watch Company's 6 Size, Hunting, Stem-Wind Movements.

Gilt, 15 jewels, same description as No 152.
No. 160 ...... $18 00

Nickel, 11 jewels, jewels in settings, tempered hair spring, sunk second dial.
No. 153 ...... $50.00 ...... $13 50

Gilt, 11 jewels, same description as No. 153
No. 161 ...... $40.00 ...... $12 50

Gilt, 9 jewels in settings, tempered hair spring.
No. 162 ...... $30.00 ...... $11 00

All of the above 6 size can be used either in Pendant or Lever Set cases. They fit either way.

All adjusted movements have D. S. dials, except 83x, 86x, 85x, 89x, 82 and 62, which have S. S. red marginal figures. We furnish all grades in 18 size non-magnetic in lots of 5 or more at $4.00 extra. Quality considered, Rockford Watches are the cheapest. In railway service they are superior to all others.

$550.00

$200.00

BUSIEST HOUSE IN AMERICA

$185.00

1906 JEWELRY SUPPLY CATALOG

18 Size ①
No. 800 Hunting ② $60.00
No. 900 Open Face ③

18 Size ③
No. 805 Hunting ④ $50.00
No. 905 Open Face

18 Size ⑤
No. 918 Open Face Only $40.00

24 extra fine ruby and sapphire jewels in gold settings, sapphire jewel pin, double roller escapement, steel escape wheel, sapphire exposed pallets, compensating balance in recess, adjusted to temperature, isochronism and five positions. Breguet hair spring, patent micrometric regulator. Safety pinion. Handsomely damaskeened nickel plates, gold lettering, champfered steel parts, double sunk glass enamel dial with red marginal figures, Roman or Arabic, elegantly finished throughout. Certificate of rating furnished upon application.

21 extra fine ruby jewels in gold settings, sapphire jewel pin, double roller escapement, steel escape wheel, sapphire exposed pallets, micrometric regulator, compensating balance in recess, adjusted to temperature, isochronism, five positions, Breguet hair spring. Safety pinion. Dust band, steel parts champfered, double sunk glass enameled dial with red marginal figures, beautifully nickel damaskeened plates, gold lettering.
A perfectly finished watch throughout. Certificate of rating furnished upon application.

21 fine ruby jewels, in settings double roller escapement, steel escape wheel, sapphire pallets, sapphire jewel pin, micrometric regulator, compensating balance in recess, adjusted to temperature, five positions, and isochronism, Breguet hair spring, safety pinion, polished steel work, double sunk glass enamel dial with red marginal figures, nickel damaskeened plates with gold lettering, finely finished throughout. Finished and adjusted to meet the most exacting Rail Road requirements. Certificate of rating furnished upon application.

$165.00

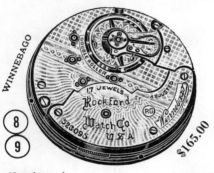

WINNEBAGO $165.00

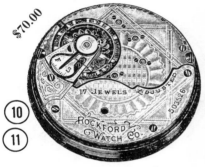

$70.00

No. 810 Hunting ⑥ $37.00
No. 910 Open Face ⑦

Hunting ⑧ $33.00
Open Face ⑨

No. 820 Hunting ⑩ $24.00
No. 920 Open Face ⑪

21 jewels in settings, elegantly damaskeened nickel plates, gold lettering, adjusted to temperature and five positions, Breguet hair spring, steel escape wheel, exposed pallets, micrometric regulator, compensating balance in recess. Safety pinion. Dust band, double sunk glass enameled dial, with red marginal figures, finely finished throughout. Certificate of rating furnished upon application.

17 ruby jewels in setting. Double roller escapement, sapphire exposed pallets, steel escape wheel, ground and polished on all acting surfaces, compensating balance, adjusted to temperature, isochronism and five positions. Breguet hair spring, patent micrometric regulator. Safety pinion. Handsomely damaskeened nickel plates, gold lettering, polished steel parts, double sunk glass enamel dial, with red marginal figures, Roman or Arabic. A 17 jewel watch, elegantly finished and equipped with all modern improvements. Certificate of Rating furnished on application.

17 jewels in settings, nickel, handsomely damaskeened, adjusted to temperature and position, steel escape wheel, Breguet hair spring, patent micrometric regulator, compensating balance in recess. Safety pinion. Dust band, glass enameled double sunk dial with red marginal figures.

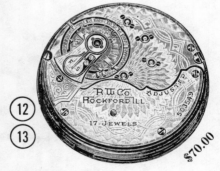

$70.00

$70.00

$50.00

No. 825 Hunting ⑫ $20.00
No. 925 Open Face ⑬

No. 830 Hunting ⑭ $16.80
No. 930 Open Face ⑮

No. 835 Hunting ⑯ $13.00
No. 935 Open Face ⑰

17 jewels in settings nickel gilt damaskeened adjusted to heat and cold, Breguet hair spring, micrometric regulator, compensating balance in recess. Safety pinion. Dust band, double sunk dial, with red marginal figures.

17 jewels in settings, nickel damaskeened, adjusted to heat and cold, Breguet hair spring, micrometric regulator, compensating balance in recess. Safety pinion. Dust band, sunk second dial with red marginal figures.

17 jewels in settings, nickel damaskeened, Breguet hair spring, micrometric regulator, compensating balance in recess. Safety pinion. Dust band, sunk second dial, marginal figures.

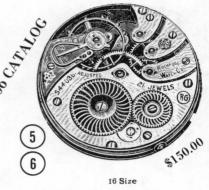

BUSIEST HOUSE IN AMERICA

1906 CATALOG

① ② 21 J – $200.00 23 J – $265.00

16 Size

No. 500 Hunting } Bridge $100.00
No. 505 Open Face }

Nickel, 21 high colored ruby jewels, gold settings, accurately adjusted to temperature, all positions and isochronism. Closely rated in pocket position. Compensating balance with gold screws, gold beveled polished train, double roller escapement, sapphire jewel pin, steel escape wheel ground and highly polished on all frictional surfaces. Red ruby pallets, patent micrometric regulator, positive action. Breguet hair spring of best quality. Safety pinion. Beveled and rayed winding wheels, all steel work elegantly polished and cornered. First quality mainspring, double sunk glass enamel dial, bronzed hands, gold lettering and artistically damaskeened.

A watch made especially for comparison in general finish and time-keeping qualities. Certificate of rating furnished upon application.

③ ④ $165.00

16 Size

No. 510 Hunting } Bridge $60.00
No. 515 Open Face }

Nickel, 21 high colored ruby jewels, gold settings, accurately adjusted to temperature, five positions and isochronism. Compensating balance, with gold screws. Gold beveled polished train, double roller escapement, sapphire pallets. Steel escape wheel ground and highly polished on all acting surfaces. Patent micrometric regulator. Breguet hair spring of best quality. Safety pinion. Beveled and rayed winding wheels, all steel work highly polished and cornered. First quality mainspring, double sunk glass enamel dial, gold lettering and richly damaskeened.

A most highly finished watch, up-to-date in all modern requirements, and an unexcelled timekeeper. Certificate of rating furnished upon application.

⑤ ⑥ $150.00

16 Size

No. 520 Hunting } Bridge $50.00
No. 525 Open Face }

Nickel, 21 ruby jewels, gold settings, accurately adjusted to temperature, five positions and isochronism. Compensating balance with gold screws, red beveled train. Double roller escapement, sapphire jewel pin, sapphire pallets, steel escape wheel ground and polished on all acting surfaces. Patent micrometric regulator. Breguet hair spring of best quality. Safety pinion. Beveled winding wheels, all steel work highly polished and cornered, double sunk glass enamel dial, gold lettering and attractively damaskeened.

A high-grade watch to meet most stringent railroad service demands. Certificate of rating furnished upon application.

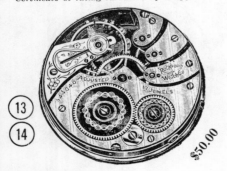
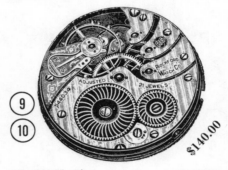
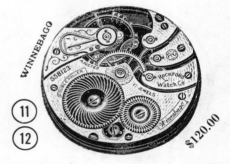

⑦ ⑧ $140.00

No. 530 Hunting } ¾ Plate $45.00
No. 535 Open Face }

Nickel, 21 ruby jewels in settings, accurately adjusted to temperature, five positions, and isochronism. Compensating balance, red beveled train, sapphire pallets, steel escape wheel ground and polished on all acting surfaces. Patent micrometric regulator. Breguet hair spring of best quality. Safety pinion. Beveled winding wheels, double sunk glass enamel dial, gold lettering, and handsomely damaskeened.

A high-grade watch for railway service. Certificate of rating furnished upon application.

⑨ ⑩ $140.00

No. 540 Hunting } Bridge $45.00
No. 545 Open Face }

Nickel, 21 ruby jewels, in settings, accurately adjusted to temperature, five positions, and isochronism. Compensating balance, red beveled train, double roller escapement, sapphire pallets, steel escape wheel ground and polished on all acting surfaces. Patent micrometic regulator. Breguet hair spring of best quality. Safety pinion. Beveled winding wheels, double sunk glass enamel dial, gold lettering, and handsomely damaskeened.

A high-grade watch for railway service. Certificate of rating furnished upon application.

WINNEBAGO

⑪ ⑫ $120.00

Hunting } Bridge $37.50
Open Face }

Nickel, 17 Ruby jewels in settings, accurately adjusted to temperature, isochronism and five positions. Compensating balance with gold screws. Red beveled train, double roller escapement, sapphire pallets, steel escape wheel, ground and polished on all acting surfaces, patent micrometric regulator. Breguet hair spring, beveled winding wheels, polished steel work. Safety pinion. Double sunk glass enamel dial, gold lettering, attractively damaskeened. A 17 jewel watch elegantly finished and equipped with all modern improvements. Certificate of Rating furnished on application.

⑬ ⑭ $50.00

No. 550 Hunting } Bridge $33.00
No. 555 Open Face }

Nickel, 17 jewels, in settings, adjusted to temperature and three positions, closely timed. Compensating balance, bevel train, steel escape wheel, Breguet hair spring of best quality. Safety pinion. Patent micrometric regulator, double sunk glass enamel dial. A well finished watch and a durable timekeeper.

Pendant Set

⑮ ⑯ $40.00

No. 561 Hunting } Bridge $23.50
No. 566 Open Face }

Nickel, 17 jewels, in settings, adjusted to temperature, closely timed. Compensating balance, beveled center wheel, beveled and rayed winding wheels. Breguet hair spring, patent micrometric regulator. Safety pinion. Double sunk glass enamel dial, bridge model, pendant set. The finest finished and most reliable time keeper on the market for the money.

⑰ ⑱ $40.00

No. 560 Hunting } ¾ Plate $21.00
No. 565 Open Face }

Nickel, 17 jewels, in settings, adjusted to temperature, closely timed. Compensating balance, beveled center wheel, Breguet hair spring. Safety pinion. Patent micrometric regulator, sunk second glass enamel dial. A well finished, reliable timekeeper.

12 Size

1908 FACTORY CATALOG

12 Size

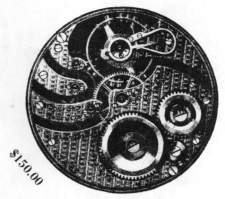

$200.00

$150.00

300 Hunting   305 Open Face

23 Jewels   Pendant Set

Adjusted to Temperature and Positions

WUAS—$67.50

Twenty-three specially selected ruby and sapphire jewels in raise gold settings, adjusted to temperature, five positions and isochronism, gold round arm train, compensating balance with gold screws, double roller escapement, steel escape wheel, sapphire jewel pin, sapphire pallets, safety pinion, patent micrometric regulator, Breguet hair spring, double sunk glass enamel dial, gold lettering, beautifully damaskeened and extra finely finished throughout.

310 Hunting   315 Open face

21 Jewels   Pendent Set

Adjusted to temperature and positions

UASS—$40.00

Twenty-one extra fine ruby and sapphire jewels in gold settings, adjusted to temperature, five positions and isochronism, double roller escapement, steel escape wheel, gold center wheel, sapphire jewel pin, sapphire pallets, compensating balance with gold screws, round arm train, safety pinion, patent micrometric regulator, Breguet hair spring, double sunk glass enamel dial, gold lettering, handsomely damaskeened and finely finished throughout.

12 Size

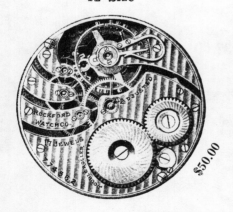

$50.00

12 Size

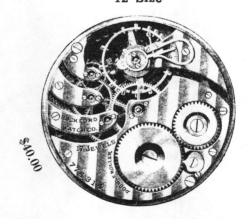

$40.00

320 Hunting   325 Open Face

17 Jewels   Pendant Set

Adjusted

OUAS—$20.00

Seventeen ruby and sapphire jewels in settings, adjusted to heat and cold, double roller escapement, steel escape wheel, gold center wheel, sapphire jewel pin, sapphire pallets, compensating balance, Breguet hair spring, safety pinion, patent micrometric regulator, gold lettering, handsomely damaskeened, double sunk glass enamel dial.

330 Hunting   335 Open Face

17 Jewels   Pendant Set

EAS—$15.00

Seventeen ruby and sapphire jewels in settings, double roller escapement, steel escape wheel, sapphire jewel pin, sapphire pallets, compensating balance, Breguet hair spring, safety pinion, patent micrometric regulator, gold lettering, double sunk glass enamel dial.

16 Size

$40.00

Pendant Set

No. 572 Hunting
No. 573 Open Face } Bridge $19.00

Nickel, 17 jewels in settings, compensating balance, beveled and rayed winding wheels. Breguet hair spring. Safety pinion. Micrometric regulator, double sunk glass enamel dial Closely timed and may be relied on.

16 Size

$40.00

Pendant Set

No. 570 Hunting
No. 575 Open Face } ¾ Plate $18.00

Nickel, 17 jewels in settings, compensating balance. Breguet hair spring. Safety pinion. Micrometric regulator, sunk second glass enamel dial. A watch trustworthy and durable.

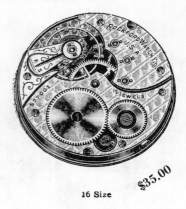

16 Size

$35.00

Pendant Set

No. 584 Hunting
No. 585 Open Face } ¾ Plate $15.00

Nickel, 15 jewels, in settings, compensating balance, Breguet hair spring. Safety pinion. Micrometric regulator, sunk second dial.

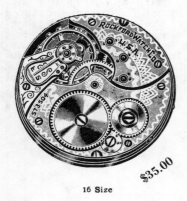

16 Size

$35.00

Pendant Set

No. 590 Hunting
No. 595 Open Face } ¾ Plate $11.90

Nickel, 11 jewels in settings, compensating balance. Breguet hair spring. Safety pinion. Micrometric regulator, sunk second dial.

$75.00

0 Size

Pendant Set

No. 140　　　　$37.00

Hunting, Nickel, 17 ruby jewels adjusted to temperature and position, gold round center wheel, steel escape wheel, double roller escapement, compensating balance, Breguet hair spring, micrometric regulator, gold lettering, handsomely damaskeened sunk second glass enamel dial.

$60.00

0 Size

Pendant Set

No. 150　　　　$25.00

Hunting, Nickel, 17 ruby jewels, gold round arm center wheel, steel escape wheel, double roller escapement, compensating balance, Breguet hair spring, micrometric regulator, gold lettering handsomely damaskeened, sunk second glass enamel dial.

$50.00

0 Size

Pendant Set

No. 160　　　　$20.00

Hunting, 15 ruby jewels, round arm center wheel, red train, steel escape wheel, double roller escapement, compensating balance, Breguet hair spring, micrometric regulator, handsomely damaskeened, sunk second glass enamel dial.

0 Size
Bridge Model
1906

This watch is manufactured in three grades, 15 jewel, 17 jewel and 17 jewel adjusted "All of which are made with 'Steel Escape Wheel.'" All Grades being equipped with Double Roller Escapement.

The jewels in these movements are all of the very best, and are made from "Ruby and Sapphire" only, thus reducing breakage to a minimum and insuring the life of the jewel against "Wear" to an unlimited degree.

The Pendant Set is designed with a view to simplicity and durability, being composed of four parts only, two levers and two wire springs. This will be found easy to case, especially care having been taken in its design to meet any ordinary variation that occur in the many makes of cases.

The patent Micrometric Regulator is made in two parts, thus affording an opportunity for lightness and delicacy of design, harmonizing with the beauty and grace of curves carried out in the plates and bridges of this 1906 O size model. Should the spring portion of the regulator become lost or break at any time, same can be replaced without any change in the rate of the watch, this being a decided advantage in this two piece micrometric regulator.

The train and escapement have been so carefully and correctly designed that the power required to give to the balance its proper motion is imparted by the weakest of main springs, of which is used nothing but the very best quality.

Elegance of design, accuracy of train, and "Double Roller with Steel Wheel Escapement" all parts finely finished, make the ROCKFORD MODEL O size the best ladies watch on the market and a "Time Keeper."

12 SIZE COMPLETE WATCHES

Value for movement only given on this page.

$125.00

$70.00

340 Hunting   345 Open Face
"Pocahontas"
21 Jewels   Pendent Set
Adjusted to temperature and positions

Twenty-one extra fine ruby and sapphire jewels in gold settings, adjusted to temperature, five positions and isochronism, double roller escapement, steel escape wheel, gold center wheel, sapphire jewel pin, sapphire pallets, compensating balance with gold screws, round arm train, safety pinion, patent micrometric regulator, Breguet hair spring, double sunk glass enamel dial, gold lettering, handsomely damaskeened and finely finished throughout.

350 Hunting   355 Open Face
"Iroquois"
17 Jewels   Pendant Set

Seventeen ruby and sapphire jewels in settings, steel escape wheel, double roller escapement, sapphire jewel pin, sapphire pallets, compensating balance, Breguet hair spring, safety pinion, patent micrometric regulator, gold lettering, double sunk glass enamel dial.

COMPLETE CASED
UP—DOWN
INDICATORS

16-S	17J	$550.00
16-S	21J	450.00
18-S	21J	550.00

$50.00

$75.00

O SIZE COMPLETE
WATCHES

190 Hunting "Winona"
15 Jewels   Pendant Set

Fifteen ruby and sapphire jewels in settings, double roller escapement, steel escape wheel, compensating balance, Breguet hair spring, patent micrometric regulator, sunk second glass enamel dial.

185   Hunting   "Iroquois"
17 Jewels   Pendant Set

Seventeen ruby and sapphire jewels in settings, double roller escapement, steel escape wheel, gold center wheel, compenating balance, Breguet hair spring, patent micrometric regulator, sunk second glass enamel dial, handsomely damaskeened and extra finely finished throughout.

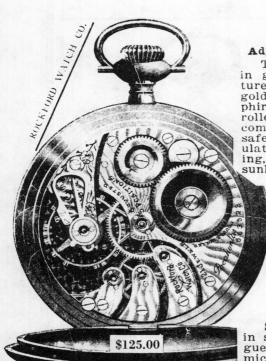

620 Hunting   625 Open Face
"Pocahontas"
21 Jewels   Pendent Set
Adjusted to temperature and positions

Twenty-one ruby and sapphire jewels in gold settings, adjusted to temperature, five positions and isochronism, gold center wheel, gold pallet cap, sapphire jewel pin, sapphire pallets, double roller escapement, steel escape wheel, compensating balance with gold screws, safety pinion, patent micrometric regulator, Breguet hair spring, gold lettering, handsomely damaskeened, double sunk glass enamel dial.

16 SIZE COMPLETE

WATCHES

630 Hunting   635 Open Face
"Iroquois"
17 Jewels   Pendant Set

Seventeen ruby and sapphire jewels in settings, compensating balance, Breguet hair spring, safety pinion, patent micrometric regulator, double sunk glass enamel dial.

$125.00

$70.00

16 SIZE COMPLETE

WATCHES

Cat. No.	Description	17 Jwl. Iroquois	21 Jwl. Pocahontas
82	18K S.G. O.F. Jtd. E.T. Ex. Hvy. With Cap Lip. Pend.	135.00	165.00
83	25 yr. Gold Filled Htg. E. T.	35.00	57.50
83	14K Solid Gold Hunting E. T. Extra Heavy	95.00	120.00
83	18K Solid Gold Hunting E. T. Extra Heavy	175.00	200.00
84	25 yr. Gold Filled Hunting Engraved	30.00	52.50
84	25 yr. Gold Filled O. F. S. B. & B. Engraved	27.50	50.00
85	25 yr. Gold Filled Hunting Engraved	30.00	52.50
85	25 yr. Gold Filled O. F. S. B. & B. Engraved	27.50	50.00
86	25 yr. Gold Filled Hunting Engraved	30.00	52.50
86	25 yr. Gold Filled O. F. S. B. & B. Engraved	27.50	50.00
87	25 yr. Gold Filled Hunting Engraved	30.00	52.50
87	25 yr. Gold Filled O. F. S. B. & B. Engraved	27.50	50.00
88	25 yr. Gold Filled Hunting Engraved	30.00	52.50
88	25 yr. Gold Filled O. F. S. B. & B. Engraved	27.50	50.00
89	25 yr. Gold Filled Htg. Eng.	30.00	52.50
89	25 yr. Gold Filled O. F. S. B. & B. Engraved	27.50	50.00
90	25 yr. Gold Filled Htg. E. T.	27.50	50.00
90	25 yr. Gold Filled O. F. Jtd. E. T. With Cap	27.50	50.00
90	25 yr. Gold Filled O. F. S. B. & B. E. T.	25.00	47.50
91	25 yr. Gold Filled Htg. Pln.	27.50	50.00
91	25 yr. Gold Filled O. F. Jtd. Plain With Cap	27.50	50.00
91	25 yr. Gold Filled O. F. S. B. & B. Plain Bassine	25.00	47.50
91	25 yr. Gold Filled O. F. S. B. & B. Pl. Fcy. Ctr.	25.00	47.50
92	25 yr. Gold Filled O.F. S.R. Dust Proof Plain or E. T.	27.00	50.00
92	25 yr. Gold Filled O.F. S.R. Dust Proof Engraved	30.00	52.50

I have shown part of the charts from the 1908 Factory Catalog that gave the descriptions and prices of the cased watches the Rockford Company offered at this time. The up and down indicators as far as I can tell were offered after 1908. I have not attempted to value these cased watches. Most of these cases are marked Rockford and are very desirable to collectors.

12 SIZE COMPLETE WATCHES

Cat. No.	Description	17 Jwl. Iroquois		21 Jwl. Pockahontas	
1	14K Solid Gold Diam. Raised	TSSS	$100.00	CWAS	$125.00
2	14K " " "	AHSS	95.00	CUAS	120.00
3	14K " " "	ACSS	92.50	COAS	117.50
3	18K " " "	AAAS	90.00	CSSS	115.00
4	14K Diamond Inlaid	TUUA	105.00	CTCA	130.00
2	14K Raised	WWSS	72.50	AHAS	97.50
3	14K Hunting Plain Heavy Lip Pendant	WSAS	65.00	AASS	90.00
3	18K Hunting Plain Heavy Lip Pendant	TASS	110.00	CESS	140.00
3	14K Hunt. Plain Ex. Heavy Lip Pendant	WAUA	70.00	AECA	100.00
3	18K Hunt. Plain Ex. Heavy Lip Pendant	CASS	130.00	HESS	160.00
57	25 yr. Gold Filled Htg. Eng.	OHSS	$27.50	RRSS	52.50
57	25 yr. " " O. F. S. B. & B. Engraved	OCSS	25.00	RUSS	50.00
58	25 yr. Gold Filled Htg. Eng.	OHSS	27.50	RRSS	52.50
58	25 yr. " " O. F. S. B. & B. Engraved	OCSS	25.00	RUSS	50.00
59	25 yr. Gold Filled Htg. Eng.	OHSS	27.50	RRSS	52.50
59	25 yr. " " O. F. S. B. & B. Engraved	OCSS	25.00	RUSS	50.00
60	25 yr. G.F. O.F. Knife Edge No Cap Jtd. B. S.B. Plain	OTAS	25.00	ROAS	50.00
61	25 yr. Gold Filled Htg. Eng.	OHSS	27.50	RRSS	52.50
61	25 yr. " " O. F. S. B. & B. Engraved	OCSS	25.00	RUSS	50.00
62	25 yr. Gold Filled Htg. Eng.	OHSS	27.50	RRSS	52.50

O SIZE COMPLETE WATCHES

Cat. No	Description	15 Jwl. Winona		17 Jwl. Iroquois	
1	14K Solid Gold 32 Diamonds	OOSSS	$200.00	OOUUA	$210.00
2	14K " 10 "	ATSS	90.00	AHUA	95.00
3	14K " 33 "	OUESS	235.00	OROUA	245.00
4	14K " Lge Diam. Star	WUSS	67.50	WWUA	72.50
5	14K " 11 Diamonds	ARSS	85.00	AAUA	90.00
6	14K " 12 "	AWUA	87.50	ATCA	92.50
7	14K " Diam. Raised	WOSS	65.00	WRUA	70.00
8	14K "	UEAS	47.50	ROCA	52.50
9	14K " Inlaid	ROSS	50.00	RRUA	55.00
10	14K " Inlaid Eng.	UTAS	42.50	UHCA	47.50
11	14K " Diam. Inlaid	UWAS	40.00	UTUA	45.00

No. 1.

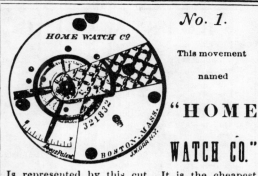

This movement

named

"HOME

WATCH CO."

Is represented by this cut. It is the cheapest grade made at Waltham. Lever movement, jewelled and extra jewelled, patent dust band, and substantially made.

No. 1.	Plain (7) Jeweled, Patent Dust Band, in Coin Silver Open Case............	$15.00
"	In 2 oz. Coin Silver, Hunting Case, plain or engine turned.................	16.00
"	In 3 oz. Coin Silver, Hunting Case, plain or engine turned............	19.00
No. 1 1-2.	Same as No. 1, but Extra Jeweled, in 2 oz. Coin Silver Hunting Case, pl. or eng. tr.	19.00
"	In 3 oz. Coin Silver Hunting Case, pl. or eng. tr..........	21.00
"	In 4 oz. Coin Silver Hunting Case, pl. or eng. tr...........	23.00

All Waltham Watches now have tempered hair springs. Tempered hair springs make a watch hold its rate better, and more lively motion.

Jewels make a watch wear longer.

Fogg's Patent Safety Pinion prevents the breaking of the wheels in case the main spring breaks.

No. 1
Model 57
$40.00
18-Size

No. 2
Model 57
18-Size
$35.00

$75.00
85.00

80.00
75.00

80.00
85.00

No. 2.

Named

"WM.

ELLERY."

This is a full plate, lever movement, and has late improvements, Fogg's patent pinion, patent dust band, sprung-over regulator, silver index, sunk second dial compound balance, and is plain and extra jewelled.

No. 2.	Plain (7) Jeweled, late improvements, in Coin Silver Open Cases, plain or engine turned...........................	$19.00
"	In 2 oz. Coin Silver Hunting Case, pl. or eng. tr.	20.00
"	" 3 oz. "	23.00
"	" 14k Gold "	60.00
"	" 18k "	70.00
No. 2 1-2.	Same as No. 2, but extra jeweled, in Coin Silver Open Case, pl. or eng. tr.	21.00
"	In 2 oz. Coin Silver Hunting Case, pl. or eng. tr.	22.00
"	" 3 " "	25.00
"	" 3 " " Flat Glass Crystals........	27.00
"	" 14k Gold Hunting Case, pl. or eng. tr.......	62.00
"	" 18k "	72.00
No. 2 3-4.	Same as No. 2 1-2, but with compound balance, in Coin Silver Open Case, pl. or eng. tr.	22.00
"	In 2 oz. Coin Silver Hunting Case, pl. or eng. tr.	23.00
"	" 3 " "	26.00
"	" 4 " "	28.00
"	" 14k Gold " "	65.00
"	" 18k " "	75.00

Both gold and silver cases come either plain or engine turned as desired. Richly engraved gold cases cost from $3.00 to $5.00 extra.

No. 3
Model 57
18-Size
$35.00

No. 4
Model 57
18-Size
$40.00

These early Walthams and all of the watches before the 1870's in the original cases are very good collector watches. These are the antiques over 100 years old. I have tried to give you some idea on these first 3 Waltham pages of the value of these early Walthams. I have in some instances valued the movement and you must add the value of the case. A watch in the original case is worth much more than a recase.

No. 3.

Named

P. S. BARTLETT.

The most Popular

Watch for the
Million.

Full plate, lever movement, has the late improvements, Fogg's patent pinion, patent dust band, sprung-over regulator, with silver-index, sunk second dial and steel and expansion balance. This grade is more widely known than any made at Waltham, and is a very close timer.

No. 3.	Plain (7) Jeweled, with late improvements, in Coin Silver Open Case, plain or engine turned.....	$23.00
"	In 2 oz. Coin Silver Hunting Case, pl. or eng. tr.	24.00
"	" 3 " "	27.00
"	" 4 " "	29.00
"	" 14k Gold, 2 oz. "	66.00
"	" 18k "	75.00
No. 3 1-2.	Same as No. 3, but with extra jewels, in Coin Silver Open Case, pl. or eng. tr..........	24.00
Same in 2 oz. Hunting Case, pl. or eng. tr.........		25.00
"	" 3 " "	28.00
"	" 4 " "	31.00
"	" 14k Gold, 2 oz. "	68.00
"	" 18k "	78.00
No. 3 3-4.	Same as No. 3 1-2, but with expansion balance, in 2 oz. Coin Silver Hunting Case, pl. or eng. tr.........	27.00
"	In 3 oz. Coin Silver Hunting Case, pl. or eng. tr.	30.00
"	" 4 " "	32.00
Same in 14k Gold, 2 oz. "		70.00
"	18k " "	80.00
"	18k " 2 1-2 oz. "	

14k gold, $1.00, and 18k $1.25 per dwt. for extra weight.

No. 4.

Named

"WALTHAM

WATCH CO."

This is a full plate, lever movement, four pairs extra jewels, late improvements, and expansion balance.

No. 4.	Sprung-Over Regulator, Fogg's Patent Pinion, Patent Dust Band, and Expansion Balance, in Coin Silver Open Case, plain or engine turned...................	$31.00
Same in 2 oz. Coin Silver Hunting Case, pl. or eng. tr.		32.00
"	" 2 1-2 oz. " "	33.50
"	" 3 " " "	35.00
"	" 4 " " "	37.00
In 2 1-2 oz. Coin Silver Open Case, Flat Plate Glass Crystals, pl. or eng. tr.......................		35.00
In 3 oz. "		38.00
In 14k, 2 oz. Solid Gold Hunting Case, pl. or eng. tr.		75.00
In 18k, " " "		85.00
In 14k, 2 1-2 oz. " "		85.00
In 18k, (18 dwts) " "		95.00

This Movement is soon to have Stem-Winding Attachment applied.

In 2 oz. Coin Silver Hunting Case.....

In 3 oz. ....

Cases with flat glass crystals can be furnished, when desired, for any grade of Waltham Watches.

No. 5.

Named

"APPLETON TRACY & CO."

Full plate, lever movement, four pairs extra jewels, late improvements and expansion balance, and made adjusted and not adjusted. This is the first grade watch which is made adjusted, and is a very accurate time-keeper.

No. 5. With Fogg's Patent Pinion, Sprung-over Regulator, Sunk Second Dial, Silver Index and Expansion Balance, in Coin Silver Open Case, plain or engine turned................ $39.00
" In 2 oz. Coin Silver Hunting Case, pl. or eng. tr. 40.00
" 3 " " " 43.00
" 4 " " " 46.00
" 14k Gold, " " 85.00
" 18k " " " 95.00
No. 5 1-2. Same as No. 5, but adjusted to heat and cold, in 2 oz. Coin Silver Hunting Case, pl. or eng. tr............................. 45.00
" In 3 oz. Coin Silver Hunting Case, pl. or eng. tr. 48.00
" 4 " " " 50.00
" Coin Silver Open Case, with Flat Plate Glass Crystal................ 50.00
No. 5 1-2. In 2 oz. 14k Gold Hunting Case, pl. or eng. tr. 90.00
" 2 1-2 oz. 11k " " 100.00
" 2 " 18k " " 100.00
" 44 dwt " " 105.00
" 48 dwt " " 110.00
" 60 dwt " " 125.00

We have open cases for $2.00 less than the hunting case, but those on the list for $1.00 less are none too heavy to protect the movement.

LADY'S WATCH.
No. 8.

Named

P. S. BARTLETT.

Three-quarter Plate.

This cut represents the size and style of this movement.

There are at present only two grades of ladies' watches, named P. S. Bartlett and Appleton, Tracy & Co., they are very reliable timekeepers, substantially made, and durable.

This is made with four pairs extra jewels, is a straight line lever movement, patent pinion, both gold and expansion balance and sunk second dial.

No. 8. Gold Balance and late improvements, in Coin Silver Open Case, plain or engine turned 32.00
" In Coin Silver Hunting Case, pl. or eng. tr.... 33.00
" 11k " " 55.00
" 18k " " 65.00
No. 8 1-2. Same as No. 8, but with Expansion Balance, in Coin Silver Hunting Case, pl. or eng. tr.... 35.00
" In 11k Gold " " 58.00
" 18k " " 68.00
" Open Case, with Flat Glass Crystals, pl. or eng. tr......$55.00-$85.00

Gold cases weigh from 23 to 25 dwts. each.
Extra heavy cases cost $1.00 per dwt. extra for 11k. and $1.25 for 18k gold. Engraved cases cost $2.00 and $5.00 extra. Engraved and enameled cases cost from $5.00 to $10.00.

No. 5
Model 57
18-Size
$40.00

No. 5½
Model 57
18-Size
$50.00

No. 7
Keywind
14-Size
$35.00
H.T.C.

No. 8
Keywind
10-Size
$35.00
H.T.C.

No. 9
Keywind
10-Size
$35.00
H.T.C.

Any of these early Walthams in original solid gold or silver cases in extra fine or better condition bring a premium to serious collectors. There is hardly any way I could value each of the many variations and case combinations shown on these 3 pages. I tried not to destroy or alter any of the original type for historical reasons. The brochure was very old and yellow and very hard to read in certain sections.

BOYS' WATCH.
No. 7.

Named AMERN. WATCH CO., Adams Street.

Three-quarter Plate, Lever Movement, 14 Size.

This is a new watch for boys and young men. A very low price has been made for this watch because it is a Boy's Watch, and also with the object of bringing it within the means of boys of all classes. This watch will suit all those who have hitherto objected to Waltham watches on account of their large size, it being a size between the 3-4 plate gent's 16 size and the lady's watch, and modeled the same. Is thorough and substantially made. Price considered, no such watch in quality and beauty has ever been produced in this country, and is better adapted to rough usage than any foreign watch yet produced.

No. 7. Seven Jewels, Patent Pinion, Sunk Second Dial, Hands setting from the back, Steel Balance, in Coin Silver Open Case, plain or engine turned................ $19.00
Same in Coin Silver Hunting Case, pl. or eng. tr.... 20.00
" 11k Gold Hunting Case, pl. or eng. tr. " extra jewels.
" 18k " "
No. 7 1-2. Same as No. 7, but with Gold Balance, in Coin Silver Open Case, pl. or eng. tr..... 21.50
In Coin Silver Hunting Case, pl. or eng. tr.........22.75
In 14k Gold
In 18k
No. 7 3-4. Same as No. 7 1-2, but with Expansion Balance, in Coin Silver Open Case, pl. or eng. tr.............................. 25.00
In Coin Silver Hunting Case, pl. or eng. tr......... 24.50
In 14k Gold " " 60.00
In 18k " " 70.00

A New Grade of the same watch has been issued since April 1st called Gent's 14 size, and differs from the Boy's Watch in having 4 pair extra jewels, expansion balance, and finished extra, late improvements.

In Coin Silver Open Case, pl. or eng. tr........... 34.00
In " Hunting Case pl. or eng. tr......... 35.00
In 14k Gold " " 75.00
In 18k " " " 85.00

LADY'S WATCH.
No. 9.

Named

"APPLETON TRACY & CO."

Three-quarter plate, lever movement, four pair extra jewels, straight line lever, patent pinion, and expansion balance.

In 11k Gold Open Case, plain or engine turned..... $62.00
" Hunting Case, pl. or eng. tr............ 65.00
In 18k " Open Case, " 70.00
" Hunting Case, " 75.00
" " Open & Hunt'g, Flat Glass Crystals. 70.00-100.00
Richly enameled cases cost from $10.00 to $15.00 extra.

WATCH REPAIRING.

In our repairing department we have facilities that no other house has, being practical Watchmakers, and provided with tools of all kinds of the latest improvement, and material selected direct from the different watch factories, we are able to do first-class work with promptness and dispatch, and at a low rate. At our factory we make and repair all kinds of Clocks, including the beautiful Ball Clock. Orders through the Post Office, or at our Store, for Clock Repairing, will be immediately attended to.

Particular attention given to Pocket Chronometers and Horse-Timeing Watches, Repeating, and Music and Bird Boxes. As we are aware of the necessity of a prompt execution of all orders to our care, we shall take special pride in giving speedy returns to those entrusted to us.

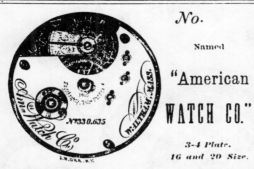

No.

Named

"American WATCH CO."

3-4 Plate.
16 and 20 Size.

This cut represents the 20 size. which differs from the 16 size, in being larger in circumference. they being exactly alike in all other respects. All those wanting a large, heavy watch, the 20 size would please, and those preferring a medium, the 16 size would be the one to buy.

No. 11. Best quality three-quarter Plate, with five pair extra fine Ruby Jewels, exposed Ruby Pallets, Compensation Balance, accurately adjusted to heat, cold, isochronism and position, in 18k Gold Hunting Case, plain or engine turned.................$269 to $300.00

In 18k Gold Open Face, Flat Plate Glass Crystals, pl. or eng. tr.....................$250 to $300.00

No 12. Same as No. 11, but Nickel Movement, 16 size, and Patent Stem-Winding and Hand Setting Attachment, in 18k Gold Hunting Case pl. or eng. turned............$375 to $450.00

In 18k Gold Open Case, Flat Back and Glass, with Monogram, pl. or eng. tr.........$400 to $425.00

These movements are the most perfect specimens of fine mechanism ever made in this country, and are not excelled in principle, finish, or performance by any watches of foreign manufacture.

No. 11
16-Size
Keywind
$175.00
H.T.C.

No. 11
20 Size
Keywind
$275.00
H.T.C.

No. 10
16-Size
Keywind
$150.00
H.T.C.

No. 10
Keywind
20-Size
$250.00
H.T.C.

No. 10.

Named

"A Mⁿ WATCH CO."

3-4 Plate.
16 and 20 Size.

This grade is modeled like the above cut, with the exception of the name, which is "Amn. Watch Co., Waltham, Mass., instead of "American Watch Co." Three-quarter plate watches differ from the full plate, in being much thinner, owing to the balance being set between the two plates, whereas in the full plate the balance is above the top plate, which necessitates the difference in thickness. This is made with and without stem-winding attachment.

No. 10. Four pair extra Jewels, Expansion Balance, adjusted to heat and cold, hardened and tempered Hair Spring, Fogg's Pat. Pinion, in Coin Silver Open case, plain or engine turned......$ 78.00
In 3 oz. Coin Silver Hunting Case, pl. or eng. tr.... 80.00
In 14k (2 oz) Gold " " 120.00
In 14k (45 dwts) " " " 125.00
In 14k (50 dwts) " " " 130.00
In 18k (42 dwts) " " " 130.00
In 18k (45 dwts) " " " 135.00
In 18k (50 dwts) " " " 140.00
No. 10 1-2. Same as No. 10, but with Stem-Winding and Hand Setting Attachment, in 18k (45 dwts) 16 size, Gold Hunting Case, pl. or eng tr........ 152.00
In 18k (50 dwts) 16 size, Gold Hunting Case, plain or engine turned.......................... 158.00

Extra heavy cases cost $1.25 per dwt. for 18k, and per dwt. for 14k gold.

The new style of plain flat cases, with plate glass crystals, is very popular, the back engraved with monogram gives a very handsome finish.

The price of the stem-winding movement, in case engraved with monogram, is from $175 to $225. This style of case can be made for any of the full plate movements, either of gold or silver, and hunting or open case when desired.

The New Plate Watch -- Railroad Timekeeper.

THE WATCH

For Business Men.

This, the highest grade of full plate watches, made at Waltham, in size and appearance, finish and general excellence, is especially intended for and recommended to business men, and in particular to railroad and expressmen, constant travellers, in fact all wanting such a watch should get the "AMERICAN WATCH CO., CRESCENT STREET." Counting on such destination for this variety of their manufacture, the Company devote the greatest care to its construction, employing upon it only their best men and machinery, and issue it with their reputation at stake upon its success.

No. 6. Full Plate, Straight line Lever Movement, 18 size, 4 pair extra Jewels, Expansion Balance, adjusted to heat and cold, Patent Regulator and Patent Rachet Click, in Coin Silver Open Case, pl. or eng. tr... $ 50.00
In 3 oz. Coin Silver Hunting Case, pl. or eng. tr.. 53.00
In 4 oz. " " 56.00
In 14k (2 oz.) Gold " " 93.00
In 14k (50 dwts) " " " 103.00
In 14k (60 dwts) " " " 112.00
In 14k (50 dwts) " " " 112.00
In 18k (60 dwts) " " " 125.00
In 18k " Flat Plate Glass Crystals, pl. or eng. tr.......................$120.00 to $140.00
No. 6 1-2. Same as No. 6, but with Stem-Winding and Hands Setting Attachment, in Coin Silver Hunting Case 70.00
In Coin Silver Hunting Case, " 73.00
In 14k (50 dwts) Gold Hunting Case, " 118.00
In 14k (60 dwts) " " 128.00
In 18k (50 dwts) " " 125.00
In 18k (60 dwts) " Flat Plate Glass Crystals, pl. or eng. tr..........$115.00 to $150.00

No. 6
1870
Keywind
18-Size
$250.00

No. 6½
1870
Stem Wind
18-Size
$200.00

The watches on this page are all high grade and very good collector pieces. A rough rule of thumb for watches in mint condition might be 4 times their original cost. Only the buyer and seller can set the final value. At the present time any early Waltham movement with a serial number below 1500 will bring $500.00 to $1000.00 from advanced collectors. A fine article in the bulletin of the NAWCC, October 1958, Vol. 8, No. 6, Whole No. 76, deals with these early Walthams.

TRADE MARKS.

The trade marks used to distinguish the different grades are engraved on the upper plates, viz:

American Watch Co., Waltham, Mass.
Amn. Watch Co., Waltham, Mass.
Appleton, Tracy & Co., Waltham, Mass.
P. S. Bartlett, Waltham, Mass.
Amern. Watch Co., Adams St.,
Waltham, Mass.
American Watch Co., Crescent Street,
Waltham, Mass.
Waltham Watch Co., Waltham, Mass.
Wm. Ellery, Waltham, Mass.
Home Watch Co., Boston, Mass.

Every genuine Waltham Watch is warranted by special certificate from the Factory Office, excepting the "Home Watch Co.," the lowest grade, that we warrant to keep good time.

The following is a fac-simile of the Company's certificate:

"AMERICAN WATCH COMPANY,

Waltham, Mass...........18

THIS IS TO CERTIFY THAT

Lever Watch Movement No._____ engraved with our Trade Mark, ...Waltham, Mass., was manufactured at our works and is guaranteed by us to be made of the best materials, on the most approved principle, and possesses every requisite for a reliable Time Keeper.

For any defect in material, workmanship, or performance under fair usage we at all times hold ourselves responsible.

For the American Watch Company,
R. E. ROBBINS, Treasurer."

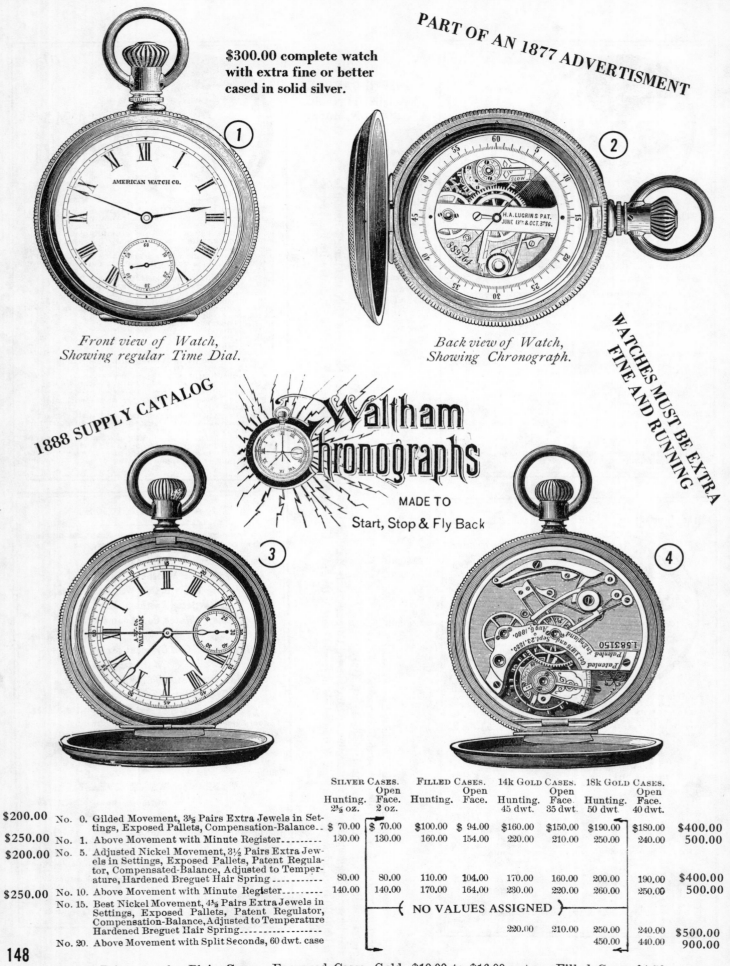

PART OF AN 1877 ADVERTISMENT

$300.00 complete watch with extra fine or better cased in solid silver.

① Front view of Watch, Showing regular Time Dial.

② Back view of Watch, Showing Chronograph.

WATCHES MUST BE EXTRA FINE AND RUNNING

1888 SUPPLY CATALOG

Waltham Chronographs

MADE TO

Start, Stop & Fly Back

③

④

		SILVER CASES.		FILLED CASES.		14k GOLD CASES.		18k GOLD CASES.		
		Hunting. 2½ oz.	Open Face. 2 oz.	Hunting.	Open Face.	Hunting. 45 dwt.	Open Face. 35 dwt.	Hunting. 50 dwt.	Open Face. 40 dwt.	
$200.00	No. 0. Gilded Movement, 3½ Pairs Extra Jewels in Settings, Exposed Pallets, Compensation-Balance..	$70.00	$70.00	$100.00	$94.00	$160.00	$150.00	$190.00	$180.00	$400.00
$250.00	No. 1. Above Movement with Minute Register.........	130.00	130.00	160.00	154.00	220.00	210.00	250.00	240.00	500.00
$200.00	No. 5. Adjusted Nickel Movement, 3½ Pairs Extra Jewels in Settings, Exposed Pallets, Patent Regulator, Compensated-Balance, Adjusted to Temperature, Hardened Breguet Hair Spring............	80.00	80.00	110.00	104.00	170.00	160.00	200.00	190.00	$400.00
$250.00	No. 10. Above Movement with Minute Register.........	140.00	140.00	170.00	164.00	230.00	220.00	260.00	250.00	500.00
	No. 15. Best Nickel Movement, 4½ Pairs Extra Jewels in Settings, Exposed Pallets, Patent Regulator, Compensation-Balance, Adjusted to Temperature Hardened Breguet Hair Spring................		NO VALUES	ASSIGNED		220.00	210.00	250.00	240.00	$500.00
	No. 20. Above Movement with Split Seconds, 60 dwt. case							450.00	440.00	900.00

148

Above Prices are for Plain Cases. Engraved Cases, Gold, $10.00 to $16.00 extra. Filled Cases, $1.50 to $2.00 extra. Extra Weight in Gold, 14k., $1.60 per Dwt.; 18k., $2.00 per Dwt ; Box Joints, $10.00 extra.

WALTHAM WATCH CO.'S MOVEMENTS.

1888

18 Size Full Plate, Gilded, Hunting or Open Face.

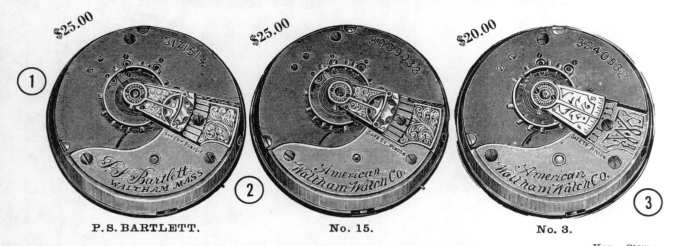

P. S. BARTLETT.　　　　No. 15.　　　　No. 3.

	Key Wind.	Stem Wind.
APPLETON, TRACY & CO., 15 jewels, 4 pairs in settings, adjusted to heat, cold and position ; patent regulator ; hardened Breguet hair spring, double sunk dial	$30.00	$40.00
P. S. BARTLETT, 15 jewels, 4 pairs in settings, patent regulator, hardened Breguet hair spring	19.00	25.00
R. E. ROBBINS, 13 jewels, 3 pairs in settings, patent regulator	17.00	40.00
WM. ELLERY, 11 jewels, 2 pairs in settings	13.50	25.00
STERLING, 7 jewels	11.00	25.00
BROADWAY, 7 jewels	$7.00	30.00
No. 15.　Nameless (same as Bartlett)	17.00	25.00
"　3.　"　　(same as Ellery)	12.50	20.00
"　1.　"　　(same as Sterling)	10.00	10.00

18 Size, Full Plate Nickel, Hunting or Open Face.

CRESCENT STREET.　　　APPLETON, TRACY & CO.　　　No. 35.

	Stem Wind.	
CRESCENT STREET, 15 ruby jewels, 4 pairs in settings, adjusted to heat, cold and position, patent regulator, hardened Breguet hair spring, double sunk dial	$50.00	$50.00
APPLETON, TRACY & CO., 15 jewels, 4 pairs in settings (same as gilt movement)	40.00	50.00
WALTHAM WATCH CO., 15 jewels, 4 pairs in settings (same as gilt movement)	30.00	30.00
No. 35.　Nameless.　15 ruby jewels, patent regulator adjusted to all positions	36.00	40.00
"　25.　"　　15 jewels　"　"　"　three　"	24.00	30.00
"　15.　"　　15　"　　"　"	18.00	25.00
"　3.　"　　11　"	14.00	25.00

Waltham Open Face Movements are made Pendant Set only, and to wind at XII.

149

WALTHAM WATCH CO. COMPLETE WATCHES.

CENTER ENGRAVED.
Assorted Patterns.

VERMICELLI STAR.

6 Size, Stem Wind.

1888 LAPP & FLERSHEM CATALOG CHICAGO

FULL OPEN FACE OR SKYLIGHT.

Hunting Only.

	No.					
$60.00	846.	Crescent Filled, "E" Movement,			$32.00	
	847.	"	"	" D "	"	34.50
to	848.	"	"	" F "	"	35.00
	849.	"	"	" C "	"	38.00
$80.00	850.	"	"	" B "	"	40.00
	850½.	"	"	" A "	"	51.00

Hunting Only.

	No.					
851.	Crescent Filled, "E" Movement,			$34.00	$60.00
852.	"	"	" D "	"	36.50	
853.	"	"	" F "	"	37.00	**to**
854.	"	"	" C "	"	40.00	
855.	"	"	" B "	"	42.00	$80.00
855½.	"	"	" A "	"	53.00	

AMERICAN WALTHAM WATCH Co.
3015031
SAFETY PINION

THE QUEEN

$60.00

AMERICAN WALTHAM WATCH Co.
3015030
SAFETY PINION

"E."

$20.00	E.	7 Jewel Gilt Movement.
20.00	D.	11 " " "
25.00	F.	9 " Nickel "

No. 856. Crescent Filled, Engraved, $27.00
" 857. 14K., Gold Engraved...... $38.00
N.B.—The above contains " E " Movement.

"C and B."

C.	13 Jewels in Gold Settings, Gilt.
B.	13 " " " Nickel.
A.	15 " " " Adjusted "

ASSORTED ENGRAVINGS.

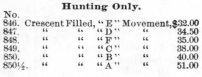

ASSORTED ENGRAVINGS.

10K	No.				10k. 16 dwt.	14k. 18 dwt.	18 K
$120.00	858.	With " E " Movement,			$44.00	$53.00	$140.00
	859.	"	" F "	"	47.00	56.00	
to	860.	"	" D "	"	46.50	55.50	**to**
	861.	"	" C "	"	50.00	59.00	
$140.00	862.	"	" B "	"	52.00	61.00	$160.00
	863.	"	" A "	"	63.00	72.00	

	No.				14k. 18 dwt.	14 K
	864.	With " E " Movement			$64.00	$130.00
	865.	"	" F "	"	67.00	
	866.	"	" D "	"	66.50	**to**
	867.	"	" C "	"	70.00	
	868.	"	" B "	"	72.00	$150.00
	869.	"	" A "	"	83.00	

Variations in weight will be added or deducted at rate of $2.00 per dwt. for 18k, $1.60 for 14k, $1.20 for 10k.

American Waltham Watch Co.'s Movements.

18 SIZE, FULL PLATE, HUNTING OR OPEN FACE.

See Page 4

Named and Nameless, Stem Wind. All Open Face Stem Wind are Pendant Set. Fit all 18 Size American Cases.

LIST PRICES EACH.

$80.00

$50.00

$50.00

$30.00

(1)

VANGUARD NICKEL. 21 Extra Fine Ruby Jewels in Raised Gold Settings; Double Roller; Pat. Reg.; Adjusted to Temperature, Isochronism and Position; Patent Safety Barrel; Patent Breguet Hairspring, Hardened and Tempered in Form; Plate and Jewel Screws Gilded; Steel Parts Chamfered. The Finest 18-size Movement in the World....$87 50

(2)

No. 214. CRESCENT STREET. Nickel, 21 Ruby Jewels in Gold Settings; Compensation Balance, Adjusted to Temperature. Isochronism and Position; Pat. Reg.; Patent Breguet Hairspring, Hardened and Tempered in Form; Fine Glass Enamel; Double Sunk Dial........$62 50

(3)

No. 209. APPLETON, TRACY & CO. Nickel, 17 Ruby Jewels in Gold Settings; Compensation Balance, Adjusted to Temperature, Isochronism and Position; Pat. Reg.; Pat. Breguet Hairspring. Hardened and Tempered in Form; Double Sunk Dial....................$46 25

(4)

No. 207. P. S. BARTLETT. Nickel, 17 Jewels in Settings; Compensation Balance. Adjusted; Pat. Reg. Patent Breguet Hairspring, Hardened and Tempered in Form. Double Sunk Dial.................$23 75
No. 206. P. S. BARTLETT. Gilded. Same as above............$20 63

$25.00

$20.00

$15.00

(5)

No. 87. Nickel, 17 Jewels in Settings. Adjusted; Compensation Balance, Pat. Reg.; Patent Breguet Hairspring, Hardened and Tempered in Form; Double Sunk Dial.$23 75
No. 85. Gilded. Same as above.. 20 63

$20.00

(6)

No. 84. Nickel. 15 Jewels in Settings, Compensation Balance; Pat. Reg.; Patent Breguet Hairspring, Hardened and Tempered in Form...$18 13

(7)

No. 81. Gilded. 15 Jewels in Settings; Compensation Balance; Patent Micrometric Regulator; Patent Breguet Hairspring, Hardened and Tempered in Form................$15 63

$15.00

(8)

No. 18. Nickel. 7 Jewels; Compensation Balance; Oval Regulator; Polished and Gilded Index Plate; Patent Breguet Hairspring, Hardened and Tempered in Form....................$10 00
No. 1. Gilded. Same as above.. 10 00

18 SIZE, NON-MAGNETIC MOVEMENTS.

$90.00

$35.00

White Non Magnetic Hairspring

$20.00

(9)

18 SIZE.
VANGUARD NICKEL, Non-Magnetic. 21 Extra Fine Ruby Jewels in Gold Settings; Double Roller; Pat. Reg.; Adjusted to Temperature, Isochronism and Position; Patent Safety Barrel; Patent Breguet Hairspring, Hardened and Tempered in Form; Plate and Jewel Screws Gilded; Steel Parts Chamfered. The Finest 18-Size Movement in the World........... $100 00

(10)

18 SIZE.
No. 45. Nickel, Non-Magnetic. 17 Fine Ruby Jewels, Gold Settings; Double Roller; Escapement; Patent Micrometric Regulator; Compensation Balance in recess. Adjusted to Temperature and Position. Tempered Steel Safety Barrel; Exposed Winding Wheel Breguet Hairspring; Double Sunk Dial.....$62 50

(11)

18 SIZE.
No. 1. Gilded Non-Magnetic, 7 Jewels; Compensation Balance. Dealers can safely guarantee Waltham Non-Magnetic Watches to possess all the qualities that are claimed for them. They will resist the most powerful magnetism...............$15 00

Any of the Above Movements Fitted with Fancy Dials Without Extra Cost, except 7 Jewels, 88c. Extra.

American Waltham Watch Co.'s Movements.

16 Size, 3-4 Plate, Hunting and Open Face.

Stem Wind, Pendant Set Movement.   Fit all 16 Size American Cases.

Model 88 $275.00 $300.00 $75.00 $60.00

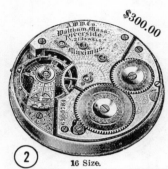
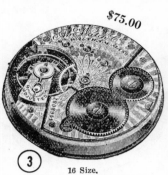

(1) **16 Size.**
"AMERICAN WATCH CO."
First Quality Nickel, 21 extra Fine Ruby Jewels in Gold Settings; Gold Train; Exposed Ruby Pallets; Patent Regulator; Compensation-Balance; Adjusted to Temperature, Isochronism and Position; Patent Breguet Hair-Spring, Hardened and Tempered in Form $125 00

(2) **16 Size.**
"RIVERSIDE MAXIMUS" NICKEL.
21 Diam. and Ruby Jew.; 2 pairs Diam. Caps; Both Bal. Piv. Run. on Diam. · Rais. G. Sett ; Gold Train; Jew. Pin Set without Shell.; Double Roll. Esc ; Exp Pall.; Pat. Micr. Reg.; Comp. Bal.; Acc. Adj. to Temp., Iso. and Pos. and caref. Tim.; Pat. Br. H.-Sp., Hard. and Temp. in Form ; Fine Glass Hand Pain Dial of Most Mod. and Art. Des. The sup. const. of this mov. adapts it to the most exacting service $112 50

(3) **16 Size.**
"AMERICAN WATCH CO."
Fine Nickel, 17 Fine Ruby Jewels in Gold Settings; Exposed Pallets, Patent Regulator; Compensation-Balance. Adjusted to Temperature, Isochronism and Position; Patent Breguet Hair-Spring, Hardened and Tempered in Form .. $75 00

15J $50.00

(4) **16 Size.**
"RIVERSIDE."
Nickel, 17 Jewels in Settings; Exposed Pallets; Patent Regulator; Compensation-Balance; Adjusted to Temperature. Isochronism and Position; Patent Breguet Hair-Spring; Hardened and Tempered in Form $46 25

THIS MODEL 88 TAKES A THICKER CASE THAN LATER 16S STANDARD MOVEMENTS.

$50.00   Model 88 $35.00 $30.00 $15.00

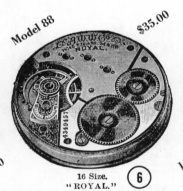

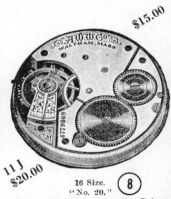

(5) **16 Size.**   15J $40.00
"RIVERSIDE."
Gilded and Nickel Damaskeened, 17 Jew. in Settings; Exposed Pallets; Patent Regulator; Compensation-Balance; Adjusted to Temperature Isochronism and Position; Patent Breguet Hair-Spring Hardened and Tempered in Form $37 50

(6) **16 Size.**
"ROYAL."
Nickel, 17 Jewels in Settings; Patent Regulator; Compensation-Balance; Patent Breguet Hair-pring Adjusted; Hardened and Tempered in Form $31 25

11J $25.00
(7) **16 Size.**
"No. 28."
Nickel, 15 Jewels in Settings ; Compensation-Balance ; Patent Breguet Hair-Spring, Hardened and Tempered in Form $19 38

11J $20.00
(8) **16 Size.**
"No. 20."
Gilded, 7 Jewels; Compensation-Balance; Patent Breguet Hair-Spring, Hardened and Tempered in Form $10 63

16 SIZE NON=MAGNETIC MOVEMENTS.

$300.00   Has White Hairspring $310.00 $70.00

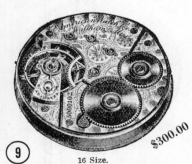
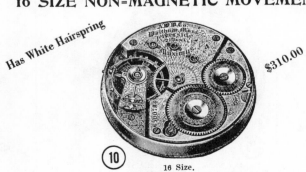
Model 88

(9) **16 Size.**
"AMERICAN WATCH CO."
Non-Magnetic. First Quality Nickel, 19 Extra Fine Ruby Jewels in Gold Settings; Gold Train; Exposed Ruby Pallets; Patent Regulator; Compensation-Balance, Adjusted to Temperature, Isochronism and Position ; Patent Breguet Hair-Spring; Hardened and Tempered in Form. $162 50

(10) **16 Size.**
"RIVERSIDE MAXIMUS" NICKEL.
Non-Magnetic. 21 Diam. and Ruby Jew.; 2 pairs Diam Caps; Both Bal. Piv. Run. on Diam.; Rais. G. Sett.; Gold Train; Jew. Pin set without Shell.; Double Roll. Esc.; Exp. Pall.; Pat. Micr. Reg.; Comp. Bal.; Acc. Adj. to Temp., Iso. and Pos. and caref. Tim.; Pat. Br. H.-Sp., Hard. and Temp. in Form; Fine Glass Hand Pain Dial ot Most Mod. and Art. Des. The sup. const. of this mov. adapts it to the most exacting service $137 50

(11) **16 Size.**
"RIVERSIDE."
Non-Magnetic. Nickel, 17 Jewels in Settings; Exposed Pallets; Patent Regulator; Compensation-Balance; Adjusted to Temperature, Isochronism and Position ; Patent Breguet Hair-Spring; Hardened and Tempered in Form 62 50

AMERICAN WALTHAM WATCH CO.'S MOVEMENTS.

0, 6 and 12 Sizes.   3-4 Plate, Hunting or Open Face.   Stem Wind, Pendant Set.   Fit all American Cases of Similar Sizes.

List Prices Each.

Model 90   Model 91

Rare $200.00 $50.00 $40.00 $30.00

① 6 Size.
"Riverside" Maximus, Nickel; 21 Diam. and Ruby Jew.; 2 pairs Diam. Caps; Both Bal. Piv. Run. on Diam.; Rais. G Sett; Gold Train; Jew. Pin set without Shell.; Double Roll. Esc.; Exp. Pall.; Pat. Micr. Reg.; Comp. Bal.; Acc. Adj. to Temp., Iso. and Pos.; Pat. Br. H-Sp., Hard. and Temp. in Form........ $68 75

② 6 Size.
"S," Fine Nickel; 17 Fine Ruby Jewels in Raised Gold Settings; Exposed Pallets; Compensation Balance; Adjusted; Patent Breguet Hair-Spring, Hardened and Tempered in Form.................... $56 25

③ 6 Size.
"Riverside," Nickel; 17 Fine Ruby Jewels (Raised Gold Settings); Exposed Pallets; Patent Regulator; Compensation Balance; Adjusted; Patent Breguet Hair-Spring, Hardened and Tempered in Form........ $46 25

④ 6 Size.
"Royal," Nickel; 16 Ruby Jewels (in Settings); Exposed Pallets; Patent Regulator; Compensation Balance; Adjusted; Patent Breguet Hair-Spring, Hardened and Tempered in Form................ $31 25

⑤ 0 Size.
"Riverside" Maximus, Nickel; 21 Diam. and Ruby Jew.; 2 pairs Diam. Caps; Both Bal. Piv. Run on Diam.; Rais. G. Sett.; Gold Train; Jew. Pin set without Shell.; Double Roll. Esc.; Exp. Pall.; Pat. Micr. Reg.; Comp. Bal.; Acc. Adj. to Temp., Iso. and Pos.; Pat. Br. H.-Sp., Hard. and Temp. in Form $68 75

$125.00

Model 90

$25.00 $20.00 $15.00 $20.00

⑥ 6 Size.
"X," Nickel; 15 Jewels (in Settings); Exposed Pallets; Compensation Balance...................... $20 00

⑦
"Y," Nickel; 7 Jewels; Exposed Pallets; Compensation Balance............. $12 50

⑧ 6 Size.
"J," Gilded; 7 Jewels; Exposed Pallets; Compensation Balance............. $12 50

⑨ 6 Size.
"N," Gilded and Nickel; Damaskeened; 15 Jewels; Exposed Pallets; Compensation Balance............. $18 75

⑩ 0 Size.
"No. 70," Fine Nickel; 17 Fine Ruby Jewels; Raised Gold Settings; Exposed Pallets; Compensation Balance; Adjusted; Patent Breguet Hair-Spring, Hardened and Tempered in Form........ $56 25

$50.00

$50.00 $40.00 $25.00 $25.00 $20.00

⑪ 0 Size.
"Riverside," Nickel; 17 Fine Ruby Jewels (Raised Gold Settings); Exposed Pallets; Patent Regulator; Compensation Balance; Adjusted; Patent Breguet Hair-Spring, Hardened and Tempered in Form........ $46 25

⑫ 0 Size.
"Royal," Nickel; 16 Ruby Jewels (in Settings); Exposed Pallets; Patent Regulator; Compensation Balance; Adjusted; Patent Breguet Hair-Spring, Hardened and Tempered in Form................. $31 25

⑬ 0 Size.
"No. 65," Nickel; 15 Jewels (in Settings); Exposed Pallets; Compensation Balance.............. $21 25

⑭ 0 Size.
"No. 63," Gilded and Nickel; Damaskeened; 15 Jewels (in Settings); Exposed Pallets; Compensation Balance $20 00

⑮ 0 Size.
"No. 60," Gilded; 7 Jewels; Exposed Pallets; Compensation Balance........ $14 38
"No. 61," Nickel, same as above.................. 14 38

$200.00   Model 94 $25.00

$40.00

⑯ 12 Size.
"Riverside" Maximus, Nickel; 21 Diam. and Ruby Jew.; 2 pairs Diam. Caps; Both Bal. Piv. Run. on Diam.; Raised G. Sett.; Gold Train; Jew. Pin set without Shell.; Double Roll. Esc.; Exp. Pall.; Pat Micr. Reg; Comp. Bal.; Acc. Adj. to Temp., Iso. and Pos.; Pat. Br. H.-Sp., Hard and Temp. in Form...................................$112 50

⑰ 12 Size.
"Riverside," Nickel; 17 Ruby Jewels (Gold Settings); Exposed Pallets; Patent Regulator; Compensation Balance; Adjusted to Temperature and Pos. Patent Breguet Hair-Spring, Hardened and Tempered in Form.............................. $46 25

⑱ 12 Size.
"Royal," Nickel; 17 Jewels (Gold Settings); Exposed Pallets; Patent Regulator; Compensation Balance; Adjusted; Patent Breguet Hair-Spring, Hardened and Tempered in Form................ $31 25

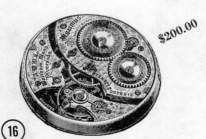

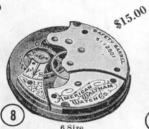

Essential Features Found in all Waltham Watches

All Nickel plates are made of Nickel, not Brass Nickel-Plated.

All Waltham watches have Breguet Hairsprings, hardened and tempered in form.

All Waltham watches, except 1883 Model, in 7 Jewel, are fitted with Meantime Screws.

All Waltham watches, double roller, Riverside grade and above, have Sapphire Roller Pins permanently driven into the roller.

All Waltham watches, except 1883 Model, have Steel Tempered Safety Barrels.

All Waltham watches in Vanguard and Maximus grades have Diamond Endstones.

All Waltham watches have Plate Jewels in Settings.

All Waltham watches, with steel escape wheels, have Sapphire Pallet Stones.

---

18 SIZE

1917 OSKAMP—NOLTING
The Great American Jewelry Co.

With up and down Indicator $300.00

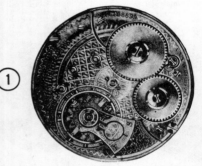

VANGUARD. Nickel

Adjusted to temperature, isochronism and five positions; double roller; steel escape wheel; diamond, fine ruby and sapphire jewels.

$160.00	23 Jewels, Hunting, Lever Setting ..	$60.00
160.00	23 Jewels, Open Face, Lever Setting	60.00
80.00	21 Jewels, Hunting, Lever Setting ..	56.60
80.00	21 Jewels, Open Face, Lever Setting	56.60
80.00	19 Jewels, Hunting, Lever Setting ..	52.00
80.00	19 Jewels, Open Face, Lever Setting .	52.00
180.00	23 Jewels, Non-magnetic, Hunting, Lever Setting	67.80
180.00	23 Jewels, Non-magnetic. Open Face, Pendant Setting	67.80

$150.00

17 Jewels

Premier

No. 845. Nickel

Adjusted to temperature, isochronism and five positions; double roller; steel escape wheel; fine ruby and sapphire jewels.

21 Jewels, Hunting, Lever Setting ..	$40.00	$70.00
21 Jewels, Open Face, Lever Setting.	40.00	70.00

CRESCENT STREET. Nickel

Adjusted to temperature, isochronism and five positions; double roller; steel escape wheel; fine ruby and sapphire jewels.

21 Jewels, Hunting, Lever Setting..	$46.60	$70.00
21 Jewels, Open Face, Lever Setting	46.60	70.00
19 Jewels, Hunting, Lever Setting ..	45.00	70.00
19 Jewels, Open Face, Lever Setting	45.00	70.00

$70.00

early Ser. No.'s

APPLETON, TRACY & CO.
Nickel

Adjusted to temperature and three positions; double roller; steel escape wheel.

17 Jewels, Hunting, Lever Setting..	$30.00
17 Jewels, Open Face, Lever Setting.	30.00

P. S. BARTLETT
Gilded and Nickeled Damaskeened

Adjusted to temperature.

17 Jewels, Open Face, Pendant Setting	$21.00	$45.00
17 Jewels, Hunting, Pendant Setting	21.00	45.00

Non-magnetic movements, extra, $7.80
Above movements supplied either Lever or Pendant Setting.
All orders accepted subject to prices ruling on date of delivery.

1916

OSKAMP—NOLTING CO.
1917

18 SIZE

$30.00
30.00
25.00
25.00

P. S. BARTLETT or No. 87. Nickel
Adjusted to temperature.
P. S. B. 17 Jewels, Hunting, Lever Setting $17.00
P. S. B. 17 Jewels, Open Face, Pendant or Lever Setting 17.00
No. 87. 17 Jewels, Hunting, Lever Setting 17.00
No. 87. 17 Jewels, Open Face, Pendant or Lever Setting 17.00

No. 85. Gilded $20.00
Adjusted to temperature.
17 Jewels, Open Face, Pendant or Lever Setting $15.00

$20.00

No. 825. Nickel
17 Jewels, Hunting, Lever Setting .. $13.00
17 Jewels, Open Face, Pendant Setting 13.00

$20.00
20.00
25.00
25.00

No. 820. Nickel
15 Jewels, Hunting, Lever Setting .. $11.00
15 Jewels, Open Face, Pendant Setting 11.00
15 Jewels, Non-magnetic, Hunting, Lever Setting 18.80
15 Jewels, Non-magnetic, Open Face, Pendant Setting 18.80

No. 81. Gilded $15.00
15 Jewels, Hunting, Lever Setting . $10.00
15 Jewels, Open Face, Pendant Setting 10.00

$15.00

No. 18. Nickel
7 Jewels, Hunting, Lever Setting ... $8.00
7 Jewels, Open Face, Pendant Setting 8.00

Model 1908

Model 1899

$300.00

MAXIMUS. Nickel
Adjusted to temperature, isochronism and five positions; double roller; steel escape wheel; gold train; diamond, fine ruby and sapphire jewels.
23 Jewels, Hunting, Pendant Setting $136.70
23 Jewels, Open Face, Pendant Setting 136.70
23 Jewels, Open Face, Lever Setting 136.70
23 Jewels, Non-magnetic, Hunting, Pendant Setting 144.50
23 Jewels, Non-magnetic, Open Face, Pendant Setting 144.50

16 SIZE

$220.00
Movement only
R R Grade

VANGUARD
With Winding Indicator
23 Jewels, Open Face, Pendant or Lever Setting $67.80

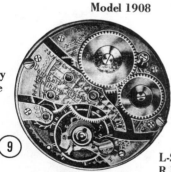

L-Set
R R Grade

VANGUARD. Nickel
Adjusted to temperature, isochronism and five positions; double roller; steel escape wheel; diamond, fine ruby and sapphire jewels.
23 Jewels, Hunting, Pendant Setting $60.00 $90.00
23 Jewels, Hunting, Lever Setting.. 60.00   110.00
23 Jewels, Open Face, Pendant Setting 60.00   90.00
23 Jewels, Open Face, Lever Setting 60.00   110.00
19 Jewels, Hunting, Lever Setting.. 52.00   110.00
19 Jewels, Open Face, Lever Setting 52.00   90.00
19 Jewels, Hunting, Pendant Setting 52.00   90.00
19 Jewels, Open Face, Pendant Setting 52.00   80.00

Non-magnetic movements, extra, $7.80
All orders accepted subject to prices ruling on date of delivery.

1916

Waltham Watches

Model 99   17 J Riv.
$40.00

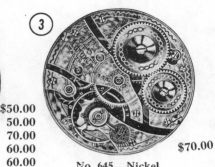

$50.00
70.00
50.00
50.00

$50.00
50.00
70.00
60.00
60.00

$70.00

CRESCENT ST. Nickel

Adjusted to temperature, isochronism and five positions; double roller; steel escape wheel; fine ruby and sapphire jewels.

21 Jewels, Hunting, Pendant Setting	$46.60
21 Jewels, Hunting, Lever Setting	46.60
21 Jewels, Open Face, Pendant Setting	46.60
21 Jewels, Open Face, Lever Setting	46.60

RIVERSIDE. Nickel

Adjusted to temperature, isochronism and five positions; double roller; steel escape wheel; fine ruby and sapphire jewels.

19 Jewels, Hunting, Pendant Setting	$47.80
19 Jewels, Open Face, Pendant Setting	47.80
19 Jewels, Open Face, Lever Setting	47.80
19 Jewels, Non-magnetic, Hunting, Pendant Setting	55.60
19 Jewels, Non-magnetic, Open Face, Pendant Setting	55.60

No. 645. Nickel

Adjusted to temperature, isochronism and five positions; double roller; steel escape wheel; fine ruby and sapphire jewels.

21 Jewels, Open Face, Pendant or Lever Setting	$44.50

$30.00

$30.00

$30.00

No. 630
$30.00

ROYAL. Nickel

Adjusted to temperature and three positions.

17 Jewels, Hunting, Pendant Setting	$29.00
17 Jewels, Open Face, Pendant Setting	29.00

P. S. BARTLETT. Nickel

Adjusted to temperature; steel escape wheel; sapphire pallets.

17 Jewels, Hunting, Pendant Setting	$25.00
17 Jewels, Open Face, Pendant Setting	25.00
17 Jewels, Open Face, Lever Setting	25.00

No. 635. Nickel

Adjusted to temperature; steel escape wheel; sapphire pallets.

17 Jewels, Hunting, Pendant Setting	$22.30
17 Jewels, Open Face, Pendant Setting	22.30
17 Jewels, Open Face, Lever Setting	22.30

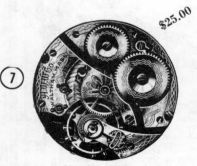

$25.00

$25.00

$20.00

No. 625. Nickel

17 Jewels, Hunting, Pendant Setting	$19.70
17 Jewels, Open Face, Pendant Setting	19.70

No. 620. Nickel

15 Jewels, Hunting, Pendant Setting	$15.50
15 Jewels, Open Face, Pendant Setting	15.50

No. 610. Nickel

7 Jewels, Hunting, Pendant Setting	$9.80
7 Jewels, Open Face, Pendant Setting	9.80

1916

Non-magnetic movements, extra, $7.80
All orders accepted subject to prices ruling on date of delivery.

OSKAMP—NOLTING CO.
1917

See Page 4

12 SIZE

$40.00

① MAXIMUS $225.00
Nickel

Adjusted to temperature, iso-chronism and five positions; double roller; steel escape wheel; gold train; diamond and fine ruby jewels.
23 Jewels, Hunting, Pendant Setting . $136.70
23 Jewels, Open Face, Pendant Setting . 136.70

② RIVERSIDE
Nickel
$30.00

Adjusted to temperature and five positions; double roller; steel escape wheel; fine ruby jewels.
19 Jewels, Hunting, Pendant Setting .. $47.80
19 Jewels, Open Face, Pendant Setting .. 47.80

ROYAL ③
Nickel

Adjusted to temperature and three positions; steel escape wheel; sapphire pallets.
17 Jewels, Hunting, Pendant Setting .. $29.00
17 Jewels, Open Face, Pendant Setting .. 29.00

④ No. 235 $25.00
Nickel

Adjusted to temperature; steel escape wheel; sapphire pallets.
17 Jewels, Hunting, Pendant Setting .. $22.30
17 Jewels, Open Face, Pendant Setting .. 22.30

$25.00

⑤ No. 225
Nickel

17 Jewels, Hunting, Pendant Setting $19.70
17 Jewels, Open Face, Pendant Setting . 19.70

⑥ No. 220 Nickel
15 Jewels, Hunting, Pendant Setting $15.50
15 Jewels, Open Face, Pendant Setting . 15.50

$20.00

⑦ No. 210 $15.00
Nickel

7 Jewels, Hunting, Pendant Setting $10.90
7 Jewels, Open Face, Pendant, Setting . 10.90

6 SIZE

$20.00

⑧ LADY WALTHAM. Nickel
$40.00

Adjusted; ruby jewels.
16 Jewels, Hunting, Pendant Setting $17.00
16 Jewels, Open Face, Pendant Setting . 17.00

⑨ V. Nickel
15 Jewels, Hunting, Pendant Setting $12.30
15 Jewels, Open Face, Pendant Setting . 12.30

⑩ Y. Nickel $20.00

7 Jewels, Hunting, Pendant Setting. $8.70
7 Jewels, Open Face, Pendant Setting . 8.70

J. Gilt
7 Jewels, Hunting, Pendant Setting. $8.50
7 Jewels, Open Face, Pendant Setting . 8.50

0 SIZE

⑪ MAXIMUS. Nickel
$120.00

Adjusted; double roller; steel escape wheel; gold train; diamond and fine ruby jewels.
19 Jewels, Hunting, Pendant Setting $64.50
19 Jewels, Open Face, Pendant Setting . 64.50

⑫ RIVERSIDE. Nickel
$50.00

Adjusted; double roller; ruby jewels; steel escape wheel; sapphire pallets.
17 Jewels, Hunting, Pendant Setting $44.50
17 Jewels, Open Face, Pendant Setting . 44.50

⑬ LADY WALTHAM. Nickel
$40.00

Adjusted; double roller; ruby jewels; steel escape wheel; sapphire pallets.
16 Jewels, Hunting, Pendant Setting $26.00
16 Jewels, Open Face, Pendant Setting . 26.00

1916 All orders accepted subject to prices ruling on date of delivery.

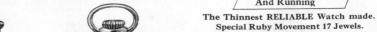

Thin Watches for Men

14S Dial
12S Mvt.

COLONIAL SERIES

RIVERSIDE MAXIMUS, 23 Jewels, adjusted to temperature, isochronism and five positions.
RIVERSIDE, 19 Jewels, adjusted to temperature, isochronism and five positions.
ROYAL, 17 Jewels, adjusted to temperature, isochronism and three positions.
No. 1425, 17 Jewels.   No. 1420, 15 Jewels.

PRICE LIST—COMPLETE WATCHES

18K. SOLID GOLD HUNTING CASE

$300.00   No. 101 Riverside Maximus $238.00
175.00   103 Riverside 144.50
150.00   105 Royal 131.00

14K. SOLID GOLD HUNTING CASE

No. 107 Riverside Maximus $205.60
109 Riverside 122.30
111 Royal 100.00
113 No. 1425...............89.00

$275.00
150.00
130.00
110.00

GOLD FILLED HUNTING CASE

No. 209 Maximus $151.10 $180.00
211 Riverside 72.30   80.00
213 Royal 55.60   70.00
215 No. 1425.............45.60   60.00

GOLD FILLED OPEN FACE WITH CAP

No. 219 Maximus $152.30
221 Riverside 71.10
223 Royal 54.50
225 No. 1425.............44.50
227 No. 1420.............37.80

18K. SOLID GOLD OPEN FACE JOINTED CASE—WITH CAP

No. 102 Riverside Maximus $210.00
104 Riverside 124.50
106 Royal 111.10

14K. SOLID GOLD OPEN FACE JOINTED CASE—WITH CAP

No. 108 Riverside Maximus $186.70
110 Riverside 106.70 $110.00
112 Royal 89.00   100.00
114 No. 1425...............76.70   100.00
116 No. 1420...............68.00

14K. SOLID GOLD OPEN FACE CALUMET CASE

No. 117 Maximus..........$179.00
118 Riverside 93.50
120 Royal 75.50
122 No. 1425..........60.00
124 No. 1420..........53.50

GOLD FILLED OPEN FACE CALUMET

No. 228 Maximus..........$152.30
229 Riverside 71.10
231 Royal 54.50
233 No. 1425..........44.50
235 No. 1420..........37.80

All Gold Filled Colonial Series cases are Guaranteed for Twenty-five years. The above cases are Bassine Plain Polished or Engine Turned. Engraved Hunting cases, $2.00 extra. Engraved Open Face cases, $1.60 extra. Colonial Series Enamel, Gilded or Silvered Dials, no extra charge. Colonial Series Watches are Cased and Timed at the Factory and are sent out in either Mahogany or Leather Display Boxes.

"COLONIAL A" WATCHES

18K. OPEN FACE JOINTED CASE

No. 254 Maximus 21 Jewels, 5 positions $266.70 $275.00
256 Riverside, 19 Jewels, 5 positions 156.00   165.00

14K. OPEN FACE JOINTED CASE

No. 262 Maximus, 21 Jewels, 5 positions $244.50 $265.00
264 Riverside, 19 Jewels, 5 positions 138.90   165.00

Supplied with Gilded or Silvered Metal Dials only.
"Colonial A" Watches can be supplied in special hand-made cases. Prices on application.
Delivered from factory in attractive display boxes.

THE OPERA WATCH

Complete Watches Must be Extra Fine And Running

The Thinnest RELIABLE Watch made.
Special Ruby Movement 17 Jewels.
Adjusted to Temperature and 2 Positions.

18K. OPEN FACE CASE $150.00
No. 708 Regular, Plain Polished ...$120.00

14K. OPEN FACE CASE $140.00
No. 730 Regular, Plain Polished ... $96.00
735 Decorated (Prices on application)

25-YEAR O. F. FILLED CASE $75.00
No. 740 Regular, Plain Polished ... $62.50
745 Regular, Engraved 65.00

Supplied with Gilded or Silvered Metal Dials only.
Delivered from the factory in attractive display boxes.

1916

OSKAMP—NOLTING CO.
1917
O SIZE — *(Continued)*
See Page 4

$25.00

$20.00

No. 165, HUNTING and No. 115, OPEN FACE—Nickel
Double roller;
15 Jewels, Hunting, Pendant
  Setting $18.00
15 Jewels, Open Face, Pendant
  Setting 18.00

No. 161, HUNTING and No. 110, OPEN FACE—Nickel
7 Jewels, Hunting, Pendant
  Setting $12.00
7 Jewels, Open Face, Pendant
  Setting.................... 12.00

No. 165, HUNTING
No. 115, OPEN FACE

No. 161, HUNTING
No. 110, OPEN FACE

3/O SIZE
$100.00 $40.00 $40.00 $25.00 $20.00

MAXIMUS — Nickel
Adjusted; double roller; steel escape wheel;
sapphire pallets; gold train; diamond and
fine ruby jewels.
19 Jewels, Hunting or Open Face
  Pendant Setting $64.50

LADY WALTHAM — Nickel
Adjusted; double roller; steel escape
wheel; sapphire pallets; ruby jewels.
16 Jewels, Hunting or Open Face,
  Pendant Setting $26.00

No. 365, HUNTING and No. 315 OPEN FACE — Nickel
Double roller;
15 Jewels, Pendant Setting $18.40

RIVERSIDE — Nickel
Adjusted; double roller; steel escape
wheel; sapphire pallets; ruby jewels.
17 Jewels, Hunting or Open Face,
  Pendant Setting $44.50

No. 361, HUNTING and No. 310 OPEN FACE—Nickel
Double roller;
7 Jewels, Pendant Setting $12.30

JEWEL SERIES
$120.00 $120.00
$60.00   60.00

Priced as if cased
in solid 14K
plain polished case

$140.00
$ 80.00

RIVERSIDE   RUBY

$120.00
$ 60.00

DIAMOND — Nickel
Adjusted; steel escape wheel; sapphire pallets; gold train; diamond and ruby jewels.
17 Jewels, Hunting, Pendant Setting $66.70
17 Jewels, Open Face, Pendant Setting 66.70

RIVERSIDE — Nickel
Adjusted; steel escape wheel; sapphire
pallets; fine ruby jewels.
17 Jewels, Hunting, Pendant Setting $46.70
17 Jewels, Open Face, Pendant Setting 46.70

RUBY — Nickel
17 Jewels, Hunting, Pendant Setting $30.00
17 Jewels, Open Face, Pendant Setting 30.00

SAPPHIRE — Nickel
15 Jewels, Hunting, Pendant Setting $27.00
15 Jewels, Open Face, Pendant Setting 27.00

Prices given are for movements only.
Prices for complete Jewel Series watches
given on application.

Equity—16 Size
JOINTED OPEN FACE
The Equity is the most thoroughly con-
structed and finely finished low-priced
watch ever put on the market.
No. 1013 15 Jewels, in Silver, Plain
  Bassine $17.80
  999 7 Jewels, in Silver, Plain
  Bassine 13.40

$50.00
$45.00

S. B. & B. OPEN FACE
1008 15 Jewels, in Gold Filled,
  Plain Bassine 17.80
$40.00 1014 15 Jewels, in Nickel, Plain
25.00   Bassine 11.70
40.00 1002 7 Jewels, in Gold Filled,
20.00   Plain Bassine 13.40
      1000 7 Jewels, in Nickel, Plain
        Bassine 7.40
Equity Filled Cases are 20-Year Quality.

GUN METAL OPEN FACE
Jointed Back, Snap Bezel.
With American-made Gold Bows, Crowns
and Joints.
$25.00 1024 15 Jewel movement, Gun
          Metal Case $14.50
20.00 1020 7 Jewel movement, Gun
          Metal Case 8.40

16 Size

Equity—12 Size
S. B. & B. OPEN FACE
No. 1030 7 Jewels, in Nickel, Plain
$20.00   Bassine $8.50
        1040 7 Jewels, in Gun Metal,
20.00   Plain Bassine 10.00

1916

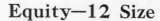
ACTUAL SIZE

Marsh Patent Watches
12 Size

14K. Open Face Plain Polished or Engine
Turned Cases, Nickeled and Gilded Pro-
tector.
No. 1250 Riverside 19 Jewels, 5 Positions $70.00 $100.00
  1225 225 Movement, 17 Jewels.. 41.10 85.00
  1210 210 Movement, 7 Jewels.. 32.30 75.00
20-Year Gold-Filled Open Face Plain
Polished Case.
No. 1206 225 Movement, 17 Jewels.. $26.00 40.00
  1200 210 Movement, 7 Jewels.. 17.80 30.00
No. 1250 is supplied with Gilded or Silvered
Metal Dials at no extra charge.

All orders accepted subject to prices ruling on date of delivery.

PRESENTATION WATCHES

WHAT Presentation Piece could be more fitting than one of the distinguished Waltham Watches illustrated on this page? Its beauty will be appreciated daily . . . its dependable time-keeping service a source of lifetime satisfaction.

PREMIER MAXIMUS. This is Waltham's finest Watch; a superb movement magnificently cased. The Premier Maximus is recognized as the crowning triumph of the watchmaker's art; an unsurpassed Presentation Piece whose bestowal recognizes supreme achievement.

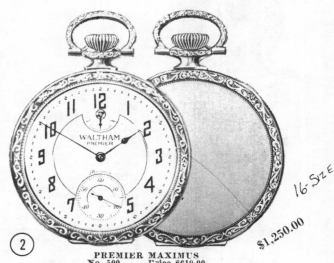

16-Size

$1,250.00

PREMIER MAXIMUS
No. 500   Price $610.00
Movement: 23 Jewels, fine Diamonds, Rubies, and Sapphires. Winding Indicator. Adjusted to Isochronism, changes in Temperature and 6 Positions.
Case: Heavy hand-made of 18K solid Gold; White, Green, or Yellow Plain or Hand-Carved.
Dial: Enamel Hand-Painted or Fine Silver with Applied Numerals of 18K Gold.
Delivered from the Factory in a Special Leather Presentation Box with two extra Mainsprings and Crystal.

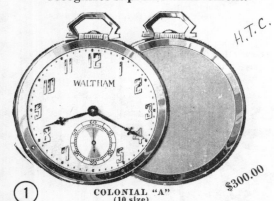

H.T.C.

$300.00

① COLONIAL "A"
(10 size)
No. 250   Price $297.00
Movement: Maximus, 23 Jewels. Adjusted to Temperature and 5 positions.
Dial: Fine Sterling Silver, 18K applied Gold Figures.
Case: 14K White Gold, Knife Edge, Plain Back and Bezel.

EXTRA THIN
Waltham's thinnest Pocket Watches are offered in the Colonial "A" No. 250 and No. 200. These distinguished Timepieces combine modern thin-model designs with the dependability which has characterized Waltham for three-quarters of a century.

Movement Only $100.00

③

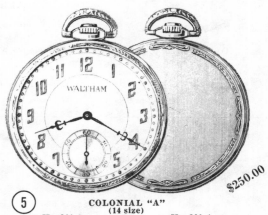

H.T.C.

$250.00

⑤ COLONIAL "A"
(14 size)
No. 200-3   No. 200-4
Green Gold   White Gold
Price $237.60
Movement: Riverside, 21 Jewels, Adjusted to Temperature and 5 positions.
Dial: Fine Sterling Silver 18K Applied Gold Figures.
Case: 14K Green or White, exquisitely hand carved or severely plain.

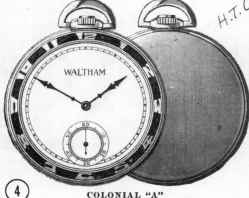

$250.00

④ COLONIAL "A"
(14 size)
No. 200   Price $237.60
Movement: Riverside, 21 Jewels, Adjusted to Temperature and 5 positions.
Dial: Silver Matt Finish.
Case: 14K White Gold only. Enamel Bezel.

WALTHAM

① $100.00

No. 150-3   Price $160.40   No. 150-4
Green Gold   White Gold
Riverside 21 Jewels, Temperature Adjusted and 5 Positions. 14K Green or White Gold Case, Burnished Bezel, Butler Back, Enamel Track Dial with Seconds Indicator.
Dial No. 1410

Add $10.00 for Seconds indicator

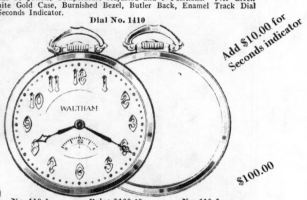

③ $100.00

No. 150-5   Price $160.40   No. 150-6
Green Gold   White Gold
Riverside 21 Jewels, Temperature Adjusted and 5 Positions. 14K Green or White Gold Case, Burnished Bezel, Butler Back. Sterling Silver Seconds Indicator Dial with 18K Gold Applied Figures.
Dial No. 150

⑤ $90.00

No. 100-7   Price $107.00   No. 100-8
Green Gold   White Gold
Royal 19 Jewels, Temperature Adjusted and 3 Positions. 14K Green or White Gold Case, Border Engraved, Butler Back. Sterling Silver Dial with 18K Gold Applied Figures.
Dial No. 460

⑥ $85.00

No. 100-9   Price $107.00   No. 100-10
Green Gold   White Gold
Royal 19 Jewels, Temperature Adjusted and 3 Positions. 14K Green or White Gold Octagon Case, Engraved Bezel, Butler Back. Sterling Silver Dial with 18K Applied Gold Figures.

Waltham Colonial Watches are Cased and Timed at the Factory. Each is supplied in a handsome Presentation Box.

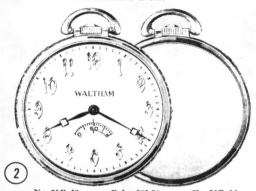

②

No. 75R-13   Price $85.90   No. 75R-14
Green Gold   White Gold
Royal 19 Jewels, Temperature Adjusted and 3 Positions. 14K Green or White Gold Case, Engraved Center, Burnished Bezel, Etched Dial.
Dial No. 1409—Seconds Indicator

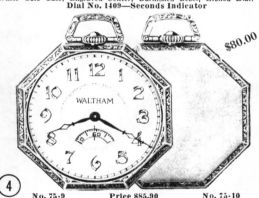

④ $80.00

No. 75-9   Price $85.90   No. 75-10
Green Gold   White Gold
17 Jewels, Temperature Adjusted. 14K Green or White Octagon Case, Engraved Bezel, Butler Back, Etched Dial.
Dial No. 727—Seconds Indicator

⑦ $70.00

No. 60R-15   Price $64.10   No. 60R-16
Green Gold   White Gold
Royal 19 Jewels, Temperature Adjusted and 3 Positions. 14K Filled Green or White Gold Cushion Case, Engraved Bezel, Butler or Straight Line Back, Etched Dial.
Dial No. 1411

WALTHAM

1937

① $ 30.00
100.00
45.00
50.00
45.00

16 Size. 10k Yellow Gold Filled Railroad Model.
Screw Back and Bezel. Dust-Proof Case.
Open Face.
No. 17272—Case Only $18.90
Fitted With:
No. 17273—21 Jewel Waltham. $53.00
No. 17274— 9 Jewel Waltham. 37.50
No. 17275—15 Jewel Elgin. 41.50
No. 17276— 7 Jewel Elgin. 38.00

② $ 30.00
100.00
45.00
50.00
45.00

16 Size. 10k Yellow Gold Filled Railroad Model.
Screw Back and Bezel. Dust-Proof Case.
Open Face.
No. 17277—Case Only $16.80
Fitted With:
No. 17278—21 Jewel Waltham. $51.00
No. 17279— 9 Jewel Waltham. 35.40
No. 17280—15 Jewel Elgin. 39.40
No. 17281— 7 Jewel Elgin. 35.70

③ $ 30.00
100.00
45.00
50.00
45.00

16 Size. 10k Yellow Gold Filled Screw Back and
Bezel, Engraved Case. Open Face.
No. 17282—Case Only $16.00
Fitted With:
No. 17283—21 Jewel Waltham. $50.00
No. 17284— 9 Jewel Waltham. 34.50
No. 17285—15 Jewel Elgin. 38.70
No. 17286— 7 Jewel Elgin. 35.00

Case $15.00
21 J 85.00
9 J 30.00
15 J 35.00
7 J 30.00

④

16 Size. 10k Yellow Rolled Gold Plate, Screw
Case. Concealed Dust-Proof Cap. Open Face.
No. 17287—Case Only $8.00
Fitted With:
No. 17288—21 Jewel Waltham. $41.00
No. 17289— 9 Jewel Waltham. 25.50
No. 17290—15 Jewel Elgin. 29.60
No. 17291— 7 Jewel Elgin. 26.00

$15.00
85.00
30.00
35.00
30.00

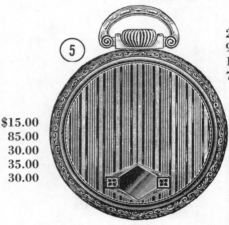

⑤

16 Size. 10k Yellow Rolled Gold Plate, Screw
Case. Concealed Dust-Proof Cap. Open Face.
No. 17292—Case Only $8.00
Fitted With:
No. 17293—21 Jewel Waltham. $41.00
No. 17294— 9 Jewel Waltham. 25.50
No. 17295—15 Jewel Elgin. 29.60
No. 17296— 7 Jewel Elgin. 26.00

21 J Waltham = 21 J Cresent
9 J Waltham = 9 J Waltham
15 J Elgin = 313 Model
7 J Elgin = 291 Model

CASE AND MOVEMENT MUST BE EXTRA FINE OR BETTER

⑥ $15.00
85.00
30.00
35.00
30.00

16 Size. 10k Yellow Rolled Gold Plate, Screw
Case. Butler Finish, Concealed Dust-Proof Case.
Open Face.
No. 17297—Case Only $7.00
Fitted With:
No. 17298—21 Jewel Waltham. $40.50
No. 17299— 9 Jewel Waltham. 24.80
No. 17300—15 Jewel Elgin. 28.80
No. 17301— 7 Jewel Elgin. 25.20

⑦ $ 5.00
75.00
25.00
30.00
25.00

16 Size. Base Metal, Plain Screw Case.
Open Face.
No. 17302—Case Only $2.30
Complete With:
No. 17303—21 Jewel Waltham. $35.40
No. 17304— 7 Jewel Waltham. 19.80
No. 17305—15 Jewel Elgin. 24.00
No. 17306— 7 Jewel Elgin. 20.00

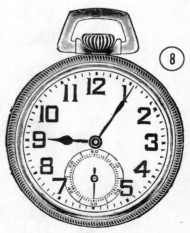

⑧ $ 7.50
77.50
25.00
30.00
25.00

16 Size. Base Metal, Plain Railroad Model Case.
Open Face.
No. 17307—Case Only $2.90
Complete With:
No. 17308—21 Jewel Waltham. $36.00
No. 17309— 7 Jewel Waltham. 20.30
No. 17310—15 Jewel Elgin. 24.40
No. 17311— 7 Jewel Elgin. 20.70

Waltham

1937

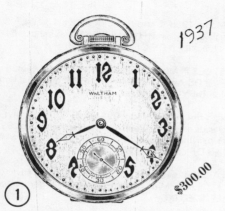

EACH WATCH
DELIVERED
IN
PRESENTATION
CASE

$110.00

$65.00

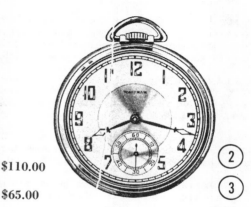

WATCHES MUST BE EXTRA FINE AND RUNNING

$300.00

WALTHAM COLONIAL "A"
No. 17210 . . . . $198.00
10 Size, 23 Jewel Waltham Maximus Movement, Adjusted to Temperature and 5 Positions. 14k Solid Yellow Gold Case, Snap Bezel, Hinged Back, Butler Finish. 18k Applied Gold Numerals, Sterling Silver Dial.

WALTHAM
No. 1721.1—14k Solid Yellow Gold. $88.00
No. 172.12—14k Yellow Gold Filled. 56.50
12 Size, 21 Jewel Waltham Colonial Movement, Adjusted to Temperature and 5 Positions. Silver Dial, Etched Gold Numerals. 14k Solid Yellow Gold or 14k Yellow Gold Filled Case. Snap Bezel, Hinged Back, Butler Finish.

① ② ③

④ ⑤

$80.00
$50.00

WALTHAM
No. 17213—14k Solid Yellow Gold. $78.00
No. 17214—14k Yellow Gold Filled. 46.50
12 Size, 17 Jewel Waltham Colonial Movement, Adjusted to Temperature. Silver Dial, Etched Gold Numerals. 14k Solid Yellow Gold or 14k Yellow Gold Filled Case. Snap Bezel, Hinged Back, Butler Finish.

$80.00
$45.00
$40.00

WALTHAM
No. 17215—17 Jewel, 14k Solid Yellow Gold $78.00
No. 17216—17 Jewel, 14k Yellow Gold Filled 46.50
No. 17217—17 Jewel, 10k Yellow Gold Plate 37.50
12 Size, 17 Jewel Waltham Colonial Movement. Silver Dial, Etched Gold Markers. 14k Solid Yellow Gold, 14k Yellow Gold Filled or 10k Yellow Rolled Gold Plate Cases. Butler Finish.

⑥ ⑦ ⑧

$40.00

⑨

WALTHAM
No. 17218 . . . . $37.50
12 Size, 17 Jewel Waltham Colonial Movement, Adjusted to Temperature. Silver Dial, Etched Gold Numerals, 10k Yellow Rolled Gold Plate Case. Snap Back and Bezel, Butler Finish.

34500122

WALTHAM WATCH COMPANY
Waltham, Mass.   **1850 to Mid 1900's**

SERIAL NO.	DATE	SERIAL NO.	DATE	SERIAL NO.	DATE
1,000	1857	900,000	1876	15,000,000	1907
14,000	1858	1,000,000	1877	17,000,000	1908
17,000	1859	1,160,000	1878	18,000,000	1910
20,000	1860	1,351,000	1879	19,000,000	1913
23,000	1861	1,499,000	1880	20,000,000	1914
34.000	1862	1,675,000	1881	21,000,000	1917
46,000	1863	1.837,000	1882	22,000,000	1918
118,000	1864	2,000,000	1883	23,000,000	1919
190,000	1865	2,356,000	1884	24,000,000	1921
262,000	1866	2,650,000	1885	26,000,000	1927
335.000	1867	3.300,000	1887	27,000,000	1929
410,000	1868	4,000,000	1889	28,000,000	1934
470,000	1869	6,000,000	1892	29,000,000	1936
500,000	1870	7,000,000	1895	30,000,000	1939
550,000	1871	9,000,000	1899	31,000,000	1942
600,000	1872	10,000,000	1901	32,000,000	1945
691,000	1873	12,000,000	1903	33,600,000	1951
720,000	1874	13,000,000	1904	33,830,000	1953
800,000	1875	14,000,000	1905	35,000,000	1957

18-S, 15-J Moedl 57, OF Keywind & Keyset, Foggs patent P. S. Bartlett, mvt. 439,443. Large jewels in gilt plate runs good. Mint flat, hand lettered Roman dial, except second bit repaired. Fine Duber 303 silverline double back OF keywind case. A nice solid old watch. $85.00

18-S OF 7-J A.W.C. Co. BROADWAY Model 57. Extra fine gilted mvt. 814,240. KEYWIND smooth bal. Extra fine plain flat glass dial and hands. Extra fine GWL OF KEYWIND YGF engraved case "G.W. Ladd" Pat. June 11, 1867. $135.00.

18-S OF 23-J VANGUARD Model 92 Mint nickel mvt. 12,011,066. LS adj. gold cups and bal. screws with diamond caps jewel. Mint DS Antique glass dial with hands. Mint Fahy's YGF OF case. $175.00

18-S OF 21-J VANGUARD Model 92 Extra fine nickel mvt. 12,081,152 LS adj. Extra fine DS glass dial. Extra fine Keystone, Victory 10 K RGP case. $110.00

18-S OF 21-J No. 854. Model 92 Mint nickel mvt. 15,039,459 LS Adj. 5 pos. gold cups and bal. weights. Mint DS Antique Arabic glass dial. Extra fine Crescent Planet 20 yr. YGF OF case. $95.00

18-S OF 17-J APPLETON TRACY Model 83 Mint gilt mvt. 6,002,772 LS Adj. gold cups and balance weights. Extra fine DS. AWW Co. glass Roman numberal dial with gold hands. Extra fine ALD English made 14 K YGF 25 yr. OF case $100.00

18-S OF 17-J CRESCENT STREET Model 83. Extra fine highly Damasceened nickel mft. 5,726,982. LS adj. Fine DS Antique Arabic glass dial. Extra fine Philadelphia Silveroid OF case with steam engine engraved on back. $75.00

18-S OF 15-J SPECIAL RR KINK Model 83. Fine nickel mvt.4,589,672 LS Adj. DS glass RR dial marked for RR SERVICE slight discoloration on dial. Extra fine Star W C Co. 925/1000 fine. Sterling silver OF case. $85.00

18-S 17-J PS BARTLETT Adj. Fancy silver plates mvt. 9,511,981. Cased in Waltham extra heavy 18 K solid gold hunting case. Glass enclosed movement. Fancy engraving - near mint. $300.00

18-S OF 17-J Model 83. Mint nickel mvt. 10,093,376. LS Adj. gold cups and balance weights. "CANADIAN PACIFIC RAILWAY" insignia on mvt. Unusual DS glass dial with Roman numerals 1 thry 12, 13 thru 24. under each Roman numeral. Repaired spot at 7 and 8. Extra fine Philadelphia YGF 20 yr. OF case. $110.00

16-S OF 23-J VANGUARD UP AND DOWN INDICATOR Model 1908 Extra fine nickel mvt. 20,030,308. LS adj. 5 pos. gold cups and balance weights, DIAMOND cap jewel. Mint DS glass indicator dial. Fine Keystone J. Boss YGF swingout case. Warrented 25 yrs. $185.00

16-S OF 23-J RIVERSIDE MAXIMUS Model 99. Mint nickel mvt. 16,071,449. LS Adj. 6 pos. Has "Lossier inter-terminal hair spring". Gold cups and balance weights. DIAMOND caps. Mint DS RR glass dial with hands. Extra fine Keystone J. Boss 10 K YGF swing out case. $300.00

16-S OF 23-J VANGUARD Model 99 Extra fine nickel mvt.11,064,715. SL Adj. gold cups and balance weights. DIAMOND Cap on balance. Mint DS glass RR dial and original hands. Extra fine Keystone guaranteed 585 fine YG 14 K swing out RR case. $250.00

16-S OF 21-J CRESCENT STREET Model 1908 Mint nickel mvt. 25,178,633. LS Adj 5 pos. gold cups and balance weights. Mint DS glass Montgomery dial with hands. Mint Keystone J. Boss 14 K WGF OF case. $95.00

16-S OF 21-J RIVERSIDE. Extra fine nickel mvt. 27,659,898. LS Adj. temp. Fine single sunk MONTGOMERY enamel dial. Fine Keystone Victory 10 K RGP Y OF case. $85.00

16-S OF 19-J RIVERSIDE Fine nickel mvt. 22,201,569. LS Adj. 5 pos gold cups and balance wieghts. Fine DS glass dial with one small hairline. Extremely fine Gruen National Watch Case Co. 14 K double back OF case. $200.00

16-S OF 17-J RIVERSIDE Model 88 Extra fine nickel mvt. 6,506,580. Pendent set Mint single sunk plain Roman Numeral glass dial. Extra fine ALD English made 14 K YGF 25 yr. OF case. $125.00

16-S OF 21-J No. 645 Model 1908 Extra fine nickel mvt. 17,174,799. LS Adj. 5 pos. Mint single sunk glass RR dial with original hands. Extra fine Crescent 25 yr. Double back YGF OF case. $95.00

16-S OF 17-J P. S. BARTLETT Model 99 Extremely fine nickel mvt. 17,073,522. LS Adj. Fine DS Antique MONTGOMERY glass dial with small chip at 5. Fine Monitor YGF. OF case. $60.00

16-S 15-J AWW Co. Extra fine nickel Model 99. Grade 620. HC mvt. 15,681,035. Running, needs cleaning. Pendant set. Extra fine flat SS Roman, red track dial, 1 hairline. Discolored filligree hands. Fine white base metal screw and B&B OF case. $25.00

14-S OF 21-J Maximus A. Mint mvt. 22,123,144. Mint sterling silver with 18 K applied gold Arabic figures. Mint white 14 K Waltham double back partially decorated case. $250.00

14-S OF 7-J Model 84 Pin Set BOND STREET. Fine gilded mvt. 2,926,87 mint flat Roman dial and hands. Jine original screw B&B silverode OF case. C & O and running. $50.00

14-S OF 19-J RIVERSIDE A. Model COL. A. Extremely fine nickel mvt. 20,189,963. Pendant set Adj. 5 pos. Extra fine Waltham gold tint metal dial. Extremely fine WALTHAM COLONIAL A 14 K 585/1000 Fine double back OF case. $160.00

12-S HC 21-J AWW Co. RIVERSIDE MAXIMUS Mint nickel mvt. 71,557,742. Pendant set. Gold cups and balance weights, diamond cap jewels. Mint single sunk Arabic glass dial with hands. Mint WADSWORTH 14 K highly engraved HC. $300.00

12-14-S OF 17-J ROYAL COL. SERIES Extra fine nickel mvt. 14,124,977. Pendant set, adj. Gold cups and balance weights. Extra fine gold metal, fancy dial. Mint Roy 14 K Y double back OF case. $125.00

12-S OF 19-J P S BARTLETT Extra fine nickel mvt. 24,845,244. Pendant set adj. Fine 2-tone metal dial with gold numbers. Mint WADSWORTH 14 K WGF Unusual Bell Shaped OF Case. $80.00

8-S HC 7-J RIVERSIDE Model 73 Extra fine gilt mvt. 841,467. LS Fine single sunk "AMERICAN WATCH CO" glass dial with hairlines. Extra fine O. Bl and H. 18 K Y engraved HC. $200.00

8-S 11-J WILLIAM ELLERY Gilted mvt. ¾ plate 2,743,585. Waltham 14 K S E case boxed, hinge hand engraved. Mint condition. $175.00

6-S 7-J Nickel mvt. 8,381,746. 14 K solid gold case with MULTICOLORED gold decorations. Fancy decorated dial near mint. $230.00

6-S OF 7-J WILLIAM ELLERY Model 73 Extremely fine gilt mvt. 2,878936. LS Mint AW Co. WALTHAM Flat glass dial. Extra fine engraved CWC Co. Trademark YGF OF case. $100.00

6-S HC 16-J AWWC LADY WALTHAM Model 90 Mint nickel mvt. 18,058,984. Adj. Mint BWC Co. Warrented 14 K box hinge HC with MULTICOLOR Birds and flowers on both lids. In Waltham carring box. $375.00

0-S HC 17-J LADY WALTHAM Model 1900 Mint nickel mvt. 14,103,554 Pendant set adj. gold cups and balance weights. Mint single sunk Roman numeral glass dial with hands. WWC Mgf. Col Mint highly engraved 14 K Y HC. $200.00

0-S 19-J RIVERSIDE MAXIMUS Adj. Gold train Diamond caps mvt. 16,096,108. Keystone 14 K solid gold hunting case. Hand engraved seenes and birds. Mint condition. $275.00

RIVERSIDE A 19-J Adj. 5 pos. Gold train raised gold settings. Mvt. 20,303,653. 14 K solid gold Waltham Case. Advertised as thinnest watch in America. Mint condition. $175.00

0-S OF 7-J MODEL 91 Extra fine gilt mvt. 713,093,938. Mint Roman numberal AW Co. glass dial with hands. Extra fine OF YGF. case.$75.00

0-S 15-J OPERA WATCH Mvt. 17,803,876. Wadsworth 25 yr. case. Fancy engraving. Mint condition. $85.00

0-S 17-J RIVERSIDE Junters case. mvt. 13,026,033. Phay six. 14 K Extra case. Fancy engraving. Scenes and flowers. scalloped edges. Mint. $125.00

Encourage the Pennsylvania Watch Manufacture.

THE Great State of Pennsylvania ranks with the First in the Union in Population and Resources, and in the importance of her Agricultural, Mining, and Manufacturing interests. Her Manufactures, keeping pace with her other interests, have grown steadily, until they are now on the most extensive scale and of the most varied character. To crown them all, the Manufacture of the Finest Grades of Watches, in all their Perfection of Detail, Delicacy of Finish, and Wonderful Accuracy of Adjustment, is already a triumphant success at the City of Lancaster. Dealers and Experts, at home and abroad, pronounce them the Best American Watches yet produced. The Lancaster Watch Company is resolved to take the lead in the manufacture of Fine Watches. They think that every Pennsylvanian will have good reason to be proud of his native State in her Watch Manufacture, and they ask the People of Pennsylvania to second their great effort to add this New and Valuable Industry to the noble list for which our old Keystone State is already famous. This can be done by inquiring for the Lancaster Watch; by insisting resolutely upon seeing it before purchasing a Watch; and, if it is equally satisfactory—as the Company have no doubt it will be—by buying it in preference to any Watch manufactured in New England, in the West, or in Europe. Let Pennsylvanians stand by Pennsylvania, and we will build up here a Great Industry that, in its more complete development, may secure to our State, in this interest, a world-wide reputation for the next Hundred Years.

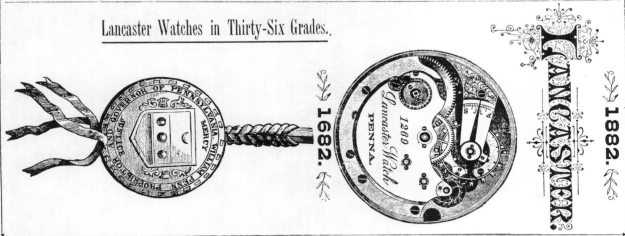

Lancaster Watches in Thirty-Six Grades.

1682.   1882.

Adams and Perry Watch Mgf. Co. 1874 to 1876
Lancaster Watch Co. 1877 to 1878
Lancaster Pa. Watch Co. 1878 to 1879
Lancaster Watch Co. 1879 to 1886
Keystone Standard Watch Co. 1886 to 1890
Sold to Hamilton in 1891

** The original aim of the projectors of the Lancaster Watch Company was to make such a Watch Movement as should be superior to any other thus far produced in America, and to offer to the Public the Finest and Most Reliable Time-Keepers, with all latest improvements, at a price as low as such Movements could be afforded with the aid of the Best Machinery and Most Skilful Workmen to be had in the country. Eight years

have elapsed since the great enterprise was originated, and more than Three-Quarters of a Million Dollars have thus far been expended at the Works. The Watches have been received in the Trade with extraordinary favor. Wherever examined by Dealers and Experts in Watches they have been heartily approved, many, after thorough examination, pronouncing them the Finest American Movements yet brought to their notice.

A man, like a Watch, is to be valued by his goings. —*Penn's Maxims.*

"PENN'S TREATY WITH THE INDIANS"—BY BENJAMIN WEST.

The Lancaster Watches welcome this Test of their Quality.

The Pennsylvania Watch Manufacture.

The Lancaster, Pa., Watch Factory.

INQUIRE FOR AND EXAMINE THE LANCASTER WATCHES.

Lancaster is one of the Most Eligible Localities for a Watch Factory to be found in America, and here it is proposed to build up such a reputation for the State of William Penn as Waltham has made for Massachusetts, and Elgin for Illinois.

An Extensive Addition to the Buildings of the Lancaster Watch Company has just been completed, which will more than double the capacity of the Factory. This Extension of the Works has been made to meet more fully the rapidly increasing demand for the various grades of the Lancaster Watches.

Our Dust and Damp Proof Watch (for which application for Letters-Patent has been filed) will be placed on the Market in Eleven Grades, about November 1st, 1882. Our Ladies' Size, in Nine Grades, will be the hand-somest Ladies' Watch yet produced in the United States. It will be ready for delivery about January 1st, 1883. The finest Movement of this size is named "Lady Penn," in honor of the Mother of the Founder, who bore this gracious title, her husband being Admiral Sir William Penn.

THE patron saint of Pennsylvania is William Penn—and this, indeed, with propriety, since to no other man does she owe so great a debt of gratitude. No grander character has ever been within her borders, be it for a day or for a life-time. American history boasts no nobler name than his; the history of England has no more glowing page than that which tells of his heroic struggle with the powers of darkness in Church and State; and the record of the World's progress is brighter for the chapter which he made possible in the founding of his Free Commonwealth. And yet—revered as is his memory—his character and work are, in themselves and in their abiding influence, far too little known or appreciated in these days and in this land of political and religious freedom, which has been in so great degree an heritage from himself. In the realm of history, as in that of nature, distance is an element essential to the proper estimate of any figure of colossal proportions. As William Penn stands apart from us to-day, with two centuries of unparalleled progress of the race between, the World is more and more impressed with the greatness of the man to whom alone, in modern times, is given the title of Founder, and with the goodness of him who, upon the dark background of an evil age, "shines resplendent in the lustre of unsullied virtue."

The historic picture of William Penn at the age of twenty-two, which is given on the first page of this circular, is a very fine reproduction of the most precious canvas in Philadelphia —perhaps the most precious in the United States. This painting, which was more than a half century old before Washington was born, hangs in the commodious rooms of the Historical Society of Pennsylvania, at 820 Spruce Street, Philadelphia. Though a portrait from life, it is an ideal face of such rare human type that the thought of sex hardly suggests itself—a face of such winning goodness, suggesting large possibilities, as might be painted for Joan of Arc clad in armor, or for John the Beloved, "the youngest and most woman-like of all the disciples." It grows upon one strangely, as he looks often and earnestly into it, and we turn to it for the hundredth time with the feeling that it is his mother's face no less than his own that looks out upon us from the silent page. And what a mother he must have had! It is a face that has a future, one of the rarest pictured faces we have ever seen—one that could grow to that which is given on a succeeding page, now to be seen at Independence Hall, on Chestnut Street, Philadelphia, and said to have been painted at the age of fifty-two years, but never to certain caricatures that have so long passed current as "William Penn."

Of the two more recent biographies, by Janney and by Dixon, the latter regards William Penn as a great historical character, and his Holy Experiment, in the founding of Pennsylvania, as "one of the most precious heirlooms of time;" while the former traces his enlightened policy as a legislator to his religious principles, and attributes far more influence to the ministry of George Fox than to the counsels of Algernon Sidney. They are books to be read.

The Bi-Centennial Edition of "William Penn: Sketches and Papers," just published in paper covers, at Fifty Cents per copy, by J. B. Lippincott & Co., is a book of absorbing interest. This valuable compilation, which is issued in good type and on good paper, selects matter of greatest interest from each of his four best-known biographers, Dixon, Janney, Weems, and Clarkson. While condensing as much as seemed necessary to bring it within given space—it aims to give the style and spirit of each writer, the 208 large octavo double-column pages—it aims to give the style and spirit of each writer, the sequence of chapters having due regard to the order of time. William Penn himself is represented in certain letters of most interest to the American public, especially those written in 1682 to his Wife and Children, and to the Society of Free Traders. The Frame of Government of Pennsylvania, with its noble preface, and the laws accompanying, not else where accessible to the ordinary reader, and which indeed but few men of our day, even among lawyers, have ever seen, are here given in full. The original text of the Charter of Pennsylvania is also found here, with its unique and varied spelling, as compared with the four original elaborate parchments in the office of the Secretary of State of Pennsylvania, at Harrisburg. This original parchment is, with a single exception, the most precious State document in America. Here, also, are "Penn's Maxims," a work little known outside the Society of Friends, and the second part of "No Cross, No Crown," the garnered experience of the best and wisest men and women of Greece and Rome, of the early Christian era, and of more modern times—a mine of wealth to the thoughtful. The book is "a contribution to the Bi-Centennial Era, in the hope that it may aid in arousing more intelligent interest in the character, and in disseminating broader knowledge of the life-work and lasting influence, of the illustrious Founder of Pennsylvania." Our space being limited to a single page, we can do little more than point the way to this full source of information.

Stem-Winding and Stem-Setting
THREE-QUARTER PLATE MOVEMENTS.

All 18-Size, Quick-Train, Making 18,000 Beats to the Hour. The Finer Movements, Nickel or Gilded, Adjusted to Position, as desired.

No. 1. Fine Nickel Movement. Double-Roller Escapement, Exposed Pallets, Patent Self-Adjusting Centre Pinion, Patent Stem-Wind, Patent Regulator, Improved Let-down, Twenty Extra Fine Ruby Jewels, Three pairs Conical Pivots, Breguet Hair Spring, Compensation Balance, Adjusted to Heat, Cold, and Isochronism. Name, "**Lancaster Watch.**"

No. 15. Fine Nickel Movement. Straight-line Escapement, Exposed Pallets, Patent Self-Adjusting Centre Pinion, Patent Stem-Wind, Patent Regulator, Improved Let-down, Twenty Extra Fine Ruby Jewels, Three pairs Conical Pivots, Compensation Balance, Adjusted to Heat, Cold, and Isochronism. Name, "**Melrose,**" Lancaster, Pa.

No. 2. Fine Nickel Movement. Straight-line Escapement, Patent Self-Adjusting Centre Pinion, Patent Stem-Wind, Patent Regulator, Four pairs Fine Ruby Jewels in Gold Settings, Improved Let-down, Expansion Balance, Adjusted to Heat, Cold, and Isochronism. Name, "**Record,**" Lancaster, Pa.

No. 14. Nickel Movement. Quick Train, Straight-line Escapement, Exposed pallets, Improved Let-down, Patent Pinion, Expansion Balance, Four pairs Ruby Jewels. Name, "**Record,**" Lancaster, Pa.

No. 3. Fine Gilded Movement. This very fine movement is identical in all respects with No. 1. Name, "**Lancaster Watch,**" Pa.

No. 16. Fine Gilded Movement. This very fine movement is identical in all respects with No. 15. Name, "**Lancaster, Pa.**"

No. 4. Fine Gilded Movement. Quick Train, Straight-line Escapement, Exposed pallets, Patent Self-Adjusting Centre Pinion, Patent Stem-Wind, Patent Regulator, Four pairs Ruby Jewels in Gold Settings, Improved Let-down, Expansion Balance, Adjusted to Heat, Cold, and Isochronism. Name, "**West End,**" Lancaster, Pa.

No. 5. Fine Gilded Movement. Quick Train, Straight-line Escapement, Exposed pallets, Patent Self-Adjusting Centre Pinion, Patent Stem-Wind, Patent Regulator, Improved Let-down, Two pairs Ruby Jewels in Settings, Expansion Balance, Adjusted to Heat, Cold, and Isochronism. Name, "**Keystone,**" Lancaster, Pa.

No. 6. Fine Gilded Movement. Quick Train, Straight-line Escapement, Exposed Pallets, Patent Self Adjusting Centre Pinion, Patent Stem-Wind, Improved Let-down, Two pairs Ruby Jewels, Expansion Balance. Name, "**Franklin,**" Lancaster, Pa.

No. 12. Gilded Movement. Quick Train, Straight-line Escapement, Exposed Pallets, Patent Pinion, Improved Let-down, Top Plate Ruby Jeweled, Expansion Balance. Name, "**West End.**"

No. 13. Gilded Movement. Quick Train, Straight-line Escapement, Exposed pallets, Patent pinion, Improved Let-down, Plain Jeweled, Expansion Balance. Name, "**New Era,**" Lancaster, Pa.

No. 7. Fine Gilded Movement. "**Keystone**" Key-wind. In all other respects this Movement is identical with No. 4.

No. 8. Fine Gilded Movement. "**Fulton**" Key-wind. In all other respects this Movement is identical with No.5.

No. 9. Fine Gilded Movement. "**Franklin**" Key-wind. In all other respects this Movement is identical with No. 6.

No. 10. Fine Gilded Movement. "**West End**" Key-wind. In all other respects this Movement is identical with No. 12.

No. 11. Fine Gilded Movement. "**New Era**" Key-wind. In all other respects this Movement is identical with No. 13.

Dust and Damp Proof Watches,
With or Without Patent Regulator.

No. 17. Fine Nickel Movement. Quick Train, Straight-line Escapement, Patent Self-Adjusting Centre Pinion, Patent Stem-Wind, Patent Regulator, Improved Let-down, Twenty Extra Fine Ruby Jewels, Three pairs Conical Pivots, Compensation Balance, Adjusted to Heat, Cold, and Isochronism. Name, "**Wm. Penn,**" Lancaster, Pa.

No. 18. Fine Nickel Movement. Quick Train, Straight-line Escapement, Patent Self-Adjusting Centre Pinion, Patent Stem-Wind, Four pairs Fine Ruby Jewels in Gold Settings, Improved Let-down, Expansion Balance, Adjusted to Heat, Cold, and Isochronism. Name, "**Stevens,**" Lancaster, Pa.

No. 19. Nickel Movement. Quick Train, Straight-line Escapement, Improved Let-down, Patent Pinion, Expansion Balance, Four Pairs Ruby Jewels. Name, "**Sidney,**" Lancaster, Pa.

No. 20. Nickel Movement. Quick Train, Straight-line Escapement, Improved Let-down, Patent Pinion, Expansion Balance, Top Plate, Ruby Jeweled. Name, "**Paoli.**"

No. 21. Fine Gilded Movement. Quick Train, Straight-line Escapement, Patent Self-Adjusting Centre Pinion, Patent Stem-Wind, Patent Regulator, Improved Let-down, Twenty Extra Fine Ruby Jewels, Three pairs Conical Pivots, Compensation Balance, Adjusted to Heat, Cold, and Isochronism. Name, "**Delaware,**"

No. 22. Fine Gilded Movement. Quick Train, Straight-line Escapement, Patent Self-Adjusting Centre Pinion, Patent Stem-Wind, Patent Regulator, Four pairs Ruby Jewels in Gold Settings, Improved Let-down, Expansion Balance, Adjusted to Heat, Cold, and Isochronism. Name, "**Girard.**"

No. 23. Fine Gilded Movement. Quick Train, Straight-line Escapement, Patent Self-Adjusting Centre Pinion, Patent Stem-Wind, Patent Regulator, Improved Let-down, Two pairs Ruby Jewels in Settings, Expansion Balance, Adjusted to Heat, Cold, and Isochronism. Name, "**Malvern.**"

No. 24. Fine Gilded Movement. Quick Train, Straight-line Escapement, Patent Self-Adjusting Centre Pinion, Patent Stem-Wind, Improved Let-down, Two pairs Ruby Jewels in Settings, Expansion Balance. Name, "**Radnor.**"

No. 25. Fine Gilded Movement. Quick Train, Straight-line Escapement, Patent Self-Adjusting Centre Pinion, Patent Stem-Wind, Improved Let-down, Two pairs Ruby Jewels in Plates, Expansion Balance. Name, "**Chester.**"

No. 26. Gilded Movement. Quick Train, Straight-line Escapement, Patent Pinion, Improved Let-down, Top Plate Ruby-Jeweled, Expansion Balance. Name, "**Elberon.**"

No. 27. Gilded Movement. Quick Train, Straight-line Escapement, Patent Pinion, Improved Let-down, Plain-Jeweled, Expansion Balance. Name, "**Denver.**"

LADIES' WATCHES.

All 8-Size, Three-Quarter Plate, Quick-Train Movements.

No. 28. Fine Nickel Movement. Three-Quarter Plate, Quick Train, Straight-line Escapement, Breguet Hair Spring, Exposed Pallets, Safety Pinion, Five pairs Fine Ruby Jewels in Raised Gold Settings, Compensation Balance, Finely Adjusted to Heat, Cold, and Isochronism. Name, "**Lady Penn.**"

No. 29. Fine Nickel Movement. Three-quarter Plate, Quick Train, Straight-line Escapement, Exposed Pallets, Safety Pinions, Four pairs Fine Ruby Jewels in Gold Settings, Compensation Balance, Adjusted to Heat, Cold, and Isochronism. Name, "**Red Rose of Lancaster.**"

No. 30. Nickel Movement. Three-quarter Plate, Safety Pinion, Four pairs Fine Ruby Jewels in Gold Settings, Compensation Balance. Name, "**Diamond.**"

No. 31. Fine Gilded Movement. Three-quarter Plate, Straight-line Escapement, Exposed Pallets, Safety Pinion, Four pairs Fine Ruby Jewels, Compensation Balance, Adjusted to Heat, Cold, and Isochronism. Name, "**Ruby.**"

No. 32. Fine Gilded Movement. Three-quarter Plate, Straight-line Escapement, Exposed Pallets, Safety Pinion, Four pairs Fine Ruby Jewels, Compensation Balance. Name, "**Pearl.**"

No. 33. Fine Gilded Movement. Three-quarter Plate, Straight-line Escapement, Exposed Pallets, Safety Pinion, Three pairs Fine Ruby Jewels, Compensation Balance. Name, "**Iris.**"

No. 34. Fine Gilded Movement. Three-quarter Plate, Straight-line Escapement, Exposed Pallets, Safety Pinion, Two pairs Ruby Jewels, Compensation Balance. Name, "**Echo.**"

No. 35. Fine Gilded Movement. Three-quarter Plate, Straight-line Escapement, Exposed Pallets, Safety Pinion, Top Plate Ruby Jeweled, Compensation Balance. Name, "**Flora.**"

No. 36. Gilded Movement. Three-quarter Plate, Straight-line Escapement, Exposed Pallets, Self-Adjusting Safety Pinion, Plain-Jeweled, Compensation Balance. Name, "**Cricket.**"

See page _____ For a picture of the dust and damp proof movement.

The 3 preceding pages are part of a factory advertising booklet. At present these watches are for the most part being overlooked by collectors. Seldom have I seen one priced for over $100.00 and most around $50.00 in a silver or base metal case. I have not attempted to value these watches.

DOLLAR WATCHES

New Model Yankee

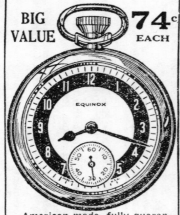

BIG VALUE 74c EACH

EQUINOX

American made, fully guaranteed Pocket Watch. Thin model, nickel plated, plain polished case. Two-tone dial with etched silver figures on a black track. The greatest value for the least money.
No. 1W57. Each..........74

New Haven Gilt Streamline Watch. A new composition case of excellent appearance, fancy silvered two-tone dial, unbreakable crystal. Each in a box.
No. 1W29. Each............. .95

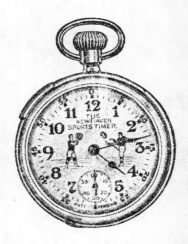

The Dollar watches pictured on this page are not to scale. These watches are just a few of the hundreds of different kinds and names used on Dollar watches. You will also run into a foreign import now and then. A Dollar watch can be recognized as usually being non Jeweled with the case and movement being one complete unit and the dial is usually inexpensive such as paper, brass, or tin. The watches pictured on this page are from 1925 to 1935 Hardware and Jewelry Supply Catalogs and are in the $3.00 to $7.50 class except the Sports Timer and the Ansonia. There are some very large collections of these in the U.S. Remember they still make them (of course they cost more than "Dollar" now), so do your homework.

New Model Midget

New Model Junior

Bull's Eye

Waterbury

Waterbury Radiolite

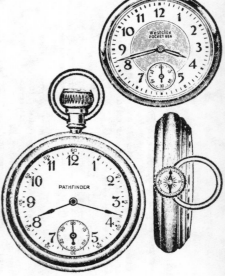

The popularity of dollar watches is steadily increasing. At the present time most of them can be picked up at Flea Markets, Antique Car Swaps, Gun Shows, etc. at about $2.00 to $5.00 each. Once into antique dealers or knowledgeable collectors hands the price goes up to $7.50 to $15.00. Comic character watches were also dollar watches and here the value will climb up to $150.00 or more for the more desireable. The better dollar watches to look for are AUBURNDALE $300.00 to $500.00, ANSONIA $15.00 to $30.00, INGERSOLL backwind $35.00 to $60.00, NEW YORK WATCH CO., crank pendant $100.00 plus, E. N. WELCH MFG. CO. 1893 Chicago Exposition Landing of Columbus $100.00 plus, Bennedict and Burnham Mfg. Co., skelton long wind, $150.00 plus, Waterbury Watch Co. series A through E, $75.00 plus. Collectors want dollar watches with an unusual dial, winding system or a picture, special dedication, etc. engraved or stamped on the case. The common watches make a very inexpensive and interesting collection. There is a new book " The Watch That Made The Dollar Famous", contaives history, line drawings, some serial numbers etc. But no retail values on 45 (5"x 8") pages Order from George Townsend, 212 Adahi Road, Vienna, Va. 22180.

SOLID GOLD HOWARD CASES.

For 18 and 16 Size Howard Movements.

E. T. JURGENSEN.   FANCY VERMICELLI.

Actual scrap value with gold at $165.00 an ounce on the world market.

	14K	18K
50 DWT	241.00	309.50
55 DWT	265.10	340.45
60 DWT	289.20	371.40

The cases on this page are J Boss and may not be marked Howard. The 6 size were Dueber.

N or 18-Size		
	14 K	18K
NO 600	350.00	425.00
NO 601	375.00	460.00
NO 602	500.00	
NO 603	550.00	

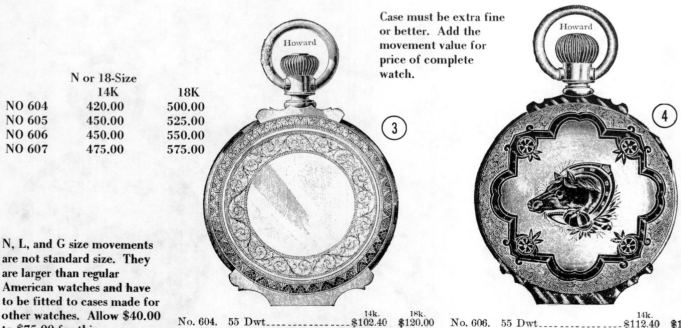

			14k.	18k.
No. 600.	50 Dwt		$80.00	$ 96.00
" 601.	60 "		92.80	112.00

For 16 Size, 5 Dwts. lighter, deduct from above prices $6.40 for 14k., $8.00 for 18k.

			14k.
No. 602.	55 Dwt		$110.40
" 603.	60 "		116.80

Full Vermicelli Engraved, Same price as above.

VERMICELLI BORDER.   BORDER AND CENTER.

N or 18-Size		
	14K	18K
NO 604	420.00	500.00
NO 605	450.00	525.00
NO 606	450.00	550.00
NO 607	475.00	575.00

Case must be extra fine or better. Add the movement value for price of complete watch.

N, L, and G size movements are not standard size. They are larger than regular American watches and have to be fitted to cases made for other watches. Allow $40.00 to $75.00 for this.

			14k.	18k.
No. 604.	55 Dwt		$102.40	$120.00
" 605.	60 "		108.80	128.00

			14k.	18k.
No. 606.	55 Dwt		$112.40	$131.00
" 607.	60 "		118.80	139.00

For 16 Size Cases, 5 Dwts. lighter, deduct from above prices $6.40 for 14k., $8.00 for 18k.

NOTE.—For Howard 6 Size Gold Cases add $4.00 extra for Regular Cases, and $8.00 extra for Louis XIV., to prices on pages 201 to 207.

For values of L or 16 Size cases deduct $25.00 to $50.00.

For values of G or 6 Size cases duduct $100.00 to $150.00.

SOLID GOLD AND "CROWN" PATENT GOLD FILLED HUNTING CASE
GENTS'
Stem Winding Howard Watches.
PENDANT SETTING.

Deduct $25.00 for the same case in 16 Size

"N" – 18-Size

$600.00

Style P.
Scalloped, Full Engraved.
14 Carat. 55 Dwt.

$800.000

Style R.
Raised Colored Gold Ornaments
and Three Real Diamonds.
14 Carat. 62 Dwt.

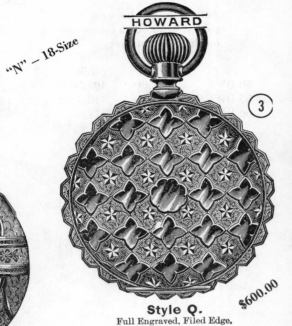

$600.00

Style Q.
Full Engraved, Filed Edge.
14 Carat. 55 Dwt.

Case only must be extra fine condition. See preceding pages for scrap gold value.

NOTE.—Our Gold Cases are all made perfectly dust proof, and those quoted above are warranted to be full 14 Carat Fine, precisely as represented.

NOTE.—We can furnish Engine Turned 14 K. Gold Filled Case similar to style S, at same price as style T.

The cases on this and the page before are made for Howard Watches special and are a little larger than standard 16-S and 18-S cases.

$350.00

Style S.
Plain Engine Turned.
14 Carat. 50 Dwt.

$200.00

18 SIZE NO. 7.
Chron. Bal., Pat. Reg., adj. to H., C., Position
and Isochronism, Nickel . . .

$150.00

Style T.
Fancy Engraved, "Crown Patent,"
14 K. Gold Filled.
(Case Warranted to Wear 20 Years.)

SOLID GOLD AND "CROWN" PATENT GOLD FILLED HUNTING CASE

Gents' Stem Winding Howard Watches.

"N" — 18-Size

Complete watch, movement dial and case must be extra fine and running.

Howard Movement NO. 1

No. 410. "E. Howard & Co." Fine Gilt Movement, full jeweled, chronometer balance, patent regulator, in 14 carat Solid Gold Case, weighing 62 dwt., style R, on page 45 ....$280.00 $875.00
No. 411. The same movement as No. 410, in 55 dwt., 14 carat case, styles P or Q..... 176.00   675.00
No. 412. The same movement as No. 410, in 50 dwt., 14 carat case, style S............ 146.00   425.00
No. 413. The same movement as No. 410, in "Crown" gold filled case, style T....... 96.00   225.00

Howard Movement NO. 2

No. 414. "E. Howard & Co." Fine Gilt Movement, full jeweled, chronometer balance, patent regulator, in 14 carat Solid Gold Case, weighing 62 dwt., style R, on page 45 .... 300.00 $900.00
No. 415. The same movement as No. 414, in 55 dwt., 14 carat case, styles P or Q..... 196.00   700.00
No. 416. The same movement as No. 414, in 50 dwt., 14 carat case, style S.......... 166.00   450.00
No. 417. The same movement as No. 414, in "Crown" gold filled case, style T....... 116.00   250.00

Howard Movement NO. 3

No. 418. "E. Howard & Co." Fine Gilt Movement, full jeweled, chronometer balance, patent regulator, adjusted to heat and cold, in 14 carat Solid Gold Case, weighing 62 dwt., style R, on page 45.................................. 320.00 $950.00
No. 419. The same movement as No. 418, in 55 dwt., 14 carat case, styles P or Q..... 216.00   750.00
No. 420. The same movement as No. 418, in 50 dwt., 14 carat case, style S............ 186.00   500.00
No. 421. The same movement as No. 418, in "Crown" gold filled case, style T....... 136.00   300.00

Howard Movement NO. 4

No. 422. "E. Howard & Co." Fine Nickel Movement, full jeweled, chronometer balance, patent regulator, in 14 carat Solid Gold Case, weighing 62 dwt., style R, on page 45 .... 330.00 $950.00
No. 423. The same movement as No. 422, in 55 dwt., 14 carat case, styles P or Q 226.00   750.00
No. 424. The same movement as No. 422, in 50 dwt., 14 carat case, style S........... 196.00   500.00
No. 425. The same movement as No. 422, in "Crown" gold filled case, style T........ 146.00   300.00

Howard Movement NO. 5

No. 426. "E. Howard & Co." Fine Nickel Movement, full jeweled, chronometer balance, patent regulator, adjusted to heat and cold, in 14 carat Solid Gold Case, weighing 62 dwt., style R, on page 45............................... 350.00 $975.00
No. 427. The same movement as No. 426, in 55 dwt., 14 carat case, styles P or Q..... 246.00   775.00
No. 428. The same movement as No. 426, in 50 dwt., 14 carat case, style S............ 216.00   525.00
No. 429. The same movement as No. 426, in "Crown" gold filled case, style T........ 166.00   325.00

Howard Movement NO. 6

No. 430. "E. Howard & Co." Fine Gilt Movement, full jeweled, chronometer balance, patent regulator, adjusted to heat, cold, position and isochronism, in 14 carat Solid Gold Case, weighing 62 dwt., style R, on page 45......... 370.00 $975.00
No. 431. The same movement as No. 430, in 55 dwt., 14 carat case, styles P or Q..... 266.00   775.00
No. 432. The same movement as No. 430, in 50 dwt., 14 carat case, style S............ 236.00   525.00
No. 433. The same movement as No. 430, in "Crown" gold filled case, style T........ 186.00   325.00

Howard Movement NO. 7

No. 434. "E. Howard & Co." Fine Nickel Movement, full jeweled, chronometer balance, patent regulator, adjusted to heat, cold, position and isochronism, in 14 carat Solid Gold Case, weighing 62 dwt., style R, on page 45.......... 406.00 $600.00
No. 435. The same movement as No. 434, in 55 dwt., 14 carat case, styles P or Q...... 302.00   800.00
No. 436. The same movement as No. 434, in 50 dwt., 14 carat case, style S............ 272.00   550.00
No. 437. The same movement as No. 434, in "Crown" gold filled case, style T....... 222.00   350.00

HOWARD MOVEMENTS.

These are a lot more Howard movements than there are cases available. These movements are prices as if they are in a case of some kind. If you are considering a movement alone that you will have to find a case for, deduct $40.00 to $60.00 from these values. These old Howard movements also have a special stem and crown. Deduct $20.00 if missing.

18 SIZE HUNTING.

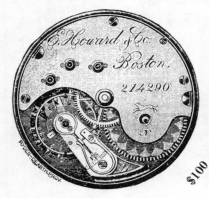

No. 2, Gilded, Pat. Regulator
$66.00

18 SIZE HUNTING.

No. 3, Gilded, Heat and Cold
$82.00

18 SIZE HUNTING.

No. 6, Gilded, Fully Adjusted
$122.00

18 SIZE HUNTING.

No. 4, Nickel, Pat. Regulator
$90.00

18 SIZE HUNTING.

No. 5, Nickel, Heat and Cold
$106.00

18 SIZE HUNTING.

No. 7, Nickel, Fully Adjusted
$150.00

18 SIZE OPEN FACE.

No. 2, Gilded, Pat. Regulator
$66.00

18 SIZE OPEN FACE.

No. 3, Gilded, Heat and Cold
$82.00

18 SIZE OPEN FACE.

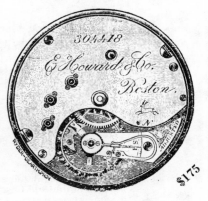

No. 6, Gilded, Fully Adjusted
$122.00

E. Howard Watch Co.'s Movements.

6, 14, 16 and 18 Size, Stem Wind and Pendant Set, Hunting or Open Face.

All of the movements described on this page are pictured on the two preceding pages except the No. 8 and No. 10 and the J or 12 size.

18 SIZE, HUNTING OR OPEN FACE.

N $ 75.00	No. 1 Gilt, Three-quarter Plate, Patent Pendant, Setting and Winding Device, 15 Ruby Jewels, Hardened and Tempered Hair-Spring...	$33 75
N $100.00	No. 2 Gilt, Three-quarter Plate, Patent Pendant Setting and Winding Device, 15 Fine Ruby Jewels, Raised Gold Settings, Patent Regulator, Hardened and Tempered Hair-Spring......................	38 75
N $150.00	No. 3 Gilt, Three-quarter Plate, Patent Pendant Setting and Winding Device, 15 Fine Ruby Jewels, Raised Gold Settings, Patent Regulator, Hardened and Tempered Hair-Spring, Compensated Balance, Adjusted to Heat and Cold	45 00
N $150.00	No. 4 Nickel, Three-quarter Plate, Patent Pendant Setting and Winding Device, 15 Fine Ruby Jewels, Raised Gold Settings, Hardened and Tempered Steel Barrel, Patent Regulator, Hardened and Tempered Hair-Spring	56 25
N $175.00	No. 5 Nickel, Three-quarter Plate, Patent Pendant Setting and Winding Device, 15 Fine Ruby Jewels, Raised Gold Settings, Patent Regulator, Hardened and Tempered Hair-Spring, Compensated Balance, Adjusted to Heat and Cold.......	62 50
N $175.00	No. 6 Gilt, Three-quarter Plate, Patent Pendant Setting and Winding Device, 15 Fine Ruby Jewels, Raised Gold Settings, Hardened and Tempered Steel Barrel, Patent Regulator, Hardened and Tempered Hair-Spring, Compensated Balance, Adjusted to Heat and Cold, Isochronism and Position	60 00
N $200.00	No. 7 Nickel, Three-quarter Plate, Finely Damaskeened, Patent Pendant Setting and Winding Device, 15 Fine Ruby Jewels, Raised Gold Settings, Hardened and Tempered Steel Barrel, Patent Regulator, Hardened and Tempered Hair-Spring, Compensated Balance, Adjusted to Heat and Cold, Isochronism and Position......	87 50
N $450.00	No. 8 Nickel, Divided Three-quarter Plate, Finely Damaskeened, Patent Pendant Setting and Winding Device, 17 Fine Ruby Jewels, Raised Gold Settings, Hardened and Tempered Steel Barrel, Compensated Balance, Adjusted to Temperature and Isochronism, Patent Regulator, Hardened and Tempered Breguet Hair-Spring, Poised Pallet, Patent Cannon Pinion and Center Arbor, Double Sunk Dial, Roller Action Sight Cut	175 00
N $550.00	No. 10 Nickel, Divided Three-quarter Plate, Finely Damaskeened, Patent Pendant Setting and Winding Device, 17 Fine Ruby Jewels, Raised Gold Settings, Hardened and Tempered Steel Barrel, Compensated Balance, Adjusted to Temperature, Isochronism and Position, Patent Regulator, Hardened and Tempered Breguet Hair-Spring, Poised Pallet, Patent Cannon Pinion and Center Arbor, Double Sunk Dial, Roller Action Sight Cut	250 00

16 SIZE, HUNTING.

L $100	No. 2 Gilt—	Same as above No.	2	$38 75
L $150	No. 3 Gilt—	" " " "	3	45 00
L $150	No. 4 Nickel—	" " " "	4	56 25
L $175	No. 5 Nickel—	" " " "	5	62 50
L $175	No. 6 Gilt—	" " " "	6	60 00
L $200	No. 7 Nickel—	" " " "	7	87 50
L $350	No. 8 Nickel—	" " " "	8	175 00
L $450	No. 10 Nickel—	" " " "	10	250 00

16 SIZE, OPEN FACE.

L $350	No. 8 Nickel—	Same as above No.	8	$175 00
L $450	No. 10 Nickel—	" " " "	10	250 00

14 SIZE, OPEN FACE.

Thin, Small, Beautifully Proportioned and Fine Timekeepers.

J 12 – Size $300		
K $200	No. 4 Nickel, Three-quarter Plate, Patent Pendant Setting and Winding Device, 15 Fine Ruby Jewels, Raised Gold Settings, Hardened and Tempered Steel Barrel, Patent Regulator, Hardened and Tempered Hair-Spring	$56 25
K $250	No. 5 Nickel, Three-quarter Plate, Patent Pendant Setting and Winding Device, 15 Fine Ruby Jewels, Raised Gold Settings, Patent Regulator, Hardened and Tempered Hair-Spring, Compensated Balance, Adjusted to Heat and Cold......	62 50
K $275	No. 7 Nickel, Three-quarter Plate, Finely Damaskeened, Patent Pendant Setting and Winding Device, 15 Fine Ruby Jewels, Raised Gold Settings, Hardened and Tempered Steel Barrel, Patent Regulator, Hardened and Tempered Hair-Spring, Compensated Balance, Adjusted to Heat and Cold, Isochronism and Position......	87 50

LADIES' 6 SIZE STEM WIND.

G $225	Gilded, Patent Regulator	$57 75
G $250	Nickel, Patent Regulator	78 75

HOWARD MOVEMENTS.

18 SIZE OPEN FACE.

$150

No. 4, Nickel, Pat. Regulator
$90.00

18 SIZE OPEN FACE.

$175

No. 5, Nickel, Heat and Cold
$106.00

18 SIZE OPEN FACE.

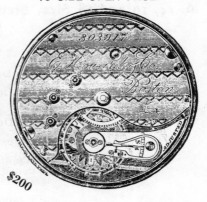

$200

No. 7, Nickel, Fully Adjusted
$150.00

16 SIZE HUNTING.

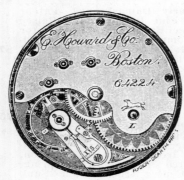

$100 No. 2, Gilded, Pat. Regulator
$66.00
$150 No. 4, Nickel, Pat. Regulator
90.00

16 SIZE HUNTING.

$150

$175

No. 3, Gilded, Heat and Cold
$82.00
No. 5, Nickel, Heat and Cold
106 00

16 SIZE HUNTING.

No. 6, Gilded, Fully Adjusted
.$122 00 $175
No. 7, Nickel, Fully Adjusted
150.00 $200

14 SIZE OPEN FACE ONLY.

HTC

$200 No. 4, Nickel, Pat. Regulator
$90.00
$225 No. 5, Nickel, Heat and Cold
106.00
$250 No. 7, Nickel, Fully Adjusted
150.00

18 SIZE HUNTING ONLY.

$75.00

No. 1, 18 size Hunting only,
15 Jeweled, Pat. Regulator
$50 00

6 SIZE HUNTING.

No. 1, 6 size, Plain Regulator
$60 00 $200
No. 2, Gilded, Pat. Regulator
66 00 $225
No. 4, Nickel, Pat. Regulator
90 00 $250

All 14, 16 and 18 size Howard Movements are Pendant Set, and 6 size are Lever Set.

Howard Watches on this page (except the Keywind) were made by the Keystone Watch Case Co., using the Howard name and trademarks. The Preceding Howard pages were made by the old Howard Factory before 1903.

HOWARD WATCHES

(13) Keywind Keyset

18-S

(14) 16-S $150 up   Old Howard

(15) Early serial numbers & series $400.00 up. Howard Keywinds hard to case but still very desirable when recased.

MODELS OF MOVEMENTS

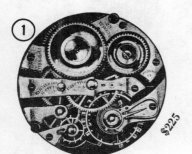

(1) $225

16 Size—Model A
Series O
23 Jewel   Htg. & O. F.

(2) $225.00

16 Size—Model B
Series O
23 Jewel   Htg. & O. F.

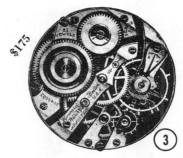

$175

(3)

16 Size—Model C
Series 10
21 Jewel   Open Face

Keystone
Howards

(4) $185

16 Size—Model D
Series 10
21 Jewel   Open Face

(5) $175

16 Size—Model E
Series 11
21 Jewel   Open Face

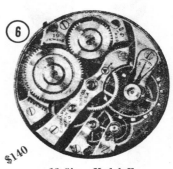

(6) $140

16 Size—Model F
Series 5
19 Jewel   Open Face

C. & E. MARSHALL CO.   PARTS CATALOG

(7) $140

16 Size—Model G
Series 5
19 Jewel   Htg. & O. F.

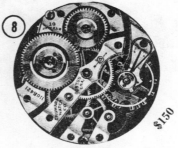

(8) $150

16 Size—Model H.
Series 5
19 Jewel   Htg. & O. F.

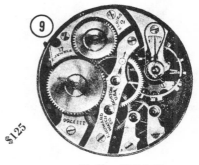

(9) $125

16 Size Model K
Series 2
17 Jewel   Open Face

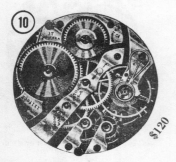

(10) $120

16 Size—Model M
Series 2
17 Jewel   Open Face

(11) $120

16 Size—Model N.
Series 9
17 Jewel   Htg. & O. F.

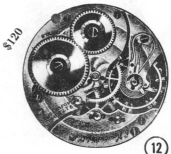

$120

(12)

16 Size—Model P
Series 3
17 Jewel   Htg. & O. F.

HOWARD WATCHES

1921   HTC

$50.00

10 Size, Thin Model

The following marks with arrow indicate number of Jewels and adjustments in each grade:

✠ Cross—23 Jewel, 5 Positions
✶ Star—21 Jewel, 5 Positions
△ Triangle—19 Jewel, 5 Positions
○ Circle—17 Jewel, 3 Positions

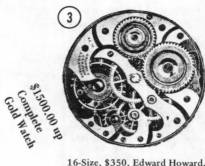

$1500.00 up
Complete
Gold Watch

16-Size, $350, Edward Howard.

$150.00

12 Size—Model R
Series 8
23 Jewel   Hunting
Going Barrel

$150.00

12 Size—Model S
Series 8
23 Jewel   Open Face
Going Barrel

$100.00

12 Size—Model T
Series 8
21 Jewel   Htg. & O. F.
Stop Works

$100.00

12 Size—Model W
Series 8
21 Jewel   Open Face
Safety Barrel

This page all Keystone Howards

$75.00

12 Size—Model X
Series 8
21 Jewel   Open Face
Going Barrel

$75.00

12 Size—Model Y
Series 6
19 Jewel   Htg. & O. F.
Stop Works

$75.00

12 Size—Model Z
Series 6
19 Jewel   Htg. & O. F.
Safety Barrel

$75.00

12 Size—Model AA
Series 6
19 Jewel   Htg. & O. F.
Going Barrel

$70.00

12 Size—Model BB
Series 7
17 Jewel   Htg. & O. F.
Stop Works

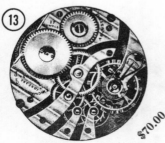

$70.00

12 Size—Model CC
Series 7
17 Jewel   Htg. & O. F.
Safety Barrel

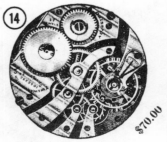

$70.00

12 Size—Model DD
Series 7
17 Jewel   Hunting
Going Barrel

$70.00

12 Size—Model EE
Series 7
17 Jewel   Open Face
Going Barrel

Parts of 1915 Howard Factory Catalog

$225

①

$150

②

16-SIZE, 23-JEWEL, NEW BRIDGE (1907) MODEL

Hunting or Open-Face

The finest practical timepiece in the world, very generally used by Railroad Men, Field Engineers and others whose needs are most exacting. Specially adjusted to five positions, temperature and isochronism. Every HOWARD Watch is cased and adjusted in its own case before leaving the factory. HOWARD movements and cases are not sold separately.

JEWELS

23 extra-fine jewels, all pigeon-blood rubies except the oriental sapphire pallet stones. Balance, pallet arbor and escape wheel have cone pivots, revolving on cap jewels. Going parts of the barrel are ruby-jeweled.

BALANCE, ESCAPEMENT AND SAFETY BARREL

Celebrated Howard Balance Wheel, specially hard tempered, will not knock out of true with the jar and jolt of the most severe use. Double-roller escapement and recessed steel escape wheel. Patent safety barrel.

DIAL

Dial is hand-made, double sunk, of finest first-quality enamel, with distinctive Howard hour and minute figures.

HUNTING AND OPEN-FACE

Made in both Hunting and Open-Face. Hunting watches are pendant setting only—Open-Face either pendant or lever setting. The Howard lever set in this grade is the highest grade railroad watch in the world.

16-SIZE, 19-JEWEL, NEW BRIDGE (1907) MODEL

Escapement has cone pivots running on Fine Ruby End Stone Jewels

Hunting or Open-Face

This is the finest adjusted 19-jewel watch made to-day with extra adjustment to five positions, temperature and isochronism. Each watch is cased and adjusted in its own case before leaving the factory. Movements and cases are not sold separately.

JEWELS

19 jewels, all selected rubies except the oriental sapphire pallet stones. Balance and escape wheel have cone pivots revolving on cap jewels.

BALANCE, ESCAPEMENT AND SAFETY BARREL

Celebrated Howard Balance Wheel, specially hard tempered, running true and giving a very close rate under jar and vibration. Double-roller escapement and steel escape wheel. Patent safety barrel.

DIAL

Dial is hand-made, double sunk, of the first-quality enamel, with distinctive Howard hour and minute figures.

HUNTING AND OPEN-FACE

Made in both Hunting and Open-Face, pendant setting only.

Values below are for case only extra fine or better. Complete and Market Howard.

18 K. SOLID GOLD, EXTRA HEAVY

Hunting		*Open-Face*	
No. 112, Plain	$300.00	No. 122, Plain	$200.00
No. 113, E. T.	325.00	No. 123, E. T.	225.00

14 K. SOLID GOLD, EXTRA HEAVY

No. 110, Plain	$250.00	No. 115, Plain	$117.00
No. 120, E. T.	275.00	No. 125, E. T.	

14 K. SOLID GOLD, HEAVY

No. 130, Plain	$200.00	No. 135, Plain	$150.00
No. 140, E. T.	225.00	No. 145, E. T.	175.00

"JAS. BOSS" OR "CRESCENT" GOLD FILLED

(Guaranteed 25 Years)

No. 150, Plain	$75.00	No. 155, Plain	$50.00
No. 160, E. T.	65.00	No. 165, E. T.	60.00
Screw Bezel, Solid Back, }		{ No. 175, Plain	50.00
Swing Ring, Dust-Proof }		{ No. 185, E. T.	60.00

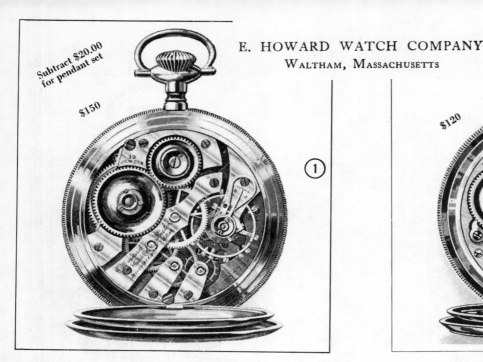

Subtract $20.00 for pendant set

$150

16-SIZE, 19-JEWEL, NEW BRIDGE (1907) MODEL
Going Parts of Barrel Jeweled
Hunting or Open-Face

The Open-Face Lever-Setting model of this movement is recommended for use by Railroad Men. It is supplied with the HOWARD Railroad Dial with marginal minutes (see illustration, page 26) and fitted in the HOWARD Special Dust-Proof, Swing Ring, Gold Filled Case when desired for Railroad Service. Extra adjustment to five positions, temperature and isochronism. Cased and timed in its own case before leaving the factory.

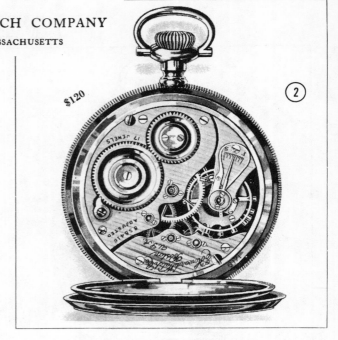

$120

16-SIZE, 17-JEWEL, 3-4 PLATE (1905) MODEL
Double Roller.   Fine Five Position Adjustment
Hunting or Open-Face

Very close adjustment to temperature, isochronism and five positions. Each watch is cased and timed in its own case before leaving the factory. Movements and cases are not sold separately.

Parts of 1915 Howard Factory Catalog

Add $20.00 for lever set

$100.00

16-SIZE, 17-JEWEL, 3-4 PLATE (1905) MODEL
Double Roller.   Five Positions Adjusted
Hunting or Open-Face

Closely adjusted to temperature, isochronism and five positions. Every HOWARD Watch is cased and adjusted in its own case before leaving the factory. HOWARD movements and cases are not sold separately. This grade meets all requirements for railroad service and is accepted by general inspectors.

$100.00

16-SIZE, 17-JEWEL, 3-4 PLATE (1905) MODEL
Single Roller.   Three Positions Adjusted
Hunting or Open-Face

Adjusted to three positions, isochronism and temperature—the HOWARD keeps accurate time despite extremes of heat and cold. A dependable timepiece for daily pocket use. Every HOWARD Watch is cased and timed in its own case at the factory. HOWARD movements and cases are not sold separately.

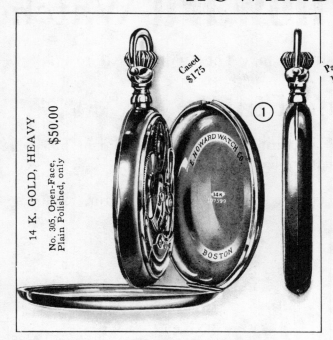

14 K. GOLD, HEAVY

No. 305, Open-Face,
Plain Polished, only $50.00

Cased $175

①

Parts of
1915 Factory
Catalog

16-SIZE, EXTRA-THIN MODEL HOWARD CARVEL WATCH

The watches on this page and the two preceding, except the Keywind, were at this time advertised as coming only from the factory cased. I have given a value for the movement only and for the case only. You must add the two together to get a value for your watch. I assume all of these cases were marked Howard. I wonder about this because I have seen a lot of Keystone Howards that were in Jas Boss or Cresent cases that were not marked but looked original to me. Collectors had, rather have the marked Howard cases. You should, I think, discount your watch some from these values if your case is not marked.

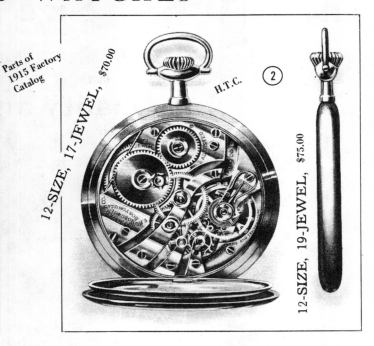

12-SIZE, 17-JEWEL, $70.00

H.T.C.

②

12-SIZE, 19-JEWEL, $75.00

H.T.C. 12-SIZE, 21-JEWEL, EXTRA-THIN $100 BRIDGE (1908) MODEL

Hunting or Open-Face, Pendant Setting

The finest thin model timepiece in the world, and the first thin model to achieve the HOWARD standard of accuracy as a timekeeper. Especially adjusted to five positions, temperature and isochronism.

18 K. SOLID GOLD, HEAVY

Hunting		*Open-Face*	
No. 812, Plain	$165.00	No. 822, Plain	$110.00
No. 813, E. T.	175.00	No. 823, E. T.	120.00

14 K. SOLID GOLD, HEAVY

No. 830, Plain	$165.00	No. 835, Plain	$100.00
No. 840, E. T.	165.00	No. 845, E. T.	110.00

"JAS. BOSS" OR "CRESCENT" GOLD FILLED
(*Guaranteed 25 Years*)

No. 850, Plain	$70.00	No. 855, Plain	$50.00
No. 860, E. T.	80.00	No. 865, E. T.	50.00

"CAVETTO" CASE "CRESCENT" GOLD FILLED
(*Guaranteed 25 Years*)

No. 850C, Plain	$70.00	No. 855C, Plain	$50.00
No. 860C, E. T.	80.00	No. 865C, E. T.	50.00

1892   GARDEN CITY WATCH CO., CHICAGO, ILL.

Gents' Howard Stem Winding Watches
HAND ENGRAVED LATEST DESIGNS.

These 4 cases are
N size for Howard

$400.00

$475.00

No. 922.
14k. Gold, 50 dwt.

No. 923.
14k. Gold, 60 dwt.

$140.00

$150.00

No. 925.
14k. Gold Filled, warranted to wear 20 years.

No. 926.
14k. Gold Filled, warranted 20 years.

These NEW 16 Size Howard Watches

are now in the hands of our Jobbers for distribution. They will appeal to all Jewelers whose first thought is for

Quality and Finish

These high-grade goods will be sold only as **Complete Watches,** cased in heavy 18 K. or 14 K. **Solid Gold** and **Boss or Crescent** 25-year Filled Cases.

No publishing of trade prices allowed.

The **retail** selling price of each Watch is fixed by the manufacturer, assuring the Jeweler an attractive profit.

No cutting of prices will be permitted.

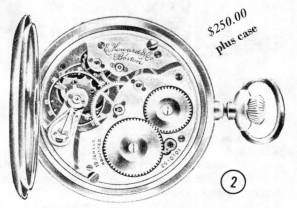

$550.00 plus case.

23 ruby and sapphire jewels (raised gold settings); adjusted to 5 positions, temperature and isochronism; breguet hairsprings; micrometric regulator; gold train wheels; double roller; steel escape wheel; sapphire pallet stones; all steel parts highly finished; extra fine, hand-made, double-sunk dial; **timed in the case and certificate of rating furnished with each watch.**

$250.00 plus case

19 ruby and sapphire jewels (gold settings); adjusted to 3 positions, temperature and isochronism; breguet hairspring; micrometric regulator; gold center wheel; double roller; steel escape wheel; sapphire pallet stones; all steel parts highly finished; extra fine, hand-made, double-sunk dial; **timed in the case and certificate of rating furnished with each watch.**

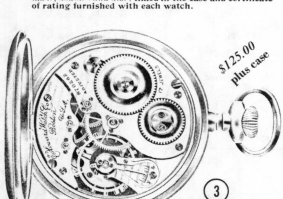

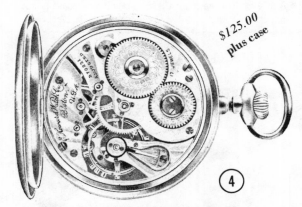

$125.00 plus case

$125.00 plus case

17 ruby and sapphire jewels (gold settings); adjusted to 3 positions and temperature; breguet hairspring; micrometric regulator; gold center wheel; double roller; steel escape wheel; sapphire pallet stones; all steel parts highly finished; extra fine, hand-made, double-sunk dial; **timed in case.**

17 ruby and sapphire jewels (gold settings) adjusted to temperature; breguet hairspring; micrometric regulator; gold center wheel; steel escape wheel; sapphire pallet stones; all steel parts highly finished; extra fine, hand-made dial; **timed in case.**

Each Watch is enclosed in a highly finished, silk=lined Mahogany Box

Write to us for Booklet giving full descriptions and the prices at which these Watches are to be sold to the consumer; also a list of **Wholesalers** from whom these Watches can be obtained.

E. Howard Watch Company, Waltham, Mass.

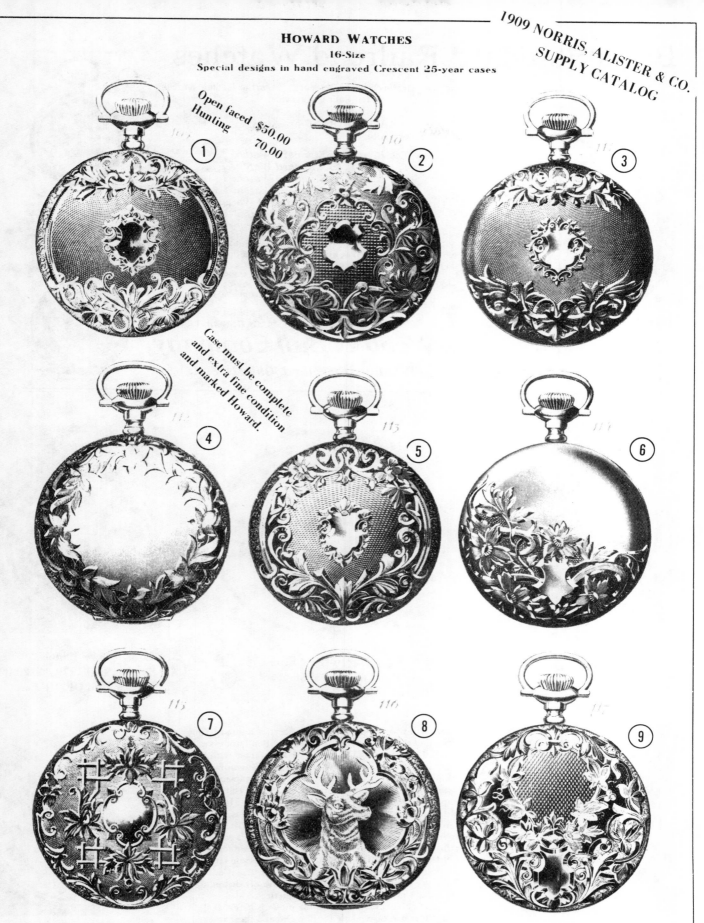

HOWARD WATCHES
16-Size
Special designs in hand engraved Crescent 25-year cases

Open faced $50.00
Hunting   70.00

Case must be complete
and extra fine condition
and marked Howard.

Numbers given specify patterns of engraving only. Any of these styles can be had with any 16-size HOWARD movement
The HOWARD is sold as a complete watch. Movements and cases not sold separately.

Ball's Standard Railroad Watches

Ball's Model Antique Pendant and Bow.

HAMILTON

The B. of L. E. Standard Watch.
A New Model Lever-Set Watch.
17 and 21 Ruby Jewels.   Sapphire Pallets.
Ball's Improved Safety Double Roller.

<u>WATCH MANUFACTURERS</u>

Bearing the "Brotherhood Trade-Marks," are the leading Watches for Railroad service.

The following "TRADE-MARKS" are favorites and easy sellers. They win friends rapidly.

The B. of L. E. Standard Watch.	WALTHAM BALL
The B. of L. F. Standard Watch.	0-Size complete
The B. of R. T. Standard Watch.	Extra fine or better
The O. of R. C. Standard Watch.	Gold filled Open Face $100.00
The Official R. R. Standard Watch.	Hunting Case $150.00
The O. of R. T. Standard Watch.	

Trade-Marks Registered in U. S. Patent Office.

One grade, one quality and one price only. A standard Watch at a standard price. No one can be deceived as to quality or over-charged in price.

We do not sell movements or cases separately, all our watches are cased up, and sold as complete watches, at an established uniform standard price.

We want an up-to-date reputable agent in every railroad center—to such houses we are prepared to make appointments on an equitable basis.

Write us for facts and further information.

OCTOBER 1899
MAGAZINE ADVERTISEMENT

The Webb C. Ball Company,

Ball Building, Cleveland, Ohio, U. S. A.

Ball's Model Antique Pendant and Bow.

① 17 Ruby Jewels.

Hunting or Open-Face.

Four Dainty Little Queens { The B. of L. E. Queen. / The B. of L. F. Queen. / The O. of R. C. Queen. / The B. of R. T. Queen.

Ball's Model Antique Pendant and Bow.

17 Ruby Jewels.

Hunting or Open-Face.

16-S 23 Jewel Illinois
Ser. No. 802,108
Official Standard ②

18-S 16-Jewel Elgin
Commercial Standard
Grade 331 ③

12-S 19 Jewel Illinois
Ser. No. B403,279 $125.00
In Near Mint GF, OF Case ④

16-S 17 Jewel Waltham
Ser. No. B208,930
Official Standard ⑤

Webb C Ball was one of the early pioneers of Railroad Time Service and the company he founded is still in business at 7101 N. Lincoln Ave, Chicago, Ill. He contracted with both American and later Swiss watch companies to manufacture both Railroad grade (Official Standard) and commercial standard watches for him to his specifications. The American companies were Howard (rare), Hampden (rare), Hamilton, Waltham, Elgin, and Illinois. I've seen Jewel series, O-size, 12-size, 16-size, and 18-size pocket watches and small wrist watches. The serial numbering system works this way: Waltham left off the million numerals and put a B instead. Early Hamiltons used the full factory numbers and later the same method as Waltham, Elgin, Hampden and Howard used full factory numbers, all of the Illinois leave off the million and used a B prefix. It takes a little practice to identify the maker and dateing the ones with the prefix is hard. Ball also at times had cases made for him also and these marked cases are very desireable to Railroad Collectors and therefore make the watch worth more. I'm working on this and if you can help, write me. They made a very interesting collection.

18-S 17 Jewel Hamilton
Grade 999 Ser. No. 534,340
Official Standard ⑥

Complete watch must be extra fine and running

Waltham Pictured

Hamilton Pictured

BALL
20th CENTURY MODELS

EVERY important watch manufacturer admits that Webb C. Ball, of Cleveland, has done more than any other one person to raise the standard of watch-making in this country.

❡ The modern railroad watch was developed by the requirements of railroad time inspection and Mr. Ball is a pioneer in that field. Today he is executive head of the watch inspection and time service systems on a majority of railroads in the United States, and the leading manufacturers cheerfully admit that railroad time service requirements, as brought about by Mr. Ball, have been responsible for the present high standard in watch-making.

❡ Mr. Ball's twenty years' experience developing railroad time inspection service placed him in position to know more about the various watches carried by railroad men than even the makers knew.

❡ The actual performance of thousands of individual watches, their faults and weaknesses, and their good points, have been carefully recorded by Mr. Ball. *He then designed a watch based on the facts as shown by his records, anticipating the needs of railroad service for a generation to come.*

The Ball Watch
21 JEWELS
16 or 18 Size

① 16-S Ball $100.00	
② 18-S Ball 100.00	
③ 16-S Ball $125.00	
④ 18-S Ball 125.00	
⑤ 16-S Ball $135.00	
⑥ 18-S Ball 135.00	

In extra quality silveroid, open face case, screw back and bezel............ **$67.00**

In extra quality 20-year gold filled case, screw back and bezel.................... **77.00**

In extra quality 25-year 14k gold filled jointed case................................ **85.00**

In heavy, solid, 14k gold, open face case...............(Price on application)

The Ball Watch
23 JEWELS
16 or 18 Size

This grade is specially cased in "Permanent" gold filled case with patent safety bow, (shown above), which prevents chain becoming entangled with pendant................................. **$93.00**

⑦	16-S 23-J Hamilton Ball $275.00	⑧
⑨	16-S 23-J Waltham Ball 300.00	
	16-S 23-J Illinois Ball 325.00	
	18-S 23-J Hamilton Ball 400.00	⑩

The values shown on these Ball pages are for Railroad Watckes.
Deduct $15.00 to $25.00 if watch is commercial standard.

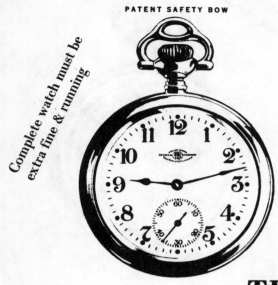

PATENT SAFETY BOW

Complete watch must be extra fine & running

THE
RAILROAD STANDARD

BALL WATCHES contain individual patented improvements and are sold at established standard prices under the following Trade Marks, registered in U. S. and Canadian Patent Offices:

Official 999 Standard	**Official B. of L. E. Standard**	**Official O. R. C. Standard**
Official R. R. Standard	**Official B. of R. T. Standard**	**Official O. R. T. Standard**
	Official B. of L. F. and E. Standard	

℄ Sold as complete watches only, in *Ball Model cases*, made to fit properly, and sent out in reliable time-keeping order.

℄ Every modern machine or tool that will contribute to accuracy and safety, is used in building Ball Watches—but after machines have done all that machines can do, human skill must finish the work. It is impossible to produce Ball Watches in large quantities. Naturally, watch-making of *this* kind is more expensive than if *quantity* were aimed at.

℄ The marvelous results of the Ball Watch are largely due to the tempered steel of the Ball Model balance wheel. The double roller escapement is another one of the many safety improvements which were first adopted in Ball Railroad Watches. No other watch is so carefully adjusted and timed as the Ball Model Railroad Watch, *after it is fitted to the case.*

℄ This Company's policy has always been progressive. If an improvement could be made, it was done at once. *The Ball Watch Company are leaders in railroad watch improvements.*

The Ball Watch				The Ball Watch			
17 JEWELS				**19 JEWELS**			
16 or 18 Size				*16 or 18 Size*			
16-S Ball 18-S $70.00	In extra quality silveroid, open face case,			In extra quality silveroid, open face case,		16-S Ball $90.00	
18-S Ball 16-S 70.00	screw back and bezel.................. **$52.00**			screw back and bezel.................. **$61.00**		18-S Ball 90.00	
16-S Ball 18-S $90.00	In extra quality 20-year gold filled case,			In extra quality 20-year gold filled case,		16-S Ball $120.00	
18-S Ball 16-S 90.00	screw back and bezel or jointed...... **62.00**			screw back and bezel or jointed...... **71.00**		18-S Ball 120.00	
16-S Ball 18-S $110.00	In extra quality 25-year 14k gold filled			In extra quality 25-year 14k gold filled		16-S Ball $130.00	
18-S Ball 18-S 110.00	jointed case................................. **70.00**			jointed case................................. **79.00**		18-S Ball 130.00	
	In heavy, solid, 14k gold, open face case..............(Price on application)			In heavy, solid, 14k gold, open face case..............(Price on application)			

The 18-size Elgin 333 seems to be the hardest to find.

MANHATTAN WATCH COMPANY,

MANUFACTURERS OF

1886 MAGAZINE $50.00
ADVERTISEMENT   SEE PAGE 167

TIFFANY STEM-WINDING WATCHES,

NICKEL MOVEMENTS, IN 18Kt. GOLD CASE.

19 Line Tiffany Movement,
PATENT REGULATOR.

18 Line Open Face Watch,
WITH DAUPHIN DIAL.

19 Line Tiffany Movement,
PLAIN REGULATOR.

19 Line Hunting Watch,
WITH ROMAN DIAL.

The cuts on this page are, as nearly as possible, the exact size of the Watches they represent; the movements are adjusted to heat, cold and position, and guaranteed time-keepers.

The 19 line movements are cased in sixty dwt. 18kt Gold Cases, and with either Roman or Dauphin Dials.

The 18 line movements are usually put up in open face Watches, with flat crystals, in cases weighing 50dwt. 18kt. gold.

Tiffany Patent Regulator Watch, ¾ plate movement
"   Patent Escapement Watch, bridge movement.
"   Chronograph, double, for two simultaneous observations.
"   "   { with minute hand for observations during
          { more than one minute.
"   Five Minute Repeater.
"   Five Minute Repeater, with Chronograph.
"   Perpetual Calendar, with the phases of the moon.

Tiffany Plain Regulator Watch, ¾ plate movement.
"   Chronograph, plain, exposed works.
"   "   split second (not with minute hand).
"   Quarter Repeater.
"   Quarter Repeater, with Chronograph.
"   Minute Repeater.
"   Minute Repeater, with Chronograph.
"   Quarter Independent Split Seconds.

Tiffany Fifth Independent Split Seconds, &c.

and 19 *Line Patent Escapement, Bridge Movements, finely adjusted, especially for Railroad use, in Open Face and Hunting Sterling Silver Cases.*

TIFFANY & CO.,

MAKERS OF

Fine and Complicated Watches for Ladies and Gentlemen.

Wholesale Office, 14 John Street, New York.   Works at Geneva, Switzerland.

GEO. R. COLLIS, MANAGER.

☞ *Also, just received an elegant assortment of Ladies' Watches, of our own make, 10, 12, 13, 14, 15 and 16 lines, both Hunting and Open Face, artistically cased in 18kt. gold.*

186

Tourbillon Chronometer.

16 Size Movement.

Ours is the only school in America
which produced such a watch.
For the second time,

We Challenge Denial.

Canadian
Horological Institute

115 to 121 King St. East
TORONTO, ONT.

The BOWMAN TECHNICAL SCHOOL now at Duke
and Chestnut Streets, Lancaster, Pa. began in 1877.
Also was a HOROLOGICAL SCHOOL and is still in
business. EZRA R. BOWMAN himself and others
tried a commercial venture and made about 50 watches
Mr. and Mrs. E. H. Parkhurst, Jr. provided me with
much of the original old advertising material found in
this book. A very special thanks for your help.

ı have included this page to point out that there are
many fine hand made one of a kind American watches
just waiting to be found and put in a collection. Be
careful of carelessly trading a watch you have not
fully identified. Even though it may look foreign
you might find one of these watches. I cannot place
a value on them.

Southern Horological Institute, 253 Main Street, Dallas, Texas

NOTE.—Cut No. 1, calculated for a railroad watch, was designed and made by C. E. DeLong; it contains several valuable improvements not found in other watches of similar type, and is protected by four U.S. patents. It has a balance staff that can be removed and a new one inserted in from one to two minutes without disturbing in the least the hairspring, roller, truth or poise of balance. An indicator hand is located underneath the second-hand, which indicates at all times the exact time elapsed since the watch was wound. It also contains improved banking pins and regulator.

This new and modern equipped school, with the latest approved methods for the rapid advancement of the young beginner in Jewelry, Watchmaking and Engraving, offers as a special inducement for the enrollment of the **first thirty students only,** a two-third rate of tuition. This special reduction, together with the cheapness at which room and board can be obtained here, would make a saving to the student of at least fifty per cent. on his course, and should be a great inducement to the young man of limited means desirous of learning a good trade.

No. 1. Front view, showing indicator ha[nd]

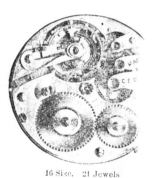

No. 1. Rear view

16 Size.   21 Jewels

16 Size.   21 Jewels

THE CHESHIRE WATCH.

"THE BEST WATCH IN THE WORLD FOR THE PRICE."

Movements, Nos. 21 and 25.

THE NEW NICKEL CHESHIRE.

Thoroughly American.

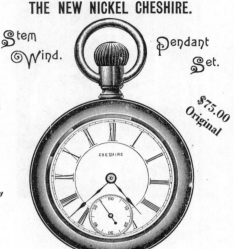

Stem Wind. *Pendant Set.*

$50.00

NON-MAGNETIC BALANCE.

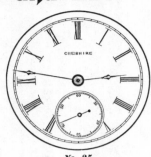

$75.00 Original

No. 21.

No. 25.

18 Size, Full Plate, Stem-Wind, HUNTING and OPEN-FACE, Quick Train, Straight Line Lever, Safety Winding Barrel, SUNK SECONDS, ENAMEL DIAL, Four Jewels. Fitting any 18 Size Standard Case.

THE BEST STEM-WIND MOVEMENT MADE FOR THE PRICE.

FOR SALE BY ALL JOBBERS.

With Second Hand, Back Rachet in Winding, in Solid Nick l Silver Case, not Nickel Plated, with Hinge Bezel, Imitation GOLD JOINT.

ALL OUR WATCHES ARE THOROUGHLY WARRANTED.

THE CHESHIRE WATCH CO.

FACTORY: Cheshire, Conn.

All orders should be addressed to New York Office.

L. W. SWEET, Gen'l Selling Agent,

40 Maiden Lane, New York.

HIGHEST DIPLOMA AND MEDA !

At the Centennial International Exhibition.

PHILADELPHIA WATCH COMPANY

Incorporated in 1868.

E. PAULUS, President
A. C. RAEFLE, Treas.

Superior Watches,

STEM & KEY WINDERS,

FOR LADIES & GENTLEMEN !

618 CHESTNUT STREET, PHILADELPHIA.

NEW YORK AGENCY:

L. H. KELLER & CO.,

No. 64 NASSAU STREET.

AUBURNDALE, MASS.,

CHRONOGRAPH TIMER,

WM. B. FOWLE, Maker.

Designed for Sporting, Scientific and Mechanical purposes ; $\frac{1}{4}$ and $\frac{1}{8}$ seconds, fly back.

List Price, - - $15.00

Positively Accurate.

Put up in German Silver Cases, Nickel Plated, *size of an ordinary watch*. Very neat and handsome, supplying a want long felt by those desiring to measure the flight of time with scientific accuracy to the fraction of a second. It indicates positively minutes, seconds, quarters or eighths of seconds, the only instrument registering one eighth of a second made. It is substantially constructed, positive in its action, and will not easily get out of order.

These Chronographs can be obtained from the principal Jobbing Houses in the Trade.

Arburndale Timer in working order and all original $300.00

American Made Watches & Cases.

Made by patent machinery, and plated by the new process upon Composition, both sides alike, and of equal thickness, the process known only to the Inventor. Warranted 18k. Plate. Having every appearance of Watches costing $200.00

Over 30,000 Sold in the Last Twelve Months.

(Fac Simile of the Bristol Watch.)

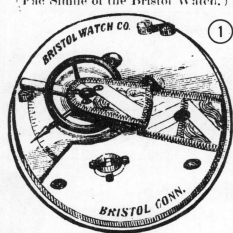

Our Watch Cases are an entirely new article and we are enabled to sell them at about half the usual price of such goods; the material of the cases is composed of Nickel (or Albata) Silver, making the most perfect metal to plate upon. They are heavily plated all over with fine Silver, by our new patent process, making to all intents a SILVER WATCH, strong and durable and will compare with any Watch costing $45.00

The Gold Cases are plated in the same style with 18k. Gold, in such a manner as to defy detection by an expert, which makes them as valuable as pure gold and silver cases. These Watches are just as fine in appearance as Watches sold for $200. to $250.

Prices of the Bristol Watch.

(To only those who Buy to Sell again.)

Case of Six in Sterling Silver Cases, - $96.00
" " " Silver Plated Cases, - - 72.00
" " " Gold Cases, - - - 120.00
" " " Gold, with Chains & Charms 153.00
" " " Silver " " " " 105.00

LADY'S WATCH.

THE DATE OF THIS IS UNKNOWN

In fourteen line Hunting Cases, full Jeweled, in Gold Plate and richly Enameled, made from the same material as the Bristol Watch.

Price in case of six $108.00 or $18.00 Single.

We take this method of introducing the **Bristol Watch** into the market, and instead of having customers pay three or four profits we prefer to sell direct, giving our patrons **Bottom Prices**, which is at least one half lower than all other Watches are sold for. All could sell at the same prices, if they sold direct, saving the enormous expenses of fine stores, large advertising bills, losses, &c If this does not interest you, please hand it to some one whom it may: thus doing them and us a kindness.

N. B. When you order, be sure and say "from Catalogue No. 75," as the prices are different from previous catalogues.

Address, SALISBURY BROS. & CO,
Providence, R. I,

BOGLE BROTHERS,

White River Junction, Vt.,

Carry in Stock

ADVERTISEMENT

Everything Needed by Jewelers.

Agents for the New Model 18 size key wind New Haven movements. Nicely engraved plates. Every movement warranted to run and take a good motion. Orders promptly filled.

Bogle Brothers,

White River Junction, - Vermont.

$2.50 Regular.

I hesitate to place a value on the watches on this page. I thought the Bristol was a Swiss watch. Now I am not sure. You usually see them priced cased at about $35.00

If this is the American "New Haven" it is scarce. If it is Swiss, about $35.00 cased.

Illustrated Watch Movement Parts

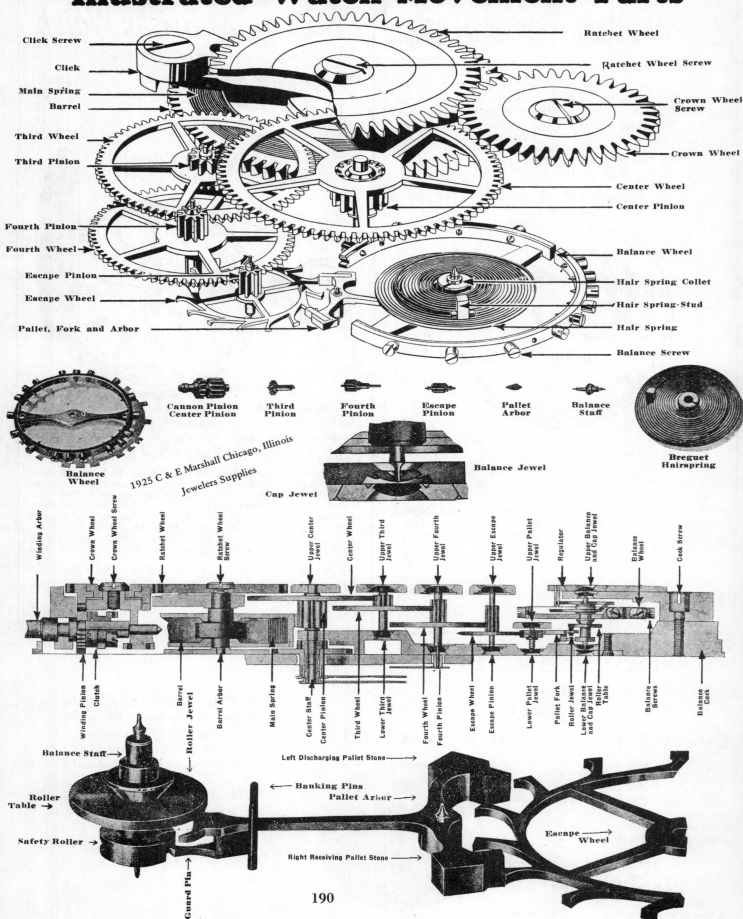

Click Screw

Click

Main Spring

Barrel

Third Wheel

Third Pinion

Fourth Pinion

Fourth Wheel

Escape Pinion

Escape Wheel

Pallet, Fork and Arbor

Ratchet Wheel

Ratchet Wheel Screw

Crown Wheel Screw

Crown Wheel

Center Wheel

Center Pinion

Balance Wheel

Hair Spring Collet

Hair Spring-Stud

Hair Spring

Balance Screw

Cannon Pinion Center Pinion

Third Pinion

Fourth Pinion

Escape Pinion

Pallet Arbor

Balance Staff

Balance Wheel

1925 C & E Marshall Chicago, Illinois

Jewelers Supplies

Balance Jewel

Cap Jewel

Breguet Hairspring

Winding Arbor

Crown Wheel

Crown Wheel Screw

Ratchet Wheel

Ratchet Wheel Screw

Upper Center Jewel

Center Wheel

Upper Third Jewel

Upper Fourth Jewel

Upper Escape Jewel

Upper Pallet Jewel

Regulator

Upper Balance and Cap Jewel

Balance Wheel

Cock Screw

Winding Pinion

Clutch

Roller Jewel

Barrel

Barrel Arbor

Main Spring

Center Staff

Center Pinion

Third Wheel

Lower Third Jewel

Fourth Wheel

Fourth Pinion

Escape Wheel

Escape Pinion

Lower Pallet Jewel

Pallet Fork

Roller Jewel

Lower Balance and Cap Jewel

Roller Table

Balance Screws

Balance Cock

Balance Staff

Roller Table

Safety Roller

Guard Pin

Left Discharging Pallet Stone

Banking Pins

Pallet Arbor

Right Receiving Pallet Stone

Escape Wheel

190

F1 — 16-S 23-J E. HOWARD & CO. Boston. Mint nickel mvt. no. 1,005,429. Pendant set, gold train, cups and balance screws. Faint hairline in double sunk Howard dial. Gold fili- gree hands. Mint 20 year YGF OF Dueber. Fully engraved dress case. This movement was called 1903 Model and was made by Waltham for Howard. $150.00

F2 — 14-S 17-J WALTHAM ROYAL Mint hunting mevement. Mint SS Roman dial. Beau- tiful factory new heavy raised solid gold design on 14 K solid YG case. A beautiful watch. $525.00

F3 — 16-S 21-J ELGIN Grade 91. Bridge model convertible mvt. Black letters gold train, gold escape wheel and reg. screw. Philadelphia GF 20 yr. case. Engraved DS Roman dial. Watch mint. $385.00

F4 — 16-S 21-J 992-B HAMILTON RAILROAD WATCH. Movement no. C-523,867. Model no. 17 Hamilton 10 K YGF RR OF case. Factory new. Never been carried. $175.00

F5 — 0-S 15-J ELGIN Mint gilded movement no. 19,229,291. Mint Arabic red track dial & hands. Mint 14 K U.S. Assay YG hunting case. Monogram front cover, beautiful hand en- graved star and leaves set with ruby and 12 small rose cut diamonds. $600.00

F6 — 16-S 15-J HAMDEN Mint plus nickel mvt. no. 2,370,555. Beautiful mint gold and pink decorated dial and original hands, no case. Mvt. $20 00 Dial $25.00

F7 — 18-S 21-J 6 pos GRADE 260 SETH THOMAS Beautiful mint gilt lettered lever set Railroad mvt. no. 210,742. Gold cups and screws. Perfect mint DS Arabic dial and hands. Beautiful fully decorated Keystone 14 K 25 yr. YGF screw B&B case. An absolute mint watch. $300.00

B9 — 18-S ILLINOIS 17-J Adjusted nickel full plate mint mvt. Mint single sunk Arabic dial and hands. Mint frosted and fully decorated hunting case with gold inlay on both front and back. No initial on gold shield. Very universal case. Mvt. $30.00 Case $150.00

B10 — 18-S ILLINOIS 24 ruby jewels, adj. BUNN special. Mint mvt. no. 1,605,963. DS antique style Arabic RR. Mint dial, mint Daw Co. 20 yr. YGF OF decorated case. Watch is mint. $450.00

B11 — 12-S HAMILTON 21-J Model 400. Mint nickel bridge mvt. no. H1,177. Adj. 5 pos. Extra large ruby jewels, near mint flat original Hamilton dial. Almost factory new 10 K RGP Keystone Victory OF case. This was originally an Illinois watch standard 12-S Illini mvt. marked and sold by Hamilton. A very nice high grade watch. $200.00

B1 — ELGIN 18-S 21-J 5 pos. OF FATHER TIME. Extra fine LS RR mvt. no. 13,505,820. Scarce ¾ plate with gold train, raised gold cups, gold weights and gilt lettering. Mint plus DS FERGUSON DIAL & hands. Extra fine Dueber Silverine Swing Ring Case. $200.00

B2 — 16-S 23-J ILLINOIS 163A 60 HOUR BUNN SPECIAL 6 pos leverset Mint Railroad mvt. no. 5,456,734. Finished by Hamilton and marked 163A ELINVAR. Perfect original DS dial and hands marked ILLINOIS 23 J BUNN SPECIAL 60 HOUR 6 positions. Fine J Boss 10 K YGF. LIghtly decorated RR case. This is a scarce watch. $225.00

B3 — 3-0-S Open Face NEW ENGLAND WATCH CO. Elfin movement. Funning. Mint blue skylight dial with gold hands. Mint 14 K solid yellow gold sunburst decorated case. $100.00

B4 — 16-S Model 88 OF WALTHAM Gilted 11-J Mint mvt. no. 5,301,459. Mint AWW Co. Waltham. Fully hand painted and gold decorated dial. Mint yellow gold filled decorated full hinged CWC CO. OF case. A beauty $165.00

B5 — 12-S HAMPDEN 17-J Adj. PAUL REVERE, new nickel mvt. no. 3,430, 328. DR, gold center wheel, cups and balance screws. Very high grade thin movement. New silver colored decorated dial marked Dueber Hampden. Like new white 14 K GF Deuber hinged back fully hand engraved case. A beauti- ful watch. $150.00

B6 — 3-0-S OF NEW ENGLAND WATCH CO. Elfin mvt. gilted duplex escapement running. Mint decorated Arabic dial and hands. Beautiful green enamel with silver and gold inlay. $150.00

B7 — 16-S 23-J LORD ELGIN. Beautiful mint mvt. 12,718,386. Gold train and trim. Mint perfect DS dial and hands. Mint 14 K solid gold OF case. $525.

B8 — 0-S WALTHAM 7-J Mint nickel mvt. no. 8,593,263. Mint original gold leaf decorated dial and hands. Mint YGF hunting case marked 14 K gauran- teed 25 years. Front lid multicolored decoration with no initial in shield. Back (shown) raised multicolored floral motif with 10 point mine cut dia- mond set in raised rose. Every watch collectors wife should own a beautiful piece of jewelry like this watch. $525.00

B12 — 6-S 16-J WALTHAM Box hinge hunting case. Beautiful mint nickel mvt. no. 18,058,984. Ajf. Gold train cups and balance screws. Mint Roman dial and hands. Mint plus 14 K U.S. Assay raised multicolor flowers, bird and shield. A fine piece of jewelry.

B13 — 0-S Open Face WALTHAM 19-J RIVERSIDE MAXIMUS. Complete watch mint 14 K solid case. 10 point mine cut diamond in center of plain polish back of case. $200.00

B14 — N-S HOWARD Keywind Key set 15-J gilt mvt. no. 23,066. Mint, but plates dark, gold balance weights. Mint SS Roman hand lettered dial and original hands, dust band, no case. $150.00

B15 — 10-S ELGIN 17-J 5 pos. Mint mvt. and double sunk porc. dial. Factory new 6 sided fully decorated split case. 14 K solid yellow gold. A fine heavy watch. $100.00

B16 — 18-S SETH THOMAS (see F7) $300.00

B17 — 16-S ELGIN 21-J 5 pos. FATHER TIME lever set Railroad mint mvt. no. 15,327,767. Gold train, cups and weights. Beautiful gilt lettered plates, mint SS MONTGOMERY dial with factory "SANTA FE" emblem. Near mint orig. Elgin 12-J YGF RR case. A dandy keeper for any RR collection. $200.00

B18 — 16-S ELGIN 23-J 6 pos. BW RAYMOND up and down indicator. Near mint lever set Railroad mvt. 34,682,715. Gold train cups etc. trace of rust on rachet wheels. Mint dial and hands, extra fine original Elgin 12 K YGF RR case shows wear but no brass. A fine watch. $225.00

B19 — 0-S ROCKFORD OF 17-J New nickel mvt. no. 909,094. Mint plus SS dial and hands. Factory new yellow gold filled permanent ROCKFORD case. Frosted back with blue enamel and fine antique stem and bow. A beautiful little watch. $150.00

B20 — 18-S OF ELGIN 15-J Keywind and keyset. Mint gilted BW RAYMOND adj. mvt. no. 38,939. Mint SS hand painted dial and hands. Beautiful original push button 18 K solid W P & CO. Double back case, old fashioned square cornered engine turned decorated case. Shows some wear. A very handsome and impressive watch. $350.00

The picture above includes me and my family, our motor home and the way we sometimes set up at an outdoor flea market. My wife Alpha is seated holding a copy of her book on cut glass she wrote last year. My 17 year old son, Larry, is holding a copy of his book on Winchester and Marble Hardware Collectibles. My daughter, Sherry, who is 15, has worked many hours with me on puting this book together. Without their help and understanding this book would not be possible. My family has always been interested in antiques of one kind or another and when I buy old advertising material usually a lot of other subjects are also included. Interest in many catagories of antiques has been acquired through looking through my old catalogs. We find this to be the surest way of identifying and dating collectables.

I'm always ready to buy, sell or trade watches, parts and advertising material so don't ever hesitate to ask me in person or drop me a line telling me what you have in mind. Please send a self addressed envelope. I sell watches through mail order to help people build collections who for one reason or another don't get to see many watches for sale. In my travels looking for research material, attending shows and flea markets I see hundreds of watches in a years time that are sleepers because most people who have them don't know what they **have** and go mostly by what they have paid for them, or what someone tells them when they price them. I can't afford to buy and keep them all so I believe these examples of American Craftsmanship should be in your collection where they can be enjoyed and appreciated. Also if the past few years is any indication of the future you should be able to enjoy them for years and then sell at a profit.

I will continue with my research on Pocket watches and will publish what I find. If you will send me your name and address I will put it on file and will write you when I have something ready. Book 3 will contain foreign watches and much more detail on American cases, and their values. I had many more pages prepared for this book and had to leave out because of publication costs and the resulting higher cost of this book. I am working on ways to make them available to you. Thank you for buying this book and when you see me come up and say hello.

Roy

HEART OF AMERICA PRESS

P. O. Box 9808 — 10101 Blue Ridge Blvd.
Kansas City, Missouri 64134

Order Form

Telephone: 816-761-0080

ISBN Prefix 9-913902-

QUANTITY	AUTHOR	TITLE	ISBN NO.	PRICE EACH	TOTAL AMT.
	R. Ehrhardt R. Rabeneck	Clock Identification & Price Guide, Book 1	-23-3	$15.00	
	R. Ehrhardt	1979 Clock Price Up-Date and Index to Clock Book 1 (Published 1977) (18 loose sheets to be inserted in your old book)	-28-4	$ 4.00	
	R. Ehrhardt R. Rabeneck	Clock Identification & Price Guide, Book 2	-27-6	$15.00	
	R. Ehrhardt E. Atchley	Violin Identification & Price Guide (1850-1977), Book 1 Violin Identification & Price Guide (1850-1977), Book 2 Violin Identification & Price Guide (Antique), Book 3	-22-5 -24-1 -25-X	$25.00 $25.00 $15.00	
	S. Ehrhardt D. Westbrook	American Collector Dolls Price Guide, Book 1	-14-4	$ 8.95	
	A. Ehrhardt	American Cut Glass Price Guide (Revised 1977)	-04-7	$ 6.95	
	R. Ehrhardt J. Ferrell	Pocket Knife Book 1&2 Price Guide (Revised 1977)	-02-0	$ 6.95	
	L. Ehrhardt	Pocket Knife Book 3 Price Guide, Winchester—Marbles—Knives & Hardware	-08-X	$ 6.95	
	R. Ehrhardt	American Pocket Watch Id. & Price Guide, Book 2 (Beginning Collector)	-09-8	$15.00	
	R. Ehrhardt	1976 Pocket Watch Price Indicator	-15-2	$ 5.00	
	R. Ehrhardt	1977 Pocket Watch Price Indicator	-21-7	$ 7.00	
	R. Ehrhardt	1978 Pocket Watch Price Indicator	-26-8	$10.00	
	R. Ehrhardt	1979 Pocket Watch Price Indicator	-29-2	$10.00	
	R. Ehrhardt	1980 Pocket Watch Price Indicator (NEW)	-32-2	$12.00	
	R. Ehrhardt	Foreign & American Pocket Watch Id. & Price Guide, Book 3	-16-0	$10.00	
	R. Ehrhardt	Waltham Pocket Watch Identification & Price Guide	-17-9	$10.00	
	R. Ehrhardt	Elgin Pocket Watch Identification & Price Guide	-10-1	$10.00	
	R. Ehrhardt	Illinois Springfield Watches Identification & Price Guide	-20-9	$10.00	
	R. Ehrhardt	Hamilton Pocket Watch Identification & Price Guide	-12-8	$10.00	
	R. Ehrhardt	Rockford Pocket Watch Identification & Price Guide	-11-X	$10.00	
	R. Ehrhardt	Trademarks (Watch Makers and Case Metal Identification)	-06-3	$10.00	
	Reprint	The Perfected American Watch—Waltham	-19-5	$ 4.00	
	Reprint	The Timekeeper—Hamilton Watch Company	-03-9	$ 3.00	
	Reprint	1858 E. Howard & Company	-18-7	$ 3.00	
	R. Ehrhardt	Master Index to Watch Books (16 loose pages to be inserted in your book)	-31-3	$ 4.00	
	R. Ehrhardt	American Pocket Watch Companies (Pocket Book) (NEW)	-30-6	$ 3.00	
	G. E. Townsend	Everything You Wanted to Know about American Watches and Didn't Know Who To Ask		$ 6.00	
	G. E. Townsend	The Watch That Made The $ Famous		$ 6.00	
	G. E. Townsend	The American Railroad Watch Encyclopedia		$ 6.00	

PLEASE RUSH THIS ORDER TO:

TOTAL For Books	
Less Applicable Discount	
Sub-Total	

Add 81 cents Postage
& Handling 1st Book, 25 cents each additional book

Add 70 Cents for Special Handling

Missouri residents add 4.625% tax

SEND CHECK OR MONEY ORDER FOR THIS AMOUNT

NAME _____

ADDRESS _____

CITY _____

STATE ——————————— ZIP ——————————

Books for Pocket Watch Collectors

AMERICAN POCKET WATCH IDENTIFICATION & PRICE GUIDE, BOOK 2. Ehrhardt, 1974. (Prices Revised in 1979). 192, 8½x11 Pages. $15.00. 1 lb. 10 oz.

FOREIGN & AMERICAN POCKET WATCH IDENTIFICATION & PRICE GUIDE, BOOK 3. Ehrhardt, 1976. 172, 8½x11 Pages. $10.00. 1 lb. 8 oz.

1976 POCKET WATCH PRICE INDICATOR. Ehrhardt, 1975. 64, 8½x11 Pages. $5.00. 14 oz.

1977 POCKET WATCH PRICE INDICATOR. Ehrhardt, 1976. 96, 8½x11 Pages. $7.00. 1 lb.

1978 POCKET WATCH PRICE INDICATOR. Ehrhardt, 1978. 110, 8½x11 Pages. $10.00. 1 lb. 2 oz.

1979 POCKET WATCH PRICE INDICATOR. Ehrhardt, 1979. 110, 8½x11 Pages. $10.00. 1 lb. 2 oz.

1980 POCKET WATCH PRICE INDICATOR. Ehrhardt, 1980. 110, 8½x11 Pages. $12.00. 1 lb. 2 oz.

AMERICAN POCKET WATCH COMPANIES (Pocket Book) Ehrhardt, 1979. 96, 3½x5½ Pages. $3.00. 2 oz.

MASTER INDEX TO POCKET WATCHES. Ehrhardt, 1979. 16, 8½x11 Pages. $4.00. 6 oz.

ELGIN POCKET WATCH ID. & PRICE GUIDE. Ehrhardt, 1976. 120, 8½x11 Pages. $10.00. 1 lb. 2 oz.

ILLINOIS SPRINGFIELD WATCHES ID. & PRICE GUIDE. Ehrhardt, 1976. 136, 8½x11 Pages. $10.00. 1 lb. 4 oz.

WALTHAM POCKET WATCH ID. & PRICE GUIDE. Ehrhardt, 1976. 172, 8½x11 Pages. $10.00. 1 lb. 4 oz.

HAMILTON POCKET WATCH ID. & PRICE GUIDE. Ehrhardt, 1976. 53, 8½x11 Pages. $10.00. 14 oz.

ROCKFORD GRADE & SERIAL NUMBERS WITH PRODUCTION FIGURES. Ehrhardt, 1976. 44, 8½x11 Pages. $10.00. 12 oz.

TRADEMARKS. Ehrhardt, 1976. 128, 8½x11 Pages. $10.00. 1 lb. 2 oz.

THE PERFECTED AMERICAN WATCH—WALTHAM (Reprint). $4.00. 6 oz.

THE TIMEKEEPER—HAMILTON WATCH COMPANY (Reprint). $3.00. 6 oz.

1858 E. HOWARD & COMPANY (Reprint). $3.00. 6 oz.

EVERYTHING YOU WANTED TO KNOW ABOUT AMERICAN WATCHES & DIDN'T KNOW WHO TO ASK. Col. George E. Townsend, 1971. 88, 6x9 Pages. $6.00. 8 oz.

AMERICAN RAILROAD WATCHES. Col. George E. Townsend, 1977. 44, 6x9 Pages. $6.00. 8 oz.

THE WATCH THAT MADE THE DOLLAR FAMOUS. Col. George E. Townsend, 1974. 45, 6x9 Pages. $6.00. 8 oz.

Clock Books

CLOCK IDENTIFICATION & PRICE GUIDE, BOOK 1. R. Rabeneck & R. Ehrhardt, 1977. (Prices Revised in 1979). 198, 8½x11 Pages. $15.00. 1 lb. 12 oz.

1979 CLOCK PRICE UP-DATE & INDEX TO CLOCK BOOK 1. Ehrhardt, 1979. 18, 8½x11 Pages. $4.00. 6 oz.

CLOCK IDENTIFICATION & PRICE GUIDE, BOOK 2. M. "Red" Rabaneck & R. Ehrhardt, 1979. 192, 8½x11 Pages. $15.00. 1 lb. 10 oz.

Violin Books

VIOLIN IDENTIFICATION & PRICE GUIDE, BOOK 1. E. Atchley & R. Ehrhardt, 1977. 192, 8½x11 Pages. $25.00 1 lb. 10 oz.

VIOLIN IDENTIFICATION & PRICE GUIDE, BOOK 2. E. Atchley & R. Ehrhardt, 1978. 206, 8½x11 Pages. $25.00 1 lb. 12 oz.

VIOLIN IDENTIFICATION & PRICE GUIDE, BOOK 3. R. Ehrhardt, 1978. 152, 8½x11 Pages. $15.00. 1 lb. 5 oz.

Misc. Books

AMERICAN COLLECTOR DOLLS PRICE GUIDE, BOOK 1. S. Ehrhardt & D. Westbrook, 1975. 128, 8½x11 Pages. $8.95 1 lb. 2 oz.

AMERICAN CUT GLASS PRICE GUIDE, Rev. 1977. Alpha Ehrhardt. 120, 8½x11 Pages. $6.95. 1 lb. 2 oz.

POCKET KNIFE BOOK 1 & 2 PRICE GUIDE. J. Ferrell & R. Ehrhardt, Rev. 1977. 128, 8½x11 Pages. $6.95 1 lb. 2 oz.

POCKET KNIFE BOOK 3 — PRICE GUIDE TO 2000 WINCHESTER & MARBLES, HARDWARE COLLECTIBLES. L. Ehrhardt, 1974. 128, 8½x11 Pages. $6.95. 1 lb. 2 oz.

The books listed above are available from HEART OF AMERICA PRESS. All are sold on a satisfaction guarantee. If you are not sure about the books you want, send a self-addressed, stamped envelope and we will send you detailed brochures on all of the publications.

For orders in the U.S. and Canada, send the price of the book plus 81 cents postage and handling for the first book and 25 cents for each additional. Foreign countries—Check with your Post Office for rate, your choice, Air or Sea Mail, Book Rate. Book and carton weights listed above. Send orders to:

HEART OF AMERICA PRESS
P. O. BOX 9808
KANSAS CITY, MISSOURI 64134

MASTER INDEX TO WATCH BOOKS

This is a master index to 13 of the pocket watch books by Roy Ehrhardt.

By title, the books included are: **American Pocket Watch Identification & Price Guide, Book 2; Foreign & American Pocket Watch Identification & Price Guide, Book 3; 1976, 1977 1978 & 1979 Price Indicators; Elgin Pocket Watch Identification & Price Guide; Hamilton Pocket Watch Identification & Price Guide; Illinois-Springfield Identification & Price Guide; Rockford Watch Company Grade & Serial Numbers with Production Figures; Waltham Pocket Watch Identification & Price Guide; Trademarks; and American Pocket Watch Companies.**

The page numbers in the Index are prefixed with a number or letter to indicate the book (or books) in which the listing is found. The prefixes are shown below — also on Page 13-15.

Prefix	Title of Book	Date Published
2	American Pocket Watch Id. & Price Guide, Book 2	1974
3	Foreign & Amer. Pocket Watch Id. & Price Guide, Book 3	1976
6	1976 Price Indicator	1975
7	1977 Price Indicator	1976
8	1978 Price Indicator	1978
9	1979 Price Indicator	1979
E	Elgin Pocket Watch Id. & Price Guide	1976
H	Hamilton Pocket Watch Id. & Price Guide	1976
I	Illinois-Springfield Id. & Price Guide	1976
R	Rockford Watch Co. Grade & Serial Nos. with Production Figures	1975
W	Waltham Pocket Watch Id. & Price Guide	1976
T	Trademarks	1976
P	American Pocket Watch Companies	1979

The following abbreviations appear after each of the pocket watch names so that you can tell at a glance what company made the watch in case you don't happen to have the book that shows the picture.

Abbr.	Company	Abbr.	Company
Ball	Webb C. Ball	M	United States W. Co. & Marion W. Co.
BWC	Boston Watch Co.		
Cornell	Cornell Watch Co.	NEWC	New England W. Co.
CWC	Columbus W. Co.	NYS	New York Standard
D	Dollar Watches	NYWC	New York W. Co.
DH	Hampden & Dueber W. Co.	NWC	Newark W. Co.
E	Elgin	PWC	Peoria W. Co.
EHC	E. Howard	RHI	Robert H. Ingersoll
HWC	Hamilton W. Co.	S	Swiss
Ill.	Illinois W. Co.	TWC	Trenton W. Co.
IWC	Independent W. Co.	USW	U.S. W. Co., Waltham
LWC	Lancaster Watch Co.	W	Waltham
		WWC	Waterbury W. Co.

AMERICAN MADE & FOREIGN MADE WATCHES ARE INDEXED SEPARATELY.

4

6

7

VIOLIN IDENTIFICATION & PRICE GUIDE, BOOK 1
EHRHARDT & ATCHLEY, 1977. 192, 8½x11 Pages. $25.00. No. -22-5

This book contains carefully selected actual pages from original sales catalogs, violin maker advertisements, musical instrument supply house catalogs and sales brochures. It covers violins and related instruments, both American and imported, sold in the United States from about 1880 to the present time. The following information is given for each violin: The year it was offered for sale—The original description—The price it sold for originally—The present retail value. Over 95% of all violins offered for sale in the United States since 1880 can be identified and a reasonably close retail value determined by comparing your violin with an actual picture of it or a similar one in this Book 1 or in Book 2. There are 1536 violins and 552 bows pictured or described. Most of the violins you come in contact with every day are included.

VIOLIN IDENTIFICATION & PRICE GUIDE, BOOK 2
EHRHARDT & ATCHLEY, 1978. 206, 8½x11 Pages. $25.00. No. -24-1

More or less a continuation of Book 1, with all new and different violins pictured and described. Most of the information contained herein was supplied by interested individuals throughout the United States who saw that they had new and valuable material that should be published. The book follows essentially the same format and the same time period as Book 1. There are 17 pages covering the very important French violins exported to the U.S. during the period 1891-1926. One change in format is that the current prices are not listed by each violin but rather included in a section at the back of the book. There are 2661 violins and 121 bows pictured or described.

·THESE TWO BOOKS, VIOLIN IDENTIFICATION & PRICE GUIDE BOOK 1 AND BOOK 2, WILL GIVE YOU A DEFINITE ADVANTAGE OVER A PERSON WHO DOES NOT HAVE THEM. INFORMATION NOT AVAILABLE ANYWHERE ELSE IN THE WORLD.

VIOLIN IDENTIFICATION & PRICE GUIDE, BOOK 3
EHRHARDT, 1978. 152, 8½x11 Pages. $15.00. No. -25-X

*Contains 6808 rare and antique violins by 1450 different makers, described with original selling prices. Price Guide pages to assist you in determining the current value of old violins. The original, rare violin catalogs copied or reproduced are: Lyon & Healy 1896, 1897, 1900, 1901, 1902, 1903, 1904, 1909, 1913, 1915, 1919, 1922 and 1949—Wurlitzer 1915 and 1931 Book 1—Lewis & Son 1946, 1952, 1953 and 1955—August Gemunder 1913 and 1927—Ernest Doring 1940 and 1941—Ferron & Kroeplin 1915 and 1925—Carl Fisher 1928—Musician's Supply 1930—Elias Howe 1888—Cremona Violin Shop 1914—Jenkins Music Co. 1926—Francis D. Ballard 1940—W. R. Ford 1927—John Friedrich & Bro. 1920—V. C. Squire 1930—Earsel V. Atchley 1965—and St. Louis Music Supply 1969. Some of the above 32 original catalogs were obtained at a cost of over $100.00 each. You get the best part of them all for $15.00. **This book is invaluable when trying to identify your old antique violin and will help you determine the current value.***

AMERICAN COLLECTOR DOLLS PRICE GUIDE, BOOK 1. S. EHRHARDT & D. WESTBROOK, 1975. 128, 8½x11 Pages. $8.95. No. -14-4

Very valuable information to dealers and collectors or an individual who has a doll to value. A reprint of carefully selected pages taken from old factory sales catalogs, factory advertisements, wholesale supply house and hardware catalogs and sales brochures. Information given by each doll pictured is: Year offered for sale—Original costume—Original selling price— Complete description—and, very important, Today's Retail Value. Many dolls are seen here in print for the first time. Includes a very high percentage of all dolls sold during the period 1890 to 1930 through the use of wholesale catalogs.

AMERICAN CUT GLASS PRICE GUIDE, BOOK 1
A. EHRHARDT, (Revised 1977). 120, 8½x11 Pages. $6.95. No. -04-7

Illustrated pages showing over 1500 pieces of old American Cut Glass. A description of each piece, its original selling price, the year it was sold, and the current market value is shown by each picture. Any collector or dealer of the very popular American Cut Glass will find this book a valuable reference. A small section is devoted to comments on reproductions, quality, age, and four pages of trademarks to round out this important guide.

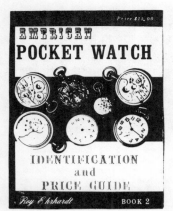

AMERICAN POCKET WATCH IDENTIFICATION & PRICE GUIDE, BOOK 2
EHRHARDT, 1974. 192, 8½x11 Pages. $15.00. No. -09-8
* * * FIRST PRINTING 1974.* * * PRICE GUIDE SECTION REVISED 1979. * * *

The **AMERICAN WATCH COLLECTOR'S BIBLE.** *This book was immediately accepted by everyone interested in watches who saw it. You can identify your watch, its age and the retail value by comparing it with an original picture. It contains selected pages from original factory sales, supply house, and parts catalogs, along with various advertisements and brochures dating back to 1865, the beginning of serious watchmaking in the U. S. Over 1900 pocket watches are pictured and described. Completely new and different from the 1972 Edition of BOOK 1— nothing is duplicated. No collector, dealer, or anyone who has a good watch for sale can afford not to look up your watch in this book before acting, if you have any doubts about what you are doing.* (**For beginning collectors. If you own no other watch books, buy this one first.)**

Prefix 2   POCKET WATCH PRICE INDICATORS

IF YOU WANT TO KEEP UP TO DATE ON ALL OF THE INFORMATION THAT HAS BEEN PUBLISHED ON AMERICAN MADE POCKET WATCHES AND CASES, YOU NEED TO HAVE ALL OF THE INDICATORS. THE YEARLY PUBLICATIONS ARE DESCRIBED BELOW.

1976 POCKET WATCH PRICE INDICATOR
EHRHARDT, 1975. 64, 8½x11 Pages. $5.00. No. -15-2   *Prefix 6*

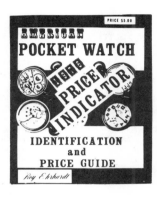

This is the first of a yearly "Price Indicator". Mr. Ehrhardt is using this means to make available to the watch collectors and dealers new information acquired during the year. This issue updates the 1974 Edition of **American Pocket Watch Identification & Price Guide, Book 2,** *and contains 40 additional pages of pictures, advertisements and new material not shown in* **BOOK 2.** *1875 Illinois brochure showing all keywinds with descriptions—Four pages of Illinois—Ben Franklin, including 23J—1877 watch cases—1877 Howard—1864 Waltham factory price list with descriptions—All Webb C. Ball serial numbers and production figures and dates—25J Columbus—More Hampdens, Walthams, 14J Seth Thomas, etc.—Elgin, New York Standard, Trenton, Elinvar Hamilton, etc.—Cases (13 page section)—And a 1975 summary of what's been happening to prices of American watches. This book will not make much sense if you do not have* **BOOK 2.**

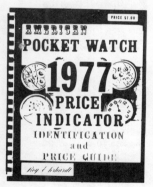

Prefix 7   **1977 POCKET WATCH PRICE INDICATOR**
EHRHARDT, 1976. 96, 8½x11 Pages. $7.00. No. -21-7

Updates prices for the **American Pocket Watch Identification & Price Guide, Book 2,** *published in 1974, and the* **1976 Pocket Watch Price Indicator.** *Additional new material on Hampden—The Ball Watch Company—Ben Franklin 1910 Catalog—United States Watch Company—Special Railroad Watches—Burlington Watch Company—Sears Roebuck watches—Montgomery Ward watches—Columbus Watch Company—E. Howard Watch Company—Waltham —Sante Fe Special—Washington Watch Company—with material on 145 Antique Watch Keys, Chrondrometers, Up-Down Indicators, and a complete price guide to all American companies and individuals who made watches (282 listings).*

1978 POCKET WATCH PRICE INDICATOR
EHRHARDT, 1978. 110, 8½x11 Pages. $10.00. No. -26-8   *Prefix 8*

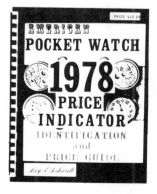

The third in a series of Indicators updating prices for pocket watches. This book updates prices for the **American Pocket Watch Identification & Price Guide, Book 2,** *published in 1974, the* **1976 Pocket Watch Price Indicator,** *and the* **1977 Pocket Watch Price Indicator.** *Forty-six (46) pages of new reprints never before seen are presented, including pages on Mermod Jaccard—Freeport—Waltham Indicator parts—Mainsprings—E. Howard Cases—Non-Magnetic—Rockford—Interstate Chronometer—Waterbury—Standard American—Monarch—Webb C. Ball. Forty-two (42) pages of* **Unusual, Scarce,** *and* **Rare** *American watches never shown in print before. This last section contains photographs of unusual watches that were taken during the last two years. Finally, the author's comments on "American Watches, 1977 and 1978, in Summary"*

Prefix 9   **1979 POCKET WATCH PRICE INDICATOR**
EHRHARDT, 1979. 120, 8½x11 Pages. $10.00. No. -29-2

The fourth in a series of Indicators updating prices for pocket watches. Updates prices for the American Pocket Watch Identification & Price Guide, Book 2, published in 1974, and the 1976, 1977, and 1978 Pocket Watch Price Indicators. I have been carrying my camera to all the Regionals and collectors have been bringing their watches that, for the most part, I have never seen before. The new material presented in this Indicator consists of photos of these watches. Another very interesting and important section covers the watches shown by drawing in Col. George E. Townsend's book, "Almost Everything You Wanted to Know about American Watches and Didn't Know Who to Ask." He was gracious to give me the original pictures from which he had made the drawings. This is the most interesting of all the Indicators.

WALTHAM POCKET WATCH IDENTIFICATION & PRICE GUIDE
EHRHARDT, 1976. 172, 8½x11 Pages. $10.00. No. -17-9

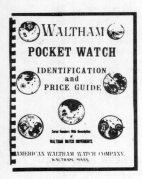

Prefix W

Waltham, being the first American watch factory beginning in the 1850's and continuing to the 1960's and manufacturing over 33 million watches, takes a book by itself to cover their production properly. This book is for the advanced collector or dealer who wants to get the most enjoyment out of his hobby or the most money for his watches. Partial material presented: Complete 1954 Waltham serial numbers with descriptions—Selections from 1890 Waltham Products Catalog (watches & cases)—1874 Waltham Illustrated Price List—1901 Waltham Mainspring Catalog (giving model numbers to KW16, KW20, KW14, etc.)—1948 Waltham Watch & Clock Material Catalog—1952 E. & J. Swigart Co. Manual of Watch Movements. All of the important models, along with all of the grades in each model and a value for each, are given. This book does not leave many questions about Waltham unanswered.

ELGIN POCKET WATCH IDENTIFICATION & PRICE GUIDE
EHRHARDT, 1976. 120, 8½x11 Pages. $10.00. No. -10-1

At last—for the first time ever available—all of the Elgin pocket watch grades with the number of each produced. (A minor miracle in itself). With the help of John Miller of Springfield, Illinois and his computer,I am very proud of this work on Elgin. Partial material presented: All named & numbered grades with classification & description as originally made. Also shown for each grade is the total production, the first and last serial number, and the current value. In addition, the first and last serial number of all the runs for all grades with production of less than 10,000. The complete Elgin serial number list of 50 Million is also included; line drawings of the Elgin models; and on and on with information that the advanced collector and dealer needs to know.

Prefix E

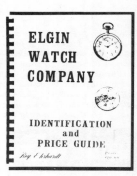

ILLINOIS SPRINGFIELD WATCHES IDENTIFICATION & PRICE GUIDE. EHRHARDT, 1976. 136, 8½x11 Pages. $10.00. No. -20-9

Prefix I

More collectors have asked for this book than any other single company I have done. Contains the following: All of the Illinois serial numbers from 1 to 5,698,801, with the Size, KW, Pendant or Lever Set, Open Face or Hunting, Jewels, Model Number, Grade Number shown for each number—First Serial Number for each model—Line drawing of all 54 different models—Watch dial foot locations—Complete illustrations of 154 watch dials—Production date table—Illustrated watch hands—Mainspring Chart—and 21 pages of movements illustrated with current price guide. Illinois is a very fascinating company and they have done everything that makes it an interesting company to collect. They started early, used names for grades, made high jeweled (24,25 & 26), made hundreds of watches with other grade names and other company names, and, of course, made a full line of excellent railroad watches. There are a lot of rare grades. Illinois made runs of 5, 10, 15 & 50 watches of one grade, one time. A book any advanced collector will enjoy.

ROCKFORD GRADE & SERIAL NUMBERS WITH PRODUCTION FIGURES. EHRHARDT, 1976. 44, 8½x11 Pages. $10.00. No. -11-X

This Rockford book and all the other single company books, contains specific information impossible to present in any other way. The 1907 Rockford Serial Number List and Parts Catalog, with all serial numbers up to 824,000, has been completely reproduced. Without a doubt the most important section is the breakdown of how many were produced of each grade. This enormous task was undertaken and completed by Roger Weiss, Jr. of Yorkville, Illinois. Most of you know the value of the 24J, 18S Rockford. There are 50 grades with less production than the 24J Open Face. There are literally hundreds of sleepers out there waiting to be found. Without the proper method of identification, the one you are holding is just another old watch.

Prefix R

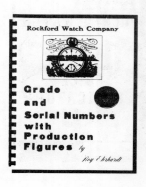

The first pocket watch price guide ever written. Fine book for beginners. Great for dealers to use as a buying reference. Investors use it to see what watches have shown the most improvement in value. Over 2600 watches priced, values from $5.00 to $16,000.00, with 95% being common everyday watches you need to know the value of. Still a very popular, strong selling book. List of all major American and foreign watches showing descriptions and retail prices. Charts of production dates, grading movements and cases; how to determine size; and other useful information.

Book 1 Out of Print - Not Indexed

This is the original book and the one that is owned by most of the antique dealers. Because the prices are so low, it is still possible to get good buys from the people who own only this book. When there is a reference needed to aid you in the purchase of a watch, this is the book to use, since (for the most part) the prices shown are only about one-third of today's value.

FOREIGN & AMERICAN POCKET WATCH IDENTIFICATION & PRICE GUIDE, BOOK 3
EHRHARDT, 1976. 172, 8½x11 Pages. $10.00. No. -16-0

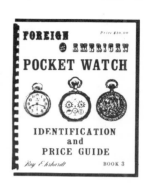

By popular request—everything from "soup to nuts" on foreign watches, including the current collector value. Know how to identify your watches by comparing them with original manufacturers' pictures and descriptions. Also included is a section on American cases of 1893 and one of 1929. Other information covered: How to value cases—Conditions that affect value—Mail order dealers—How current values were determined—Grading of movements & cases—Reproduction of an 18-page illustrated antique watch catalog of expensive watches currently for sale—List of hundreds of foreign watch names—80 Swiss fake railroad names—two pages of American watch company names (merchandisers only). This book contains carefully selected, original, fully illustrated pages from factory sales catalogs and advertisements, supply house catalogs, and sales brochures. The original antique pages have not been altered except for the current value, issue date of page, and author comments added in bold type. A must for every foreign and American watch collector. This book, as well as BOOK 1 and BOOK 2, has a world of information for both beginners and advanced collectors. No duplication in either of the three books.

Prefix H

Prefix 3

HAMILTON POCKET WATCH IDENTIFICATION & PRICE GUIDE
EHRHARDT, 1976. 53, 8½x11 Pages. $10.00. No. -12-8

How much is my old pocket watch worth? * * How many were made, and when? * * *Three questions very important to anyone interested in pocket watches. With this and the other single company books, you first look up the serial number of your watch to find the grade, then look up how many were made, and finally, how much it is worth. The complete Hamilton serial number list is included, along with everything else you need to know.*

TRADEMARKS
EHRHARDT, 1976. 128, 8½x11 Pages. $10.00. No. -06-3

This book is so absolutely necessary to the advanced watch collector, dealer, or trader that you will wonder how you ever managed without it. Contains sections on the following subjects: American Pocket Watch Case Trademark (probably the most important section). Records all of the marks known to the author, and especially the marks used on solid gold cases that do not specifically say gold—American pocket watch trademarks and makers names—Foreign import pocket watch trademarks and makers names—American and foreign clock trademarks and names—Diamonds, How to buy and trade without expensive equipment—Scrap gold, how to find, recognize, buy and sell—Many other useful charts, tables, etc.

Prefix T

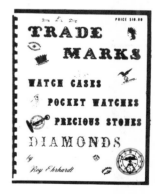

Prefix P

MASTER INDEX

AMERICAN POCKET WATCH COMPANIES
EHRHARDT, 1979. 96, 3½x5½ Pages. $3.00. No. -30-6

This little pocket book contains all of the following: **Names of all the known companies. * * How many watches were made by each company and when by serial number. * * Inventory space for 80 pocket watches.** *This is a handy "must have" little book for all collectors. Many dealers use this as a "give away" to their customers after marking "Compliments of" and their name on the inside cover.*

This little book is new. If you want a copy, send $3.00 plus 50 cents postage. No postage if you order it with another book. Write for special volume dealer price.

MASTER INDEX TO WATCH BOOKS
R. EHRHARDT, 1979. 16, 8½x11 Pages. $4.00. -31-3.

This is a master index to 13 of the pocket watch books by Roy Ehrhardt. By title, the books included are: **American Pocket Watch Identification & Price Guide, Book 2; Foreign & American Pocket Watch Identification & Price Guide, Book 3; 1976, 1977, 1978 & 1979 Price Indicators; Elgin Pocket Watch Identification & Price Guide; Hamilton Pocket Watch Id. & Price Guide; Illinois-Springfield Identification & Price Guide; Rockford Watch Company Grade & Serial Numbers with Production Figures; Waltham Pocket Watch Identification & Price Guide; Trademarks; and American Pocket Watch Companies.**

CLOCK IDENTIFICATION & PRICE GUIDE, BOOK 1
R. RABENECK & R. EHRHARDT, 1977. 198, 8½x11 Pages. $15.00. No. -23-3
* * * FIRST PRINTED 1977. * * * PRICE GUIDE SECTION REVISED 1979. * * *

This book follows the format of Mr. Ehrhardt's price guides on pocket watches, in that the material is selected from original factory sales catalogs, etc. It covers American and imported clocks from 1850 to the 1940's, with the following information for each clock: The year offered for sale—The factory description—The price it sold for originally—The present retail value. Most of the clocks you see every day are pictured or described (4,000 in all). Over 95% of all clocks manufactured or sold in the United States since 1850 can be identified and a reasonably close retail value determined by comparing your clock with a picture of it or a similar one in this book or in **BOOK 2.** *Of interest is the comments on "Conditions or Considerations as they Affect Value", "Periods in Clock Production", and "Replicas, Reproductions and Fakes". In addition, identification and dating of 150 of the most important clock makers is shown in chart form, beginning with Thomas Harland in 1773, down to the present time.* **THE ONLY BOOK OF THIS KIND EVER PUBLISHED. TWO YEARS IN PREPARATION. A MUST FOR EVERY CLOCK COLLECTOR.** *This book is now considered the best all-around for identification and prices, and collectors who have it won't leave home without it. Revised, 1979, to include 1979 Price Up-Date and a complete index.*

1979 CLOCK PRICE UP-DATE & INDEX TO BOOK 1
EHRHARDT, 1979. 18, 8½x11 Pages. $4.00. No. -28-4

Price Revisions for CLOCK IDENTIFICATION AND PRICE GUIDE, BOOK 1 (Published 1977). These 18 pages are punched for insertion in the back of the book. Makes the book current with today's retail prices.

CLOCK IDENTIFICATION & PRICE GUIDE, BOOK 2
R. RABENECK & R. EHRHARDT, 1979. 192, 8½x11 Pages. $15.00. No. -27-6

A continuation of Book 1, with practically all new clocks not pictured in Book 1. Many additional clock companies are covered. Some examples are: Jennings Bros.—Western Clock Company—1873 Terry Clock Company—more complete Ansonia, New Haven, Gilbert, Seth Thomas, Ingraham, Sessions, Welsh—more Jeweler's Regulators and Battery Regulators—Hall—Grandfathers—Calendars—Connecticut Shelf—Novelty and Statue, etc. In addition, a complete unillustrated price guide to all known calendar clocks, with references to all books containing calendar clocks. Also, interesting articles, comments and sidelights to clock collecting and values.

FULL PAGE BROCHURES ARE AVAILABLE BY REQUEST.

**ALL BOOKS ARE GUARANTEED TO PLEASE. YOUR MONEY BACK
IS ASSURED. JUST RETURN THE BOOK IN GOOD CONDITION.**

POCKET KNIFE BOOK 1 & 2 PRICE GUIDE
J. FERRELL & R. EHRHARDT, (Revised, 1977).
128, 8½x11 Pages. $6.95. No. -02-0

Originally published in 1973, with prices and format revised in 1977. A very popular book and a "must have" for anyone interested in buying, selling, or collecting pocket knives. Contains carefully selected pages from old factory and hardware catalogs and sales brochures. Knives are shown actual size with the original factory description and selling price, and, most important, **today's retail value** *shown by each knife. Most knives can be valued by comparing your knife with one in the book, even if made by a different maker. Over 1,790 American and foreign Pocket, Bowie, and Hunting knife makers shown, with a mint price by each that will indicate the quality of the known examples. This book was completely revised in September 1977, updating the prices to the current collector value.*

**POCKET KNIFE BOOK 3 - PRICE GUIDE TO 2000
WINCHESTER & MARBLES, HARDWARE COLLECTIBLES
LARRY EHRHARDT, 1974. 128, 8½x11 Pages. $6.95. -08-X**

This book was compiled of selections from various product sales catalogs of both WINCHESTER and MARBLE companies. The catalogs date from 1903 through the 20's and 30's. Most of the items that are now collectible are shown, along with today's current retail value. **If you are interested in Pocket Knives, Hunting Knives, Fishing Equipment, Sporting Equipment, Hardware Tools, etc., you need this book.** *Hardware Collectibles of WINCHESTER & MARBLES are real sleepers and if you get into any old houses or go to Flea Markets be sure and pick them up.*